# BRITISH
# AND AMERICAN
# NAVAL POWER

*Politics and Policy, 1900–1936*

PHILLIPS PAYSON O'BRIEN

Praeger Studies in Diplomacy and Strategic Thought
*B.J.C. McKercher, Series Editor*

**Westport, Connecticut**
**London**

**Library of Congress Cataloging-in-Publication Data**

O'Brien, Phillips Payson, 1963–
    British and American naval power : politics and policy, 1900–1936
/ Phillips Payson O'Brien.
        p.   cm.—(Praeger studies in diplomacy and strategic
thought, ISSN 1076–1543)
    Includes bibliographical references and index.
    ISBN 0–275–95898–1 (alk. paper)
    1. United States—Military relations—Great Britain.  2. Great
Britain—Military relations—United States.  3. United States—
History, Naval—20th century.  4. Great Britain—History,
Naval—20th century.  5. United States.  Navy—History—20th
century.  6. Great Britain.  Royal Navy—History—20th century.
I. Title.  II. Series.
E183.8.G7037   1998
359′.00973—dc21         97–7180

British Library Cataloguing in Publication Data is available.

Library of Congress Catalog Card Number: 97–7180
ISBN: 0–275–95898–1
ISSN: 1076–1543

First published in 1998

Praeger Publishers, 88 Post Road West, Westport, CT 06881
An imprint of Greenwood Publishing Group, Inc.

Printed in the United States of America

The paper used in this book complies with the
Permanent Paper Standard issued by the National
Information Standards Organization (Z39.48–1984).

10 9 8 7 6 5 4 3 2 1

# Contents

# Acknowledgments

Many people and institutions contributed to making this book possible. Before all of them I must thank Dr. Zara Steiner of New Hall, Cambridge. Over the past years Dr. Steiner has been my sternest critic, my greatest supporter, and my friend. Without her this book could not have been written.

I must also thank a number of other people for their learned advice. In particular I would like to mention Dr David Reynolds of Christs College, Cambridge, Professor Richard Langhorne of Rutgers University, Dr. John A. Thompson of St. Catherine's College, Cambridge and Professor Geoffrey Till of the Royal Naval College. I would also like to thank Dr. John Parry and Dr. Mark Kaplanoff of Pembroke College, Cambridge, Dr. Brendan Simms of Peterhouse, Cambridge, Dr. R. A. C. Parker of the Queens College, Oxford, Dr. Brian McKercher of Royal Military College, Kingston, Ontario, and Mr. Justin Barker. I owe a special debt to Dr. Susan Pennybacker of Trinity College, Hartford Connecticut, who first encouraged me to work in history.

A number of institutions contributed generously toward helping me in my research and writing. First and foremost I must thank the history faculty of Cambridge University and Pembroke College, Cambridge. By awarding me the

Mellon Research Fellowship in American History, the faculty provided me with the perfect environment from which to proceed with my work. The master and fellows of Pembroke College, who honored me with the Drapers Research Fellowship, helped me immeasurably with their support, good cheer, and friendship.

I must also thank the master and fellows of Peterhouse, Cambridge for their award of a research studentship. My gratitude extends to the Herbert Hoover Presidential Library in West Branch, Iowa, the Franklin and Eleanor Roosevelt Library in Hyde Park, New York, and the Stanley Baldwin Fund in Cambridge for their assistance. A special thanks is extended to the Naval Historical Center. By awarding me a research fellowship they provided an excellent base from which to do my months of research in Washington, D.C.

Over the past years I have visited a host of libraries and archives. I would like to thank the staffs of the Cambridge University Library, the Seeley Historical Library, Cambridge, the Churchill Archives Centre, Churchill College, Cambridge, the Public Records Office, the Bodleian Library, Oxford, the National Library of Scotland, the National Maritime Museum, Greenwich, the British Library, the Library of Congress, the National Archives, Washington, D.C., the Massachusetts Historical Society, the Franklin and Eleanor Roosevelt Presidential Library, Hyde Park, New York, and the Naval Historical Society, Washington, D.C., for their professionalism and courtesy. I would particularly like to thank the staff of the Herbert Hoover Presidential Library in West Branch, Iowa, for services above and beyond the call of duty.

On a personal note I would like to record my deep gratitude to Dr. Robert Ojemann, Dr. Michael McKenna, and their entire surgical team at Massachusetts General Hospital and Massachusetts Eye and Ear. Their skill and commitment allowed me to continue working. Finally, I must thank my family. The constant support of my parents, sisters, brother, aunt, and uncle, especially over the more trying times during the last two and a half years, kept me going. Without them this book would really not have seen the light of day.

# Abbreviations

| | |
|---|---|
| AANR | Anglo-American Naval Relations 1917-1919 |
| ADM | Admiralty Papers (UK) |
| AMPUS | Annual Messages of the President of the United States |
| ARSN | Annual Report of the Secretary of the Navy (US) |
| Beatty Papers | *The Beatty Papers*, ed. B. M. Ranft |
| BFP Documents | Documents on British Foreign Policy 1919–1939 |
| CAB | Cabinet Papers (UK) |
| CR | Congressional Record (US) |
| FDR Mss | Franklin D. Roosevelt Papers |
| FO | Foreign Office Papers (UK) |

Abbreviations

| | |
|---|---|
| GBDC | General Board Disarmament Conference Papers (US) |
| GB Letters | General Board Letter Books (US) |
| GBSF | General Board Subject File (US) |
| NDGC | Navy Department General Correspondence (US) |
| NID | Naval Intelligence Department Papers (US) |
| PPPUS | Public Papers of the President of the United States |
| SCCCNO | Secret and Confidential Correspondence of the Chief of Naval Operations (US) |
| TR Letters | *The Letters of Theodore Roosevelt*, ed. E. E. Morison |
| WPL | War Plans Division (US) |
| WSC | *Winston S. Churchill*, R. Churchill or M. Gilbert |
| WW Papers | *The Papers of Woodrow Wilson*, ed. A. S. Link |

# Introduction

The year 1897 is one that historians just love. It was that rare kind of year that contained both evocative and subtle premonitions of upcoming changes in the balance of national power. From the pageantry of Queen Victoria's Diamond Jubilee to the almost unnoticed arrival of Theodore Roosevelt at the Navy Department, 1897 served notice that one great era was ending, and another was poised to open up. For both the United States and Royal Navies it marked the end of decades of convenient assumptions and comfortable procedures. In Great Britain it saw the final as well as the most lavish celebration of the Pax Britannica. On 20 June all of London seemed to turn out to pay their respects to the longest serving monarch in English history. Six days later, in what must have been one of the great spectacles of the age, the Royal Navy paraded in front of Queen Victoria at Spithead. Lined up in five columns that stretched for almost thirty miles were 165 of the most modern and powerful warships in the world. Yet, this enormous force represented only part of the Royal Navy, drawn, as it was, predominantly from ships stationed in home waters. The overseas squadrons remained at their far-flung posts silently and remorselessly standing guard over the vast shipping lanes of the British Empire.

In the United States it was an altogether less dramatic, but just as momentous, year. 1897 was the last full year for the unimpressive, unimportant, and much unloved U.S. Navy of the late nineteenth century. At the end of the Civil War the American fleet had been second only to the Royal Navy. Since then it had been allowed to slip into disrepair and obsolescence. By 1897 the United States had fewer battleships than Great Britain, France, Russia, Germany, or Italy. Now, however, there was a new president, William McKinley, who chose Theodore Roosevelt as his new assistant secretary of the navy. At the time it would have been impossible to guess that this appointment heralded great changes, but one year later the United States found itself in a naval war with Spain, and four years later Theodore Roosevelt found himself in the White House. Things would never be the same for the U.S. Navy again.

Because of all of these events 1897 has been used to mark the beginning of the transition of the British and American navies from traditional, insular nineteenth-century organisms into modern, unsentimental fighting machines. Queen Victoria's Diamond Jubilee has been seen as the last hurrah for Britain's naval supremacy. In the coming years the Admiralty and Cabinet would have to turn their attention to the grubby and unromantic business of fending off a number of formidable and determined challengers. This, the traditional view, holds that the next forty years of British history were one long struggle, as the governments of the day did their best to protect Britain's position in the face of the nation's relative decline. It is the picture accepted by many historians, a small sample of whom would have to include Paul Kennedy, Corelli Barnett, Max Beloff, and Sir Harry Hinsley. Even the two great historians of the Royal Navy between 1900 and 1939, Arthur Marder and Stephen Roskill, write mainly of the exhausting efforts undertaken by the Admiralty and the Cabinet to maintain Britain's maritime supremacy in the face of stiff international competition.

Recently, however, there has been a move to challenge many of the orthodox assumptions about British decline, naval or otherwise. Sidney Pollard has argued that Britain's relative economic performance was very respectable and that the country maintained important advantages for much of the period.[1] Brian McKercher and John Ferris, furthermore, have claimed that the reports of Britain's overall decline before 1939 have been greatly exaggerated.[2] In a series of articles it was argued that the British successfully defended their position between 1900 and the outbreak of the Second World War.[3]

Anyone delving into the secondary literature will therefore be given two quite contrasting pictures of Britain and the British Empire between 1900 and 1939. The first is of an aging lion that, while still possessing a considerable bite, is growing increasingly exhausted defending his large pride and is slowly slipping into a steady, inevitable, and almost magisterial dotage. The second is of a well maintained sports car, no longer the unchallenged leader but with the most complete set of extras available. It is a vehicle that was able to negotiate a very tricky course successfully until the Second World War, after which it plunged headlong off a very steep cliff.

Historians of the U.S. Navy, including Harold and Margaret Sprout, William Braisted, Robert Love, and George Davis, are less divided.[4] To them this is a period of steady and sometimes spectacular growth for the U.S. Navy. The United States, which possessed the world's largest economy by 1890, still had only a token naval force until the Spanish American War. After 1898, however, the American navy under the beneficent tutelage of Theodore and, later, Franklin Roosevelt, began its ascent to the top of the world's naval tables. By 1907 it had become the second largest in the world, by 1921 it was recognized as Great Britain's equal, and by the end of World War II it reigned supreme. While this was not always the smoothest of journeys, it was supposedly as inevitable and unstoppable as Britain's decline.

What should one make of these different views? It is probably best to begin with the basics and move on from there. In 1897, as mentioned before, the Royal Navy was far and away the world's largest while the American fleet toiled down in the minor leagues. The British had at least as many battleships as their most serious competitors, France and Russia, combined and more than Germany, Italy, Japan, and the United States put together. By 1945 the situation had changed substantially. Great Britain was a clear, if respectable, second while the United States had a larger navy than the rest of the world combined. Since then the Royal Navy has slipped even further down the rankings, falling behind the fleets of Russia and even the "auld enemy" France, while the United States has maintained its worldwide preeminence. The question that historians have asked is whether the years between 1900 and 1939 witnessed this transition in naval power or whether the British were able to withstand the challenge by the United States and others until the Second World War, only to collapse dramatically afterward.

It is a difficult and tricky question. There is some compelling evidence for both views. While this book will not be able to settle this debate, hopefully it will provide a different way of looking at the evolution of naval power. This will not be done through a comprehensive survey of all aspects of American and British naval policy. That would be entirely superfluous after the magisterial efforts of Marder, Roskill, and Braisted, to name just a few. Instead, only specific peacetime incidents and issues are examined in detail. This is mainly because in both countries naval policy often drifted along unchecked for years at a time and then had to be dramatically reevaluated in the face of new and often unforeseen developments. By looking at these specific moments of reevaluation, one can see both the changes in the perceptions of the naval policymakers and the actual evolution of the naval balance of power.

To do this it is best to divide the years in question into three different periods: the first from the turn of the century to the First World War, the second from the end of the war until the conclusion of the First London Naval Conference in 1930, and the third from 1930 until the end of the naval arms control process. Since these periods saw the United States and Great Britain wrestle with different problems, the narrative will be broken down into sections. Between

1900 and 1914 the Anglo-American naval balance, while interesting, was not
the most pressing issue for either nation. There will therefore be separate sections for each country. The changes in Britain's naval position are examined by
looking at two issues, the evolution of the two-power standard and the 1909 naval estimates crisis, while the growth of the U.S. Navy is seen by evaluating the
presidency of Theodore Roosevelt and the famous 1916 naval program.

The two-power standard is one of the most famous policies in naval history.
Though it had existed unofficially since the late eighteenth century, it was not
formally adopted by a British government until 1889. It has often been assumed
that the standard was an ironclad commitment on the part of the British to
maintain the Royal Navy at a strength equal to that of the second and third largest fleets in the world. When the British were thereupon forced to replace the
two-power standard with the 160 percent ratio in 1910 and the one-power standard in 1921, this was seen as a clear indication of the slow, but inevitable, decline of British naval power. In reality, the two-power standard, in practice if not
in public, was constantly reinterpreted and redefined by different governments.
Within seven years of its announcement the Cabinet began to weaken it. A few
years later the Balfour government changed the standard's meaning completely
by counting only the combined strengths of France and Russia. Four years later,
though, Prime Minister Asquith took the extraordinary step of redefining the
standard as the combined strength of the next two naval powers, including the
United States, plus an additional margin of 10 percent. It was the most ambitious
standard ever promulgated, though it had a shelflife of only a number of months.

This was because of the 1909 naval estimates crisis. This event, a bitter
Cabinet and public debate over the number of battleships to be laid down in
1909, was the single most important event in shaping British naval policy before
World War I. The crisis occurred after a three-year period of extreme confidence
that followed the destruction of the Russian navy by the Japanese and the development of HMS Dreadnought. In a matter of a few weeks in late 1908 and early
1909 this confidence evaporated, and the Cabinet and Admiralty were confronted by the possibility that the Germans might be able to build enough dreadnought battleships to wrest naval supremacy from Great Britain. This realization
caused a wholesale reexamination of Britain's naval position and the adoption of
a new policy that the Asquith government would follow faithfully until 1914.

American naval policy was also prone to similar swings. The first of these
was because of the energetic presidency of Theodore Roosevelt. Roosevelt has
been hailed by most historians as the godfather of the modern U.S. Navy. It is
true that he had some gratifying successes early in his term, especially when he
was able to cajole the Congress into authorizing enough capital ships to make
the American fleet the world's second largest. It is also true, however, that his
legacy needs to be looked at with a more skeptical eye. It is still an open question
whether the advent of Theodore Roosevelt represented a permanent change or a
pleasant aberration in the development of American naval power. By the end of
his second term Congress was proving increasingly recalcitrant and was sub-

stantially reducing the president's building programs. After he left office, his chosen successor, William Taft, and the next president, Woodrow Wilson, refused to follow on with Roosevelt's ambitious plans for the American navy. The two of them were quite happy to see the fleet slip back down the world's naval rankings. This period of drift and decline lasted for almost six years and was brought to a sudden halt only by the extraordinary impact of the First World War. In 1915 Wilson, who had previously resisted appeals to increase America's naval strength, had a startling change of heart and called for the construction of a navy "second to none." The result of this wholly unforeseen turn of events was the 1916 naval program, which would have made the U.S. Navy the world's strongest by 1921.

If the Anglo-American naval balance was not a great worry to the two countries before the First World War, it was their paramount concern between 1918 and 1930. It makes sense, therefore, to combine the narrative for this period and discuss each country's reactions to the same events. The most important of these were the various naval arms control conferences. These were the meetings at Washington in 1921-22, Geneva in 1927 and London in 1930. The first established the famous 5-5-3 ratio in capital ship strength between the United States, Great Britain and Japan. The second, also known as the Coolidge Conference, was called by the United States to try and extend this ratio to cruisers, destroyers and other auxiliary vessels. Unfortunately this second meeting ended in acrimony and led to the worst level of Anglo-American hostility in the twentieth century. Eventually the rift was healed in 1930 at the London conference, when the British and the Americans agreed on a formula for overall naval parity.

These conferences have been the object of some rather bitter criticism, especially by historians of British naval power. The various British governments have been accused of unnecessarily ceding naval parity to the United States, letting idealistic and misguided notions cloud their strategic vision, and allowing the Royal Navy to fall dangerously below its minimum acceptable level of strength.[5] American naval historians, however, are more divided. Some have argued that the conferences, Washington in particular, allowed the United States to formally establish its right to naval parity at little cost.[6] Others, however, have been critical of the ratios for giving the Japanese too large an allocation and allowing them to dominate the western Pacific.

One of the great difficulties facing anyone trying to sort through these various arguments is the increasing fragmentation of naval power in the interwar period. Before 1914 capital ship numbers and technology were universally accepted as the key measurements of a nation's naval power. The experiences of the First World War, specifically, the improvements made in submarine warfare and naval airpower, complicated this equation enormously. Naval power was made a much more volatile and uncertain commodity. One of the great hopes for the arms control conferences was that they would help regulate the growth of these new technologies and prolong the useful life of Britain's and America's large capital ship fleets. Before too much criticism is heaped upon the agreements, it should be noted that both America's and Britain's naval position would invariably have been much more complicated had there been no arms control agreements at all.

The First London Conference settled almost all the outstanding naval issues between Great Britain and the United States and allowed them to focus their attentions on more likely enemies such as Germany and Japan. Worrying about each other was a luxury that neither country wished to purchase between 1930 and 1936. So once again the narratives about Great Britain and the United States divide. For both it was a period of contrasting developments. On one hand, there were the British and American rearmament programs, called reluctant and insufficient by many and adequate by only a few. On the other hand, there was a joint, final attempt to keep alive the naval arms control process at the second London Conference of 1935-1936. Since these developments were crucial for determining the strengths of the American and British navies at the outbreak of the Second World War, it is important to examine what both countries decisionmakers were thinking at the time and what they expected to accomplish by their actions. The view one takes about these issues determines how one answers the overarching question about the rise and fall of British and American naval power between 1900 and the outbreak of the Second World War.

At this point it does not make sense to jump too far ahead and try to give an answer. However, one thing should be said. Any attempt to describe the rise and fall of naval power as a linear phenomenon is bound to fail. Naval power did not move in gradual, incremental phases like two lines on a graph moving slowly, but evenly, to bisect. Naval power was, in fact, extremely volatile, subject to unexpected and dramatic swings and often the hostage of chance or luck. Take the Royal Navy, for instance. Whether you believe that the British were in a period of decline or that they were able to maintain their supremacy, it is clear that the Royal Navy's position swung back and forth quite substantially between 1900 and 1939. At the beginning of the twentieth century it could be argued that the Royal Navy was in a more precarious situation than any it would have to face again until 1940. It is true that it still outnumbered the Franco-Russian navies, but the United States and Germany were in the process of greatly enlarging their fleets, and Britain had no reliable allies other than Portugal. It was a time of pessimistic reevaluation as the Balfour government weakened the two-power standard and sought alliances with almost every major naval power in the world. Just a few years later, after 1905, the Admiralty would be flush with confidence, even creating war plans for a war against an alliance of Germany and the United States. Six months after these plans were drawn British confidence would plummet to its lowest depths in almost a century, when it was thought that the Germans were secretly plotting to outbuild the Royal Navy. This assumption, which proved entirely groundless, was responsible for Britain's largest yearly peacetime construction program in the twentieth century, which provided the Royal Navy with the crucial edge it would need in the first few months of World War I. This pattern repeated itself in the interwar period. Great confidence coming out of the war quickly changed to pessimism when it was thought that the United States would press ahead with its enormous building program. Later, when it was thought that the Americans had lost interest and that the Royal Navy had maintained its supremacy, the Baldwin government rather rashly chose to provoke the United States. This action precipitated another period of British pessimism and reevaluation.

For the United States the evolution of naval power was no more smooth or even. Extreme confidence under Roosevelt gave way to gloom and despair under Taft and Wilson. The First World War provided a completely unexpected fillip to the American navy, and plans were drawn up for at least parity with Great Britain. After the war it seemed even greater things beckoned when the president threatened to use the American fleet as his "big stick" to bludgeon the Europeans. This bravado soon disappeared. After the Washington Conference the American Navy languished without direction for years, until a British blunder enraged Calvin Coolidge and set in motion another round of American naval construction. Therefore, by the outbreak of the Second World War both the perceptions about, and the reality of, American and British naval power had swung back and forth dramatically a number of times.

Finally, two other areas will receive special attention. The first is the decision-making processes in Britain and the United States. Naval power was the single greatest manifestation of national power for both countries. Their armies were small, and their air forces existed for only part of the period covered. For Great Britain naval power was vital to its very existence, and for the United States naval power was far and away the most effective tool it could use to exercise armed influence around the world. Therefore, the decisions taken about the relative strengths of the two navies were in many ways the most important strategic choices the British and American governments ever took.

Yet, beyond this one similarity they had little else in common. The British had a compact, streamlined, and highly confidential way of formulating naval policy. There were only two bodies intimately involved, the Cabinet and the Admiralty, and the total number of individuals who participated in their deliberations was probably no more than thirty. Of this number only a handful, the prime minister, the foreign secretary, the chancellor of the exchequer, the first lord of the admiralty, the first sea lord, the director of naval intelligence, and few other Cabinet members and sailors, were really influential. Even though the British system was so centralized, the people involved had to be very careful, for they knew that naval issues had great resonance in the public, and any shortcoming on their part could quickly be used against them.

In the United States the situation was totally different. Since the public knew little and cared less about the American navy, there was little control or accountability in the naval decision-making process. Three different institutions had some influence over policy, the presidency, the Congress, and the Navy Department. Of these three the Navy Department was undoubtedly the weakest. Since the secretary of the Department was not usually a personality with great political credibility, the navy generally had to hope that the president and the Congress would take an interest in naval issues. The president was vital because only he, except in times of national emergency, had the political capital needed to make naval issues part and parcel of the national debate. Members of Congress, on the other hand, were inclined to look on the naval budget as a source of "pork" for their districts and had little inclination to spend large sums of money building up the fleet's fighting strength. They preferred bases to battleships, and only the strenuous efforts of a committed president could persuade them to approve a consistent plan of naval building.

The final issue that is discussed in some detail is the specific role that naval issues played in the Anglo-American relationship. If either America or Britain had to say which country represented its most formidable naval challenger, it would have to have been the other. Britain was the only country with bases that could have supported a large fleet in the western Atlantic or the Caribbean. The United States, alternatively, stood astride Britain's most vital trade routes and had the industrial capability to construct a fleet much larger than the Royal Navy. This does not mean that an Anglo-American war was ever considered likely or desirable. It was not. In fact, the trend was very much in the opposite direction. Much has been made of the growth in Anglo-American friendship and cooperation in the first part of the twentieth century. Yet, the relationship was much more complex than it might seem. A number of important sailors and politicians in both countries, such as William Benson, America's first chief of naval operations, Edmond Slade the British director of naval intelligence during the 1909 naval crisis, and well known figures such as Winston Churchill, Neville Chamberlain, Calvin Coolidge, and Henry Cabot Lodge, at different times were very skeptical of the embryonic "special relationship." While they did not counsel war, they did exert a great deal of influence over the course of their country's naval development. In the end their influence was another reason for the instability and swings in American and British naval power.

# NOTES

1. S. Pollard, *Britain's Prime and Britain's Decline: The British Economy 1870-1914.*

2. Ferris, "The Symbol and Substance of Seapower: Great Britain and the United States and the One-Power Standard, 1919-1921," in B. McKercher, ed. *Anglo-American Relations in the 1920s*: B. McKercher, "Wealth, Power and the New International Order: Britain and the American Challenge in the 1920's". *Diplomatic History.*

3. Neilson, "Greatly Exaggerated: The Myth of the Decline of Great Britain before 1914;" J. Ferris, "The Greatest Power on the Earth, Great Britain in the 1920's;" B. McKercher, "Our Most Dangerous Enemy: Great Britain Preeminent in the 1930's," *International History Review.*

4. H. and M. Sprout, *The Rise of American Naval Power 1776-1918*; W. R. Braisted, *The United States Navy in the Pacific, 1897-1909*, and *The United States Navy*

*in the Pacific, 1909-1922*; R. W. Love, *History of the United States Navy*, G. Davis, *A Navy Second to None*.

5.  C. Hall, *Britain America and Arms Control 1921-37*; A. Marder, *Old Friends, New Enemies*, vol. I, F. H. Hinsley, *Command of the Sea: The Naval Side of British History 1918-45*, P. M. Kennedy, *The Rise and Fall of British Naval Mastery*, C. L. Mowat, *Britain Between the Wars, 1918-40*.

6.  T. Buckley, *The United States and the Washington Conference, 1921-22*.

# 1

# Naval Policy in Great Britain and the United States

In Parliament I would always speak, in general terms, of not falling below the Two-Power Standard. To the Cabinet I would suggest that if we make such provision as will offer us the reasonable certainty of success in a war with France and Russia, we shall have fully provided for all contingencies

Lord Selborne, "Navy Estimates," 16 November 1901[1]

There is in the American government, considered as a whole, a want of unity. Its branches are unconnected; their efforts are not directed to one aim, do not produce one harmonious result. The sailors, the helmsman, the engineer, do not seem to have one purpose or obey one will, so that instead of making steady way the vessel may pursue a devious or zigzag course, and sometimes merely turn round and round in the water.

James Bryce, *The American Commonwealth*, Vol. I, p.294[2]

To examine the differences in how Great Britain and the United States made naval policy is to examine some of the basic differences in their whole systems of governance. There was only one important similarity. In both countries naval policy was made through a three-step process. Annual naval programs were drawn up by the navies and forwarded to an executive, and they ended up in the legislatures. The British Admiralty and the American Navy Department decided upon a set of recommendations; these were passed on to the Cabinet and the president, respectively, and then sent to Parliament and Congress for final approval. Beyond this superficial schematic resemblance, however, the systems had little in common.

In Britain naval policy was decided in private by a small group of politicians and sailors. This streamlined process allowed British governments a great deal of flexibility. They could change or redefine policy very quickly, just so long as the public remained convinced that the Royal Navy's supremacy was not threatened. In 1901 Lord Selborne eagerly took advantage of the highly confidential nature of British naval policy. He was able to make a major change in the definition of the famous two-power standard but had to inform only the Cabinet. He admitted that the public and Parliament would be told nothing. The American system, meanwhile, was as chaotic as the British system was controlled. There was no finer proof of Bryce's commentary on American government than its annual struggle over warship construction. For the American navy to get what it wanted it first had to convince the president—no easy task—and he in turn had to convince both houses of Congress, an even harder proposition. If any link in this chain gave way, the whole system broke down.

The question might very well be asked what is meant by the term "naval policy." A whole of host of topics from minute technical details to grand political questions could fit under its rubric. Within the context of this book "naval policy" refers mainly to the debates and decisions surrounding the annual naval construction programs. Both Britain's and America's publicly stated naval policies, like the two-power standard or a navy "second to none," were usually just vague guidelines that were rarely, if ever, strictly followed. Only during the annual discussions about new shipbuilding did American and British politicians and sailors reveal their perceptions of the present and their expectations for the future. This was when they were forced to ponder the crucial questions of naval power. How strong are our potential enemies? How strong are we? How strong should we be? In answering these questions, British and American naval policy was "made."

In Britain only two bodies had real influence in this process: the Royal Navy and the Cabinet. At the turn of the century the Royal Navy was probably the single most respected national institution in the country. The average British subject seemed to have more confidence in the fleet than in any other group or individual.[3] At the time the executive office in charge of the Royal Navy was the Admiralty. The Admiralty was controlled by the Admiralty Board, a committee made up of professional sailors, politicians, and civil servants. The board was chaired by the first lord of the Admiralty, a member of the Cabinet who was appointed by the prime minister. The fleet was represented by the four sea lords. The first sea lord, or chief of the naval staff, was the most important officer in the fleet. He was responsible for maintaining the strength and efficiency of the navy, distributing ships into fleets, and advising the first lord on policy. The other sea lords were responsible for personnel, materiel, and supplies and transport, respectively. There was also one civil lord in charge of works and building, with a second appointed in 1912 to oversee Admiralty contracts and dockyards. The chief civil servant was the permanent secretary, who took control of the Admiralty's bureaucratic affairs and looked after its correspondence. The permanent secretary was not made a full member of the Admiralty Board until 1921. The last member was the parliamentary and financial secretary. He was a member of Parliament, in essence a junior secretary of state, with responsibility for overseeing the Admiralty's budget. The parliamentary and financial secretary was not formally made a member of the Admiralty Board until 1929.

The Admiralty Board was not a committee of equals. During the nineteenth century more and more power had been concentrated in the hands of the first sea lord. He dominated areas such as warplanning and strategic policy. In making his decisions the first sea lord was chiefly assisted not by members of the board but by the Naval Intelligence Department (NID). Founded in 1886, the NID, usually in the person of the director of Naval Intelligence, became responsible for supplying the first sea lord with the data he needed to formulate and defend his policies. The other sea lords were generally left to look after their own departments and were wheeled out by the first sea lord only when he needed extra support.

The man who took most advantage of the position's power was Admiral John "Jacky" Fisher, first sea lord from October 1904 to January 1910. Fisher's dynamic, aggressive personality allowed him to dominate the Royal Navy. He not only instituted the wide-ranging reforms for which he is famous but he also monopolized the formulation of the Admiralty's annual building programs and war plans. He was particularly sensitive about his control of the latter. He constructed war plans in private and refused to divulge little of their details. In one instance he concocted a plan for a war between Great Britain and an alliance of Germany and the United States. Later he drew up a plan to land a large force on the Pomeranian coast only sixty miles from Berlin.[4] He was so secretive that he even refused to share his plans with the Committee for Imperial Defence, the organization established by Arthur Balfour to coordinate British strategic planning.

During the era of "Splendid Isolation" Fisher and the other first sea lord's could get away with such independence. As the British began to work more closely with allies such as France, however, the system became unworkable. The problem came to a head in 1911, when Admiral Arthur Wilson was first sea lord. Wilson had been no more forthcoming with his war plans than Fisher, and his taciturn and gruff exterior made him seem even more forbidding. In August 1911, during the Agadir crisis, he was called up before the Committee for Imperial Defence to describe his plans for a possible war with Germany. All Wilson could manage was a brief and unconvincing outline. To members of the committee his plans seemed incoherent. Indeed Wilson's halting performance caused such alarm that Asquith, the prime minister, decided to remove the first lord, Reginald McKenna, in favor of Winston Churchill.[5]

In hoisting Churchill upon the Admiralty, Asquith was hoping to change the unequal relationship that had grown up between the first lord and the first sea lord. The first lord of the Admiralty was supposed to be the superior of the first sea lord. The first lord was a relatively senior post in any government. It tended to be filled by younger, ambitious politicians on the way up, such as McKenna and Churchill, or party grandees such as Lords Selborne and Tweedmouth. Though all the first lords before the First World War, with perhaps the sole exception of Tweedmouth, were able and opinionated men, they immediately became committed, vocal supporters of a larger navy as soon as they took up their post. Even if they had previously opposed increases in the navy's budget, they quickly metamorphosed into ardent supporters of a "big navy."

This metamorphosis had been a crucial component of the first sea lord's power prior to 1914. When it came to drawing up the Admiralty's yearly construction programs, the first sea lord dominated proceedings, but the first lord had to explain and defend the Royal Navy's plans to the Cabinet. One of the first sea lord's most important tasks was therefore to butter up his civilian superior. Fisher was particularly assiduous in this respect. He spent a great deal of his time alternately flattering and cajoling his first lords. Only when he believed that he had the confidence of the first lord would Fisher reveal his building plans and send the first lord off to defend the Admiralty's position.

For Fisher, or any other first sea lord, the task of preparing the upcoming year's budget and building program was a never-ending process. In Britain the financial year runs from the 1 April to 31 March. The Admiralty would therefore begin preparing its plans by at least the summer and often the spring of the year before. These plans took shape in the form of sketch estimates that outlined the Royal Navy's expected spending and desired new construction. Once the first sea lord determined the number of new ships he wanted, he had to persuade the first lord. Before the First World War the first lord almost always agreed with the first sea lord, and so the Admiralty quickly came together in a united front to support the proposed building program.

The Cabinet usually had its first discussions about the naval sketch estimates in November or December. In a quiet year any problems could be settled through direct negotiations between the Admiralty and the Treasury, so that the Cabinet had to have only a brief discussion of the issue. At other times, such as the debates over the 1908-1909 and 1909-1910 estimates, the issue could split the Cabinet in two. Yet, no matter how deep the divisions were, the Cabinet had to reach some decision by early March to give the first lord enough time to introduce and defend the budget in Parliament.

The debates in Cabinet were almost always about one thing—money. Invariably leading the charge against the Admiralty's estimates was the chancellor of the exchequer. In much the same way that the first lord automatically mutated into a "big-navy" man, the chancellor, regardless of his earlier views, instantly assumed that the Admiralty was unduly alarmist and that its budget was full of waste and extravagance. Yet, before the First World War the chancellor was almost always thwarted and had to give in to the Admiralty's demands. Though the Liberal government in power after 1905 consistently pledged itself to retrenchment, only Asquith, chancellor from 1905 to 1908, oversaw a reduction in the Admiralty's budget. The experiences of his successor, Lloyd George, were more typical. He lost every battle he ever fought with the Admiralty.

Lloyd George's lack of success had much to do with the strategic positioning of "Liberal Imperialists" in the Asquith government. Once Campbell-Bannerman was forced to step down by illhealth, the Cabinet offices with the greatest influence over foreign and military affairs were held by Liberal imperialists. Not only was Asquith prime minister, but Sir Edward Grey, the Cabinet's most consistent supporter of a large navy, was foreign secretary, Richard Haldane was war secretary, and the First marquess of Crewe was colonial secretary. Traditional Liberals who by nature were more skeptical of the Admiralty, men like Lewis Harcourt, John Morley, and John Burns, were given domestic portfolios and were not well placed to resist the Royal Navy's demands. Asquith's and Grey's support for the Royal Navy were particularly important.

After the First World War there were some important changes in both the substance and structure of British naval policymaking. Within the Admiralty the first sea lord lost some of his independence and had to rely more and more on professional bureaucratic structures. The Finance Committee, chaired by the parliamentary and financial secretary, closely monitored the spending proposals of each Admiralty department. The Committee of Imperial Defence (CID) was called in to examine the Admiralty's strategic and war plans and to adjudicate disputes. Finally, in the 1930s the Defence Requirements Sub-Committee (DRC) was established to force the army and navy to coordinate their planning.

Even with all the changes the first sea lord remained the most important single man in the fleet. First sea lords like Admirals David Beatty and Ernle Chatfield were particularly prominent and had a great deal of influence. However, the Admiralty had undoubtedly lost some of its ability to sway the Cabinet. Various governments felt emboldened enough by victory in the First World War to now dictate limits to the Royal Navy. In the 1920s the Admiralty was forced to draw up its budgetary plans within the stiff requirements of the "Ten-Year Rule," which assumed that Britain would not be engaged in a war for at least ten years. During the Great Depression the Admiralty was also compelled to reduce its budget significantly.

One thing, however, did not change in the interwar period. No one outside the Cabinet or Admiralty was able to gain any influence over the process of making naval policy. Parliament remained what it had been prior to the First World War, a compliant rubberstamp for the Cabinet's naval policy. Though the opposition and, occasionally, members of the governing party might grumble about the direction of British naval policy, the governments of the day always had their way. British party discipline was a crucial component to the success of a government's naval policy. Because the British public had such a keen interest in naval issues, the party in power had to present a united front to assure the country that the fleet was being properly maintained. The role of Parliament in the process was to provide this assurance.

This automatic compliance on the part of the House of Commons was one of the great differences between Britain and the United States. In America the Senate and House of Representatives were fiercely independent institutions. They had great power to shape American naval policy, and a number of congressmen used their authority, often capriciously, to foist their personal predilections on the fleet. Congress was often able to get its way because of the political and structural weaknesses of the American navy. While the Royal Navy had the ancient and venerable Admiralty Board to argue its case, its American counterpart had to make do with only the quasi-legal General Board.

It was quasi-legal because even though the General Board was founded in 1900, it was never sanctioned by Congress. It was established by executive order, and even though successive administrations urged Congress to approve its existence, the legislators did nothing. This inaction left the General Board in a permanent state of limbo. It could debate and give advice about American naval policy, but it could never issue orders.

The General Board was created to try to end the chaos that had gripped the American navy since the Civil War. In 1900 the navy was still organized along lines laid down in the age of wind and sail. Instead of having a central coordinating body, the American navy had a vast collection of independent bureau chiefs. The bureau chiefs ran their departments like personal empires and were under little pressure to coordinate their activities. By the twentieth century the number of bureaus had ballooned to ten: navigation, construction and repair, yards and docks, engineering, ordinance, supplies and accounts, naval intelligence, medicine and surgery, the marines, and a solicitor general. Of these the Bureau of Navigation had taken control of much of the American navy's strategic planning. Captain Henry C. Taylor, one of the greatest Chiefs of the Bureau of Navigation, had been mainly responsible for the creation of the General Board.[6]

Taylor, one of the most perceptive officers of his generation, was acutely aware of the deficiencies in the fleet's administration and pressed for a coordinating body to give direction to American naval policy. The result was the General Board, founded on 13 March 1900. The board was originally composed of Admiral George Dewey, the victor at Manila Bay and the most famous sailor of his generation, the chief of the Bureau of Navigation, the chief of Naval Intelligence, the president of the Naval War College, and other officers who were brought in on an ex officio basis. Because of Congress' refusal to sanction its existence, however, the General Board functioned only as an advisory body until the First World War. It was unable either to curb the power of the bureau chiefs or to present itself to the administration and Congress as the official voice of the fleet.

This last weakness might have been the General Board's greatest failing. The U.S. Navy needed to speak with one voice to its civilian leadership. Under the bureau system, however, very different noises emanated from the fleet, making the navy seem indecisive, fractious, and quarrelsome. During 1908 congressional hearings on American design faults some senior admirals and bureau chiefs defended American designs, while various junior officers bitterly attacked them. The General Board, meanwhile, was forced to stand on the sidelines completely mute.

In the absence of a united front, the job of articulating naval policy often fell to the secretary of the navy. The secretary was the civilian head of the American navy and was appointed by the president. Unlike in Britain, where the first lord of the Admiralty tended to be an important and intelligent politician, in America the president often appointed an undistinguished political ally to be secretary of the navy. Most of the time the appointees had no knowledge of, or interest in, naval affairs, and very few of them made lasting contributions. Theodore Roosevelt appointed six different secretaries during his seven years in power. Taft was the exception to the rule and appointed George von Lengerke Meyer, a man of real ability who served for an entire term and achieved some important successes. Wilson returned to form with his appointment of Josephus Daniels, an eccentric, southern, populist, white supremacist, prohibitionist, newspaper editor. While Daniels undoubtedly had the ear of the president, he was also unsuited to the job of running a modern navy. He remains to this day the most controversial secretary of the navy in American history.

A weak secretary of the navy was a great problem for the General Board because the secretary was the main conduit for information going from the fleet to the president. The secretary explained the General Board's proposed building programs to the White House. However, instead of defending his board's plans, like a British first lord, the secretary of the navy often decided to scale them back substantially. For any secretary it was more important to keep favor with the president than with the General Board. They were all therefore willing to slash the General Board's requests if it would make them more politically acceptable.

This kind of weakness led to the first attempts to reform the Navy Department in the twentieth century. William Sims in 1908 and then Bradley Fiske in 1914-1915 hatched plans for the appointment of an American equivalent of the first sea lord. Their hope was that any such appointee would relieve the secretary of the navy from having to make technical decisions while at the same time impose order on the bureau system. It should be recognized, however, that while these men have been lauded as "reformers" their plans were far from perfect. Both Sims and Fiske tended to be contemptuous of the politically appointed secretaries and wanted to drastically reduce civilian control over the navy. Both probably went too far in this direction, and their plans to weaken civilian control were divisive and possibly dangerous.

When change did occur, it was at first much more moderate than Sims or Fiske had hoped. In 1915 Congress approved the appointment of a chief of naval operations (CNO), one of the most significant reforms in American naval history. While the first CNO, William Benson, was at first starved of staff and authority, he transformed his position during the First World War. By 1918 he was undoubtedly the most important officer in the navy, with a large and efficient staff and a great deal of authority over the bureau chiefs. Since that time, the CNO has been the undisputed professional head of the navy and one of the most powerful military officers in the United States.

No matter how powerful the CNO was, he could achieve little without the support of the president. The chief executive, more than any other individual, was ultimately responsible for changes in American naval policy. This was because the U.S. Navy, unlike the Royal Navy, could not draw upon popular opinion for support. Except for a few short bursts of interest, Americans remained uninterested in naval issues. While the average citizen might have reflexively stated that he or she favored a large navy, this support was usually without depth and, more important, rarely influenced how he or she voted. There is no evidence that naval issues ever played a major role in the outcome of an American political campaign. In fact, the opposite seems to be the case. When the Republicans made support for a large navy part of their campaigns in 1908 and 1912, their share of the vote and the number of their elected senators and representatives went down.

Since the U.S. Navy could not draw upon public opinion for support, only the president could supply the necessary muscle to persuade Congress to increase naval strength. However, since different presidents had very different views, the fortunes of the U.S. Navy waxed and waned with successive administrations. Theodore Roosevelt was probably the greatest supporter that the American navy ever had in the White House, and during his tenure the American navy became the second strongest in the world. However, the next five presidents, Taft, Wilson, Harding, Coolidge, and Hoover, were not inclined to accord naval issues high priority. For most of their administrations naval building was neglected and the fleet withdrew from the public eye. Only when a president felt he needed the threat of a large American navy to secure his foreign policy goals, as Wilson did in 1915-1918 and Coolidge in 1928, did naval appropriations become a front-page issue, and new warships were authorized.

Things changed for the better, as far as the navy was concerned, when Franklin Roosevelt became president. Having served as assistant secretary of the navy under Wilson, this Roosevelt was also a supporter of a large American fleet. Congress once again approved large construction programs, and the United States finally began the unbroken ascent that would leave it with the largest navy in the world.

However, it should always be remembered that even if a president supported a large navy, he could not guarantee support in Congress. In his second term, Theodore Roosevelt had a series of brutal confrontations with Congress over increased dreadnought construction, confrontations in which the president was only partially victorious. Taft's conversion to a large-navy supporter proved even less successful. His attempts to increase American construction in 1911 and 1912 were dismissed contemptuously by Congress. What Roosevelt and Taft both failed to do was to forge a viable congressional coalition in favor of increased naval building. One could hardly blame them. Trying to put together such a coalition was almost impossible. Trying to put together a coalition to support increased spending on naval bases, on the other hand, was always possible.

The role that Congress played in the shaping of American naval policy separated the United States from the other great naval powers. Both senators and representatives knew that naval policy was not an issue of great political interest, which meant that they were generally immune from popular pressure. In Congress' eyes the navy was not simply an arm of national defense; it was more a source of largesse for the home folks. That meant that naval policy was as much a sectional as a partisan issue. While it was true that, on the whole, Republicans were more likely to support, and Democrats more likely to oppose, large shipbuilding programs, there were strong advocates for and against a large navy in each party. Before the First World War, Democrat Richmond Hobson was the American navy's strongest supporter in the House, while Theodore Burton, a Republican, was its most vociferous opponent. In the 1920s Republican senator William Borah often fought against the building programs drawn up by Republican presidents, while in the 1930s Democrat representative Carl Vinson led the fight for increased naval building.

These men, though, were atypical. Most members of Congress, especially those from the Midwest, the Rocky Mountain states, and the rural South, could muster little enthusiasm for naval debates. Instead, legislators from the coastal states were most concerned with naval issues,[7] though they expressed their concern in ways that did not always please the U.S. Navy. The way that a member of Congress was most likely to gain influence over naval policy was through the House and Senate Naval Affairs Committee. These committees had the greatest say over naval appropriations, the key to almost every area of naval policy. Both committees were controlled by very powerful chairmen. Of the three senators and two representatives who served as chairmen between 1900 and 1914, only one did not have a major naval base in his home state. In the Senate Eugene Hale, Republican from Maine, was chairman from 1900 to 1908, George Perkins, Republican from California, was chairman from 1909 to 1912, and Benjamin "Pitchfork" Tillman, Democrat from South Carolina, was chairman from 1913 to 1917. Hale ran the Portsmouth Naval Base like a personal fief, making sure it had all the latest materiel and trying to have it staffed with officers he preferred. Perkins, an otherwise passive man, worked assiduously to buildup the Mare Island base in San Francisco Bay. Yet, in using the naval budget as a source of "pork" and patronage, neither man could compare with Senator Tillman. Tillman, one of the most extraordinary men to ever inhabit the Senate, was a fire-breathing southern populist. He was personally loathed by most Republicans and even many members of his own party. Theodore Roosevelt was particularly unimpressed. The president, who at one point was warned by a constituent that Tillman might assassinate him, was convinced that the senator was a crook.[8] Yet, through sheer grit and determination, Tillman was able to wear down his opponents and transform Charleston Naval Base from an almost nonexistent facility into one of the largest naval bases in the United States. Tillman cared little about building new warships or recruiting new sailors, but whenever possible he added extra appropriations for his beloved Charleston. It was so well known that Tillman would stop at nothing to buildup Charleston that Senator Boies Penrose, Republican from Pennsylvania, once joked on the Senate floor "I want to say that I have never failed in 18 years to vote for the appropriations for the Charleston Navy Yard, knowing all the time that I could not get an adjournment of Congress until I did so."[9]

This kind of behavior was not limited to the Senate. One might have thought that George Foss, Republican from Illinois and chairman of the House Naval Affairs Committee from 1901 to 1910, would have been hamstrung because he came from a state without an ocean coastline. He got around this seemingly insurmountable problem in 1905 through the establishment of the Great Lakes Naval Training Station. Over the next ten years more than $3.5 million were spent on this facility.[10] The only chairman in either the Senate or the House not to use the naval budget for political gain was Lemuel Padgett. Padgett, a Democrat, was chairman of the House Naval Affairs Committee from 1911 to 1918 and came from Tennessee, a state that was physically incapable of supporting a large naval installation. This is without doubt one of the reasons that he was a navy favorite.

The fact that the Naval Affairs Committees were so fond of voting for large base appropriations did not mean, however, that they were in favor of building many new naval vessels. All the chairmen mentioned earlier, Hale, Perkins, Tillman, Foss, and Padgett, at one time in their career strongly opposed new construction plans. Hale, Perkins, Foss, and Tillman each opposed Roosevelt's plan for increasing battleship construction in 1907 and 1908, for which they were attacked by the president. Padgett, on the other hand, led the fight against Taft's construction plans in 1911 and 1912. Because of these different impulses, the United States ended up with an inordinately large shore establishment. In 1910 the United States, with a navy much smaller than Britain's and about equal to Germany's, maintained seven first class and four second class navy yards.[11] Great Britain, on the other hand, had only three first-class and three second-class yards, while the Germans had two and one, respectively.

Congress did not just use its influence to build bases and prevent the construction of new warships; it also interfered in technical decisions. By 1900 Senator Hale had developed a phobia of big battleships. For the next decade he fought strenuously to limit their size. He even tried to prevent the construction of American dreadnoughts for as long as possible. This type of congressional interference set the United States apart from Great Britain. While the naval profes-

# 2

# British Naval Power from the Two-Power Standard to 1908

The leading idea has been that our establishment should be on such a scale that it should be equal to the naval strength of any two other countries.

First Lord of the Admiralty George Hamilton, 7 March 1889[1]

Now there has never been any suggestion of equality with two naval powers. . . . The real question is as to the requisite expenditure necessary to protect the commerce of this country in time of war; and for that purpose no standard of bare equality of numbers has ever been suggested.

First Lord of the Admiralty Earl Selborne, 24 March 1903[2]

[Arthur Lee] I beg to ask the Prime Minister whether the Government accepts the Two-Power Standard of naval strength as meaning a preponderance of ten percent over the combined strengths, in capital ships, of the two next strongest powers.

[Asquith] The answer to . . . the question is in the affirmative.

House of Commons, 12 November 1908[3]

## PESSIMISM

In 1889, when George Hamilton announced that the two-power standard was the official policy of the British government, he spoke in a casual, almost perfunctory manner. What he was so casually announcing, however, was one of the most famous policies in British history. The idea that the Royal Navy should be as strong as the next two largest fleets in the world had been around since the 1770s, yet it had never been an official policy. Hamilton's move was thus a bold, almost arrogant affirmation of national power. Historians of the Royal Navy speak of the two-power standard as almost an immutable element of Britain's naval supremacy. Marder has claimed that after 1889 the standard was "confirmed time and again by responsible statesmen of both parties in the next fifteen years."[4]

For almost a decade after Hamilton's announcement this description was accurate. The two-power standard was endorsed by leading politicians from all parties, such as Lord Salisbury and Henry Campbell-Bannerman. It seemed both a tidy and logical standard with which to measure British strength. However, the two-power standard had one glaring, if hidden, weakness. When it was announced, the United States and Germany, Britain's two most powerful industrial rivals, had only small fleets. A naval challenge by either one would have taxed British resources in a manner not seen since Trafalgar. For the last few decades the Admiralty had to worry about only French and Russian naval strength. While neither was a *quantite negligible,* neither possessed the industrial or shipbuilding capacity necessary to challenge forcefully the Royal Navy.

Eventually, however, the equilibrium on which Hamilton's standard had been based started to break down. On 26 March 1898 the Reichstag approved Germany's first modern naval law. Eschewing a quick challenge, the Germans approved a building program stretching over more than a decade. The original law called for nineteen battleships, a figure doubled in 1900. Eventually, the German high seas fleet was to be capable of posing a threat to the "world's greatest naval power." At the same time the United States was beginning, though more spasmodically, to develop its naval power. By 1905 the United States had begun the construction of enough battleships to make the American navy the second largest in the world. Indeed, it first seemed as if America was to pose a greater challenge than Germany.

The Admiralty was quick to acknowledge the impact that these challenges would have upon Britain's position. In 1898, it recognized that the United States and Germany were both increasing their naval strength.[5] This is not to say that the United States or Germany quickly supplanted France and Russia. Such a shift would not occur for a few years. Instead, the Admiralty was forced to undertake a reevaluation of Britain's global naval position.

From the beginning the Germans were viewed more suspiciously than the Americans. In December 1900 Reginald Custance, the Director of Naval Intelligence, assembled all known information about the German fleet. His findings were sobering. While the Russians built their battleships in a leisurely five years, and the French in a more respectable three and a half to four,[6] the British usually assembled their capital ships in approximately three years. It was a vital British advantage that allowed for great flexibility in Admiralty planning. Custance, however, discovered that the average German battleship was also constructed in only three years. The Admiralty would therefore have to keep a close watch on the growing size of the German fleet: "In 1906 Germany will be equal in line of Battleships to Russia. After that date, unless Russia increases her navy, Germany will be the third naval power, and then, in considering the strength of our fleet; the Navies of France and Germany will have to be considered instead of those of France and Russia."

Later, in 1901, Custance brought to the attention of Lord Selborne, first lord of the Admiralty, the fact that Germany possessed only three fewer battleships than Russia.[7] Selborne was apparently quite impressed and decided to bring the issue up for discussion in the Cabinet. It was a decision that began the process of revising Hamilton's two-power standard. Selborne submitted a paper on 16 November 1901: "The Naval policy of Germany . . . is definite and persistent. The Emperor seems determined that the power of Germany shall be used all over the world to push German commerce, possessions and interests. . . . The result of this policy will be to place Germany in a commanding position if ever we find ourselves at war with France and Russia."[8]

However, at this point the Cabinet could not afford an aggressive policy toward the Germans. The Cabinet's initial impulse was quite the opposite. Joseph Chamberlain, the influential colonial secretary, had long nurtured plans for an Anglo-Saxon, Teutonic alliance involving Britain, Germany, and the United States. By 1901 the rest of the Cabinet seemed willing to give the notion a try. In December the foreign secretary, Lord Landsdowne, mooted the possibility of a defensive Anglo-Germany alliance.[9] Unbeknownst to Admiral Tirpitz, this might very well have been the one moment when his concept of a "risk fleet" came close to fulfilling its original goal. It would have been inconceivable for an alliance between Great Britain and Germany not to have entailed some satisfaction of the latter's strategic demands.[10]

In 1902, however, British thinking about the German Navy shifted. The British naval attache in Berlin, H. O. Arnold-Foster, submitted a very detailed analysis of the German fleet, a report passed on to the Cabinet.[11] He outlined the capabilities of the new German battleships, as well as the strategic considerations underlining their construction. While admitting that France and Russia still represented a greater threat to the British Empire, Arnold-Foster spelled out the special dangers posed by Germany. First, the German navy would be relatively unimportant in war with France and Russia, and thus Britain was the one power really threatened. Second, Germany possessed some of the world's most efficient shipbuilding facilities, such as those at Kiel and Wilhelmshaven. Finally, Arnold-Foster stated that German battleships might be qualitatively equal or even superior to their British counterparts. This conclusion was especially troubling. The British had always counted on their technological superiority to carry the day. If this was no longer the case, the Admiralty would have to reconsider many of its basic precepts. Selborne adopted much of Arnold-Foster's thinking.[12]

Yet, while the Germans were beginning to worry the Cabinet, the Americans were posing an even greater numerical challenge. The British reaction, however, could not have been more different. By 1900 the British government had become remarkably skillful at acquiescing to American demands. In the 1890s and 1900s the British gave way on a number of important questions. In 1895 they bowed to American pressure and allowed the United States to arbitrate a long-standing border dispute between Venezuela and British Guyana. In 1903, the British connived with Theodore Roosevelt to frustrate a Canadian border claim in Alaska. Actually, Canada, the world's largest geographical hostage, was one of the main reasons for Britain's "softly-softly" approach to the United States. America's enormous industrial muscle, its latent military power, and its position astride many of Britain's vital sea-lanes, were also powerful incentives. When the U.S. Navy began to expand, the British response was naturally cautious: "If the United States continue their present naval policy, and develop their navy as they are easily capable of developing it if they chose, it will be scarcely possible for us to raise our navy to a strength equal to that both of France and the United States combined."[13]

Lord Selborne accepted that America's latent strength was reason enough to exclude the United States from the two-power standard.[14] He expounded upon this theme in separate memoranda submitted on 6 September and 16 November 1901. His feeling of resignation was shared by politicians of all parties. Sir Edward Grey, who later proved to be a committed "big-navy" man, admitted that Great Britain should never build against the United States.[15]

In 1905 this policy was taken one step further when the Committee for Imperial Defence decided to make no further effort to defend Canada. Though the verbal acrobatics used to obscure this policy change were impressive, they could not hide the extent of British withdrawal:

In the event of an occurrence so much deprecated as the rupture of friendly relations with the United States, the position of Canada is one of extreme danger, and, so far as the navy is concerned, any effective assistance would be exceedingly difficult. . . . Generally, the more carefully this problem is considered, the more tremendous do the difficulties which would confront Great Britain in a war with the United States appear. It may be hoped that the policy of the British Government will ever be to use all possible means to avoid such a war.[16]

The rise of Germany and the United States led to a wholesale reexamination of the two-power standard. Early supporters of the standard assumed that Great Britain had to keep a fleet at least numerically equal to that of the next two strongest naval powers—whoever they might be. Now numerical equivalence began to be questioned. Arthur Balfour provided the early indications of a shift when he stated, in 1896 and 1899, that the Royal Navy needed to be strong enough only to "contend" or "deal" with the next two strongest powers.[17] This was just the beginning. A few years later Selborne admitted that the Royal Navy would now be maintained at a strength capable of defeating France and Russia.[18] In March 1903 Selborne went even further when he, somewhat mendaciously, claimed that "no standard of bare equality of numbers has ever been suggested."[19]

The great problem facing the government was whether or not to explain these changes publicly. The two-power standard had become part of Britain's national language, and the public had come to view it as a concrete commitment on the part of their leadership. It was therefore not surprising that the Balfour government eventually decided to keep these changes under wraps. When Selborne first told the Cabinet that the standard would apply only to France and Russia, he carefully stated that the public would not be informed:

In Parliament I would always speak, in general terms, of not falling below the Two-Power Standard. To the Cabinet I would suggest that if we make such provision as will offer us the reasonable certainty of success in a war with France and Russia, we shall have fully provided for all contingencies.[20]

By 1904 Britain's leadership was taking decisive action to reevaluate the Royal Navy's strategic doctrines. No longer would the fleet be able to rule the world's waves imperiously. France and Russia remained the main threats, with almost the same number of battleships as the Royal Navy. Yet, there was a real possibility that a few years hence France and Russia would themselves be surpassed. Germany was building a powerful fleet that, in terms of quality, was more advanced than that of any other European country. Finally, the United States, which had forced significant concessions from the British while unarmed, was also building a powerful fleet of its own. All these factors combined to force the British government to modify and then abandon some of the basic tenets of the two-power standard.

In November 1904 the Admiralty appointed a committee, chaired by Prince Louis Battenberg, to evaluate further certain policy changes. The committee had the unenviable task of recommending more changes to the two-power standard. It proposed a strict limit on how and when the standard would be applied. The Admiralty was now to concentrate against the "likely" combinations of either Germany and Russia or France and Russia. The United States was never included, "being regarded throughout as friendly."[21] By neglecting to include a combination of France and Germany, these changes represented a body blow to the standard. If Germany's building plans progressed on schedule, it would pass the Russians in only a few years. A pure two-power standard, even removing the United States, should thus have included both France and Germany.

This reduction in the standard was accompanied by a corresponding shift in Great Britain's diplomatic relations. The British government agreed to the Anglo-Japanese Alliance partly because it was no longer deemed prudent to keep a large naval squadron in the Pacific.[22] Though this agreement was soon to cause friction with the United States, at the time it simply seemed to be a sensible and beneficial move. Later, the British would conclude the famous entente with France, supposedly the Royal Navy's greatest rival at the time. Taken together, these moves marked the end of the period of "Splendid Isolation." Within the space of a few years attempts had been made to placate all of Britain's potential rivals, moves motivated by the assumption that the Royal Navy could no longer single-handedly protect the British Empire.

## THE RUSSO-JAPANESE WAR AND THE DREADNOUGHT

On 27 May 1905 the Japanese Navy destroyed the Russian Baltic Fleet in the Battle of Tsushima. The results of this battle did more to restore British confidence than anything since the Crimean War. All the sober and considerate thinking that had characterized British naval planning since 1900 disappeared. Instead of planning for the future, the Admiralty and the Cabinet began to revel in the Royal Navy's present supremacy. This was because the strategic ramifications of Tsushima were so dramatic. Not only had the Russian Navy been dispatched to the ocean floor, but, for all practical purposes, the French Navy had been sunk as well.

The Admiralty had long assumed that if it had to fight the French, it would also have to contend with the Russians. Now that there was no Russian fleet worth speaking of, the French would have to challenge the Royal Navy directly. By 1905 this was distinctly unlikely. After Tsushima the Royal Navy took great pleasure in showing how much stronger it was than the French Navy and stronger than even a Franco-German coalition. For Germany the results of the battle were equally significant. The Germans originally hoped that their fleet would hold the balance between Great Britain, and France and Russia. Now there was no balance to hold. If Germany was to gain concessions from the British, it would now have to be as a direct threat. Also, the destruction of the Russian fleet inevitably led the Admiralty to pay more attention to the German navy.[23] This shift was not instantaneous, but it was as unstoppable as the rising number of German battleships.[24] By 1906, Germany seems to have replaced France and Russia as Britain's most formidable challenger. The Admiralty declared that of all the powers in the world Germany was the only one viewed as a "possible enemy."[25] In his private correspondence Admiral Fisher, the first sea lord, declared three times that Germany was Britain's only possible or "probable foe."[26]

Another dramatic result of Tsushima was the reinvigoration of the two-power standard. After years of being revised downward, it was restored to its former glory. Selborne openly contradicted what he had stated just months earlier: "It is an error to suppose that the Two-Power Standard, adopted fifteen years ago, ratified by every government since, and accepted by the whole nation, has ever had reference only to France and Russia."[27] In fact, as the Admiralty realized, the destruction of the Russian navy meant that the Royal Navy actually maintained a three-power standard. A committee was established after Tsushima to look for budgetary savings. The numbers it produced about the naval balance of power were comforting, to say the least. Now Great Britain had 46 battleships, while France had 18, Germany 17 and Russia only 5. The British also had 27 armored cruisers, while the others had only 21 between them. By any stretch of the imagination, the Royal Navy was in a very secure position, and the committee proposed a £1,520,000 reduction in the 1906-1907 naval budget.[28]

The main difference between the situation now and that before the Russo-Japanese War was one of emphasis. Previously, the Admiralty spent much of its time analyzing the potential strengths of the world's other fleets, concerned as it was not only with the present but also with the future balance of naval power. Now, the focus remained firmly fixed upon the Royal Navy's present preponderance. The best sign of this was a change in Admiralty policy toward the United States. Having earlier been exempted from the two-power standard, the United States was quietly reinserted into some Admiralty calculations.[29]

Yet, the Battle of Tsushima was not the only thing that restored British confidence; there was also the building of HMS *Dreadnought*. Much has been written about this vessel, supposedly a revolutionary warship that rendered earlier ships obsolete. By dispensing with secondary armaments, the *Dreadnought* was able to mount a battery of twelve large, ten-inch guns. Its firepower was therefore considerably larger than any other ship afloat. Just as remarkable was the manner of its construction. The *Dreadnought* was laid down in October 1905 and ready for duty in December 1906. The speed of its construction was breathtaking and further reinforced British notions that their shipbuilding skills were second to none.

Whether or not the *Dreadnought* represented a revolutionary breakthrough, it is true that it was perceived as such by the other naval powers. Admiral Fisher, its creator, was quick to seize on that point. "Foreign nations have put the dreadnought type beyond controversy, . . . They have one and all decided against their own shallow water interests . . . all plunged for the dreadnought type, pure and simple."[30] Even many of the *Dreadnought's* critics conceded this point. They attacked the ship for being too powerful, thus making Britain's lead in earlier classes irrelevant.

The *Dreadnought* speeded up the process of naval realignment begun at Tsushima. The French navy, already weakened, was dealt a further blow. France was still the world's second naval power in 1905, but its fleet was showing its age. Now that fleet was considered almost totally obsolete. After the *Dreadnought* the French would have to compete on a level playing field with industrial powers like Germany and America. In British eyes the value of the French navy declined dramatically. In 1909 the Admiralty assumed that the best six French battleships under construction were not even of dreadnought caliber.[31] In the same year the Naval Intelligence Department practically dismissed the French as naval powers: "Her downfall is not only apparent; it is real. . . . It may be argued on behalf of France . . . that the future programme is not known, but it is known only too well that there is no French Programme, and no laying down of new ships has yet been provided for, with the result that no new unit can be ready to reinforce the French squadrons before 1915 or even 1916."[32]

The *Dreadnought* made naval power a more exact reflection of a country's economic and technological might. The British or, in reality, Fisher had chosen to trade the Royal Navy's present numerical preponderance for a three-year head start in construction. This trade-off, of power for time, was not necessarily a bad one. If the British had mobilized their resources to construct a large number of dreadnoughts, they might have preempted a serious challenge. However, because the *Dreadnought* was built soon after Tsushima, neither the Cabinet nor the Admiralty felt compelled to support a large new construction program. In fact, due to the surge in British confidence, capital ship construction was being scaled back. The Balfour government had proposed in 1905 that four first-class battleships should be built a year. Because of Tsushima and the *Dreadnought*, however, Henry Campbell-Bannerman's Liberal government considerably reduced this program. The *Dreadnought* was conceived in 1904 and laid down in 1905. By March 1908 only nine similar ships, six battleships, and three battlecruisers, were under construction. According to Admiralty estimates Germany was building seven dreadnoughts, and the United States four, for a total of eleven.[33] If the program of four capital ships a year had been strictly followed, the Royal Navy could have completed six dreadnoughts with eight under construction and four more ready to be laid down. The slowdown can also be seen in the reduction of the Royal Navy's construction budget. From 1893 until the Russo-Japanese War, 26.5 percent of the Royal Navy's budget was devoted to building battleships. After Tsushima until the crucial year of 1909, this figure was 14.2 percent.[34] This smaller percentage was also being taken from a smaller overall naval estimate.

However, even in the face of these cutbacks, those responsible for British naval policy maintained an extremely optimistic outlook:

the British Navy far exceeds the Two-Power Standard. . . . Great Britain is in alliance with Japan, is on the most friendly terms with France and the United States . . . Russia's Navy has been almost completely destroyed . . . a combination between Germany and France or between either of these countries and the United States against us is inconceivable.[35]

Fisher, as was usually the case, made even more dramatic claims. "Our present margin of superiority over Germany (our only possible foe for years ) is so great as to render it absurd in the extreme to talk of anything endangering our naval supremacy, even if we stopped all shipbuilding altogether!!!."[36]

This era was replete with such dramatic assertions. It represented a dramatic shift from the quiet and cautious statements that characterized British thinking before Tsushima. This is a change that has more often than not been overlooked. Most who study this period talk about either Fisher's reforms or Britain's supposed continued decline:

After jumping . . . to £36.8 million in 1904, the estimates were reduced in the following year by £3.5 million. Nevertheless, this particular aspect of the reforms should be seen for what it was—the cutting away of unnecessary expenditure. . . . Fisher's root-and-branch measures, combined with some skillful British diplomacy at this time, were to give Britain a breathing-space; but the recognition that she could no longer afford to build a navy to take on all others had already been made.[37]

The first assertion about cuts coming from "unnecessary expenditure," is confusing. The great mass of savings was made possible not by paring navy bureaucracy but by slashing naval construction. The second claim is also problematic. It ignores the significant change in thinking that did occur. What was the point of saying that Britain possessed a three-power standard, except to prove that the Royal Navy did possess the ability to take on all others? In October 1907 Fisher wrote to Edward VII: "The English Navy is now four times stronger than the German Navy! And we are going to keep the British Navy at that strength . . . [an article had been given to Prime Minister Campbell-Bannerman] showing that we don't want to lay down any new ships at all—we are so strong. It is quite true!"[38] Fisher was still boasting of British strength as late as 1909:

The unswerving intention of 4 years has now culminated in two complete fleets in home waters. Each of which is incomparably superior to the whole German fleet mobilised for war. . . . This can't alter for years even were we supremely passive in our building. . . . I might also say the Germans are not building in this feverish haste to fight you! No! it's the daily dread they have of a second Copenhagen which they know a Pitt or Bismarck would execute on them! Cease building or I strike![39]

## 1908: THE HIGH POINT OF BRITISH CONFIDENCE
The best place to begin an examination of the 1909 naval crisis is with the quarrel over the previous year's naval budget. For the first time since 1904, the Admiralty tried to secure a £1,250,000 increase in its budget for 1908-1909. The Treasury, however, had grown fond of the previous years' decreases and saw no reason why this agreeable trend should not continue. Because of Campbell-Bannerman's ill health, the Treasury's case was argued by Sir George Murray and not H. H. Asquith, who had assumed a great deal of the prime minister's functions. Murray, a senior civil servant, attacked the Admiralty's request for an increase in construction. He argued that the Royal Navy's supremacy meant that no new battleships should be laid. Murray assumed that presently the Royal Navy had a two-power standard over the United States and Germany, that neither of these powers would have a dreadnought by 1910, and that Britain's superior shipbuilding skills could cope with any unexpected developments: "If we can build a Dreadnought and commission her in fifteen months, we ought to have little difficulty in overtaking the paper programmes of any other Power which showed signs of accelerating its activities."[40]

The first lord of the Admiralty, Lord Tweedmouth, replied to Murray by arguing that the earlier reductions gave the navy no more room for maneuver: "There is only one way left to reduce the Estimates, and that is to pay off ships now in commission in our seagoing fleet, lay them up in harbour, house their crews on shore, and stop all recruiting. . . . Such measures would dislocate the whole Naval Service as now established."[41] Tweedmouth pressed the Admiralty's case for two new dreadnoughts, and the argument dragged on through late 1907. Things were at an impasse when the Admiralty was saved by the one body it could usually count on to come to its rescue—the Reichstag. On 14 November 1907, the German Navy Law was amended by lowering the statutory time for replacing battleships from twenty-five years to twenty. The previous version of the Navy Law called for three capital ships to be started each year between 1908 and 1912 and then two each year between 1913 and 1920, until thirty-eight battleships and nineteen armored cruisers would either have been built or under construction. Under the amended law four dreadnoughts, instead of three, were to be laid down annually from 1908 to 1911, with the 1912 program reduced from three to two.[42]

This change had some important implications for the Royal Navy. In 1908 the balance between the British and German navies was somewhat complicated. Britain had a very large lead in predreadnought battleships of forty-six to eighteen.[43] This advantage was usually cited by those favoring reductions in the naval budget. The dreadnought balance, however, was less clear. In November 1907, the Royal Navy had eight dreadnoughts built or being built, with one to be started. Germany had no completed dreadnoughts but was building four, the first of which was to be launched in June 1908.[44] The Germans would also lay down four dreadnoughts annually for the next four years. Since the Admiralty reckoned it took the Germans about three years to build a dreadnought, they expected the Germans to have twelve vessels built or being built in 1912.[45] Since British dreadnought construction time averaged slightly more than two years, they would have to lay down a number of new ships either this year or the next:[46]

Although it is quite true that our preponderance in battleships at the present moment justifies the omission of [the two capital ships requested for this year] . . . yet with the full knowledge and absolute certainty, now afforded by the German programme just issued, of having to commence a large battleship programme in 1909-1910 it would be unbusinesslike, and indeed disastrous to close down the armour plate industry of this country by the entire cessation of battleship building. It would be similarly disastrous to abruptly stop the manufacture of heavy gun mountings.[47]

The German Navy Law provided the Admiralty with the ammunition to get much of what it wanted. Two new dreadnoughts were approved, though its budget increase was limited to £900,000. Yet, in many ways, this increase was not a sign of concern but an example of British confidence. Even though two battleships were to be built, this was the smallest annual construction program since the Boer War. Also, the £900,000 increase was the first for three years and did not even bring the budget up to the level requested in 1907-1908. Perhaps the greatest argument against this affairs representing a change in thinking was the continuing expressions of confidence that radiated from British sources. Fisher, as usual, was the most vocal. The first sea lord boasted to Balfour that the German Kaiser admitted that: "England's Navy is _five_ times stronger than the Germans!"[48] Fisher even spread a rumor that Tirpitz was looking for a naval agreement. "Very Private Tirpitz asked a mutual friend at Berlin recently to see me whether I would agree to limit the size of gun and ship. I replied within five minutes that I would see him d--d first."[49]

Fisher was not the only person to express confidence in the balance of naval power. Lord Esher, a member of the Committee for Imperial Defence and one of the most knowledgeable members of Britain's defense establishment, spoke condescendingly of Germany's navy:

Did you see a telegram as to the British Government having approached the German authorities so as to obtain some cessation of rivalry? The impudence of these people is beyond expression, they who don't know which way to turn for money, and can't get anyone to accept office as Finance Minister, and face the storm which the next taxation will cause. From the German press I am not sure that the programme will be carried out. . . . They have character it is true, but their finances are in a terrible muddle.[50]

Perhaps the best indication of this confidence was the Admiralty's preoccupation with other distractions. There was the interminable Fisher-Beresford feud.[51] This spat was undoubtedly Fisher's greatest worry throughout 1908 and much of 1909. It brought to the fore some of the first sea lord's least attractive characteristics.[52] The other issue occupying much of the Admiralty's time was the "invasion scare." In early 1908 there was some public hand-wringing about the possibility of a German lightning invasion of Britain, or a "bolt from the blue." The chief alarmists were Charles Repington, a military correspondent for the Times, and Lord Roberts. Fisher thought their campaign was pure nonsense:

The peculiar wonder to me is the serious arguing that the German Fleet is going to hold the Straits of Dover for 48 hours and not a living soul pass any of the German frontier for 2 or 3 days. . . . The present marvelous dissemination of information, especially financial, utterly precludes the faintest possibility of that naval surprise upon which the whole case of invasion hangs, as set forth by Repington (Roberts is a cypher!) but even assuming the surprise, the case remains impossible.[53]

In response to the agitation a Cabinet committee was established in 1908 to discuss the question of a German invasion. Its findings completely vindicated the Admiralty.[54] Far from engendering concern, these arguments over invasion only seemed to reinforce Admiralty confidence. Afterward Fisher still boasted about Britain's naval dominance with his customary bravado. Now, the British "were four times stronger than Germany on any basis you liked to take."[55]

However, the best evidence of continuing British confidence is contained in the Admiralty's war plans. After the Russo-Japanese War, Fisher, assisted by the director of Naval Intelligence, Captain Edmond Slade, spent much more time planning for an Anglo-German war. Because of Britain's overwhelming naval supremacy, it was considered unlikely that the Germans would risk a maritime conflict. Instead, German aggression on the continent was considered a more likely cause of an Anglo-German war. In such a war the Admiralty assumed that Britain would continue as the traditional arbiter of the balance of power, with the Royal Navy as its chief weapon.

In plans assembled in 1906 and left basically unaltered through 1908, three different scenarios were advanced for an Anglo-German war: the attempted German absorption of Belgium and the Netherlands, a German attempt to incorporate the Austro-Hungarian Empire after the death of Emperor Franz-Joseph, and a German attempt to exert force in the Americas.[56] The Royal Navy would be assigned two main tasks in any resulting war. The first was a total blockade of German trade. This, it was assumed, would damage Germany's economy and cripple its war effort. The second, more ambitious task was a possible landing on the German coast. One plan involved landing up to 120,000 men, who, hopefully, would tie down a great number of German troops.[57] The location for this invasion was never explicitly stated, though Fisher at one time voiced a particular preference for a sandy beach on the Pomeranian Coast only ninety miles from Berlin![58] In none of these plans was the German navy considered much of a threat. It was thought there was little the Germans could do to disrupt British plans, and the Admiralty's greatest worry was that the outgunned German fleet would stay in harbor.

Not until 1908 were these optimistic assumptions put in doubt. In February Philip Dumas, the British naval attache in Berlin, submitted a detailed report that was passed on to the Admiralty and Cabinet.[59] He described the German navy as a growing force that still had a number of weaknesses. Numerically, it was growing quickly, and Dumas expected the Germans to complete ten dreadnoughts by 1911, fourteen by 1912, and thirty-four by 1920. Dumas also thought the Germans would eventually increase their fleet's statutory size from thirty-eight battleships and twenty armored cruisers to forty-eight and thirty-two respectively. Furthermore, Dumas claimed that the Germans were preoccupied with a possible war with Britain. Constant haranguing from anti-British groups like the German Navy League was beginning to hit home.

The German navy, however, still had problems. Foremost was the financial strain imposed by the fleet's expansion. The development of the *Dreadnought* had also provided an unexpected problem. The recently completed Kiel Canal would have to be enlarged to accommodate bigger ships. The 1907 amendment to the Fleet Law and the widening of the Kiel Canal would cost the Germans £49,000,000: "Such sums, especially when read in marks, must stagger even the most extravagant Government and . . . with bad times in evidence everywhere in Germany, so that the Bankers are undoubtedly very nervous and cautious, it is likely that the spirit will spread throughout the nation, when they once realise the source of this debt, some check might possibly supervene against a still greater expansion of naval power."

All in all, Dumas' picture was of a strong navy planning for a great future. Germany had followed its statutory construction laws religiously and would almost certainly continue to do so. The German navy was, however, faced with real problems and was unlikely to challenge the Royal Navy anytime in the near future. The Dumas report helped solidify a consensus that had emerged within the government. Germany was Britain's most likely enemy, and its fleet was being built up to challenge British superiority. However, so long as close attention was paid to the rate of German construction, Britain could maintain its superiority by manipulating its superior shipbuilding skills.

The United States, on the other hand, presented a much greater enigma. After Tsushima America had been reinserted into some two-power standard calculations. Yet, since 1905 little time had been spent planning for an Anglo-American war. It would be simplistic, however, to claim that all idea of such a conflict had disappeared. Many historians, Marder included, have overestimated the depth of support for the Anglo-American "special relationship": "British governments and British public opinion in the prewar decade simply refused to recognize the American Republic as a possible enemy, no matter what complications might arise."[60]

The truth was not so simple. On one hand, there were attempts by those friendly to the United States to remove America from the two-power standard.[61] On the other hand, there were some important examples of the United States' being included in Admiralty strategic thinking, including during the discussions over the 1908-1909 estimates. Then the Admiralty made a point of directly comparing the Royal Navy to a combination of Germany and France. However, the Admiralty assumed the United States would be the world's second naval power for years and refused to remove America from the two-power standard.[62]

Fisher was of two minds about the United States. At times he was a firm believer in the "special relationship." He once predicted the growth of "that great and impending bulwark against both the yellow man and the Slav, The Federation of All Who Speak the English Tongue!"[63] Later, he declared that a war between America and Britain was impossible.[64] However, in one of the finest examples of the man's erratic nature, three months later he personally drew up a complete set of war plans for a conflict with America.[65]

Fisher believed that an alliance between Germany and the United States was the only thing Britain had to fear.[66] He assumed that in any war the German and American fleets would attempt to link up, and he planned to use the Royal Navy to prevent this rendezvous. Half of the Royal Navy would be stationed in Ireland, and the other half in the North Sea. This division of the British fleet, in opposition to accepted naval thinking, was made possible by the Royal Navy's great supremacy. Fisher reckoned that the Royal Navy had seventeen first-class battleships, fifteen second-class and twenty-eight third-class, for a grand total of sixty.

He believed that the United States had eleven first-class, six second-class and seven third-class battleships, and Germany none, ten and twelve respectively. Thus, the next two strongest naval powers could muster a force of only forty-six capital ships to oppose the Royal Navy's sixty.

Fisher was not the only member of the Admiralty planning for a possible war with America. Captain Slade developed his own plan.[67] Slade was probably the most anti-American sailor in the Admiralty. Throughout his career he manifested a deep distrust of the United States. Near the end of World War I he was the catalyst behind a British attempt to maintain naval supremacy by cutting America's access to oil. In 1908 Slade had an even more intriguing scenario than Fisher: a war just between the United States and Great Britain with Germany neutral but probably unsympathetic to the British. Like Fisher, he thought the Royal Navy strong enough to split its forces. The Channel and Atlantic fleets with the first, second, and fourth Cruiser Squadrons would guard the North Sea while the home and Mediterranean Fleets with the third and fifth Cruiser Squadrons would proceed to Halifax, Nova Scotia. Slade also proposed sending 30,000 troops to bolster Canadian defenses, troops, he added hopefully, that could be used to threaten America's East Coast.

Ironically, Fisher and Slade viewed each other's plans with disdain. Slade thought Fisher's plan "hopelessly puerile" because it assumed the American and German fleets would try to merge.[68] Slade thought the Americans would stay at home and force the British to come to them. Slade also hoped that more would be done to defend Canada, and this was what Fisher ridiculed: "Whenever the United States wants to annex Canada she can do it, for no earthly power (not the world in arms!) could prevent the 70 millions of the United States accomplishing this on a land frontier extending from the Atlantic to the Pacific Ocean, and Europe 3,000 miles away . . . yet there are thousands of foolish people in England who talk of throwing in our lot with Canada against the United States!"[69] Fisher also opposed defending Canada because he did not trust Canadians: "Sir J has taken up the attitude that we ought to do nothing for Canada and abandon Bermuda. He says he knows the Canadians, that they are an unpatriotic, grasping people, who only stick by us for the good they can get out of us."[70]

The creation of these war plans, among other issues, indicates that the summer of 1908 witnessed the high point of British naval confidence after Tsushima. The Admiralty felt confident enough to ask for only two new battleships, the smallest number since before the Boer War. A breezy self-assurance characterized the private correspondence of many of those knowledgeable of British naval policy. The Admiralty also felt strong enough to assemble two separate plans for a war against the United States. Finally, confidence was so high that the government decided to reinterpret the two-power standard.

In 1907, the United States became the world's second strongest naval power,[71] and the Admiralty assumed America would try hard to maintain this position in the future.[72] So, when the German naval law was also amended in 1907, it seemed that the Royal Navy would soon be pushed very hard to retain a two-power standard including both America and Germany. If the United States kept pace with the German Naval Law the Royal Navy would need approximately eighty battleships and forty armored cruisers by 1920. The government, however, seemed oblivious to these possible developments. On 10 March 1908, much to the delight of the Foreign Office and the Admiralty, Asquith announced that Great Britain would continue to follow strictly the two-power standard.[73] The prime minister defined the standard as the combined strength of the next two navies in the world, plus an additional 10 percent. It was an extraordinary definition, more expansive than the standard originally announced by Lord Hamilton, and it would have been inconceivable to Lord Selborne just a few years earlier. The 10 percent margin was originally devised by the Admiralty committee chaired by Admiral Battenberg. However, in this case the United States was never considered, and a possible combination of France and Germany was ruled out. The 10 percent cushion was actually a concession to Britain's relative naval decline. Now Asquith was indiscriminately applying the 10 percent margin to any combination of naval powers, including the United States.

Unbeknownst to Asquith, he had chosen perhaps the least auspicious moment possible to announce his new, grand standard. Reports of a secret "acceleration" in German battleship construction began circulating in October and November 1908. If these reports were true, than the comfortable assumptions that had underpinned British policy since 1905 no longer applied. Even Asquith, who was mostly confused by naval questions, quickly grasped that surreptitious German building posed a real threat to his new two-power standard. The Conservative opposition, however, refused to let the prime minister off the hook, and Asquith was pressed in the Commons to reaffirm his earlier, bolder claims.[74]

It soon became apparent, however, that no matter how often Asquith supported the standard in public, events were slipping out of his control. It began to look increasingly likely that Britain could not maintain a full two-power standard against Germany and the United States in the future. The prime minister tried desperately to dig himself out of his self-created hole. He tried to return to the policy adopted by Selborne and once again exclude the United States from the standard. Asquith asked McKenna: "Would it not be best at once to make it clear that the United States of America has never been regarded as coming into the proposals [two-power standard] . . . it was not included in Cawdor's memo . . . [and also] by Selborne, Campbell-Bannerman, Haldane and others. Please assure me of this."[75]

Ignoring the fact that Asquith had twice refused to exempt the United States from the standard, the prime minister was now trying to cover his tracks by appealing to the more moderate policies adopted before Tsushima. It was the first sign that British confidence was beginning to erode. However, Asquith was unable to redefine the two-power standard until after the 1909 crisis. In an interesting twist Earl Cawdor, the last Conservative first lord of the admiralty, forced the government to support Asquith's enlarged standard one final time. Writing to McKenna, Cawdor asked the Admiralty to spell out how it planned to enforce the new standard: "What steps [does] H.M.'s Government propose to take in order to secure an absolute Two-Power Standard with a margin for contingencies against any combination of foreign power?"[76] The government and the Admiralty were trapped. They had constructed and boasted about this new standard to such a degree that, when they began to realize the gravity of the situation, it was impossible for them to retreat.

## 1908: CRACKS IN THE FACADE

It was obvious after the Cabinet's 1908 decision to approve only two new battle-ships that the 1909 estimates would have to provide for more. It would be impossible for Britain to maintain naval supremacy building at such a leisurely pace. Yet, there was a split between a big-navy faction and the "economists" (those opposed to large increases) about how large the increase should be. For the navy to get what it wanted, the Admiralty had to present a united front. This task was complicated, however, by the Cabinet reshuffle triggered by the resignation of the ailing Campbell-Bannerman.

Fisher knew that the appointment of the erstwhile "economist" Reginald McKenna as first lord could easily complicate matters. He wasted little time in trying to convert his new boss into a big-navy man. For the first weeks after McKenna's appointment all Fisher seems to have done is woo the new first lord:

Sir J. is very full trying to swing the new First Lord in the way he wants. He spends two hours with him every day. . . . I only hope he doesn't overdo it.

Cannot get hold of Sir J. now at all, he is so busy trying to work the First Lord around to his view that he will not touch anything.[77]

Eventually, McKenna agreed to support Fisher, a success that the first sea lord described with characteristic understatement: "Yesterday, with all Sea Lords present McKenna formally agreed to Four Dreadnoughts, And if necessary six Dreadnoughts, next year (perhaps the greatest triumph ever known!)"[78] However, this victory did not mollify all of Fisher's concerns. He still feared that McKenna's commitment to the extra dreadnoughts might weaken or, in an even more devastating move, that the first lord might strike a deal with Fisher's arch enemy, Admiral Beresford.[79]

Fisher tried to keep McKenna in line by smothering the first lord with correspondence. Whether on vacation in France or on a state visit to Russia, Fisher was careful to write McKenna regularly.[80] Convincing McKenna, however, was only his first problem. Laying in wait was David Lloyd George, now happily ensconced at the Treasury. The chancellor needed to find a great deal of extra revenue to fund old-age pensions and the other projects he had publicly championed. To do this he tried to reduce spending on the armed services, circulating a Cabinet paper on the subject only six weeks after his appointment. The situation, as Lloyd George described it, was certainly bleak.[81] The largest possible increase in revenue that could be expected was £1,500,000, while expenditures were slated to increase by a massive £9,500,000, £2,000,000 of which was earmarked for the Royal Navy. Lloyd George saw no reason to part with so much money. He compared the £14,307,000 that the Royal Navy made do with in 1893-1894 to the Admiralty's budget of £32,319,000 in 1908-1909:

I need hardly remind my colleagues that we have repeatedly pledged ourselves, both before we took office and since, to a substantial reduction of the national expenditure, and particularly that which depends upon the two combatant services. . . . I do not think any of us can regard these figures with satisfaction.[82]

The Admiralty did not respond immediately. Fisher decided to wait until December, by which time he expected the Admiralty's case to have become more compelling. Even though he expected a fight, the first lord still maintained a clear sense of optimism about the Royal Navy's relative position:

We are going to have a very difficult time of it as regards Navy Estimates. Isn't it curious how little the British people realise what Providence does for them. Germany has to keep *over 3 million* soldiers to be the first military power and to maintain her existence. England only takes *128,000* men to do the same with her Navy, and it is true what the German Emperor said—we are at least at a "three powers standard.[83]

In August 1908, however, reports began to circulate that Germany was secretly constructing an extra dreadnought. Fisher told McKenna this was being done to "take advantage of slackness of work in German dockyards."[84] At first this report caused little alarm, and the Admiralty felt no need to alter its building plans. In November, however, a new batch of reports was received. Now the number of secret German battleships had jumped from one to three:

A rumour has reached the Admiralty not long ago that the three battleships which according to the Naval programme are to be laid down in the financial year beginning 1 April 1909 had been already taken in hand. . . . Heath [the British naval attache in Berlin] has told me that as far as he can find out there seems to be a good deal of truth in the rumour; the preparation of the material—a lengthy part of the business—has . . . already begun.[85]

The question of whether the Germans were secretly accelerating their building was the most serious strategic problem that the Liberal government had to face since coming to power. If the reports were true, the British would have to reexamine their assumptions about Germany's future strength and the Royal Navy's relative position. The 1908 report by De Salis claimed that Germany would have ten dreadnoughts in July 1911 and fourteen in July 1912. In late 1908 Great Britain had twelve dreadnoughts built or being built, all of which would be ready before 1911. Assuming that the first two battleships laid down under the 1909 estimates could be constructed in two years, the largest number of dreadnoughts that the British could have by the summer of 1911 was fourteen, or four more than the expected German total in 1912. If there was no German acceleration, Britain's majority would be either two or four, depending on whether four or six new battleships were approved in 1909. If, however, the Germans were secretly accelerating, the Royal Navy might not have a majority at all.

These new stories stirred the Admiralty into action and it was decided to press for a firm construction program of six new dreadnoughts. Fisher stated the navy's case in terms of practicality, not danger: "I prefer to take the ground that our maximum output of large armoured ships is six annually . . . therefore we cannot afford to build 4 this year on the basis of building 8 next year,"[86] Slade was more pessimistic. He believed that the two-power standard was in danger of dissolving and that Britain's supremacy could soon be under siege: "If we lay down six ships a year and complete them in two years, we shall just keep the two-power standard, but we shall have no margin beyond it, and even if we lay down six ships in 1909, Germany will still be dangerously close to us in completed dreadnoughts at the beginning of 1912."[87]

The reports of a secret German acceleration had a varying impact on the Cabinet. The Admiralty's strongest supporter, Sir Edward Grey, was instantly alarmed. The foreign secretary took a close, personal interest in the reports and insisted that British diplomats acquire as much information on the subject as possible: "Admiralty believe that report that preparation of material for the next three battleships which are to be laid down this year in anticipation of next year's programme. . . . First Lord of the Admiralty is anxious that everything should be done to verify report mentioned by De Salis."[88] Lloyd George, however, remained unmoved by this flurry of activity. He continued to press for a moderate naval program. His reticence caused gloomy talk in the Admiralty of having to make due with only five or four new ships.[89]

The fate of Britain's 1909 naval program was thus very much in the balance when the Cabinet first met to discuss the issue on 18 December 1908. The Admiralty presented a sketch estimate calling for a funding increase of £2,923,200. This was to be used for the construction of six new dreadnoughts, six protected cruisers, twenty destroyers, and a submarine development program.[90] The contrast with Fisher's earlier estimates was striking. There were no allusions to the Royal Navy's immense strength. Now it was stated that if Germany was accelerating, Great Britain would barely have a one-power standard in the near future. By building three battleships at an accelerated pace Germany could have thirteen dreadnoughts by October 1911.[91] The most the British could have at the same time was fourteen.

The strategic debate had shifted ground dramatically. The United States was once again shunted aside. Planning against America was always a luxury, one that now the Admiralty could clearly not afford. Germany from now until the First World War would be the Admiralty's one and only point of comparison.

German strength would determine British strength, and all serious Royal Navy planning was directed at combating the high seas fleet: "The result of this perseverance on the part of Germany is that now she directs the Naval Policy of the world, and her strength is the standard to which all others must be compared. . . . She orders the laying-down of ships in all countries who are obliged to enter into rivalry with her."[92]

The Cabinet, however, was not so easily swayed. A number of important Cabinet members agreed with Lloyd George and put little credence in the reports of German acceleration. They also believed that the Admiralty was confusing the issue by focusing all attention on the relative dreadnought balance. For instance, official Admiralty calculations of British dreadnought strength did not include the two vessels of the Lord Nelson class. These ships were considered comparable to dreadnoughts, and members of the Cabinet quite often grouped them as such. Also, the "economists" argued, the Royal Navy's large advantage in predreadnoughts would see the country through the dangerous period, after which Britain's superior shipbuilding capacity could be brought to bear.

Winston Churchill, who had recently entered the Cabinet as president of the Board of Trade, took the lead for the "economists" and argued for four battleships, while McKenna was demanding six. The Cabinet division proved to be so great that debate had to be postponed until after Christmas. Asquith, though, was desperate to conceal the degree of division and sent a misleading description of the Cabinet meeting to Edward VII: "After much discussion the Estimates were in substance approved . . . with the reservation that the necessity of including the last two of the six dreadnoughts in next year's scheme is held over for further discussion by the Cabinet in January."[93]

This "reservation" would soon tear the government apart. For now, however, the Cabinet parted. McKenna and Churchill, the two main protagonists at the 18 December meeting, were treated like boxers returning to their corners after a particularly bruising round. The first lord was greeted by an emotional letter from Fisher.

You, yourself, being convinced from your own enquiries, have led the whole Board to the unanimous decision arrived at during their last Board meeting, and . . . they intend to stand by you! . . . I hope you will play the game off your own bat, quoting the whole Board as being absolutely with you and no compromise possible because we have gone to the very minimum.[94]

Churchill, meanwhile, received a huge dollop of well-crafted praise from Lloyd George.

I cannot go away without expressing to you my deep obligation for the assistance you rendered me in smashing McKenna's fatuous estimates and my warm admiration for the splendid way in which you tore them up. . . . I am a Celt and you will forgive me for telling you that the whole time you were raking McK's squadron I had a vivid idea in my mind that your father looked on with pride at the skillful and plucky way in which his brilliant son was achieving victory in a cause for which he had sacrificed his career and his life. Wishing Mrs. Winston Churchill and Yourself a merry Xmas.[95]

## NOTES

1. Asquith Mss, Box 21, "The Two Power Standard, 1889-1909."
2. Ibid.
3. Asquith Mss, Box 21. "Pronouncements on the Two Power Standard, 1889-1909."
4. A. J. Marder, *From the Dreadnought to Scapa Flow*, p. 123.
5. CAB 37/46, #30, "Navy Estimates and Shipbuilding," 22 February 1898.
6. Selborne Mss, Custance Memorandum, 19 December 1900.
7. Ibid. 24 September 1901.
8. CAB 37/59 #118, "Navy Estimates," 16 November 1901.
9. CAB 37/59 #141, "Anglo-German Relations," 24 December 1901.
10. G. Monger, *The End of Isolation: British Foreign Policy 1900-07*, pp. 21-45.
11. CAB 37/62 #133, "The German Navy," 15 September 1902.
12. Selborne Mss, "Navy Estimates 1903-04," 10 October 1902.
13. Selborne Mss, "Naval Estimates 1901-02," 17 January 1901.
14. CAB 37/59 #81, "The Balance of Naval Power in the Far East," 16 November 1901.
15. Asquith Mss, Box 21, "The Two Power Standard."
16. CID Papers, 21 C, Admiralty Memorandum, February 1905.
17. Asquith Mss, Box 21, "The Two Power Standard."
18. CAB 37/56 #8, 37/58 #81, 37/59 #118, 37/63 #142.
19. Asquith Mss, Box 21, "The Two Power Standard."
20. CAB 37/59 #118, "Naval Estimates," 16 November 1901.
21. Marder, *From the Dreadnought to Scapa Flow*, p. 124.
22. CAB 37/58 #81, "Naval Power in the Far East," 4 September 1901.
23. CAB 37/69 #32.
24. ADM 116/1036B, Anglo-German War Plans.
25. CAB 37/84 #80, "Admiralty Policy," October 1906.
26. A. J. Marder, *Fear God and Dreadnought*, vol. 2, #s 49, 50, 56.
27. CAB 37/69 #32, "Possible Admiralty Reductions."
28. CAB 37/81, "Report of the Navy Estimates Committee," 16 November 1905.
29. ADM 116/1043, 1908 War Plans, CAB 37/83, # 60, "Naval Estimates."
30. McKenna Mss, 6/2, Fisher to McKenna, 10 February 1909.
31. CAB 37/00 #97, "Battleship Building," 14 July 1909.
32. ADM 1/7996, Memorandum, 16 December 1908.
33. E. Woodward, *Great Britain and the German Navy*, Appendix.
34. J. T. Sumida, "British Capital Ship Design and Fire Control in the Dreadnought Era," *Journal of Modern History*, p. 206.
35. CAB 37/83 #60, "Naval Estimates 1907-08," 26 June 1906.
36. Marder, *Fear God and Dreadnought*, vol. 2, #49.
37. P. M. Kennedy, *The Rise and Fall of British Naval Mastery*, p. 218.

38. Marder, *Fear God and Dreadnought*, vol. 2, #90.

39. Esher Mss, 10/43, Fisher to Esher, 21 March 1909.

40. CAB 37/90 #98, "Naval and Military Expenditure," 18 November 1907.

41. CAB 37/90 #112, "Naval Estimates 1908-09," 18 December 1907.

42. CAB 17/61, Naval Attache Report, 12 February 1908.

43. CAB 37/83, #60.

44. CAB 37/90 #101, "Future Battleship Building," 21 November 1907.

45. CAB 37/90 #6.

46. Slade Mss, Diary Entry, 10 March 1908.

47. Fisher Mss, 5/14, Navy Estimates, 3 December 1907.

48. Balfour Mss, 49712, Fisher to Balfour, 23 February 1908.

49. Corbett Mss, Box #12, Fisher to Corbett, 11 March 1908.

50. Fisher Mss, 1/6, Esher to Fisher, February 1908.

51. Marder, *From Dreadnought to Scapa Flow*, pp. 71-104.

52. Slade Mss, Diary Entry, 24 April 1908.

53. Fisher Mss, 1/6, Fisher to Ottley, 28 January 1908.

54. Esher Mss, 16/12, Subcommittee Conclusions, November 1908.

55. Esher Mss, 10/42, Fisher to Esher, 8 September 1908.

56. ADM 116/1036b, War Plans versus Germany, 1906.

57. ADM 116/1043b, War Plans versus Germany (Potentially allied with United States), 1908.

58. Marder, *From the Dreadnought to Scapa Flow*, Vol. 1, p. 385.

59. CAB 17/61, Dumas report, 12 February 1908.

60. Marder, *From the Dreadnought to Scapa Flow*, p. 183.

61. Fisher Mss, 8/30, Report of H. King-Hill, 13 April 1907.

62. CAB 37/90, "Future Battleship Building," 21 November 1907.

63. Marder, *Fear God and Dreadnought*, #139.

64. McKenna Mss, 3/4, Fisher to McKenna, 12 May 1908.

65. ADM 116/1043B, War Plans, July 1908.

66. Marder, *Fear God and Dreadnought*, #90.

67. Slade Mss, War Plans versus United States with Germany Unfriendly, July 1908.

68. Slade Mss, Diary Entry, 22 July 1908.

69. Marder, *Fear God and Dreadnought*, #90.

70. Slade Mss, Diary Entry, 9 May 1908.

71. *Jane's Fighting Ships*, 1906.

72. FO Confidential Print #s 9265, 9483, 9657.

73. Hardinge Mss, Hardinge to Edward VII, 14 March 1908; Slade Mss, Diary Entry, 10 March 1908.

74. Asquith Mss, Box 21, "Pronouncements on the Two Power Standard," 12 November 1908.

75. McKenna Mss, 3/3, Asquith to McKenna, 14 November 1908.

76. McKenna Mss, 3/11, Cawdor to McKenna, 16 November 1908.

77. Slade Mss, Diary Entries, 4, 6 May 1908.

78. Esher Mss, 10/42, Fisher to Esher, 5 May 1908.

79. Ibid. 12 July 1908.

80. McKenna Mss, 3/4, Fisher to McKenna, 19 May 1908, 28 July 1908, 11 August 1908, 14 August 1908.

81. Lloyd George Mss, C/14/1/2, "The Financial Situation This Year and Next," 18 May 1908.

82. Ibid.

83. Fisher Mss, 1/7, Fisher Letter, 16 September 1908.

84. McKenna Mss, 3/4, Fisher to McKenna, 14 August 1908.

85. Grey Mss, De Salis to Tyrrell, 3 November 1908.

86. Marder, *Fear God and Dreadnought*, #143.

87. Slade Mss, "Present State of Shipbuilding," 10 October 1908.

88. Grey Mss, Grey to Goschen, 18 November 1908.

89. Slade Mss, Diary Entry, 17 October 1908.

90. ADM 167/42, Board Minutes, 11 December 1908.

91. Asquith Mss, "Sketch Estimates 1909-10," 8 December 1908.

92. ADM 1/7996, Memorandum, 16 December 1908.

93. Asquith Mss, Asquith to Edward VII, 19 December 1908.

94. McKenna Mss, 3/4, Fisher to McKenna, 19 December 1908.

95. R. S. Churchill, *Winston S. Churchill*, vol. 2 Companion 2, p. 937.

# 3

# Theodore Roosevelt and American Naval Power

Our battleships, oh our battleships. They remind me of the story I have somewhere read of the ancient sacrifices to Jove . . . how the ox had all his spots chalked white before being led to the altar in order that the victims might wear the appearance of unblemished whiteness.

> Captain J. H. Oliver in a letter to Lt. Sims, 30 September 1904[1]

[Senator] Hale would like to introduce into our military affairs a system of supervision based on the Aulic Council of Vienna, and flavored with the spirit of Moorfield Storey's Anti-Imperialist League, plus the heroism of the average New York financier.

> Theodore Roosevelt, 2 September 1907[2]

## THE NAVY'S FRIEND

It is one of the ironies of American history that an anarchist was responsible for Theodore Roosevelt's presidency. If Leon Czolgosz had known what he was about to unleash he would probably have stayed home that September day.

Theodore Roosevelt's ascension has been seen as a watershed for the development of federal power. This is especially true for the U.S. Navy. Roosevelt is almost universally described by historians as the driving force behind the creation of the modern American navy.[3]

A quick glance at Roosevelt's record does much to justify these opinions. Never before had a president been so interested in naval issues. Roosevelt considered the navy the "strong arm" of American government[4] and many of his most famous exploits were either in support of, or because of the growth of, the American fleet. The construction of the Panama Canal, the Roosevelt corollary to the Monroe Doctrine, and the cruise of the Great White Fleet were all the result of a desire to capitalize on the strength of the new American navy. Even his final letter written as president was a discussion of naval strategy.

Roosevelt's interest in the navy stretched from grand strategic questions to minute technical details. He was involved in decisions ranging from the height of warship smokestacks to the deployment of ships in battle groups. Under his command no area of American naval policy and power was unaffected. Steps were undertaken to improve naval gunnery and ship design, and a belated attempt was made to create a professional naval general staff. More dramatically, so much money was spent, and so many capital ships were constructed that the United States became the second strongest naval power in the world.

Roosevelt worked hard to raise the U.S. Navy's perennial low profile. Coming to power hot on the heels of the Spanish-American War, the new president enmeshed the United States in a number of foreign incidents that emphasized the navy's role as never before. His term of office began with a confrontation over the Anglo-German blockade of Venezuela in 1901-1902 and ended with an abortive war scare with the Japanese. The president seemed determined to alter permanently the fortunes of the fleet:

The one unforgivable crime is to put one's self in the position where strength and courage are needed, and then to show lack of strength and courage . . . It is perfectly allowable, although I think rather ignoble, to take the attitude that this country is to occupy a position in the New World analogous to that of China in the Old World, to stay entirely within her borders, not to endeavor to assert the Monroe Doctrine, incidentally to leave the Philippines, to abandon the care of the Panama Canal, to give up Hawaii and Porto Rico, etc., etc. It is also allowable . . . to insist therefore that the navy shall be kept up and built up as required by the needs of such an attitude. But any attempt to combine the two attitudes is fraught with the certainty of hopeless and ignominious disaster to the Nation. To be rich, aggressive, and yet helpless in war, is to invite destruction.[5]

However, the task that Roosevelt was attempting was an extraordinarily difficult one. The American navy had never had a consistent peacetime policy. Without a war it usually faded rapidly from public view and often fell into disrepair or obsolescence. Most Congresses and presidents had seen no need to appropriate large sums to maintain a first-class fleet. Roosevelt was trying to break this cycle of neglect by establishing a new consensus in favor of a strong fleet that would endure after he left office.

Roosevelt was aware of the enormity of the challenge confronting him. The very passion displayed in the preceding extract was sign of his concern. This passage comes from a letter written to Theodore Burton, a Republican congressman from Ohio. Burton had consistently supported the president on domestic matters, and Roosevelt, at first, respected him. Burton, however, was also a firm champion of disarmament and a fierce opponent of a large American navy. His opposition was grounded on a desire to separate America from Europe's petty squabbles and allow the United States to stand forth as an example of moral rectitude:

Let us continue our traditional policy, not indeed one of weakness, nor yet one of nonresistance, but one of confidence in our strength as a nation. Our military strength, though mighty in its possibilities, is but a part; our material strength is much more: but most of all we can rely upon those great moral and political principles which have made our country what it is, the eternal principles of justice to all, the equality of man. Those great ideas are stronger than battleships.[6]

Burton represented only part of the opposition arrayed against Roosevelt. Burton and his allies were vastly outnumbered by a horde of congressmen whose opposition to a large navy was motivated not by idealism but by indifference. Since most of their constituents manifested, at best, indifference and, at worst, hostility to a large American navy, these men felt no compulsion to support Roosevelt. Included in this group were stalwarts of Congress' naval affairs committees such as Eugene Hale of Maine, Ben Tillman of South Carolina, George Perkins of California, and Joseph Cannon and George Foss of Illinois, as well as those who were not usually associated with naval issues such as James Slayden of Texas, Gilbert Hitchcock of Nebraska, and Jacob Gallinger of New Hampshire. To them the naval budget represented, at best, a vehicle to enrich their districts and, at worst, an example of government waste and extravagance.

This, then, is the question that needs to be asked: did the changes wrought by Roosevelt, as dramatic as they seemed, represent a permanent shift in the fortunes of the U.S. Navy? In order to have instituted lasting changes he would have had to alter substantially the congressional and popular view of the importance of naval power to the United States. Furthermore, he needed to provide the navy with a coherent policy that Congress and the people could accept. Only If he could do this would Roosevelt really accomplish what he set out to do. It was never going to be an easy task. America seemed so happily self-contained, so impervious to outside assault, that the president was ultimately asking people to disbelieve many of their basic preconceptions.

## THEODORE ROOSEVELT—THE EARLY BUILD-UP IN PERSPECTIVE

Of all of Roosevelt's naval legacies none were as obvious as the enormous increases in ships, men, and money. During the eight fiscal years between 1902 and 1909 the president was able to persuade Congress to fund the construction of sixteen battleships and four armored cruisers. Naval appropriations grew from $48 million in 1899 to $78 million in 1901 and reached almost $137 million in 1909. In 1905 the navy discovered that when the capital ship tonnage then being built was completed, the American battle fleet would more than double in size.[7] These were the ships that would make the U.S. Navy the world's second largest by 1907. These peacetime increases were unprecedented and seemed to indicate that the United States had truly arrived as a great naval power. In 1907 the British Admiralty seemed convinced that America planned to maintain the position of the world's second naval power, even in the face of German competition.[8] One recent history of the U.S. Navy has described these increases as Roosevelt's "monument."[9] Roosevelt himself liked to boast about the changes he had wrought: "When I came in as President . . . the policy of completely stopping the further building up of the navy had been inaugurated. Not a ship had been provided for in the preceding session of Congress. We have peace now, and the chance of peace in the future, only because I secured the reversal of this policy by Congress."[10]

However, the question still remains whether these changes represent a long-term shift in the navy's fortunes. In the preceding quote, for instance, Roosevelt significantly overstated the depth of the change. While he was correct in the narrowest sense (in 1901-1902 there was no authorization for new warships), he ignored the appropriations of the three previous years. Between 1898 and 1900 eight battleships and six armored cruisers were sanctioned. These fourteen major warships were the same number as those authorized in Roosevelt's first four years, the ones that he liked to boast about.

To be fair, it should be noted that the earlier ships were approved during and immediately after the Spanish-American War. Roosevelt's success in continuing the buildup, while not as impressive as he claimed, was an important change in American behavior. It is also true, however, that the long-term impact of this change was muted. The capital ships that Roosevelt built suffered from a number of major defects. To properly understand these defects the ships should be divided into three different categories. Of Roosevelt's twenty capital ships all those approved before 1905, eight battleships and four armored cruisers, were predreadnoughts, and two, the *South Carolina* and *Michigan*, were semidreadnoughts. Only the six authorized after 1906, the *Delaware, North Dakota, Utah, Florida, Arkansas*, and *Wyoming*, were pure dreadnoughts.

The earliest ships were of limited value, especially the armored cruisers. These cruisers were less heavily protected and possessed a slightly smaller broadside than battleships but were faster and cost about the same. They were usually grouped together with battleships as the major units of the fleet, and

Roosevelt considered them an integral part of his buildup.[11] It later became apparent, however, that their value had been drastically overestimated. The dreadnought class equivalent, the battlecruiser, had a checkered career, as demonstrated by its performance during the First World War. Because these ships had sacrificed armored protection to secure greater speed, they were unable to stand the bombardment of large naval guns.

The greatest weakness with these earlier ships lay not with the armored cruisers, however, but with the battleships themselves. First, a number of them were dogged by the design flaws mentioned earlier, including the Idaho class, which made up a quarter of the predreadnought battleships laid down during Roosevelt's presidency. Beyond design problems, however, the most important defect of these earlier battleships was the fact that they were predreadnoughts. The sad truth of the Roosevelt buildup was that it was composed primarily of obsolete vessels. Of the twenty capital ships authorized during his tenure either 60 or 70 percent (depending on one's opinion of the *South Carolina* or *Michigan*) were soon considered obsolete. The difference in striking power between dreadnoughts and the predreadnoughts was startling. In 1914, when the General Board evaluated the effectiveness of its warships, it stated that the predreadnoughts authorized in 1903 and 1904 had only half the value of the *Delaware*, a dreadnought laid down in 1906.[12] This disparity only increased over time. The *Arkansas* and *Utah*, the last battleships approved during Roosevelt's term, were considered 35 percent more powerful than the *Delaware*.[13] While Roosevelt's Great White Fleet was one of the strongest in the world at the time, it had an extraordinarily early "sell-by" date.

Also, it should be noted that Roosevelt failed to provide the navy with a proper number of auxiliary ships. At the beginning of the century the U.S. Navy had an impressive list of commissioned vessels, but most were really obsolete. Of the 307 ships on official lists, only 59 were considered of "war value."[14] In 1902 the secretary of the navy, William Moody, proclaimed that the navy had only 46 vessels that would be of use in war.[15] At the time the General Board believed that the American fleet actually ranked behind the fleets of Great Britain, France, Russia, Germany, and, possibly, Japan and Italy.

A properly balanced navy at the turn of the century required a great number of auxiliary vessels such as destroyers, torpedo boats, small cruisers, colliers, and support ships. In 1900 the General Board estimated that for every two battleships and two armored cruisers there should be six gunboats, two destroyers, three torpedo boats, one transport, and two training ships.[16] In 1902 this idea was refined by the adoption of a squadron ratio. A squadron was to consist of eight battleships, six armored cruisers and twelve torpedo boats, as well as an undefined number of colliers, transports, and hospital and supply ships.[17] However, neither Congress nor Roosevelt at first paid any attention to the calls for a balanced fleet. In 1901, when the General Board requested twenty nine auxiliary ships, the president forwarded a recommendation for only eighteen and Congress authorized but four.[18]

In 1903, when the General Board formulated its famous plan for a forty eight battleship fleet, it returned to the question of auxiliary ships. Now it was stated that the navy needed forty eight protected cruisers, forty eight scout cruisers, forty eight destroyers, thirty colliers and fifty six other support vessels.[19] No one with even a passing knowledge of American naval history could have expected sanction for such a request. Yet, even a pessimist would have been surprised at the depth of congressional indifference. In 1904 the General Board requested six destroyers and eighteen other vessels. Congress approved none. Future results were hardly better. In 1905 the General Board requested four submarines and sixteen other ships and received eight submarines. In 1906, four destroyers and fourteen other vessels were requested, and two destroyers were authorized. To put the auxiliary ship question in perspective one should compare their authorization ratios with those of battleships and armored cruisers. During Roosevelt's entire term in office, he requested twenty six capital ships, and Congress authorized twenty, or 76 percent. During the same period 115 auxiliary ships were requested, and only 63 approved, or 55 percent. Professor Love has properly criticized the Roosevelt buildup as "unbalanced."[20]

Above and beyond the question of money and matériel, the final defect with the Roosevelt buildup has nothing to do with the ships themselves. Roosevelt needed to correct not just material weaknesses in the American fleet but philosophical and strategic ones as well. In particular he had to provide the U.S. Navy with a believable and coherent policy. This might not seem like a tremendous problem. The other great naval powers in the world built their fleets either for reasons of national security, to secure certain rational goals, or to keep pace with specific national rivals. Britain needed the Royal Navy to protect its economic and imperial existence. In the late nineteenth century France and Russia tried to match the Royal Navy, and Great Britain countered with the two-power standard. Germany's original intention was for its navy to hold the balance between these two groups. After the Russo-Japanese War, however, the Germans decided to make a unilateral, long-term challenge to the Royal Navy, and the British responded with the 160 percent ratio. Even smaller naval powers based their building on the strengths of their rivals. Austria-Hungary and Italy faced each other across the Adriatic, and Argentina and Brazil competed in the South Atlantic.

The United States, however, lacked a clearly defined power or group of powers against which to build. Unless Roosevelt could change this reality and provide the navy with a standard that would endure after he left office, his legacy would be incomplete. The problem, however, was to decide exactly what any American naval standard should contain. Should it be based on national defense, the Monroe Doctrine, or the protection of America's imperial possessions? Which powers should be included, and what how large should the navy be to fight them?

## THE HUNT FOR A NAVAL POLICY

The difference between the United States and the other great naval powers is best seen by looking at the American navy's frustrating attempts to articulate a naval policy. Such a policy needed a plausible threat to national safety. During the first few years of Roosevelt's tenure the fleet ignored this problem by clinging hard to the new president's coattails and hoping his efforts would sustain a continuing buildup. Until 1903 the General Board refused to spell out why the United States needed a strong fleet.[21] As the Roosevelt buildup picked up steam, however, the navy's even grew bold. In 1903 the General Board made a remarkable call for a fleet of forty eight battleships and 24 armored cruisers. Such a force would have made the United States the strongest naval power in the world. Yet this grandiose plan was described as necessary to defend "the coasts, insular possessions, commerce and general maritime interests of the United States."[22] It was an extremely optimistic gambit. The General Board was claiming that the fleet should be strong enough to protect both South and North America and all of America's Pacific possessions. However, the very boldness of the proposal belied its basic weakness. Neither the Monroe Doctrine nor the Philippines was vital to the security of the United States proper. Neither would be enough to persuade Congress to expend large sums of money building up the navy. What the U.S. Navy really needed was what every other naval power in the world possessed: a credible threat.

During the Roosevelt administration three major powers, Great Britain, Germany, and Japan, were used as examples of realistic threats. Germany and Japan are usually described as America's most threatening competitors. Great Britain must also be mentioned because of the amount of naval planning undertaken for an Anglo-American war. This was not because such a war was ever considered likely but because such a war would have presented the navy with its most formidable challenge. Also, views of the British were not as fulsome as might be supposed.

The British possessed a number of advantages that would have allowed them to fight a war against the U.S. Navy with a greater likelihood of success than anyone else. Not only was the Royal Navy the world's largest, but it also had a complete set of bases in the Western Hemisphere, from Halifax, through Bermuda, and down into the Caribbean. No other power had so much as a decent coaling station. The American navy, therefore, often used the scenario of a British attack to test its own capabilities. In these scenarios Great Britain would either be specifically mentioned, or a "European" power would be signified which could be only the British.

In 1900, when discussing the defense of the Philippines, the British were viewed as no less threatening than any other power and were specifically mentioned as a threat.[23] The American navy also assembled plans to capture Halifax, Bermuda, Esquimalt, Victoria, and Jamaica.[24] Bermuda generally received the most scrutiny. It was reported that the British appointed Sir Henry Geary governor of Bermuda because of his knowledge of fortifications.[25] One of the more common war exercises undertaken by the Americans during these years involved an attempted British landing on the American East Coast. In 1900 the selected target was Narragansett Bay.[26] In 1901 attention shifted to the islands of Nantucket and Martha's Vineyard.[27] Later, requests were made to fortify Chesapeake Bay to prevent a foreign power from capturing a base on this vital waterway.[28] It would be hard to see who, except the British, could have conceived of such ambitious plans.

In February 1906 fears of British intentions reached an unusual pitch when Charles Bonaparte, secretary of the navy, approved a plan calling for the abrogation of the 1817 Anglo-American agreement demilitarizing the Great Lakes.[29] The plan included a detailed, sixteen-page plan for a war on the lakes. It was felt that British control of the Saint Lawrence would allow the Royal Navy to bring in eighty-nine warships compared to America's two. A number of American cities, especially those on Lake Superior, like Duluth, Ashland, and Marquette, could be bombarded by the British. Potential damage was estimated at $78 million. To guard against this, the navy believed that an armed American force should be permanently stationed on the Great Lakes.

It should also be noted, however, that there were a number of well-placed, powerful Anglophiles in Roosevelt's government and navy who would have had little sympathy for these plans. Secretary of State John Hay and Admiral William Sims worked hard to improve Anglo-American relations. Roosevelt was also generally sympathetic to the British, though the depth of his affections varied. When writing to English friends like Cecil Spring-Rice or Arthur Lee, Roosevelt would speak of the great importance of Anglo-American.[30] At other times, however, he was more circumspect. Roosevelt had some serious worries about Britain's long-term prospects and spoke gloomily about England being "on the downgrade."[31] He also believed that the wealth generated by the British Empire had weakened the fighting spirit of the British public, while the Germans, correspondingly, had maintained a tough edge.[32] Roosevelt could conceive of a situation in which the United States might have to hold the middle ground between these two competing European powers.[33] As he wrote to Whitelaw Reid, American ambassador to Great Britain:

In international matters I am no great believer in the long-continued effects of gratitude. The United States must rely in the last resort upon their own preparedness and resolution, and not upon the good will of any outside nation. I think England has a more sincere feeling of friendliness for us than any other power; but even this English friendliness would be a broken reed if we leaned on it, . . . No matter how great our strength, we could of course make trouble for ourselves if we behaved wrongly. But merely to be harmless would not save us from aggression. If we keep our navy at a high standard of efficiency and at the same time are just and courteous in our dealings with foreign nations, we will be able to remain on good terms with all foreign powers.[34]

Roosevelt was also not averse to applying pressure on the British.[35] During the 1903 Alaskan boundary dispute he made it perfectly clear that he would not accept arbitration unless America's claim was guaranteed.[36] He expected British support, even though the dispute was with Canada, part of the British Empire.[37] Later, during a quarrel over fishing rights off Newfoundland, Roosevelt threatened to send a warship into Canadian waters.[38] Compared to many, however, Roosevelt was quite an Anglophile. Lodge was even more skeptical. Once he told the president that Newfoundland should be detached from the British Empire.[39]

Germany and Japan, on the other hand, were viewed with even greater distrust. Both had industrious, fast-growing, populations and since the Spanish-American War, the United States had acquired territories that brought America into possible conflict with both. Relations with Germany had been strained since 1898. Certain elements within the German government had coveted Spain's imperial possessions, particularly the Philippines. When the Spanish-American War broke out, the Germans sent a large force to Manila Bay.[40] In 1899 tension also flared up with America over Samoa, a long-standing area of dispute.[41] By 1900 attention shifted to the Caribbean and South America. South America had long been seen as a possible area for German expansion. It was the most productive part of the globe not under European control. Any German attempt to acquire South American territory, however, would have inevitably brought conflict with the United States. "The steady increase of [the German] population . . . the steady expansion of [German] home industries which must find a *protected* market abroad; the desire of the Imperial Government for colonial expansion to satisfy imperial needs . . . all lead to the conclusion that when conditions at home are no longer considered bearable and [Germany] is strong enough, [Germany] will insist upon occupation of Western Hemisphere territory."[42]

American naval planning focused on achieving naval supremacy in the Caribbean and depriving the Germans of a naval base in the Western Hemisphere. The General Board in 1900 approved an exercise to see if the United States could thwart a German attempt to capture Puerto Rico or Haiti.[43] In 1901 the navy surveyed America's ability to defend the Caribbean and the coast of South America.[44] Afterward Admiral H. C. Taylor, head of the Bureau of Navigation and one of the most able officers of his generation, called for a permanent American base in Haiti.[45]

Before taking office, Roosevelt worried about the possibility of German expansion. He considered Germany "the only power with which there is any reasonable likelihood or possibility of our clashing in the future."[46] He was impressed by the German's toughness. "Modern Germany is alert, aggressive, military and industrial. It thinks it is a match for England and France combined in war, and would probably be less reluctant to fight both those powers together than they would be together to fight it.[47] Roosevelt pushed for increased vigilance in the Caribbean. The area was combed for good base sites.[48] In 1902 the Germans and British cooperated in blockading the Venezuelan coast to force repayment of a debt. Roosevelt sent Admiral Dewey and a considerable naval force to monitor events.[49] The president later boasted that he had wanted to convince the Germans that he was willing to use power to enforce the Monroe Doctrine.[50]

American obstinacy did stir the wrath of a number of highly placed Germans. The Kaiser had, spasmodically, nurtured a grand plan for a European coalition against the United States. However, at other times he mentioned the possibility of combining with the United States against Japan and Great Britain.[51] The German armed forces seemed equally split. The navy drew up plans for an assault on various Caribbean islands, a precursor to an assault on the American coast.[52] The German army, however, had little enthusiasm for such a project and did its best to suppress the plans. But the tensions did persist. The historian with the greatest knowledge of German plans against America has claimed that by 1903 a consensus existed "among Germany's political as well as military leaders that the United States had become the most probable future opponent."[53] This antagonism gave a certain sense of immediacy to Roosevelt's naval program. Soon the rise of Japan would provide another reason for concern.

The change in American-Japanese relations occurred very rapidly. At the turn of the century relations were solid. In 1901 the General Board studied the possibility of a war between an alliance of the United States, Japan, and Great Britain and one of Germany, Russia, and France.[54] Roosevelt's accession also boded well for American-Japanese relations. The new president had a favorable opinion of the Japanese, and his feelings were reciprocated. Most Japanese leaders deeply appreciated the respect that Roosevelt always paid them.[55] After having inspected the Japanese at close quarters during the negotiations ending the Russo-Japanese War, Roosevelt's respect grew. He considered the Japanese to be tough, but honest, negotiators and paid them a great compliment when he claimed that they "had always told me the truth."[56] The achievements of the Japanese in the war also made a deep impression on the president, for he had never expected them to triumph as spectacularly as they did.[57] The completeness of their victories, the obvious efficiency of their navy, and the panache of many of their fighting men caught Roosevelt's eye. He started to refer to the Japanese as a great civilized nation that the West could learn from.[58] In 1906 Roosevelt sent to Bonaparte a laudatory letter about the Japanese admiral Togo, the victor of Tsushima. The president asked that Togo's battle message be commended "to every man who is or may be part of the fighting force of the United States."[59] On another occasion he sent Senator Lodge a Japanese poem that had caught his eye and exclaimed, "What people those Japs are!"[60]

Ironically, the strategic repercussions of the Russo-Japanese War began to bring America and Japan into conflict. After the destruction of the Russian navy, the United States and Japan were the only two nations that could afford to deploy large forces in the Pacific. The British had been withdrawing from the region since signing the Anglo-Japanese Alliance, and both they and the Germans were now concentrating in the North Sea. Any French effort in the Pacific depended on Russian support. After Tsushima this was distinctly unlikely. This lack of outside involvement did not necessarily imply that America and Japan had to fight. The Japanese made their desire for cooperation known immediately after the signing of the Treaty of Portsmouth. However, instead of being able to develop this friendship, Roosevelt found himself stymied by his own countrymen.

On 11 October 1906 the San Francisco School Board approved a plan segregating the city's schools. A separate establishment was set up for "Oriental" students, to protect white children against association "with pupils of the Mongolian race."[61] Not surprisingly, the Japanese were insulted. During the last few years they had defeated the Chinese and Russians, signed an alliance with Great Britain, and acquired a large empire. However, the enforced segregation of their countrymen showed that they were still far from being considered the equal of Caucasians. Long-simmering resentments at American attempts to restrict Japanese immigration combined with the San Francisco decision to lead to a storm of Japanese protest. A full description of the issues leading to this is unnecessary here.[62] However, it might be useful to examine the strategic ramifications of the confrontation.

The U.S. Navy began making plans for a war as soon as the crisis erupted. Until the Panama Canal was completed, the American navy would have to steam around South America before engaging the Japanese, a journey that could take months. Studies were made to determine the number of ships that would be needed to fight the Japanese.[63] Wide-ranging plans were drawn up to either build or improve existing naval facilities in the Pacific, including bases in Puget Sound, the Philippines, and Hawaii.[64] A serious, if slightly alarmist, note crept into American naval planning. Sims sent Roosevelt a report that three dreadnoughts being built in England, ostensibly for Brazil, might actually be destined for Japan.[65] Stories were circulated that Japanese had infiltrated Mexico.[66] The General Board pressed for increased security measures at American naval bases. They singled out the Philippines for particular vigilance, because Japanese agents were "readily capable of disguising themselves as Filipinos."[67] Roosevelt even made inquiries about the possibility of speeding up the construction battleships already being built.[68] This sense of urgency also played an important role in the most public demonstration of American naval strength ever undertaken to that time, the worldwide cruise of the Great White Fleet.

This cruise has often been seen as the crowning achievement of the Roosevelt buildup.[69] It was motivated by a number of reasons. One was undoubtedly Roosevelt's desire to demonstrate American resolve to the Japanese. The president made this clear when he first broached the subject with Elihu Root, his trusted secretary of state.

I am more concerned over this Japanese situation than almost any other. Thank Heaven we have the navy in good shape. It is high time, however, that it should go on a cruise around the world. In the first place I think it will have a pacific effect to show that it can be done and . . . I became convinced that it was absolutely necessary for us to try in time of peace what we could do in the way of putting a big battle fleet in the Pacific, and not make the experiment in time of war.[70]

Roosevelt also wanted to test the efficiency of his new navy and whip up public interest in the fleet. Finally, Roosevelt wanted to impress the Germans. Distrust of Germany ran high in the Navy Department, and even while the fleet traversed the globe, a close watch was kept on the Caribbean and Atlantic.

It must have seemed at the time that the navy had finally carved out a useful role for itself. Earlier policies, like the General Board's call for forty-eight battleships, had involved the use of arbitrary figures. It now seemed possible that the navy might be built up to a strength equal to that of Japan and Germany combined. The General Board wasted little time in calling for a bold new policy: "The Navy should be of such strength that there may be one fleet concentrated in the Atlantic and one fleet concentrated in the Pacific, each sufficient to cope with any emergency that may require immediate action in its own sphere."[71] There had been earlier plans to divide the fleet between the two coasts, but they had gone nowhere.[72] Now, some West Coast congressmen were clamoring for protection against a sneak Japanese attack. The General Board tried to capitalize on these worries by calling for a "two-ocean" navy.

However, this policy was far from universally accepted. Dividing the fleet ran contrary to Mahanian notions about the concentration of power. The rest of the world's navies were actually being consolidated in this period, not dispersed. Mahan himself was so worried about reports that the fleet was to be divided that he wrote the president directly. Roosevelt quickly replied that he was "incapable of such an act of utter folly."[73] For this reason alone the two-ocean navy was never going to be accepted. Indeed, Roosevelt's final letter as president, which he characterized as a "closing legacy" to Taft, contained a warning never to divide American battleships between the Atlantic and Pacific.[74]

However, the policy of the two-ocean navy is still important because it provides compelling evidence of the growth of the navy's expectations and ambitions during the Roosevelt administration. All the great increases in money, men, and matériel and the important reforms made it seem as if the navy had entered into a new era of public prominence. The two-ocean navy, following fast on the heels of the call for a forty-eight battleship fleet, seemed to indicate that the navy now had a politically acceptable policy with which to defend and promote increased naval construction.

Certainly, a number of historians have portrayed Roosevelt's naval buildup as having a firm direction. Most have assumed it was aimed at Germany.[75] The Sprouts described the president's fears of German aggressions as a "veritable nightmare" and an "obsession."[76] Hagan repeats the Sprouts' assertion of Roosevelt's supposed "obsession."[77] Herwig also describes the president as "obsessed" with German intentions in the Western Hemisphere.[78] Challener, while minimizing the likelihood of a German attack, states that "germanophobia" existed inside the American government and specifically mentions Roosevelt.[79] Even books that only briefly discuss the period often assume that the president was primarily concerned with thwarting the Germans.[80]

However, a close examination of the primary sources does little to support the idea of a Roosevelt obsessed with German strength. There is some evidence that the Germans worried Roosevelt before he took office.[81] However, his attitude changed quite quickly after McKinley's assassination. He wrote to a close German friend, Hermann Speck von Sternberg, "I am myself convinced that the United States and Germany can work in the closest intimacy and with heartiest mutual good will for the benefit of both, not only in China but in South America as well." This kind of sentiment was not exclusively reserved for German acquaintances. He was almost as positive with the Englishman Cecil Spring-Rice: "The more I have heard of the Kaiser the more my respect for him has grown."[82] On a number of occasions Roosevelt revealed a willingness to cooperate with the Germans, even going so far as to tell Taft in 1905 that he would be "glad to oblige" Germany on the Moroccan question.[83]

Contrasting Roosevelt's views about Germany and Great Britain helps show the real complexity of his positions. Roosevelt is usually described as an Anglophile as much as a Germanophobe. It is true that he preferred the friendship of Great Britain to that of Germany.[84] However, he was also realistic and unsentimental in his dealings with each country. As he told the American ambassador to Great Britain: "I like the Kaiser and the Germans. I wish to keep on terms with them. I agree with you in thinking it even more important that we should keep on good or better terms with the English."[85]

Roosevelt's preference for the British did not mean that he blindly supported them over the Germans. When Roosevelt felt that Secretary of State Hay, a committed Anglophile, was not treating the Germans fairly, he bypassed him. Later Roosevelt would state that Hay was "foolishly distrustful" of the Germans.[86] During the negotiations ending the Russo-Japanese War Roosevelt favorably compared German to British behavior.[87] Later, in 1905, he was equally critical of British and German posturing. Writing to Whitelaw Reid, American ambassador in London, he criticized both governments: "I wish that the English and the German governments did not reciprocally feel such wild manias of hatred and distrust for one another . . . I know that each side is hopelessly and foolishly wrong . . . I wish that when it comes naturally you would say a word to the German Ambassador in London to show that you are entirely friendly to Germany."[88] When describing the situation to Taft, he was even more critical of the British.[89]

Roosevelt's views on the development of national power made him wary of becoming too dependent on British friendship. He believed Britain was in a period of decline, while Germany was destined to become the most powerful European country.[90] What is often portrayed as Roosevelt's "fear" of Germany was actually a healthy respect for German strengths:

The love of pleasure, the love of ease, and the growth of extravagance and luxury among the upper classes, and a certain frivolous habit of mind and failure to fix relative values of things, all of these are very dangerous and very marked among the English-speaking peoples, as well as in France. . . . Germany alone among the modern nations of high civilisation has been able successfully to combat the more dangerous tendencies that have been at work among other peoples for the last half century.[91]

One of the best examples of the complexity of Roosevelt's feelings can be seen in his reaction to the 1902 Venezuela crisis. In response to a Venezuelan failure to honor its financial obligations, Germany and Great Britain instituted a blockade. During the First World War Roosevelt claimed to have threatened the Germans with an ultimatum. However there is little evidence to support this assertion. Not until 1905 did he first mention the existence of an ultimatum, and no hard evidence corroborating his claim has ever been found.[92] Roosevelt's own correspondence gives little hint of an ultimatum.[93] To a British friend like Spring-Rice Roosevelt claimed to have told the kaiser that infringing on the Monroe Doctrine meant "war, not ultimately, but immediately and without any delay."[94] Yet, when speaking to American confidants he was considerably less bellicose.[95] Interestingly, Roosevelt later portrayed the 1902 confrontation as a low point in German-American relations, after which the kaiser had "helped me in every way, and my relations with him and the relations of the two countries have been, I am happy to say, growing more close and more friendly."[96]

Not everything went smoothly between Roosevelt and the Germans. Late in his second term Roosevelt seemed increasingly frustrated with the kaiser. In 1908 he felt concerned enough about the behavior of Wilhelm II to send a letter of warning to a British friend, Arthur Lee. Yet, in this letter Roosevelt admitted that previously he had believed there was no need of "arming against Germany."[97] Perhaps the best evidence to rebut the argument that Roosevelt was obsessed with Germany is contained in the president's March 1909 letter to Philander Knox, the incoming secretary of state.

It may be very well that you will have acute trouble about Cuba, or with Venezuela or in Central America, or with some European power; but it is not likely that grave international complications—that is, complications that can possibly lead to serious war—can come from any such troubles. . . . I do not believe that Germany has any designs that would bring her in conflict with the Monroe Doctrine. The last seven years have tended steadily toward a better understanding of Germany on our part, and a more thoro understanding on the part of Germany that she must not expect colonial expansion in South America.[98]

The other threat that supposedly worried Roosevelt was from Japan. Thankfully, most of the works that discuss Roosevelt's view of Japan recognize the complexity of his thought. Braisted, Esthus, and Bailey all use restrained language to describe the 1906-1907 confrontation.[99] They show how Roosevelt did much to calm relations and avoid conflict. Braisted describes how the president personally lobbied San Francisco officials to revoke their segregation plan.[100]

Indeed, Roosevelt respected Japan's strength in much the same way that he respected Germany's.[101] He considered Japan a nation on the rise that would play an increasingly important role in world affairs. After Tsushima, Roosevelt demonstrated his desire to cooperate with Japan by sending Taft to discuss security arrangements with the Japanese prime minister, Katsura Taro.[102] Roosevelt's sympathy for Japan meant that when tensions did arise, he often directed his anger at his own countrymen. In 1905 Roosevelt called the California legislature "idiots" who filled him with "contempt and disgust."[103] The 1906-1907 crisis angered him even more: "These Pacific coast people wish grossly to insult the Japanese and keep out the Japanese immigrants on the basis that they are an immoral, degraded and worthless race . . . and with besotted folly are indifferent to building up the Navy while provoking this formidable new power."[104]

There is also little indication before 1906 that Roosevelt was seriously worried about the chance of a war with the Japanese. In January 1906 he concluded that a Japanese attack on the Philippines, were it to come, would not be "for a decade or two."[105] However, as the tensions between the two countries grew after the San Francisco School Board decision, Roosevelt's concern increased. He never claimed that war was imminent, but at the same time he devised the plan to send the fleet on its world-wide cruise. Roosevelt the realist was convinced that a show of America's naval strength was what was needed to keep the Japanese in line: "My own judgment is that the only thing that will prevent war is the Japanese feeling that we shall not be beaten, and this feeling we can only excite by keeping and making our navy efficient in the highest degree. It was evidently high time that we should get our whole battle fleet on a practice voyage to the Pacific."[106] Roosevelt then did his best to calm tensions and accepted a Japanese offer in 1908 to have talks. These talks resulted in the Root-Takahira agreement, whereby each nation promised to "respect" the other's possessions in the Pacific.[107] By December 1908 Roosevelt seemed satisfied that the crisis had been settled: "Indeed the agreement with Japan is an admirable thing all around. . . . My policy of constant friendliness and courtesy toward Japan, coupled with sending the fleet around the world, has borne good results!"[108]

The discussion so far might seem to imply that Roosevelt never believed in a serious German or Japanese threat or that he was not overly concerned with American security. This is not the case. The fleet Roosevelt built was the result of a personal vision. Roosevelt was firmly convinced of the need for a large American navy precisely because he could not predict who might challenge America in the future. He desperately wanted the United States to have the power to either deter or to vanquish any opponent. This could be only with a powerful American fleet. As he told Joseph Cannon, speaker of the House of Representatives:

I am not acting with a view to an emergency of the next year or two. I am acting with a view to the emergencies that there is a reasonable chance may arise within the next decade or two. . . . I do not think that in this case . . . considerations as to the need of economy should be allowed to offset the far greater need of guaranteeing the preservation both of peace and of the national honour and interest.[109]

   This lack of a specific threat eventually became a serious handicap. It fatally weakened the Roosevelt administration's push for a long-term policy. One of the reasons the Roosevelt buildup was not to have the lasting impact that the president expected was that the country was never really convinced that its safety was under threat. If Theodore Roosevelt could not come up with a believable enemy, no one else could. Congress was much less inclined to worry about security. This split in congressional and presidential perceptions had been papered over during Roosevelt's first term, when the legislators rather meekly supported his programs. This state of affairs was not destined to last.

## CONGRESS, DREADNOUGHTS AND THE ROOSEVELT LEGACY

In 1905 the British began building the famous battleship HMS *Dreadnought*.[110] The design of the *Dreadnought* did not come as a surprise to the American navy. The United States was almost the first nation to build all-big-gun battleships. The two ships of the South Carolina class, which had broadsides identical to the *Dreadnought's*, were also designed in 1905. However, construction delays meant that neither would be finished until 1910.

   To begin with, American opinion was divided on the merits of dreadnought battleships. Most of the navy, led by Admiral Dewey, strongly supported the new designs.[111] However, no less a figure than Alfred Thayer Mahan was opposed. Mahan was convinced that smaller, secondary batteries had been crucial to Japan's victory at Tsushima and attacked the all-big-gun concept.[112] President Roosevelt was initially ambivalent about the new designs.[113] He was particularly worried about the dreadnought's increased construction costs. Roosevelt was, however, generally one to err on the side of strength and asked Captain Sims to critique Mahan's arguments. Sims strongly defended the dreadnought in two detailed reports sent to Roosevelt in the fall of 1906.[114] The president, for one, seemed completely won over.[115]

   Mahan's preference for smaller, less expensive ships still had some support, most of which came, unsurprisingly, from Congress. Congress had the authority to limit the displacements of battleships, a power it had often used to reduce the cost of new vessels. Senator Hale, who was particularly fond of this device, tried to swing Roosevelt back to the antidreadnought camp:

The more I study the question the stronger I am against the monster ships. They are experimental, costly, unwieldy and I do not believe that four years from now any nation will be found building any more of them . . . I like George Dewey as everybody does and have no personal prejudice against other members of the board, but I think most of them know little about a battleship except from visiting it.[116]

   Hale failed. In the end Roosevelt who was able to convince most congressmen to support building dreadnoughts. Lodge was naturally a key supporter,[117] but a more prized convert was the chairman of the House Naval Affairs Committee, George Foss.[118] Roosevelt tirelessly worked Foss over. In the end the bewildered congressman could not resist and supported battleships without mandated limits.[119]

The result was the construction of the *Delaware* and *North Dakota*, America's first full dreadnought-class battleships. Sadly for Roosevelt, this was one of the few victories he would have over Congress during his second term. Roosevelt ran into ferocious opposition when he tried to increase the tempo of capital ship construction. Roosevelt first tried to cope with Congress' opposition by working for an international agreement limiting the size of new battleships, thus preserving the viability of America's predreadnoughts. He tried to interest the noted philanthropist Andrew Carnegie[120] and the British foreign secretary Sir Edward Grey in a plan to restrict all battleships to 15,000 tons.[121] When his efforts failed, Roosevelt was left with no other option than trying to change Congress' mind.[122]

This task was made especially difficult by Roosevelt's previous, impulsive behavior. In 1905 the United States had twenty-eight battleships and twelve armored cruisers either built or being built. At the time Roosevelt thought this number adequate, and he rashly announced that the navy was now at a "sufficient" strength.[123] All he wanted to do was maintain this level of strength by replacing ships as they became obsolete:[124] "As regards our own navy, I think in number of units it is now as large as it need be, and I should advocate merely the substitution of efficient for inefficient units. This would mean allowing for about one new battleship a year, and of course now and then for a cruiser, collier, or a few torpedo-boat destroyers."[125]

It was a foolish move that Lodge had warned Roosevelt against.[126] Roosevelt had never spelled out why twenty-eight battleships were "sufficient" number and what America's relative naval position should be. While the United States did become the second largest naval power in the world in 1907, in 1905 there was no consensus that this was America's proper position. When Roosevelt first mentioned halting the buildup, he thought America was "a good second to France and about on par with Germany."[127] Eighteen months later he told Sir Edward Grey that the American navy was smaller than France's or Germany's.[128] Lodge, in April 1906, said that the United States was either the third or fourth naval power.[129] For Roosevelt's halt to be strategically viable the rest of the powers would have to tread water as well. Unfortunately the president had picked the least auspicious moment since Trafalgar to call for a halt in naval construction. The *Dreadnought* would soon be built, the Russian fleet would be sunk, the Japanese navy would expand, and the British and Germans would embark upon a vicious building race. In a matter of months all the strategic considerations that underlined the halt melted away.

Congress, meanwhile, had eagerly taken up Roosevelt's suggestion and authorized only one battleship during each of the first two years of Roosevelt's second term. The president now believed that this tempo was insufficient.[130] In 1907 he requested four new battleships, but his earlier statements returned to haunt him. The stage was now set for two years of bitter wrangling between

Roosevelt and Congress, struggles that would leave both parties bitter and defiant. This confrontation has been described without exaggeration as "one of the bitterest legislative struggles in American naval history."[131] Roosevelt's earlier successes had obscured the fact that no national consensus existed in favor of a large American fleet. Now the navy's political weakness was uncovered for all to see. Many congressmen saw no reason to build a great fleet and considered a large navy inimical to American interests.[132] Roosevelt struggled fiercely to change these opinions, even feeling it necessary to lobby Lodge.[133] In the end he was frustrated by congressional recalcitrance and had to accept authorization for only two battleships annually in 1907 and 1908. It was a victory of sorts. Without Roosevelt's pressure Congress would probably have approved fewer capital ships. Yet, Roosevelt was running out of time.

The mood of Congress in 1908 and early 1909 shows just how difficult Roosevelt's task was. The president had failed to convince most congressmen that the U.S. Navy was vital to the nation's defense. A few legislators, such as Representative Richmond Hobson of Alabama and Senator Albert Beveridge of Indiana passionately supported a big navy.[134] But even they had difficulty describing which countries posed a threat to the United States. Beveridge, who with Lodge was the navy's most effective advocate in the Senate, was left to make the pathetic claim "that all opinions as to the possibility of war are not upon the side that it cannot *possibly* occur."[135]

However, a majority of congressmen could see little point in building a large navy. In the Senate Hale, Julius Burrows and William Smith of Michigan, Nelson Aldrich of Rhode Island, Porter McCumber of North Dakota, and others attacked Beveridge. Smith claimed, "I do not see a single cloud in the world's horizon which menaces our peace or good order."[136] Burrows remarked that "this is an era of peace; an era of international parliaments seeking to devise means to settle international differences through the peaceful instrumentality of arbitration."[137] Members from the West Coast, who were worried about the Japanese, favored the construction of coastal fortifications over extra battleships. Building fortifications employed constituents. George Perkins of California, chairman of the Senate Naval Affairs Committee, and Samuel Piles of Washington refused to support Roosevelt's plan for four battleships but backed a program to build more shore installations.[138]

The situation in the House was similar. Burton once again led the fight against building battleships.[139] He was supported by those who scoffed at the notion of a threat to the United States. One of the most vociferous, Representative Tawney of Minnesota, mocked the alarmists: "Why, Mr. Chairman, we hear a great deal at this particular time about the possibility of war with Japan. I am getting tired of these annually recurring wars with Japan. They are always simultaneous with the consideration of the naval appropriation bill in this House (Laughter and applause)."[140] Tawney and Burton were opposed by George Foss, chairman of the House Naval Affairs Committee. Even Foss, however, did not support Roosevelt's plan for four battleships but the more modest proposal for two. Foss also refused to say exactly who or what threatened the United States.[141] Roosevelt's full plan was probably doomed before it arrived. The real debate in Congress was not between four and two battleships but between two and fewer.

Most congressmen still looked upon the navy as a source of money for their constituents and not as a vital arm of national defense. In 1908 and 1909 there were periodic attempts to reduce some of the "pork" in the naval budget, but they were quickly squelched. In April 1908 Representative Lilley of Connecticut called for the creation of a commission to examine naval appropriations.[142] He painted a lurid picture of waste. At Senator Perkins' pet project of Mare Island $1,175,000 had been spent on a dry dock that no battleship could reach because of shallow water. Congress had also appropriated $1,198,984 to build a dry dock at Senator Tillman's beloved Charleston, but not only was the channel too shallow, "there is no berthing room for vessels, and no ship of any description has ever been docked there." There were also enormous discrepancies between the amount paid in salaries to the various navy yards and the total value of their work. At Mare Island $1,620,678 had been paid to employees, but only $928,582 worth of work had been performed. At Portsmouth, Senator Hale's personal fief, $792,760 had been paid, and only $418,804 worth of work performed. Unsurprisingly, Lilley's commission never materialized.

Similar efforts in the Senate failed. Senator Joseph Dixon of Montana unwisely questioned appropriations for both the Portsmouth and Charleston naval bases.[143] The response by Hale, Tillman, Gallinger of New Hampshire, and even Lodge was brutal. Dixon was ridiculed, and Tillman told him to mind his own business: "It comes with bad grace from men on that side, who have been getting their share of chicks and eggs from the National Government, to get up and captiously criticize the rest of us, who are only doing the same thing (Laughter)."[144]

The fact that Roosevelt was able to get such a Congress to approve two battleships might actually be seen as a victory.[145] On balance, however, these authorizations are more likely examples of the president's ambiguous impact. They show how little support there was for maintaining the second largest navy in the world. During the 1908 election year a very popular president was unable to persuade a Congress controlled by his own party to support a naval policy that he considered vital to national safety.

Roosevelt was aware that much still needed to be done. His belief in the importance of naval power had grown stronger during his second term. He considered the navy the "one foundation of peace we have," and "an infinitely more potent factor for peace than all the peace societies . . . together."[146] Roosevelt had wanted to "put the navy on such a basis that it cannot be shaken from it."[147] At the same time, however, he was faced with growing opposition. The president's ruminations became both bitter and gloomy. Once, he declared that America would have to withdraw from the Philippines because the "country" was unconcerned with being a world power.[148] Yet, most of his anger was directed not at the "country," but at Congress.

Roosevelt seemed incapable of understanding how a patriotic congressman could oppose his naval program. To him such opposition was dangerous and foolhardy: "It is simply criminal to act as at times Congress tends to act and put a stop to the upbuilding of the navy. The people who advocate such a course should at once stop building the canal, give up the Philippines and Hawaii, and announce that they have no concern with the Monroe Doctrine; and in short . . . they are not men at all."[149] His most eloquent denunciations were reserved for the individual congressmen he despised most. He frequently targeted Hale, Foss, Tillman, Burton, and Perkins. Foss was "an awful nuisance and . . . a corrupt influence."[150] Tillman, whom Roosevelt loathed, was a "conscienceless scoundrel."[151] Perkins, a Californian and thus a particular target of the president's wrath, fared even worse. He was a "wretched creature"[152] with "no more backbone than a sea anemone."[153] Even Theodore Burton, a firm supporter of Roosevelt's domestic agenda, was attacked as "a preposterous apostle of peace"[154] and dismissed as "not really a valuable man."[155] Yet, no one was attacked with the singular savageness that Roosevelt saved for Senator Hale. The president employed a vast vocabulary to describe Maine's senior senator. In letters to Taft, Hale was described as a "veritable national calamity"[156] whom Roosevelt wished to "maul."[157] Writing to Root, the president called Hale a "physical coward"[158] and, in an epic turn of phrase, a "conscienceless voluptuary."[159] At times mere sentences were inadequate, and Roosevelt needed paragraphs to properly express his distaste. One began by calling Hale an "arrant physical coward" and ended with an indictment of the senator's "shriveled soul."[160] Even Roosevelt's last letter as president revealed his bitterness toward Hale, Tillman, and Perkins.[161] These outbursts are important for more than their colorful nature. They show just how worried Roosevelt was about the future. They were examples not just of anger but also of frustration.

In the end it might be said that Roosevelt's impact was more of a tidal wave than a sea change. He was undoubtedly one of the greatest friends, if not the greatest friend, of the navy ever to occupy the Oval Office. For a while he had remarkable success in galvanizing support for a larger American fleet. He kept the navy in the public eye as never before. He improved the navy's efficiency in such vital areas as gunnery and design. He spent vast amounts of money and built large numbers of new ships. However, Roosevelt's early successes should not blind us to the fact that many of his changes lacked staying power.

The fleet could never really hope for a long-term change in its fortunes until it had a coherent, consistent, and "believable" policy. Until Congress or the American people believed that the navy was vital to national defense, the navy would always be politically vulnerable. Roosevelt was unable to effect this change and give the navy a policy that could endure. He was unable to convince people that a large American navy was vital for the nation's security, because it was not.

In many ways Roosevelt left at a very auspicious moment. The U.S. Navy had reached the apex of its pre-1914 strength, one it would not again attain until the end of the First World War. Had Roosevelt stayed in office, it is doubtful that he could have done anything more than Taft or Wilson to arrest the navy's decline from this height. The frustration manifested during Roosevelt's last few years shows that he was aware that much still needed to be changed. When he examined the state of American preparedness in 1913, he despaired: "I suppose the United States will always be unready for war, and in consequence will always be exposed to great expense, and to the possibility of the gravest calamity, when the Nation goes to war. This is no new thing. Americans learn only from catastrophes and not from experience."[162]

## NOTES

1. Sims Mss, Sims to TR., 4 October 1904.

2. Lodge Mss, #88, TR. to Lodge, 2 September 1907

3. See H. Sprout and M. Sprout, *The Rise of American Naval Power 1776-1918*, p. 250; G. C. O'Gara, *Theodore Roosevelt and the Rise of the Modern American Navy*, p. 109; W. R. Braisted, *The United States Navy in the Pacific, 1897-1909*, p. 10; R. W. Turk, "Defending the New Empire," in K. J. Hagan, *In Peace and War: Interpretations of American Naval History 1775-1978*, p. 186; S. Howarth, *To Shining Sea: A History of the United States Navy 1775-1991*.

4. AMPUSA 1904, p. xliii

5. TR. Letters, vol. 4, TR. to Burton, 23 February 1904.

6. CR, vol. 42, p. 4778, 15 April 1908.

7. GB Letters, vol. 3, p. 458, Present State of the Fleet, 10 July 1905.

8. CAB 37/90, "Future Battleship Building", 21 November 1907.

9. K. J. Hagan, *This People's Navy: The Making of American Seapower*, p. 240.

10. TR. Letters, vol. 5, TR. to Stone, 26 July 1907.

11. TR. Letters, vol. 5, TR. to Newberry, 10 August 1907.

12. GBSF #420, "Comparison of Ship Values," 4 December 1914.

13. Ibid.

14. GB Letters, vol. 1, p. 440, Memorandum, 27 March 1902.

15. Moody Mss, "The Navy", 9 October 1902.

16. GB Letters, vol. 1, p. 80, Dewey Letter, 12 October 1900.

17. GBSF #420, Chadwick Memorandum, September 1902.

18. See Appendix 1.

19. NDGC, 8557-37, Memorandum, 17 October 1903.

20. R. W. Love, *History of the United States Navy*, p. 416.

21. GB Letters, vol. 1, p. 80, Dewey Letter, 12 October, 1900. "Henceforth . . . certain definite proportions based upon the plans of campaign and the needs of the war fleet should be attained and maintained in material and personnel. The Board is not yet prepared to indicate these proportions in detail."

22. NDGC 8557-36, Memorandum, 9 February 1903.

23. GB Letters, vol. 1, Memorandum, April 1900.

24. GB War Portfolios: Bermuda Plan, January 1905; Kingston Plan, March 1905; Halifax Plan, October 1906.

25. Ibid.

26. GBSF, Secretary of War Letter, 9 January 1901.

27. GBSF, #434-1, Dewey to Secretary of Navy, 22 March 1901.

28. GB Letters, vol. 2, p. 416, 30 October 1903.

29. GBSF, #420, "Naval Policy on the Great Lakes", 28 February 1906.

30. TR. Letters, vol. 3, TR. to Lee, 6 June 1905; vol. 5, TR. to Spring-Rice, 1 November 1905; vol. 6, TR. to Lee, 17 October 1908, 20 December 1908.

31. TR. Letters, vol. 3, TR. to Baker, 8 July 1901; TR. to Sternberg, 11 October 1901.

32. TR. Letters, vol. 5 TR. to Reid, 11 September 1905; TR. to Spring-Rice, 21 July 1908.

33. TR. Letters, vol. 4 TR. to Lodge, 16 June 1905.

34. TR. Letters, vol. 5 TR. to Reid, 11 September 1905.

35. TR. Letters, vol. 5 TR. to Reid, 27 June 1906.

36. Lodge Mss, #87.

37. TR. Letters, vol. 5 TR. to Reid, 27 June 1905; Lodge Mss, #88, TR. to Lodge, 28 January 1909.

38. TR. Letters, vol. 5 TR. to Reid, 27 June 1905.

39. Lodge Mss, #87, Lodge to TR., 20 October 1902.

40. See Braisted, *The United States Navy in the Pacific*, pp. 33-42.

41. Ibid, pp. 58-62. See also P. M. Kennedy, *The Samoan Tangle: A Study in Anglo-German-American Relations 1878-1900*.

42. GB War Plans, Box 10, "Germany, #1, Reference # 5-4, undated.

43. GB War Plans, Box 11, 21 May 1900. See also GB Minutes, 23 May 1900.

44. GB Letters, vol. 1, p. 239, 25 June 1901.

45. Moody Mss, Box 10, Taylor Memorandum, 30 December 1903.

46. TR. Letters, vol. 3, TR. to Meyer, 12 April 1901; TR. to Lodge, 27 March 1901.

47. TR. Letters, vol. 5, TR. to Straus, 27 February 1906. See also vol. 3, TR. to Baker, 8 July 1901; vol. 5, TR. to Reid, 1 March 1906,

48. See R. D. Challener, *Admirals, General and American Foreign Policy 1898-1914*, pp. 81-110. See also D. C. Munro, *Intervention and Dollar Diplomacy in the Caribbean 1900-1921*.

49. Challener, *Admirals, General and American Foreign Policy 1898-1914*, pp. 111-119.

50. TR. Letters, vol. 5, TR. to White, 14 August 1906.

51. Braisted, *The United States Navy in the Pacific*, pp. 215, 233, 235.

52. D. F. Trask, H. H. Herwig, "Naval Operations Plans between Germany and the USA 1881-1913." pp. 50-51, in P. M. Kennedy, ed., *The War Plans of the Great Powers: 1880-1914*.

53. H. Herwig, *Politics of Frustration; The United States in German Naval Plans 1889-1914*, p. 86.

54. GB Letters, Hackett to Rodgers, 16 February 1901.

55. See R. A. Esthus, *Theodore Roosevelt and Japan*.

56. TR. Letters, vol. 5, TR. to Trevelyan, 12 September 1905.

57. TR. Letters, vol. 4, TR. to Spring-Rice, 16 June 1905.

58. Lodge Mss, #88, TR. to Lodge, 16 June 1905. Also See TR. Letters, vol. 4, TR. to Spring-Rice, 16 June 1905; vol. 5, TR. to Trevelyan, 12 September 1905.

59. TR. Letters, vol. 5, TR. to Bonaparte, 21 February 1906.

60. Lodge Mss, #87, TR. to Lodge, 15 June 1903.

61. Braisted, *The United States Navy in the Pacific*, p. 191.

62. Ibid, pp. 191-215; Esthus, *Theodore Roosevelt and Japan*, pp. 128-144, 181-195.

63. TR. Mss, Series 1, Naval War College to TR., 2 August 1907; Newberry to TR., 8 August 1907.

64. TR. Mss, Series 1, Dewey to TR., 20 February 1908.

65. The first report is in TR. Mss, Series 1, Sims to TR., 19 December 1907. A follow-up report, supporting the original allegation, was sent on 15 February 1908. A copy is contained in Sims Mss, Box 96, "TR. January-February 1908." See also TR. Letters, vol. 6, TR. to Root, 15 February 1908.

66. TR. Letters, vol. 5 TR. to Sternberg, 16 July 1907. Also See vol. 6, TR. to Tower, 12 February 1908.

67. GB Letters, vol. 5, p. 78, 17 June 1907.

68. TR. Mss, Series 1, Navy Department to TR., 30 July 1907.

69. See R. A. Hart, *The Great White Fleet*; J. R. Reckner, *Teddy Roosevelt's Great White Fleet*.

70. Root Mss, #163, TR. to Root, 13 July 1907.

71. GB Letters, vol. 5, p. 124, Memorandum, 26 September 1907.

72. Braisted, *The United States Navy in the Pacific*, pp. 149-152.

73. TR. Letters, vol. 5, TR. to Mahan, 12 January 1907.

74. TR. Letters, vol. 6, TR. to Taft, 3 March 1909.

75. G. T. Davis, *A Navy Second to None: The Development of Modern American Naval Policy*, pp. 163-166. See also Turk, "Defending the New Empire."

76. Sprout and Sprout, *The Rise of American Naval Power*, p. 253.

77. Hagan, *This Peoples Navy: The Making of American Sea Power*, p. 233.

78. Herwig, *Politics of Frustration; The United States in German Naval Plans*, p. 95. See also H. H. Herwig, *Germany's Vision of Empire in Venezuela: 1871-1914*, pp. 175-198.

79. Challener, *Admirals, Generals and American Foreign Policy 1898-1914*, pp. 32, 67.

80. See J. Chace, *America Invulnerable: The Quest for Absolute Security from 1812 to Star Wars*, p. 139.

81. TR. Letters, vol. 3, TR. to Meyer 12 April 1901. See also TR. to Lodge, 27 March 1901.

82. TR. Letters, vol. 3, TR. to Spring-Rice, 3 July 1901. See also vol. 4, TR. to Spring-Rice, 13 May 1905.

83. TR. Letters, vol. 4, TR. to Taft, 20 April 1905. See also vol. 4, TR. to Tower, 27 July 1905.

84. TR. Letters, vol. 5, TR. to Straus, 27 February 1906.

85. TR. Letters, vol. 5, TR. to Reid, 27 June 1906.

86. Lodge Mss, # 88, TR. to Lodge, 28 January 1909.

87. TR. Letters, vol. 5, TR. to Reid, 11 September 1905.

88. TR. Letters, vol. 5, TR. to Reid, 19 September 1905. See also vol. 6, TR. to Strachey, 22 February 1907.

89. TR. Letters, vol. 4, TR. to Taft, 20 April 1905.

90. TR. Letters, vol. 3, TR. to Baker, 8 July 1901; TR. to Sternberg, 11 October 1901.

91. TR. Letters, vol. 6, TR. to Spring-Rice, 21 July 1908.

92. Challener, *Admirals, General and American Foreign Policy*, pp. 111-119.

93. TR. Letters, vol. 3, TR. to Shaw, 26 December 1902.

94. TR. Letters, vol. 5, TR. to Spring-Rice, 1 November 1905.

95. TR. Letters, vol. 5, TR. to Reid, 27 June 1906. See also TR. to White, 14 August 1906.

96. TR. Letters, vol. 5, TR. to Reid, 27 June 1906. See also TR. to White, 14 August 1906.

97. TR. Letters, vol. 6, TR. to Lee, 17 October 1908.

98. TR. Letters, vol. 6, TR. to Knox, 8 February 1909.

99. T. R. Bailey, *Theodore Roosevelt and the Japanese-American Crises*, p. 330.

100. Braisted, *The United States Navy in the Pacific*, p. 196.

101. TR. Letters, vol. 6, TR. to Knox 8, February 1909.

102. Braisted, *The United States Navy in the Pacific*, pp. 181-183.

103. TR. Letters, vol. 4, TR. to Kennan, 6 May 1905; Lodge Mss, #88, TR. to Lodge, 15 May 1905; TR. Mss, Series 3B, TR. to Lodge, 5 June 1908.

104. TR. Mss, Series 3B, TR. to Lodge, 5 June 1908.

105. TR. Letters, vol. 5, TR. to Wood, 22 January 1906.

106. TR. Letters, vol. 5, TR. to Root, 23 July 1907.

107. Braisted, *The United States Navy in the Pacific*, pp. 233-235.

108. TR. Letters, vol. 6, TR. to Lee, 20 December 1908.

109. TR. Letters, vol. 6, TR. to Cannon, 29 February 1908.

110. A. J. Marder, *From the Dreadnought to Scapa Flow*, vol. 1, pp. 56-70

111. GB Letters, vol. 4, p. 49, Memorandum, 30 September 1905. See also p. 65, Memorandum, 28 October 1905.

112. See Seager, R., *Alfred Thayer Mahan: The Man and His Letters*, pp. 525-527.

113. Bonaparte Mss, #126, TR. to Bonaparte, 20 August 1906.

114. TR. Mss, Series 1, Sims to TR., 27 September, 29 October 1906.

115. TR. Letters, vol. 5, TR. to Sims, 27 September 1906.

116. TR. Mss, Series 1, Hale to TR., 31 October 1906. See also 9 December 1906.

117. G. T. Davis, *A Navy Second to None*, p. 182.

118. TR. Letters, vol. 5, TR. to Foss, 19 December 1906, 11 January 1907.

119. Davis, *A Navy Second to None*, p. 180.

120. TR. Letters, vol. 5, TR. to Carnegie, 6 September 1906.

121. TR. Letters, vol. 5, TR. to Grey, 22 October 1906, 28 February 1907.

122. Root Mss, #163, TR. to Root, 2 July 1907.

123. AMPUSA (GPO) 5 December 1905, p. xli.

124. Lodge Mss, #88, TR. to Schurz, 15 September 1905. Also see, TR. Letters, vol. 5, TR. to Bartholdt, 25 September 1905.

125. TR. Letters, vol. 5, TR. to Reid, 7 August 1906; TR. to White, 14 August 1906.

126. Lodge Mss, #88, Lodge to TR., 29 September 1905.

127. TR. Letters, vol. 5, TR. to Wood, 9 March 1905.

128. TR. Letters, TR. to Grey, 22 October 1906.

129. Lodge Mss, #24, Lodge to Meyer, 28 May 1906.

130. TR. Letters, vol. 5, TR. to Hale, 7 December 1906.

131. Sprout and Sprout, *The Rise of American Naval Power*, p. 264.

132. Ibid, pp. 264-267.

133. Lodge Mss, #88, TR. to Lodge, 22 April 1908.

134. CR, vol. 42, pp. 4805-06, 15 April 1908.

135. CR, vol. 42, p. 4169, 24 April 1908.

136. Ibid.

137. CR, vol. 42, p. 5229, 25 April 1908.

138. CR, vol. 42, p. 5225, 25 April 1908.

139. CR, vol. 42, pp. 4611-12, 11 April 1908, pp. 4777-78, 15 April 1908.

140. CR, vol. 43, p. 1305, 22 January 1909.

141. CR, vol. 42, p. 4806, 15 April 1908.

142. CR, vol. 42, pp. 4612-15, 11 April 1908.

143. CR, vol. 43, pp. 2431-36, 16 February 1909.

144. CR, vol. 43, p. 2434.

145. TR. Letters, vol. 6 TR. to White, 27 April 1908; TR. to K. Roosevelt, 23 January 1909.

146. TR. Letters, vol. 5, TR. to Otis, 8 January 1907, TR. to Eliot, 22 September 1906.

147. TR. Letters, vol. 5, TR. to A. Lodge, 20 September 1907.

148. TR. Letters, vol. 5, TR. to Taft, 21 August 1907.

149. TR. Letters, vol. 5, TR. to Otis, 8 January 1907

150. TR. Letters, vol. 5, TR. to Lodge, 1 October 1906.

151. TR. Letters, vol. 6, TR. to Taft, 3 March 1909.

152. TR. Letters, vol. 6, TR. to Knox, 8 February 1909.

153. TR. Letters, vol. 6, TR. to Kent, 4 February 1909.

154. TR. Letters, vol. 5, TR. to Trevelyan, 18 August 1906.

155. TR. Letters, vol. 6, TR. to White, 10 August 1908.

156. TR. Letters, vol. 5, TR. to Taft, 21 August 1907.

157. TR. Letters, vol. 5, TR. to Taft, 3 August 1907.

158. TR. Letters, vol. 5, TR. to Root, 31 July 1907.

159. TR. Letters, vol. 5, TR. to Root, 13 July 1907.

160. TR. Letters, vol. 5, TR. to Bonaparte, 13 July 1907.

161. TR. Letters, vol. 6, TR. to Taft, 3 March 1909.

162. T. Roosevelt, *An Autobiography*, p. 204.

# 4

# The 1909 Naval Estimates Crisis

[McKenna] When one assumes that programmes are adhered to, one perhaps forgets that if the Germans do not adhere to their programme, we have no power to keep ahead of them. If the Germans say "we are not going to keep to our programme, but we are going to build as much as we can," we cannot beat them.
[Asquith] Why?
[McKenna] Because we have not the power of constructing quicker than they.[1]

Meanwhile we have been in the throes of a navy scare. Well engineered and it will bring us our 8 dreadnoughts.[2]

Lord Esher, Diary Entry, 20 March 1909

## CABINET PERSONALITIES

The 1909 naval estimates crisis was dominated by five members of the Cabinet: Asquith, Grey, Lloyd George, McKenna, and Churchill. Other Cabinet members such as Harcourt, Morley, Burns, and Crewe took an active part in the debates, but the first five controlled events. Of the five, four had taken over their portfolios in April 1908. Only Edward Grey, foreign secretary since 1905, had been in his job for more than a year. The resignation of the gravely ill prime minister Campbell-Bannerman, led to this Cabinet shake-up. Asquith left the Treasury to become prime minister, and to keep an ideological balance in the Cabinet the more radical Lloyd George became chancellor. Winston Churchill was then promoted into the Cabinet to take over from Lloyd George as president of the Board of Trade. For the Royal Navy the most important appointment was McKenna as first lord of the Admiralty. Lord Tweedmouth, well meaning but ineffectual, had been first lord since 1905. This had suited Fisher, as the first sea lord had a free hand to run the fleet, but as time went by, Tweedmouth's weaknesses began to worry the Cabinet. After he caused a diplomatic incident by leaking the contents of a letter from Kaiser Wilhelm II, a decision was made to replace him.[3]

While these five men dominated the naval debate in 1909, they did not play equal roles. Churchill and McKenna are best described as the "advocates." They were largely responsible for writing the Cabinet memoranda and presenting oral arguments. They swapped papers throughout the crucial month of February, and their last submissions in July marked the end of the crisis. The real power to settle the Cabinet crisis, however, lay with Asquith, Grey and Lloyd George. When the prime minister, foreign secretary, and chancellor of the exchequer reached a tacit and somewhat grudging understanding, the crisis was resolved.

Of all the parts played in 1909, Reginald McKenna's was the most unexpected. His only previous experience in naval affairs had been as a blues-winning oarsman for Cambridge University. When he arrived at the Admiralty, he was forty-six, precise, slightly self-righteous, and balding. His mind was methodical and somewhat pedantic. Later in life he would be a very successful chairman of the Midland Bank. His background for the position was unorthodox, having served as a member of the 1908 retrenchment committee appointed to find reductions in the naval estimates.[4] The first time McKenna appeared in Fisher's correspondence was as an advocate for cuts in the navy's budget.[5] The first sea lord was therefore rather wary of his new boss.[6]

By December, however, McKenna had been able to mollify most of Fisher's concerns.[7] After the first lord put in a determined performance during a crucial Cabinet meeting, the first sea lord was won over. "I am going to emphasise the fact that never had we a more united Board or a stronger first lord."[8] In the end, McKenna earned all the accolades that Fisher heaped upon him. He waged a persistent, exhausting, and ultimately successful battle. He never once compromised in his fight to secure as complete a package as possible for the Royal Navy, and by the end he had even gained the grudging respect of the man he disliked more than anyone else in the Cabinet—David Lloyd George.

Perhaps it was inevitable that the emotional Lloyd George would clash with the more conventional McKenna. Indeed, the only thing the two men seemed to have in common was a strong mutual dislike. Neither man did anything to conceal the animosity between them, and their disagreements often led to acrimonious bickering in Cabinet. McKenna even expressed his sentiments to Charles Repington, a correspondent for the *Times*:

I [Repington] expressed my sympathies with Lloyd George, who, with a beggars surplus of £250,000 anticipated, would have to provide £4,800,000 for old age pensions and also such sums as McKenna required for additional building. . . . Both ministers [McKenna and Haldane] laughed a good deal at Lloyd George's predicament and rather seemed to enjoy it. Lloyd George, said McKenna, is wonderfully quick in debate or in picking up the points of an argument . . . but his defective education does not allow him to take in anything by reading: to this Haldane agreed and both said by that details were beyond Lloyd George's comprehension.[9]

McKenna's dislike of Lloyd George was so strong that Fisher feared it might harm the Admiralty's position. He worried that McKenna would change the Admiralty's building program because of "funk of Lloyd George."[10] The Lloyd George-McKenna relationship reached a particular low point in September 1908. After Lloyd George asked McKenna if the Admiralty could begin building ships earlier than anticipated to help relieve unemployment, the first lord told the chancellor to mind his own business.[11] Lloyd George fired back an indignant reply:

I have no idea in what form my wire reached you, but it must indeed have been distorted in transmission to justify your reply. . . . I am sorry to have to [rebuke?] a colleague—for the first time—on such a storm, but I rather resent being lectured on my elementary duty to my chief.[12]

Bitterness between the two continued long after 1909. They had a spectacular falling out during the First World War, and Lloyd George eventually succeeded in driving McKenna from the Cabinet. In 1909, however, Lloyd George ended up the beaten man. He thought the Admiralty's plans were too expensive, but he eventually acquiesced because of exhaustion. Part of the problem was that Lloyd George tried to be all things to all men. When asked about naval issues, he would state earnestly that the Royal Navy should remain supreme. When asked about naval spending, he would just as earnestly state that it must be reduced.

A wonderful example of Lloyd George's fickleness was seen during an amusing encounter with the German ambassador in London, Count Paul von Wolff Metternich. Lloyd George found himself in conversation with Metternich about naval power. He seems to have forgotten his earlier calls for restraint: "He told M[etternich] plainly that if he had to borrow 100 millions for the Fleet, he would do so, in order to maintain our relative strength vis a vis Germany. I wonder how the Emperor likes this! It is rather splendid of Lloyd George."[13] Esher became so excited by Lloyd George's bravado that he suggested the chancellor back up his pledge by purchasing extra dreadnoughts: "Why not buy the 3 ships building for Brazil. Nothing would be more effective as an amplification of what you said to Metternich. . . . Is this project sufficiently bold for your Celtic soul?"[14] Lloyd George's reaction to this suggestion has been lost to history.

Lloyd George's most useful ally throughout the 1909 crisis was the young and rather too self-confident Winston Churchill. Churchill was the "enfant terrible" of the Liberal Cabinet. Once in the government, he bombarded his colleagues with papers, often making suggestions about subjects entirely outside his realm of responsibility and knowledge. In 1909 he even badgered Haldane to start developing the airplane for military potential, arguing that it could lead to reductions in the naval budget.[15] He was also, at this time, probably the most "pro-German" member of the Cabinet. Throughout the crisis he never flagged in his conviction that Germany was not secretly planning to wrest naval supremacy from Great Britain.[16]

Lloyd George was also the greatest single influence over Churchill at this time. Working with the dynamic Welshman offered Churchill the tantalizing prospect of exercising real power—something that always appealed. For a while it seemed that he was completely under Lloyd George's spell.[17] Together they attacked Haldane's army estimates with such passion that the war minister thought they were planning to take over the government. "Haldane is convinced that Lloyd George and Winston have in their minds the capture of Asquith. They think that by destroying Haldane, and even Grey, they can carry the government with Asquith as a respectable figurehead. I think there is some probability in this."[18]

Asquith, who had to preside over all this wrangling, would have been much happier if it had never happened. When dealing with naval matters, Asquith was generally tentative and uneasy. In 1908 he had basked in adulation following his reaffirmation of the two-power standard but then quickly came to believe he had blundered. He tried to retreat from his more ambitious claims but was ambushed by the opposition. He also paid little attention to technical details of the naval debate, as shown in this humorous and somewhat disquieting 1909 exchange:

[Asquith] Look at that beautiful picture of yours. Look at the range of a dreadnought gun; does the German gun go as far as that?
[Lloyd George] That is not the range, that is the weight.
[Asquith] Has the German gun as much weight as that?
[McKenna] Perhaps you had better look at it closer.[19]

Asquith was also distrusted by naval supporters like Esher and Fisher because of his earlier behavior at the Treasury. While chancellor, Asquith had presided over the deep cuts made in the Admiralty budget after Tsushima. It was an unusual experience for a chancellor, though not one he found distasteful, as Asquith often took the lead in arguing for reductions.[20] Furthermore, Asquith was known to have doubts about the building of the *Dreadnought*.[21]

However, even with all these defects Asquith played a crucial role in fashioning an end to the 1909 crisis. Much to the skeptic's surprise, he made two crucial decisions that bolstered the Admiralty's position. The first was that additional dreadnoughts were needed to protect British security and, second, that Lloyd George could be browbeaten into paying for them. Asquith was partly forced into taking such a tough line because of constant pressure from Edward Grey. Throughout the 1909 crisis the foreign secretary remained convinced that Britain needed as many ships as it could build, and he blocked moves toward a substantive compromise. Grey and others in the Foreign Office were motivated by a number of concerns. The first and most important was a native distrust of German intentions. Grey had been suspicious of Germany for years, and in 1908 his fears were heightened. He received a spate of reports stating that Germany was planning for a war with Great Britain.[22] Frank Lascelles, a British attache in Berlin, claimed that German children were taught to hate England and that Germany was searching for a moment to launch "an immediate attack."[23] Later in 1908 Grey believed that an Anglo-German war might break out over the Moroccan question. The foreign secretary was worried enough to ask McKenna to keep the fleet ready for action "in case Germany sent France an ultimatum and the Cabinet decided we must assist France."[24]

The possibility of a German attack was something that Grey took very seriously. He had been an influential member of the 1908 Invasion Inquiry Committee and believed that naval supremacy was vital:

There is no doubt whatever that the Germans have studied and are studying the question [of invasion]. German officers on leave come here and explore our coast and no doubt send in reports which are interesting and welcome to their own authorities. No doubt the German staffs work out possible plans. . . . As long as we have sufficient superiority of Navy the risk will be too great for the Germans to run it in cold blood, but it is a danger to us to be borne in mind in all contingencies.[25]

In 1909 Grey's arguments usually revolved around the fact that any indecision about whether or not Germany was secretly building dreadnoughts must be met by the assumption that it was. His distrust never abated, even after being categorically assured by Metternich that there was no secret building.[26] His opinion was shared by others in the Foreign Office, particularly the permanent undersecretary of state, Charles Hardinge:

When one comes to think that, as the Germans admit, their Navy is being built at very great sacrifices in order to impose their will, it is quite conclusive to us that it is only upon us that they wish that their will should be imposed. . . . The only means by which they can be indefinitely deferred is by the construction of a very large number of battleships in this country.[27]

Hardinge and Grey worked very closely in this period, and their views about Germany seemed almost identical.[28] However, Grey and Hardinge were also concerned about the impact the naval issue could have upon Russia. The 1907 Anglo-Russian agreement negotiated by Grey was considerably less stable than the Anglo-French entente, and the Foreign Office was on guard against any

signs that Russia might be moving back into the German camp. The Foreign
Office's Annual Report for 1908 showed its concern:

It is considered that the value of France as an ally has largely diminished of recent years.
There is generally received opinion that both her naval and military forces are much
weakened by sedition and insubordination, and that they would be of no great value in
case of war. On the other hand, the power of Germany, both on land and on sea is regarded with perhaps exaggerated admiration, and it is considered prudent to live on
friendly terms with so powerful a neighbour.[29]

These worries were exacerbated during the 1908 Bosnian crisis. Russia was
shown to be powerless to stop Austria-Hungary backed up by German power. At
the same time that Russia was being humiliated over Bosnia, reports began to
reach the Foreign Office that the Russians were fearful that Britain and Germany
might improve relations:

I have it on best authority . . . that the opinion is held by at least one important Russian
that some sort of a working understanding between Great Britain and Germany on the
naval question is not so impossible as generally supposed, and that the idea disturbs him.
The Russian Government have now before them a paper pointing out that "should conversations begin between Great Britain and Germany at this point, they may lead further" and, in fact, if a rapprochement takes place the position of Russia will not be so
comfortable, as she will be too much at the mercy of Berlin.[30]

Hardinge moved decisively to quell these Russian fears:

I trust, however, that the Russians will not think for a moment that we want to improve
our relations with Germany at their expense. We have no pending questions with Germany, except that of naval construction, while our whole future in Asia is bound up with
the necessity of maintaining the best and most friendly relations with Russia—even for
the sake of a reduced naval programme. . . . I have not seen Grey, who has been away for
some time; but I am quite convinced that he is of that opinion too.[31]

Later, as the 1909 naval crisis deepened, and more reports reached the Foreign Office about Russia's doubts, Hardinge's notes began to sound more desperate:[32] "Will they [Russia] be far-sighted enough to see that the loyal support
which we have given them throughout this recent crisis may be of inestimable
benefit to Russia if repeated at the time when she is engaged in a death struggle
with Germany and Austria?"[33] These messages do not prove that Russian griev-
ances played a major part in Grey's thinking during the 1909 crisis. However, it
is probable from Hardinge's detailed knowledge of Cabinet proceedings that he
and Grey discussed the question of Anglo-German and Anglo-Russian relations
frequently. It is almost very unlikely that Grey would have been unaware of
Russian opinion and even more unlikely that Hardinge would have written Nicolson the previous statements if Grey had not given at least tacit approval. In
and of themselves, the worries about Russia might not have been enough to pro-

pel Grey to act as vociferously as he did in 1909, but when the worries about Russia are combined with Grey's basic distrust of German intentions, it becomes apparent that Grey had much to gain by being intransigent.

## THE CRISIS UNFOLDS

When the Cabinet recessed for Christmas, everyone knew a bitter fight was looming. The 18 December meeting had shown that the government was finely balanced. McKenna had the backing of Liberal imperialists like Grey, Haldane, and Crewe while the "economists" were mostly traditional Liberals such as Lloyd George, Burns, Harcourt, and Morley. Asquith had yet to reveal his personal opinion because, more likely than not, he was unsure what it was. By the time the Cabinet reconvened, however, the balance had tipped slightly, but significantly, in the Admiralty's favor. This was because of how the different factions utilized their holiday. Lloyd George cut himself off from communication with Asquith and trundled around France. McKenna and Grey, meanwhile, worked Asquith over feverishly. Grey, who had been Asquith's ally for years, took the lead. In what can only be described as a textbook example of political maneuvering, Grey reshaped Asquith's understanding of Germany and the German navy. He began by frightening the prime minister.

The foreign secretary began his campaign with a letter written two days before Christmas. He told Asquith that if there was any uncertainty about Germany's intentions the Cabinet should assume the worst: "Failing any agreement with them [Germany], we must base our programme on the assumption of what they can do."[34] Grey was always careful to speak as if some secret German acceleration was an accepted fact. Under the terms of the German naval law thirteen dreadnoughts should have been completed by July 1912. Grey told Asquith, however, that Germany could have twenty-one dreadnoughts by April 1912, or, if they collected matériel in advance, they would have seventeen.

Next, Grey urged McKenna to prepare a paper describing the effects of any German acceleration.[35] McKenna completed this task on 29 December and sent the paper to Grey for his approval.[36] The situation as McKenna described it was perilous: "I have no doubt whatever that Germany means to build up to the full extent of her capacity. . . . If by any spurt they can catch us up, we have no longer any such building capacity as would ensure supremacy." It had earlier been assumed that Britain's superior shipbuilding skills would protect the country. Those opposed to the six-dreadnought program argued that Britain could take time to assess any challenge. McKenna and Grey were hoping to preempt this argument.

McKenna also described Germany's earlier procedures for constructing warships and compared them to what he claimed was going on in 1909. Previously, German warships had been paid for in four installments, a practice that was now being disregarded:

The four ships of the 1909-10 programme are being proceeded with in quite another manner. Although they do not appear in the estimates until 1909-10 when a first install-ment of £480,000 is provided they were already ordered in October 1908 and a consider-able sum of money will have been spent on them before 1 April next. . . . Unless the building of these ships is deliberately hung-up, (which would be an expensive matter for the contractors) the heaviest cost of construction must fall upon the year 1909-10. There was a difference in time of only a few months—more than two less than six—between the orders for the ships of the 1908-09 programme and those for the ships of the 1909-10 programme . . . the only limit to the acceleration of the programme is the constructive capacity of Krupps and various shipyards.[37]

Like Grey, McKenna then listed both the statutory and possible sizes of the German fleet. According to the Navy Law, Germany should have nine dread-noughts in February 1911, thirteen in February 1912, seventeen in February 1913, and twenty-one in February 1914. If the Germans decided to build to the limit of their capacity, however, they could have thirteen dreadnoughts in April 1911, seventeen in February 1912, and twenty-one in April 1912.[38] Armed with these figures, Grey paid a personal visit to Asquith and outlined the German challenge in gory detail. He obviously alarmed the prime minister, for a worried Asquith soon wrote to McKenna asking to see his paper, saying that "nobody here can understand why Germany should need, or how she can use, 21 dread-noughts, unless for aggressive purposes and [threats?] against ourselves."[39]

McKenna dutifully passed along his report on 3 January, together with a note describing some new and ominous developments:

I am anxious to avoid alarmist language but I cannot [help?] the following conclusions which is my duty to submit to you.
1. Germany is anticipating . . . [both its construction program and the widening of the Kiel Canal].
2. She is doing so secretly.
3. She will certainly have 13 big ships in commission within the Spring of 1911.
4. She will probably have 21 big ships in commission within the Spring of 1912.
5. German capacity to build dreadnoughts is at this moment equal to ours.
The last conclusion is the most alarming and if justified would give the public a rude awakening.[40]

Grey and McKenna had taken full advantage of Lloyd George's absence to shift the whole tenor of the discussion in London. It was no longer hypothetically possible that Germany might have twenty-one dreadnoughts in 1912, now it was "probable." Asquith was unsurprisingly deeply affected by the alarming news fed to him by two of his most trusted colleagues, and by January he seems to have been convinced that the Germans were secretly building.[41]

Now that Grey had accomplished his first objective, he next had to neutral-ize Lloyd George. Having spent Christmas sampling the delights of southern France, Lloyd George soon realized that he had miscalculated badly by leaving

Asquith unchaperoned. The jaunty confidence he had exhibited in December soon gave way to uncertainty. He shared his anxiety with Winston Churchill:

The Admiralty mean to get their 6 dreadnoughts. Murray sent me a message through Clark that the Admiralty have had very serious news from their naval attache in Germany since our last Cabinet Committee & that McK is now convinced we may have to lay down 8 dreadnoughts next year!!! . . . Frankly I believe the Admirals are procuring false information to frighten us. McK feels his personal position & prestige is at stake. He has postponed his visit to the South of France in order to organise the intelligence for the next fight. . . . I do not believe the Germans are at all anxious to hurry up their building programme, quite the reverse. Their financial difficulties are already great. Why should they increase them?[42]

However, not until early February was Lloyd George able to present his arguments to Asquith in a coherent and organized form, and by then he had lost too much time. Indeed, before the Cabinet reassembled, a new element entered the debate. Now the argument was not just between those who wanted four or six dreadnoughts but between those who wanted four, six, or eight.

It is still not exactly clear when the Admiralty decided to press for eight dreadnoughts. Fisher had urged McKenna on 22 December to make a case for two extra ships.[43] However, this suggestion was pushed into the background until 18 January. On that day the sea lords handed McKenna a signed memorandum urging the construction of eight battleships. They claimed it was a "possibility" that Germany would have twenty-one dreadnoughts in 1912 and a "practical certainty" that it would have seventeen. If the Germans had seventeen, and Great Britain laid down six ships in 1909–1910, then Britain's capital ship strength would be larger than Germany's by a margin of only 4 to 3. If Germany had twenty-one dreadnoughts, the ratio would be 5 to 4.[44]

The call for eight dreadnoughts only complicated matters. When the Cabinet reopened the issue in early February, the discussions were once again very heated. Asquith, in his best deadpan style, described them to Edward VII as having a "great diversity of opinion leading to an animated discussion."[45] During these talks McKenna and Churchill repeated their roles of December and did most of the arguing. Each also wrote a number of memoranda. Churchill, for once, struck first. He circulated a paper on 4 February arguing that the Royal Navy's huge lead in predreadnought battleships allowed Britain to wait to see if Germany really was secretly building. Churchill assumed that Germany would have seventeen dreadnoughts by April 1912, and Britain, if it laid down four, would have sixteen. The Germans, however, had only ten effective predreadnoughts, while the Royal Navy had thirty-two: "Cancel like with like. The British preponderance will be 21 first class battleships; the German preponderance will be 1 Dreadnought. Assume (a large assumption) that this odd Dreadnought is equal to any two of the remaining British battleships . . . and the net preponderance in British battleships will be 19—against nothing, or a majority nearly equal to the whole existing German battleship fleet."[46]

One of the most remarkable aspects about Churchill's argument was the almost casual way in which he disregarded the two-power standard—recently defined as a 10 percent superiority over the combined strength of the next two naval powers. It was probably true that, had Churchill's scenario developed, the Royal Navy in 1912 would be marginally stronger than the German fleet. However, Britain's superiority would consist of battleships laid down mostly between 1898 and 1902. The two power standard would simply have disappeared.

There was one other serious weakness in Churchill's paper. He seemed to accept as fact that three German dreadnoughts were being laid down ahead of schedule. Even though he argued there would be no more German acceleration, he had made a serious gaffe. McKenna gratefully seized on this.[47] The first lord argued that Britain's predreadnought advantage was seventeen, not twenty-one, and instead of discussing the merits of different classes he cleverly used one of Churchill's own ploys. McKenna likewise treated two predreadnoughts as the qualitative equal of one dreadnought and argued that if Great Britain had only sixteen real dreadnoughts in 1912, its combined strength in both classes would be the equivalent of thirty-three dreadnoughts. At the same time Germany should have seventeen real dreadnoughts and the functional equivalent of eight and a half more, for a total of twenty-five and a half. Therefore, the Anglo-German ratio in battleship strength would be an alarming 5 to 4. It was not, perhaps, a completely honest description of the situation, but it was very effective. Churchill realized he had been outfoxed and tried to extricate himself by submitting another memorandum:

The First Lord proves that, in terms of "Dreadnoughts," Great Britain will . . . have in 1912 33 and Germany 25 1/2, or just over 5 to 4 in favour of Great Britain against Germany only. To avert this grave conjecture he asks that not 4, but 6 "Dreadnoughts" should be laid down this year. That is to say, if all that is asked for were conceded, the result would be Great Britain 35 "Dreadnoughts," Germany 25 1/2 "Dreadnoughts" or a balance in British favour not of over 5 to 4, but under 7 to 5. It is submitted that the difference between these two scales is too small to be material.[48]

Churchill was correct in claiming that a ratio of 7 to 5 was scarcely better than one of 5 to 4. However, he had allowed himself to be dragged into a debate over how drastically British supremacy would be reduced, in which case the general instinct would be to make the Royal Navy as strong as possible.

The exchange of papers stopped at this point. Both sides needed time to digest all the arguments. However, the struggle continued on a different and much more important level, as the main participants argued bitterly outside the Cabinet. Grey tried to consolidate his earlier gains and kept the pressure on Asquith: "The House of Commons will demand to know how many ships it will in our opinion be necessary to lay down this year to maintain the superiority which will be the declared principle of our whole building program. I, like others, advocated retrenchment at the last election, but I always excepted the Navy from my promises, and in any case promises must be subordinate to national safety."[49]

What worried Grey was the possibility that Asquith, desperate for Cabinet peace, would strike a compromise with the "economists." He was worried that Asquith might hold over any extra dreadnoughts for later Cabinet approval. He showed his fierce determination to preempt such a compromise during a meeting with Winston Churchill. Grey's single-mindedness clearly unnerved the younger man:

Are you really prepared to drive out colleagues who accept the basis you yourself laid down, when no scrap of public security is compromised, simply because you fear a naval panic? Are you willing to see the Government broken irretrievably rather than postpone for a few months during wh[ich] the facts may be proved?[50]

One of the reasons Grey was so worried was that he knew Lloyd George was also putting pressure on the prime minister. Lloyd George had sent Asquith a remarkable ten-page letter, which the prime minister had shown to Grey. In it Lloyd George threatened Asquith with the collapse of the government.

The discussion of Naval Estimates threatens to reopen all the old controversies which rent the Party for years and brought us to impotence and contempt. You alone can save us from the prospect of sterile and squalid disruption. I therefore earnestly pray you not to commit yourself to the very . . . ill considered Admiralty demands without giving full consideration to the arguments urged upon you by Morley, Churchill and other members of the Cabinet who cannot see their way to assent to these demands. . . . When the £38,000,000 Navy Estimates are announced, the disaffection of these good Liberals will break into open sedition and the usefulness of this Parliament will be at an end.[51]

Lloyd George also attacked the notion that the Germans were secretly accelerating their building program:

The only new fact we are confronted with is the alleged anticipation of the German ship-building programme. But what does this really amount to? It has occurred this year owing entirely to the well-known German practice of counter-balancing and re-dressing trade un-employment. . . . When I was in Germany some months ago, I saw some of the greatest shipbuilding yards and they were all almost empty. The German government, in accordance with its usual policy of doling out work during periods of depression, came to terms with German shipbuilders to start ships a few months in advance of the statutory period of construction, a wise and on the whole economical system.[52]

Then Lloyd George attacked the Admiralty. If the Germans were not accelerating, and the British laid down four dreadnoughts in 1909, the Royal Navy's advantage in 1912 would be sixteen to ten. If, on the other hand, the Germans were building up to the limits of their capacity, as suggested by McKenna and Grey, then "the Admiralty proposals were ludicrous." Finally, Lloyd George suggested a compromise. Instead of having yearly naval programs Lloyd George pressed for long-term programs covering a large number of ships. This way the

Cabinet could react to changes in the international situation by either speeding up or slowing down the construction of new warships.

Asquith, reading what was otherwise a threatening letter, glimpsed in this suggestion a possible way out of the impasse. He replied to Lloyd George with an encouraging letter.[53] Lloyd George took heart and actually drafted a possible footnote for the 1909 estimates. His footnote would have allowed two or four extra dreadnoughts to be laid down, but only if the Cabinet approved later.[54] However, an agreement could still not be reached. The problem was the specific wording of the footnote. The "economists" would not approve wording that guaranteed the laying down of the extra dreadnoughts in 1909-1910 while Grey and McKenna opposed giving the Cabinet any leeway to reject them.

Now McKenna and Grey's earlier lobbying of Asquith paid dividends. The prime minister seems to have decided that the only way out of the Cabinet deadlock was to separate Lloyd George from the rest of the "economists." Without the support of the chancellor those opposed to the extra ships were leaderless. Churchill was a fascinating figure, but he was also very junior and lacked the necessary stature to lead a Cabinet uprising. The effective opposition to the extra ships had lived and would die with Lloyd George. The first sign that Asquith was treating Lloyd George differently occurred in a letter sent to Edward VII on 15 February. He described Churchill, Harcourt, Burns and Morley as strongly in favor of a "four now and possibly two later" program, while Grey, Crewe, Walter Runciman, and Noel Buxton were listed as supporters of, at least, a firm six-dreadnought program. Lloyd George, while included with the "economists," was singled out as someone seeking a solution. At this point, however, Lloyd George was still unwilling to compromise enough to satisfy Asquith. On 17 February Hardinge, who almost certainly received his information from Grey, was still describing Lloyd George as a strong opponent of the extra ships.[55] On 20 February, in a letter to his wife, Asquith even fantasized about "cashiering" Lloyd George.[56]

A few days later, however, Lloyd George's resistance began to crumble. The reason was a vital meeting held on 23 February. In this meeting the question of battleship construction times was examined in detail. Construction time had always been considered Britain's ace in the hole. Slade, the director of Naval Intelligence, estimated in early 1908 that the British built their battleships in twenty-four months, and the Germans in approximately thirty.[57] Dumas assumed, in February 1908, that German battleships laid down in May 1905 would take thirty-eight months to be built.[58] McKenna even thought in early 1908 that the Germans would have great difficulty fulfilling their naval program because they could not manufacture enough heavy gun mountings.[59]

In October 1908, however, the British began to reconsider some of these optimistic assumptions. After a study of total shipyard capacity, Slade now claimed that Britain could produce six capital ships a year and that Germany could equal that number.[60] Next, in the December sketch estimates, McKenna revealed that the Germans would complete their first dreadnought, the *Nassau*, in twenty-six months.[61] This was a revision of the Admiralty's earlier estimate of thirty months or more. These new and pessimistic calculations were part of the report written by McKenna and sent to Grey and Asquith in late December.[62] McKenna now assumed that the construction time for the nine German dreadnoughts already under construction would be (in months) twenty-six, twenty-eight, thirty, thirty, thirty-one, thirty, thirty, thirty and thirty. It should be noted that McKenna was advancing as pessimistic a view of the situation as possible. He estimated that all future German dreadnoughts would be built in twenty-six months, or as fast as they had ever done so before.[63]

The government also became concerned that the growing strength of Krupp, Germany's leading industrial concern, might tip the balance away from Britain in a naval race. On 28 December 1908 Grey passed on to Asquith an alarming report about Krupp by Colonel Surtees, a British army attaché in Berlin. According to Surtees, Krupp was the largest manufacturing company in the world, employing around 65,000 people. Krupp's engineering capacity alone was larger than that of the Woolwich Arsenal, Armstrongs, Vickers, and the Coventry Ordnance Works combined. Surtees further claimed that Krupp's management was "entirely under the control of a few directors, each of whom is devoted heart and soul to the interests of the Emperor."[64] Krupp had also just made an enormous investment in the heavy machinery needed to construct large naval guns and mountings. It now had a capacity "far in excess of any requirements for the existing Naval Programme of Germany."

That British fear of Krupp played a significant role during the 1909 crisis has been recognized by Marder. He referred to "The Mulliner Affair," and concentrated on a 24 February 1909 meeting between H. H. Mulliner, director of the Coventry Ordnance Works, and Admiral Charles Ottley.[65] Yet, the information passed on by Mulliner about Krupp was almost identical to the information gathered by Surtees.[66] It came as no surprise to many in the Cabinet, especially since the issue of German construction capacity had dominated a crucial government meeting on 23 February.

This extraordinary meeting represented the culmination of Asquith's attempt to separate Lloyd George from the rest of the "economists." It took place in the prime minister's rooms in the House of Commons and was attended by Asquith, Grey, McKenna, Fisher, Lloyd George, and Captain John Jellicoe, the third sea lord.[67] Asquith had surrounded the chancellor with naval supporters and deprived him of any "economists." Thankfully, a transcript remains of the meeting, and in it one can see how Lloyd George was beaten into submission. The discussion began with the question of building costs and the need for a long-term program but quickly moved to the key issue of construction time. It was assumed that the Royal Navy could have eighteen dreadnoughts in April 1912, twenty in November 1912, twenty-two in January 1913, and twenty-four in March 1913.

Those at the meeting also agreed, Lloyd George not objecting, that if Germany accelerated the building of just three dreadnoughts, it would have twenty-one completed in early 1913. This was partly because the Germans had the ability to lay down four battleships at a time, while Great Britain had to lay down sets of two: "[McKenna] To us it is absolutely amazing that they can do it [lay down four ships at a time] and it is only possible because of the extra-ordinary power that Krupp's have. We could not do it."[68]

Discussion then turned to 1914 and 1915, when it was assumed that Germany would have twenty-three and twenty-five dreadnoughts, respectively. The maximum number that Britain could possess was twenty-seven and thirty, respectively, so at most the Royal Navy would have a ratio of superiority of 6 to 5. Lloyd George, bombarded by these pessimistic calculations, became quite unsettled: "We ought to have more, but as against Germany alone, considering nothing else, we should not be safe with anything less than 30." Worse was to come. McKenna described what would happen if the Germans threw everything into the balance, if they utilized all of their resources to build as many battleships as possible:

[McKenna] When one assumes that programmes are adhered to, one perhaps forgets that if the Germans do not adhere to their programme, we have no power to keep ahead of them. If the Germans say "we are not going to keep to our programme, but we are going to build as much as we can," we cannot beat them.
[Asquith] Why?
[McKenna] Because we have not the power of constructing quicker than they.[69]

This was the most pessimistic evaluation of the naval balance given by a first lord of the Admiralty before World War One. McKenna was claiming that Britain could not maintain even a one-power standard if fully pressed by Germany. Britain's key weakness lay not in the construction of warship hulls but in the assembly of the massive guns and gunmountings needed for dreadnoughts. Krupp alone could provide fifty-four turrets in a year, enough for eleven battleships, which was far larger than Britain's capacity. To Asquith this was "the most disquieting thing I have heard about the whole question." Lloyd George, who had already begun to waver, seemed shocked at the threat to Britain's superiority. He was so worried that he actually began badgering McKenna to take some action:

[Lloyd George] If Krupp can turn out 54 I think the capacity of this country ought to be that we could turn out 60. . . . If they [British gun manufacturers] say we will not do it, then I think we ought to make provision in the Estimates for next year and inform these firms that unless they undertake immediately to increase their capacity to a degree we shall agree upon, we will make provision for setting up machinery for setting up in our Arsenal in Woolwich for that purpose. Of course if we say that, they will do it.
[McKenna] We cannot treat them quite in that way, because they have put up their existing machinery and spent a couple of millions of money on it.
[Lloyd George] You can treat any firm in any way you like if the safety of the country depends upon it.[70]

Lloyd George pressed for a large increase in Britain's building capacity, enough to allow for the simultaneous construction of twelve dreadnoughts in a single year. This was far above the present figure of six or eight and would have been extremely expensive. Lloyd George even seemed willing to give the Admiralty's "experts" the power to speed up construction if needed, a wholesale change from his earlier position.[71] Finally, Lloyd George seemed to relent and accept the "fact" that the Germans were secretly accelerating their dreadnought construction.

[Lloyd George] Suppose that Germany, instead of having 17 in 1912, had 21 in 1912, which I understand is a possible contingency although not a likely one, then if the Admiralty were to discover this in November, and were to come to the Treasury, as they would in the first instance, and say we must anticipate next year's programme, they should have the power to make arrangements for anticipating your orders.[72]

From this point onward the 1909 crisis was bound to be settled in the Admiralty's favor. This meeting had brought to the fore issues that had not been discussed by a British government for over a century. First and foremost, it revealed just how concerned many key Cabinet members were about the future naval balance of power. The question that had occupied British governments since Trafalgar had been how much superiority the Royal Navy needed. Now the first lord of the Admiralty had stated that Britain no longer controlled its own naval destiny. The fact that that this challenge turned out to be mostly illusory did little to assuage the fears of those who had participated in the discussion. From now until 1914 the Asquith government always erred on the side of caution when dealing with Germany's potential naval threat.

This meeting was also particularly important because of its impact upon Lloyd George. By its end he had lost the will to fight on against the Admiralty. The Cabinet met the following day and agreed to a "four now, four later" mechanism to build eight dreadnoughts. The connection between the two meetings is undeniable. While Churchill and a number of the remaining "economists" continued to fight,[73] Lloyd George seemed exhausted. He revealed his disillusionment in a letter to Haldane

We went out of our way to avoid a crisis and a split that would inevitably weaken the Liberal forces. You will admit that we went much further to meet the Admiralty views than McKenna came to meet ours. But if every concession we make is used as a means of manoeuvring us into something much worse than the proposals we originally fought, the situation is hopeless. . . . Grey said after last week's Cabinet that we got the shadow and McKenna walked of with the substance. He now wants to deprive us of this poor shadow. How Fabulous.[74]

The "shadow" that Lloyd George was referring to was the "four now, four later" formula. Four new dreadnoughts would be laid down immediately, and four more would be started in the autumn if the Cabinet thought it necessary.

Instead of being an equal compromise, however, the Admiralty supporters won a key victory. Immediate steps could be taken to proceed with the extra dreadnoughts, which meant that active opposition would be required to stop their construction. Asquith sent a copy of the footnote covering their construction to Edward VII:

(1) Four new Dreadnoughts to be in any event laid down in the ensuing financial years. (2) An Act of Parliament to be passed this session providing for a programme of naval construction so calculated as to keep us always ahead of the German programme. (3) Power to be given . . . to make forward contracts for the ships of next year—so that the Government will be able (if so advised) next Autumn, to place orders for four additional Dreadnoughts, to be laid down not later than April 1st, 1910. This will ensure us having a very substantial preponderance over Germany at the critical time . . . March-June 1912.[75]

At this point the 1909 crisis entered a most unusual phase. The big-navy group could not bring itself to believe that the "economists" were in retreat and continued to fight on against almost nonexistent opposition. The reason for this was that Admiral Fisher, unbelieving in his victory, decided to press for an ironclad commitment to the extra dreadnoughts. He was primarily motivated by a deep distrust of politicians and believed that once the present furor had abated, the Cabinet might lose the political will to proceed with the contingent vessels.[76]

When McKenna first informed the Admiralty Board of the 24 February decision, Fisher pressed for an irrevocable commitment to the four extra dreadnoughts.[77] Fisher even tried to stir things up by interjecting a new piece of intelligence about German intentions into the debate. A group of Argentinean officers had been touring European shipyards trying to decide where to place their orders for new battleships. They had been given an extensive tour of the Krupp works and told the Admiralty that they had seen 100 eleven-inch and twelve-inch naval guns nearing completion.[78] If this report was accurate, and the Germans were intending to use these guns to arm their own battleships, then they must have been planning a massive construction expansion. However, all this extra maneuvering only seemed to aggravate the prime minister. When Asquith received a letter from McKenna about the extra ships, he was more than a little annoyed. To him the issue was settled. The extra ships were sure to be built, and all the Admiralty could hope to achieve through their agitation was to further embarrass the "economists."[79]

Asquith always considered that his personal threat to resign would be enough to guarantee the acceptance of the extra four ships. To McKenna, however, even this was insufficient, and he wanted a footnote capable of dealing with all contingencies. McKenna even wanted a bill that would "incur liability" for the extra ships. He wanted to deny the House of Commons any opportunity to later cancel them:

The only point of danger I see is that Parlt. may not be disposed to accept it. If it is rejected either in the Commons or in the Lords, I understood from you yesterday that you would instantly resign. I know that you would bring the whole of your authority to support the Bill and that you would stand or fall by it, but is it certain, even then, that it would pass?[80]

Asquith, however, felt that he could not completely humiliate the "economists," and tried to restrain McKenna:

It has been most painful and repugnant to me, in view of our long and close personal intimacy and (I may say) affection, even to appear to exert any kind of pressure. But you know me so well (I hope) that, in a matter like this, you will give weight to my judgment, and believe that my one predominant desire is to attain the end wh. we both have in view. I have never before made—as I make to you now—so clear and direct an appeal for trust and confidence.[81]

Finally, before Asquith could consider the issue closed, he had to deal with one final sortie from the foreign secretary. Grey, who had so superbly manipulated events so far, once again stepped in to apply his own special brand of pressure. He had been talking with Fisher and shared many of the first sea lord's concerns. Grey also wanted a stronger commitment to the extra dreadnoughts and once again threatened Asquith:

As soon as the moment arrived when in the opinion of McKenna and the Board of Admiralty time would be lost and national safety endangered, by not giving the order for these additional four ships, the matter should be brought before the Cabinet. If the Cabinet refused then to give McKenna authority to act, then would be the time for McKenna, the Admiralty and any of us to decide whether the action of the Cabinet was inconsistent with National Safety.[82]

The footnote issue remained unsettled until mid-March. Much to the discomfort of Fisher, who never could bring himself to trust Asquith,[83] the prime minister stuck to his guns. Even after all the Admiralty's efforts the words "incur liability" were not included in the final draft.[84]

## WE WANT EIGHT AND WE WON'T WAIT

Once the estimates footnote had been agreed to by the Cabinet, the 1909 crisis was essentially settled. This does not mean everything settled down.[85] Elements of the Conservative press vociferously attacked the "four now, four later" policy and cries of "We want eight, and we won't wait," echoed around. On 16 March McKenna was forced to defend the policy in the House, and on 29 March the government defeated a motion of censure tabled by the opposition. Yet, this commotion was mostly irrelevant. What the opposition did not know was that there was little or no danger of the extra ships not being laid down. To keep

Cabinet unity the illusion had to be maintained that the extra dreadnoughts still needed approval.

When the Cabinet finally did give its approval, there was little debate, even though the Admiralty's hysterical claims had been proven false. In July McKenna admitted that only one German dreadnought, instead of the three or four he had always claimed, had been laid down ahead of schedule. While he had previously stated that Germany would have at least seventeen and maybe twenty-one dreadnoughts in early 1912, now he had to resort to semantic calisthenics. "It could not be affirmed with any confidence that Germany will not have seventeen ships of the Dreadnought type ready for war some time between April and October 1912."[86]

It was McKenna's first admission of error, and Churchill tried to use it to his advantage.[87] He was flogging a dead horse. Even the discovery of the Admiralty's gross overexaggeration could not stir the bulk of the Cabinet. Lloyd George said not a word, and Asquith informed the king on 21 July that the four extra dreadnoughts would be laid down.[88] Marder claimed that the threat posed by Austrian dreadnoughts was crucial to securing final Cabinet approval.[89] Unfortunately, this is not the case. While there was some public hand wringing about the Austrians, they were never considered a serious threat. Only Edward Grey, unsurprisingly, tried to make an issue of the Austrian navy. He was still worried that the "economists" might rebel and tried to use the Austrian threat to convince Asquith to lay down the extra ships as soon as possible: "Here is what we know at present about the Austrian intentions. I think it ought to [decide?] us to use our powers as to beginning the extra four ships this year. . . . We have inquired at the Admiralty about this. They say that the rumor about the Austrian ships is regarded as well founded."[90]

Unfortunately for Grey, however, Asquith asked the Admiralty for its opinion of the Austrian navy. Fisher seemed far from concerned and told Asquith that the Austrians were capable of completing only one large ship annually and that they would be unable to complete a dreadnought until 1913.[91] Even this projection was somewhat pessimistic, for McKenna admitted that it took the Austrians approximately three and a half years to build a battleship.[92] Later, Fisher told Asquith that the Austrians would not have an open dock capable of building a dreadnought until at least 1911.[93] Fisher thought Austria's handicaps so serious that he assumed the only way the Austrian navy would acquire dreadnoughts in the short term would be to buy them from Germany.[94]

The information gathered by the various British attachés was no more threatening. The Austrian navy seemed like a fleet in stasis:

His Excellency [Head of the Austrian Marine Section] states that no vessels of the Dreadnought type are at present under construction in Austria-Hungary and that the question of their construction depends entirely upon the delegations which have not yet voted the necessary money . . . he referred to the difficulty of arousing interest in naval matters in a for the most part inland population, and he left the military attache with the impression that he was not particularly sanguine as to the prospects of getting necessary money at any rate in the immediate future.[95]

Any claim that the threat of Austrian dreadnoughts somehow caused the government to lay down the extra battleships is without foundation. Indeed, when McKenna officially informed the Cabinet in July that construction would soon begin, he hardly mentioned the Austrians.[96]

Before finishing with the 1909 crisis, it is worth asking whether or not Fisher and the Admiralty's supporters had concocted the whole affair. The fact that Germany's "acceleration" was shown to be illusory might lead one to be skeptical. Lloyd George thought in January that the Admiralty was twisting the facts.[97] The evidence to support this claim is mixed. Fisher certainly seemed as shocked as anyone when the first reports of German acceleration surfaced. There are, however, indications that he was willing to see the "darker" side of the issue if it served Admiralty purposes.

The earliest indication was seen during the Admiralty's first attempt to convince the Cabinet to support building eight dreadnoughts. Immediately after the 18 December Cabinet Fisher wrote McKenna urging him to press on with plans for the extra dreadnoughts even "if a scare autumn session becomes necessary for the eight ships."[98] There are also indications that Fisher, when speaking to his closest friends, was not as concerned about the Germans as he let on publicly. The first sea lord told Lord Esher, when the crisis was erupting, that things were under control: "Tell him [Francis Knollys, private secretary to Edward VII] very very secretly that the Navy Estimates all right. But don't breathe a word—entreat him not to."[99]

Perhaps the most interesting evidence comes from Esher. He was one of Fisher's closest confidants and the two met constantly. Fisher was never reluctant to share the most sensitive information with Esher, and on a number of occasions Esher made it seem as if the crisis was being deliberately exaggerated:

20 March 1909 . . . Meanwhile we have been in the throes of a navy scare. Well engineered and it will bring us our 8 dreadnoughts.
28 March 1909 . . . We have done well with the navy. And we will get our ships.[100]

While it is unlikely that Fisher and his supporters could have manipulated the whole crisis, it is not difficult to envisage the first sea lord deliberately fanning the flames in his quest for the extra dreadnoughts. Once Fisher, in a maneuver of dubious ethicality, used Esher as a channel of communication to the leader of the opposition, Arthur Balfour. Esher seems to have supplied Balfour with a number of questions that the Admiralty wished to have "pressed and answered."[101] Another possibility is that Fisher and Grey manipulated the course of events together. Grey was undoubtedly the most important and powerful of the Admiralty's supporters in the Cabinet. He met Fisher regularly, and they coordinated many of their activities. Once they even combined resignation threats.[102]

Their relationship became so close that Fisher was worried that McKenna might be irritated by its intimacy: "He [Grey] is a tower of strength! I would see him myself but am doubtful because of McKenna. Also, is it wise for me to tout Cabinet Ministers?"[103]

Like Fisher, Grey believed that the government's proper course was to build against all contingencies—including German lying. He was also rather selective with the Foreign Office information that he passed on to the Cabinet. During the height of the 1909 crisis, the Foreign Office received some reports that Germany, far from accelerating its shipbuilding, might soon have to reduce construction.[104] This information was duly passed along to certain British diplomats, but the reports never reached the Cabinet. Grey was also unusually slow in revealing the contents of his discussions with Count Metternich, German ambassador in London. The German was always conciliatory and assured Grey from January to March that Germany would adhere strictly to its naval law. However, the foreign secretary did not provide the Cabinet with a summary of these discussions until March.[105] None of this proves that a conspiracy existed to manipulate the 1909 crisis. However, Grey's constant meetings and coordinated activity with Fisher, his reluctance to release the German ambassador's assurances, and his refusal to inform the Cabinet of reports that German construction might be slowing down do not make the Foreign Office seem entirely evenhanded.

## THE 1909 NAVAL CRISIS AND THE FIRST WORLD WAR

When the First World War began, the Royal Navy was the strongest in the world. In September 1914 the Royal Navy outnumbered the high seas fleet by twenty-nine dreadnoughts to twenty-one.[106] Professor Marder speaks of the Germans being "intimidated" by the strength of the Royal Navy.[107] It seemed as if British naval policy in the prewar years had been vindicated. The government had been right to be suspicious of the new German Navy and had made the correct decisions in choosing to build the ships that it had. Even Winston Churchill, who had correctly argued that the Germans were not accelerating in 1909, came to believe that it was right to build all eight ships.[108]

Yet, if it was comforting to think that the First World War had vindicated the Asquith government's naval policy, it was also a delusion. Britain's eight-dreadnought advantage of September 1914 came entirely from the 1909 program. However, four of these ships had been built only because of a drastic miscalculation. Had there been no false reports of German acceleration, at most four ships and possibly three or two, would have been built. Then the British would have entered the First World War with only the barest margin of safety. Had the Battle of Jutland been fought under such circumstances, the British could have found themselves without any advantage.

It cannot be argued that if these extra ships were not built in 1909, they would have been provided for later. The "economist" faction in the Cabinet was willing to risk dreadnought parity with Germany if it could reduce naval spending. Even the rest of the Cabinet was planning for a much smaller level of superiority than Britain ended up with. At the height of the 1909 crisis McKenna had to terrify the Cabinet to secure a program that he claimed, in his most optimistic scenario, would leave Britain with twenty dreadnoughts in 1912 and Germany with seventeen.

Thankfully for the Admiralty, McKenna succeeded in terrifying the government. From 1909 until 1914, the British built to the limit of their capacity. Between 1909 and 1914 thirty dreadnought-type vessels were laid down. Since Britain's national capacity was thought to be six large ships a year, there was no margin for increase. This can hardly be called a prudent and reasonable policy. Instead, it was an unrestrained, unexpected, and drastic attempt to maintain British naval supremacy.

The 1909 crisis thus ended up dictating British naval policy until the outbreak of the First World War. There were other squabbles. The Admiralty's estimates for 1910-1911 and 1913-1914 caused major Cabinet splits.[109] Yet, during these later disputes the Cabinet rehashed the same questions that came to the fore in 1909. How strong will Germany be? How many new ships do we need to maintain our superiority over them? In both cases the pattern established in 1909 repeated itself. The Treasury, led by Lloyd George, complained bitterly about Admiralty spending. However, the Liberal imperialists, now supported by Winston Churchill, who replaced McKenna in 1911, made sure that the Royal Navy received most of what it wanted.

The supporters of the navy were so successful that the naval budget rocketed upward. Some have claimed that the decades before 1914 saw a continual, evolutionary growth in British naval spending.[110] However, except for during the Boer War, there was no significant growth in naval spending until 1909. As an example, Britain spent more for warship construction in 1896-1897 (£7,604,302), than 1908-1909 (£7,589,986). This is not to say that there was no real increase. Total Admiralty spending in 1896-1897 (£23,790,835) was only 70 percent of that in 1908-1909 (£33,511,720). However, this moderate growth paled in comparison to the increase in naval spending between 1909 and 1914. The 1896-1897 budget was only 44 percent of the 1914-1915 prewar allocation (£53,361,703).[111]

The real impact of the 1909 crisis has been consumed by the enormity of the First World War. It became an embarrassing affair for both sides in the Cabinet. The Admiralty's supporters eventually realized that their assumptions about German building were wrong, but the "economists," once the war erupted, had little reason to trumpet their earlier opposition to large building programs. Whenever the crisis is mentioned in Cabinet memoirs, it is usually passed over quickly.[112] Edward Grey has provided a particularly peculiar description of the split:

The most acute crisis in the Liberal Government came over naval expenditure in 1909. . . . For some days there was a Cabinet crisis. Eventually it was observed that all eight ships could not be laid down at once, and it was agreed that the construction should proceed in a manner that would not delay the completion of the eight ships if reflection and further knowledge proved them to be necessary, but on the understanding that reduction of the number could be made, if it became apparent that the need for them had been overestimated.[113]

Historians, as well, have yet to devote proper attention to the crisis. It has been described as just one more step along the path of British decline.[114] However, the 1909 crisis, if anything, throws doubt upon the idea of a slow, evolutionary change in behavior or policy. Its impact went far beyond just one single step on an inevitable road. For instance, it killed off the two-power standard. As the Admiralty told the Cabinet, "It may become necessary to have, apart from the two-power standard, an independent standard of strength measured by a given percentage of strength over any individual European power."[115] The year 1909 also demonstrates how quickly the perceptions and realities of national power could move in these years. Battleships were formidable and powerful weapons, but in a matter of months whole classes of them were considered obsolete. Power requires commitment, planning, and the willingness to spend scarce resources. It is also an unstable variable. Historical hindsight almost invariably causes one to discern sweeping trends in national development. We claim to see historical courses charted over decades, moving inexorably to their conclusions. Such a vision is distorting if for no other reason than that it provides for a grossly incomplete narrative. If we simply look at Great Britain as a declining power inevitably slipping first into parity and then inferiority with other powers, we are left with a misleading picture. Britain's own views were entirely more complex and in just a few months shifted from supreme confidence to paranoia. It is dangerous to ignore this perception in favor of grander trends.

## NOTES

1. Asquith Mss, Box #21, Conference, 23 February 1909.
2. Esher Mss, Diary Entry, 20 March 1909.
3. Marder A. J., *From Dreadnought to Scapa Flow*, pp. 140-142.
4. S. McKenna, *Reginald McKenna*, p. 70.
5. A. J. Marder, *Fear God and Dreadnought*, # 71.
6. Esher Mss, Diary Entry, 22 April 1908.
7. A. J. Marder, *Fear God and Dreadnought*, #150.
8. McKenna Mss 3/4, Fisher to McKenna, 21 December 1908.
9. Esher Mss 16/12, Conversation Notes, 8 May 1908.
10. Esher Mss 10/42, Fisher to Esher, 5 May 1908.
11. Lloyd George Mss C/6/5/12, McKenna to Lloyd George, 12 September 1908.
12. Lloyd George Mss C/6/5/12, Lloyd George to McKenna, 16 September 1908.
13. Esher Mss, Diary Entry, 23 July 1908.
14. Esher Mss 19/7, Esher to Lloyd George, 18 July 1908.
15. Esher Mss 5/26, Churchill to Haldane, 19 January 1909.
16. R. S. Churchill., *Winston S. Churchill*, vol. 2, pp. 511-514.
17. B. B. Gilbert, *David Lloyd George*, pp. 354-355.

18. Esher Mss, Diary Entry, 23 August 1908.

19. Asquith Mss, Box #21, Conference Minutes, 23 February 1909.

20. Cabinet Papers 37/83 #63, "Naval Expenditure," 8 July 1906.

21. McKenna Mss 3/3, Asquith to McKenna, 4 July 1908.

22. G. P. Gooch, H. Temperley, eds., *British Documents on the Origins of the War*, vol. 6, #94.

23. Admiralty 116/940B, Foreign Office Report, Lascelles to Grey, 6 August 1908.

24. Grey Mss 800/87, Grey to McKenna, 5 November 1908.

25. G. P. Gooch, H. Temperley, eds., *British Documents on the Origins of the War*, vol. 6, #80.

26. Ibid., #108

27. Hardinge Mss, Hardinge to Lascelles, 19 May 1908.

28. Z. S. Steiner, *The Foreign Office and Foreign Policy 1898-1914*, pp. 91-94.

29. FO Confidential Print, #9177, 1907 Annual Report on Russia, February 1908.

30. Hardinge Mss, De Salis to Hardinge, 25 December 1908.

31. Hardinge Mss, Hardinge to Nicolson, 4 January 1909.

32. Ibid., 16 February 1909.

33. Ibid., 30 March 1909.

34. Asquith Mss, Grey to Asquith, 23 December 1908.

35. McKenna Mss 3/19, McKenna to Asquith, 3 January 1909.

36. McKenna Mss 3/22, McKenna to Grey, 30 December 1908.

37. McKenna Mss 3/23, Memorandum, 29 December 1908.

38. Ibid.

39. McKenna Mss 3/3, Asquith to McKenna, 1 January 1909.

40. McKenna Mss 3/19, McKenna to Asquith, 3 January 1909.

41. Asquith Mss, Asquith to Edward VII, 2 February 1909.

42. R. S. Churchill, *Winston S. Churchill*, vol. 2, Companion, p. 938.

43. McKenna Mss 3/4, Fisher to McKenna, 22 December 1908.

44. Fisher Mss 1/7, Memorandum, 18 January 1909.

45. Asquith Mss, Asquith to Edward VII, 2 February 1909.

46. Cabinet Papers 37/97, #19, 4 February 1909.

47. Ibid., #24, 8 February 1909.

48. Ibid., #26.

49. Asquith Mss, Grey to Asquith, 5 February 1909.

50. R. S. Churchill, *Winston S. Churchill*, vol. 2 Companion, pp. 954-955; Churchill to Grey, 16 February 1909.

51. Lloyd George Mss C/6/11, Lloyd George to Asquith, 2 February 1909.

52. Ibid.

53. Ibid., Asquith to Lloyd George, 8 February 1909.

54. Ibid.

55. Hardinge Mss, Hardinge Letter, 17 February 1909.

56. S. McKenna, *Reginald McKenna*, p. 79.

57. Slade Mss, Diary Entry, 10 March 1908. See also Admiralty Papers 231/50.

58. Cabinet Papers 17/61, Dumas Report, 12 February 1908.

59. Esher Mss 16/12, Conversation Notes, 8 May 1908.

60. Slade Mss, "Present State of Shipbuilding," 10 October 1908.

61. Asquith Mss, Sketch Estimates, 8 December 1908.

62. McKenna Mss 3/23, Memorandum, 29 December 1908.

63. Asquith Mss, "Revised German Construction Plan," 3 January 1909.

64. Asquith Mss, Confidential Cabinet Paper, Grey to Asquith, 28 December 1908.

65. A. J. Marder, *From Dreadnought to Scapa Flow*, pp. 156-159.

66. McKenna Mss 3/14, "Note by Sir Charles Ottley."

67. Asquith Mss, "Minutes of a Conference Held in the P. M.'s Room, House of Commons on Tuesday February 23, 1909."

68. Ibid.

69. Ibid.

70. Ibid.

71. Ibid.

72. Ibid.

73. Cabinet Papers 37/98, #37, Harcourt Memorandum.

74. Haldane Mss #5921, Lloyd George to Haldane, 27 February 1909.

75. Asquith Mss, Asquith to Edward VII, 24 February 1909.

76. McKenna Mss 6/2, Fisher to McKenna, 5 March 1909. See also Jellicoe Mss #49006, Fisher to Jellicoe, 21 February 1909.

77. McKenna Mss 3/19, McKenna to Asquith, 25 February 1909.

78. McKenna Mss 6/2, Fisher to McKenna, 2 March 1909.

79. Haldane Mss, Asquith to Haldane, 27 February 1909.

80. Asquith Mss, McKenna to Asquith, 2 March 1909.

81. McKenna Mss 3/19, Asquith to McKenna, 2 March 1909.

82. Asquith Mss, Grey to Asquith, 4 March 1909.

83. Fisher Mss 1/8, Fisher to McKenna, 19 March 1909.

84. McKenna Mss 3/19, Sea lords to McKenna, 29 March 1909. See also A. J. Marder *From Dreadnought to Scapa Flow*, p. 162.

85. A. J. Marder, *From Dreadnought to Scapa Flow*, pp. 163-170.

86. CAB 37/100 #97, "Battleship Building," 14 July 1909.

87. CAB 37/100 #99, "Naval Programme," 20 July 1909.

88. Asquith Mss, Asquith to Edward VII, 21 July 1909.

89. A. J. Marder, *From Dreadnought to Scapa Flow*, pp. 170-171.

90. Asquith Mss, Grey to Asquith, 9 April 1909.

91. Asquith Mss, Fisher to Asquith, 10 April 1909.

92. McKenna Mss 3/3, McKenna to Churchill, 12 April 1909.

93. Asquith Mss, Fisher to Asquith, 11 April 1909.

94. Ibid., 10 April 1909.

95. Ibid., Cartwright Report, 11 April 1909.

96. CAB 37/100 #97, "Battleship Building," 14 July 1909.

97. R. S. Churchill, *Winston S. Churchill*, vol. 2, Companion, p. 938.

98. McKenna Mss 3/4, Fisher to McKenna, 22 December 1908.

99. Esher Mss, 10/43, Fisher to Esher, 26 January 1909.

100. Esher Mss, 10/43, Diary Entries.

101. Balfour Mss, #49719, Letter, 15 March 1909.

102. Asquith Mss, Box 21, Grey to Asquith, 4 March 1909.

103. Esher Mss, 10/43, Fisher to Esher, 14 April 1909.

104. Hardinge Mss, Hardinge to Bryce, 15 January 1909. See also De Salis to Hardinge, 25 December 1908, Hardinge to De Salis, 29 December 1908.

105. CAB 37/98 #46, "Conversations with the German Ambassador," 19 March 1909.

106. A. J. Marder, *From Dreadnought to Scapa Flow*, vol. 1, Appendix, pp. 439-442.

107. Marder. A. J., *From Dreadnought to Scapa Flow*, vol. 5, p. 330.

108. W. S. Churchill, *The World Crisis, 1911-1914*

109. A. J. Marder, *From Dreadnought to Scapa Flow*, vol. 1, pp. 214-220, 311-327.

110. W. H. McNeill, *The Pursuit of Power*, p. 287.

111. J. T. Sumida, *In Defence of Naval Supremacy*, Table 3, p. 345, & Table 8, p. 350.

112. H. H. Asquith, *The Genesis of The War*, p. 75.

113. E. Grey, *Twenty-Five Years*, pp. 199-200.

114. P. M. Kennedy, *The Rise and Fall of British Naval Mastery*, p. 237.

115. Asquith Mss, Two-Power Standard Notes, Spring 1909.

# 5

# From Taft to Wilson

The trouble has been that money has been expended in different localities and locations, probably due in many instances to political influence. . . . For instance, some miles from Bremerton navy yard a location has been acquired and a magazine station established. It is impossible for any ship to get to it and the ammunition must be moved by barges. It is, however, an ideal picnic ground.

George von Lengerke Meyer, 22 October 1910[1]

The General Board invites the attention of the Department to the fact that in the creation and maintenance of the fleet as an arm of national defense, there is not now, and has never been in any true sense, a governmental or departmental naval policy.

U.S. General Board, 28 March 1913[2]

## THE TAFT ADMINISTRATION AND THE U.S. NAVY

Historians of the U.S. Navy often find the Taft and Wilson administrations perplexing. Having heralded the beginning of a new era with Theodore Roosevelt, they are confronted with two presidents who, until 1915, accord naval issues little prominence. The Taft administration, in particular, is puzzling. Here is Roosevelt's chosen heir, a man aware of his predecessor's love for the navy, and he devotes relatively little time to the fleet. How can this phenomenon be explained? Some simply ignore the years between 1909 and 1915 and skip directly from the Roosevelt build-up to the First World War and the famous 1916 program. Another tack is to portray the Taft administration as the frustrated heir of Roosevelt's policy, struggling gamely but ultimately unsuccessfully to continue the buildup. The Sprouts speak of a "Rooseveltian policy without Roosevelt" and describe the Taft administration as a "strange chapter" in American naval history.[3] Love likewise describes Taft as "uninspiring."[4] Braisted is one of the few scholars who try to portray Taft in a more flattering light, but even he claims that Taft's endeavors ended in "partial defeat."[5]

These different views all hinge upon the assumption that Roosevelt did bring about a real change in the long-term fortunes of the U.S. Navy. Only then can Taft's and Wilson's actions be worthy of the criticism that has been heaped upon them. If, however, Roosevelt's legacy is viewed more skeptically, Taft and Wilson's naval policies become less baffling and more logical. The Taft administration in particular played a more positive role in America's naval development than is widely assumed. Under the guidance of George von Lengerke Meyer, America's most competent secretary of the navy between 1865 and the Second World War, important steps were taken to increase the fleet's efficiency. The fact that Taft and Meyer were unable to continue with a full-blooded, Rooseveltian buildup should not be seen as a failure. Instead, it should be seen as a reversion to "normalcy" in American naval policy.

## WILLIAM HOWARD TAFT AND GEORGE VON LENGERKE MEYER

One of the great problems that historians have with William Howard Taft is that he rarely said anything of substance about the U.S. Navy. When Taft did speak publicly, he resorted to uninspiring generalizations. In his nomination acceptance speech he outlined a naval policy so lacking in specifics that it was meaningless.[6] When addressing the public as president, he was no more inspiring.[7] In his first two annual messages Taft spoke more about the need for economy and rationalization than about the need to increase the fleet's strength. In the 1911 and 1912 annual messages he neglected to mention naval issues at all.

Taft did rouse himself annually to urge Congress to lay down new battleships, but these efforts were more akin to yearly trips to the legislative dentist than a welcome opportunity to champion the cause of the fleet. Taft obviously found it difficult to generate much enthusiasm for naval issues, which meant that he generally left matters to be decided by his secretary of the navy. It was a fortuitous step, better for Taft and better for the U.S. Navy. It was to the navy's real benefit to be run by George Meyer from 1909 to 1913. This was not because he achieved great things. Instead, Meyer made incremental and thoughtful changes in the way the U.S. Navy did business. No secretary of the navy between 1909 and 1913 was going to be remembered as a great builder; there was no national will to make him so. Yet, Meyer brought about as much positive change as possible.

A personal friend of both Roosevelt and Taft, Meyer had served as ambassador to Italy, ambassador to Russia and postmaster general between 1900 and 1909. When Taft chose him to be secretary of the navy, Meyer already had some idea of what he wanted to do. He was able to maintain a personal control over the navy that would have been unimaginable for one of Roosevelt's secretaries. Meyer used his power to make some much-needed changes. He tried to streamline the navy's bureau system with the appointment of four aides, one each for operations, personnel, material and inspections.[8] These aides reported directly to the secretary and, it was hoped, would lead to greater centralization of the navy's business. Unfortunately for Meyer, this reform had only limited impact at the time, as Congress, fearful of anything that smacked of a general staff, refused to give the aides statutory sanction. When Meyer left, his successor, Josephus Daniels, seemed willing to let the aide system lapse. Yet all was not lost. In 1915, with the war in Europe looming menacingly, the aide for operations was reincarnated as the chief of naval operations, the most important officer in the fleet.

Meyer also proved his worth in the areas of warship maintenance and auxiliary vessel construction. In 1909 much of the American navy was badly in need of repair.[9] Forty-four percent of all American warships were tied up in port or undergoing repairs. By 1912 this figure was down to twelve percent. Battleships were particularly well attended to. In 1909 seventeen battleships were on active duty, while ten were tied up. By 1912 all American battleships were ready for duty.[10]

Meyer also began to redress the imbalance that had grown up in the American fleet between capital and auxiliary ships. For instance, in eight years Theodore Roosevelt was able to coax Congress into authorizing only sixty-three non-capital ships. Meyer, meanwhile, was able to secure congressional approval for fifty-seven auxiliaries in four years.[11] For every capital ship approved under Roosevelt, only 3.15 auxiliary vessels were sanctioned. The corresponding figure for Meyer was one capital ship to 9.5 auxiliaries.

The last area that Meyer tried to reform was America's chaotic and wasteful base system. In 1910 the United States maintained seven first-class and four second-class navy yards.[12] The British, with a much larger fleet, had only three first-class and three-second class yards. Yet, the American bases combined had fewer dry docks than the single largest British base.[13] Compared to nations with comparable fleets, American overbasing looks ridiculous. Germany had only two first-class bases and one second-class base while France had four and one, respectively. Meyer bravely tried to consolidate some of these far-flung installations. In 1910 he visited every major domestic naval yard. The magazine station/picnic ground at Bremerton was but one example of extraordinary waste he found. Even though $14 million had been spent on Mare Island, Senator

Perkins' pet project, it was still impossible to base the fleet on the West Coast.[14] Meyer seemed particularly incensed at the money lavished on the New Orleans Navy Yard. Founded in 1849, this base was now useless. Hardly any naval vessels visited New Orleans, and almost no work was undertaken there. In 1908, while $118,978.79 had been paid to repair workers, only $7,000 worth of repairs had been performed. The base had, however, become the personal protectorate of Representative Adolph Meyer, a Confederate veteran and member of the House since 1891. Adolph Meyer was responsible for "costly buildings which have never been used, a coaling plant which is almost useless, and a large tract of unnecessary land, with improvements, being his share of the roundup with Hale and Tillman."[15]

Luckily for George Meyer, Adolph Meyer died unexpectedly in 1908. The secretary moved rapidly to shut the New Orleans yard. News of his proposal leaked, however. Senator William Bradley of Kentucky wrote to Taft complaining that if the base were closed, the whole Mississippi Valley "would be exposed to attack, and would be utterly helpless; so much is this the fact that, if an enemy's fleet should obtain possession of the mouth of the river, it would form a base from which the entire Mississippi Valley could be attacked and overrun."[16] Meyer, however, felt the tide had turned in his favor. The country was gripped by an ongoing depression, and the president was taking a strong line on public expenditures.[17] In 1910, Meyer felt confident enough to call for the closure not only of the New Orleans yard but also of the bases at Pensacola, Florida; Port Royal, South Carolina; New London, Connecticut; San Juan, Puerto Rico; and the Philippines.[18] It was the most audacious proposal made by a secretary of the navy since the Civil War and, surprisingly, largely successful. The one base that Meyer could not close down was Port Royal, situated as it was in Senator Tillman's home state. Tillman, the ranking Democrat on the House Naval Affairs Committee, proved too powerful an ox to gore.[19] The rest, however, were shut, and for the first time in decades a secretary of the navy won a battle with Congress over the maintenance of shore installations.

How, then, should George Meyer be judged? The kaiser rather dramatically referred to him as the "American von Tirpitz."[20] This characterization misses the point. The German admiral is best remembered as a naval builder, the moving force behind the tremendous growth of the German navy before the First World War. Meyer fails this test. He was unable to win large increases in American capital ship construction and eventually unable to stop Congress from reducing the tempo of American battleship construction. But the characterization is also unfair because it would have been impossible for anybody to be the United States' von Tirpitz in these years. Meyer should be remembered for improving the American navy in the limited areas that Congress allowed him to improve it. Each of his reforms was not, in and of itself, dramatic, but their sum total was undoubtedly positive.

## CONGRESS CALLS A HALT AND THE NAVY CRASHES

Congress made it apparent early in the Taft administration that it wished to revert to the pre-Rooseveltian status quo, and the incoming administration was under no illusion that it could win support for a large naval buildup. Senator Hale wasted no time in trying to reassert some of his authority. He wrote to Taft just eight weeks after the president's inauguration.[21] A few months later Hale visited Meyer and pressed for a reduction in the size of the battleships under construction.[22] Reacting to this kind of pressure, Taft and Meyer opted for a conciliatory policy. In 1909 and 1910 the president asked the Congress for programs of only two battleships. The legislators gave their assent, but only after some bitter debates. However, the tenor of the discussion in Congress had changed ominously. Most debates centered around reducing construction to one or even no ships a year. Someone like Senator Perkins, whom Roosevelt had damned and whom Taft's assistant secretary of the navy considered "very feeble," now became crucial to the passage of the administration's program.[23] Having taken over the Senate Naval Affairs Committee in 1909 (Hale moved on to chair the Appropriations Committee), Perkins provided vital support for the two-battleship-a-year program.[24]

This rebirth of opposition to a large navy quickly picked up steam. The opposition's greatest weapon was Congress' growing skepticism about any realistic threat to American security. When Richmond Hobson spoke about a German threat to the United States, he was quickly rebuffed by John Adair of Indiana, Gilbert Hitchcock of Nebraska, and James Burke of Pennsylvania.[25] Theodore Burton, who moved to the Senate in 1908, now found much greater support for his attempts to reduce naval construction:

Who is attacking us? Who would dare attack the United States? Here we are, mighty in our isolation, in our material and physical strength, in our great population . . . even if we had scarcely any navy at all . . . and no more a standing army than we had twenty years ago, this Nation for defense, would be one of the strongest in the world.[26]

A strong coalition formed to keep the United States from keeping pace in the global naval race that had been sparked by Great Britain and Germany. It was a motley group, including longtime opponents of the navy like Hale, idealists like Burton, a large number of congressmen from landlocked districts in the Midwest or Rocky Mountains, and progressives like Senator Robert Lafollette. It is very difficult to tell why each member of this coalition voted as he did. Many claimed that America had no need of a large fleet in this new era of international cooperation and understanding. As one representative put it: "This, the twentieth century, is not the age of war. It is the age of arbitration, and of judicial consideration and judicial determination of questions."[27]

This was not the outburst of an uninterested legislator. It was the considered opinion of Representative Lemuel Padgett, Democrat from Tennessee. Padgett happened to be the ranking minority member on the House's Naval Affairs

Committee. In 1910 his opinion gained even more importance when the Democrats captured the House. While naval policy did not simply break down along partisan lines, Democrats were generally less enthusiastic than Republicans about shipbuilding programs. With their base in the South, few Democrats had a material reason to support large naval appropriations. Therefore, many debates over naval policy involved confrontations between different wings of the Republican majority. By 1910 this majority was increasingly embattled. The American economy, which had been in a recession for four years, had yet to recover. Internal divisions, which in 1912 rent the party in two, deprived the Republicans of cohesiveness. In Taft the GOP had a leader who, while competent, did not engender much popular enthusiasm. Finally, after fourteen years of Republican rule the country seemed willing to give the Democrats another chance. Eventually, there was a massive swing away from the Republicans in the 1910 midterm elections. The House saw a Republican majority of forty-seven change into a Democratic advantage of sixty-seven. The Republicans also lost ten Senate seats but retained a slim majority.

The 1910 election was a waterloo for the Taft administration's naval policy. Politics in general became more partisan, with naval policy becoming a focal point for division. Taft tried to support the navy by adopting Roosevelt's methods and hosting naval reviews and parades. In 1911 he called for the construction of four new dreadnoughts. However, the president's influence had been drastically reduced. House Democrats decided to fight against any new battleship building. Padgett, though a thoughtful and considerate man whom many in the navy respected,[28] stood squarely against building any new battleships at all. The debates in the House became bitter and spiteful. This one excerpt, from a debate that was ostensibly about naval policy, demonstrates how the issue had become bogged down:

The Democratic Party has been in control of the House for a comparatively short time . . . but upon no question has the Democratic majority in this House shown its proneness to blunder and its desire to play politics and its inability to climb the heights of American statesmanship as much as it has on the naval program of this year. . . . Well you had a great convention over in Baltimore. (Applause on the Democratic side.) I refer to the Ryanized-Bryanized-Tammanyized convention. (Applause on the Republican side.) After you had nominated by nine successive ballots the Speaker of the House (general applause), who has the affection and confidence of every member of it (renewed applause), you permitted William Jennings Bryan (applause on the Democratic side) to exercise the veto power on that presidential nomination, and you did not have the courage of your convictions (applause on the Republican side) nor the nerve nor the virility as a party to override that veto with a two-thirds vote (Applause on the Republican side.)[29]

The preceding speech was delivered by another one of Roosevelt's nemeses, George Foss. The Taft administration claimed Foss was "lazy, hard to move, and inertly opposes any proposition which he does not put forth himself."[30] Now, however, Foss was one of Taft's strongest supporters in the House. However, with the Democrats in control there, most of the navy's hopes rested in the Senate. Republicans in the upper chamber dueled with the Democrats throughout 1911 and 1912. As late as July 1912 they were still voting down Democratic attempts to reduce battleship construction.[31] A fierce deadlock ensued. Tillman threatened to block any bill unless an additional $300,000 were appropriated for the Charleston Navy Yard.[32] The Republicans saw off Tillman, but were forced to make other compromises. House Democrats offered four additional submarines if the Senate would accept only one battleship, and the navy's backers gave in.[33] However, to salve everybody's wounds Congress passed the largest naval appropriation in American history, making sure there was plenty of pork for all.

There was a similar confrontation during the debate over the following year's authorization. Taft, now running for reelection, began his campaign with a large naval review. Now he called for a mammoth program of five new capital ships. Congress seemed unimpressed, especially once Taft had been defeated by Woodrow Wilson. With Wilson's inauguration only hours away Congress repeated the compromise of 1912 and approved the construction of one new battleship.[34]

The political weakness of the U.S. Navy had been clearly demonstrated. Twice within four years sitting presidents had made public, election-year appeals for large construction programs, and twice Congress had slashed their requests. In neither case did the opponents of a large fleet suffer at the polls. The Democratic Party actually increased its membership of Congress both times, and in 1912 it captured the presidency. If the American public cared at all about a strong U.S. Navy, it should have become more concerned during this time, for now Great Britain and Germany began their naval race that relegated the United States to third place.

All of this demonstrates that there was no, and had been no, coherent, consistent American naval policy. There was still no agreement as to the optimum strength of the fleet. Should it be the world's second strongest? Its third? Should it be as strong as Germany's or Japan's or both or neither? Should it be strong enough to protect both coastlines at the same time or the Philippines or the Monroe Doctrine? There was no answer.

During the Taft administration these unanswered questions returned to haunt the navy. Between 1901 and 1909 the General Board had tried to hide behind Roosevelt and pretend that it had a policy. When Roosevelt stepped down, the General Board tried to act as if nothing had changed. In 1909 and 1910 it asked for enormous construction programs built around four battleships a year. However, the navy could not convincingly articulate why it needed so many ships.

It was generally believed that the Germans would be the most "formidable" opponent the American navy would have to face.[35] Since 1910 Germany had replaced the United States as the world's second largest naval power. Germany was also seen as the "uneasy state" in Europe that would like to expand into South America if only the Monroe Doctrine did not block its path.[36] However, any move by the Germans in the Western Hemisphere would have been fraught with difficulty. First, they would need British acquiescence, which was, in the General Board's words, "most improbable."[37] Second, they would have to attack and seize a major base before confronting the United States. If they were successful in that difficult task, they then would have had to find and destroy the American fleet. Finally, they would have to conquer parts of South America and hope the United States, with its extraordinary resources, would simply give way. It was a somewhat fanciful scenario, not just "not probable"[38] but, as the General Board admitted, basically impossible:

Any war that will bring the United States to sue for peace must probably find the enemy firmly lodged in our territory as well as master of the sea. Our resources are so great in men, material and wealth, and our national spirit is so high, that it is difficult to believe that any nation whatever could afford the attempt to tire us out, and it is equally difficult to conceive of the United States yielding to anything but absolute mastery, both on sea and on land. Any European nation, other than England, must conduct operations against the continental portions of the United States by oversea expeditions pure and simple—expeditions so monumental that their transport and maintenance will be exceedingly difficult under the most favorable circumstances.[39]

Japan was considered a more likely enemy. During the Taft administration the famous American-Japanese war plan "Orange" was first developed.[40] It also seemed that American policy might cause a conflict. One of Taft's more famous foreign policy forays was his attempt to resuscitate the Open Door policy in China.[41] The navy sought to capitalize on the policy by adding the "Open Door" to its list of things to be defended.[42] In 1912 the navy went even further by listing "Asiatic exclusion" as one of its tasks.[43] In the end the changes made no difference. The main problem again was that while war with Japan was considered more probable than war with Germany, it was still thought "unlikely."[44] Japan's navy was significantly weaker than America's, and it seemed to the General Board that "no other important additions will be made for the present."[45]

In the end Congress just did not buy into the idea of a German or Japanese threat. By the end of the Taft administration the General Board seemed close to despair. In their own memoranda they demolished the idea that the United States had somehow entered a new era of naval prominence under Roosevelt:

From 1889 to the present time the authorization of vessels of war by the United States has been irregular both as to types and numbers. As a result, the United States at present time is lacking not only in battleships but in armored cruisers, protective cruisers, destroyers, and auxiliaries. . . . The navy has never recovered from the weakened condition into which it was permitted to fall after the Civil War.[46]

It also seemed that worse was in store. The advent of a Democratic president and Congress certainly did not bode well for future naval expansion. Still, the General Board mustered its arguments. In its first submission to the new administration the board admitted that "there is not now, and never has been in any true sense, a governmental or departmental naval policy."[47] It continued:

The fleet, as it exists, is the growth of an inadequately expressed public opinion; and that growth has followed the laws of expediency to meet temporary emergencies and has little or no relation to the true meaning of naval power, or to the nation's need therefore for the preservation of peace, and for the support and advancement of our national policies. . . . In 1903 the General Board formulated its opinion as to what the naval development of the nation should be. . . . This policy—as a policy—has remained a General Board policy only, without adoption by the government or even by the navy Department, and without being understood by the people or Congress.

In the end we could say that the real importance of the Taft administration was in showing not how much had changed since 1900 but how little.

## THE FIRST YEAR OF THE WILSON ADMINISTRATION

The results of the 1912 election, which brought Woodrow Wilson to the presidency and gave the Democrats comfortable majorities in both chambers of Congress, were a mixed bag for the U.S. Navy. Democratic intransigence had limited the navy to only one new battleship a year in both 1912 and 1913. Now, of the four Democrats with strong influence over American naval policy, Woodrow Wilson, Josephus Daniels, Ben Tillman, and Lemuel Padgett, only Padgett was trusted by many naval officers. Wilson seemed mainly interested in domestic affairs and ignored the navy in his inaugural address and first annual message. Also the Democratic Party platform had promised independence to the Philippines, something that threatened to deprive the navy of one of its raison d'etres. Wilson's Cabinet selections also did not bode well for the fleet. Putting William Jennings Bryan in control of the State Department indicated that, for a while at least, the "big stick" would be sheathed. Wilson's choice of Josephus Daniels to be secretary of the navy also implied big changes. Roosevelt and Taft had consistently favored well-heeled northeasterners for the post. The new secretary was an altogether different beast.

Josephus Daniels was a genial and pious white supremacist from North Carolina who had made his reputation through the editorship of the Raleigh News and Observer. A populist, Daniels was an early and enthusiastic supporter of Bryan and built up a formidable reputation within the Democratic Party. He also established a good rapport with an up-and-coming politician named Woodrow Wilson. Daniels' support helped Wilson win the Democratic nomination, and the reward for his efforts was the navy. Daniels' only previous naval experience had been as an editorial writer when he, unusually for a southern Democrat, supported President Taft's naval policy. It would be safe to say, however, that none of his previous experience had in any way prepared him to be secretary. Nevertheless, he refused to be cowed by professional officers and quite readily imposed his will on the fleet. He soon became, in the words of one naval historian, the "most controversial" secretary ever to hold the post.[48]

There was, and is, a strong division in opinion about Daniels. He was distrusted by many. When Walter Hines Page, Wilson's ambassador to London, was asked whether Daniels was "cabinet timber," he replied, "He is hardly a splinter."[49] Colonel Edward House, one of Wilson's closest confidants, also doubted Daniels' abilities. In 1916 he conspired with the president's new bride, Edith Bolling Wilson, to get Daniels fired.[50] The antipathy of these Democrats was more than matched by many naval men. Two of the most famous admirals to serve under Daniels, Bradley Fiske and William Sims, would accuse him of neglecting to prepare the fleet for the First World War. A number of historians have also portrayed Daniels in an unflattering light. Professor Love claims that Daniels "failed the most meager test of an executive" and that the outbreak of the First World War found American naval policy in "shambles."[51]

Daniels did have supporters, however. He got along famously with most Democratic congressmen. Both Tillman and Padgett were southern populists very much in the Daniels mold, and communication flowed easily between them and the Navy Department. In his second Annual Report Daniels took the unprecedented step for a secretary of the navy of praising Congress as a "forward-looking" body.[52] Daniels also won the belated respect of his assistant secretary, Franklin Delano Roosevelt. Though this Roosevelt was very critical of Daniels' reluctance to prepare the fleet for war, he eventually grew to trust the North Carolinian and for the rest of his life referred to Daniels as "Chief." Most important, however, Daniels was able to maintain the confidence of Woodrow Wilson. He is one of only a handful of American secretaries of the navy to serve for a full eight years. The fact that he was able to maintain Wilson's confidence in the face of opposition from Republicans, much of the fleet, and Colonel House is a testament to his perseverance.

One reason that Daniels presents such a perplexing picture is that he tried to reform areas that most of his predecessors avoided. As he said in his first Annual Report. "In considering the needs of the navy the secretary has given less thought to the guns than to the men behind the guns."[53] Under Daniels' direction educational opportunities for average sailors were expanded, and admission to the Naval Academy was opened to enlisted men. Also Daniels, who was a teetotaler and a firm supporter of Prohibition, infuriated many sailors by banning all alcoholic beverages from American ships, a restriction that continues to this day.

At the same time Daniels showed little interest in strategic questions. He began by requesting appropriation for two battleships annually. The General Board, trying to recover from its previous setbacks, wanted to ask for four new battleships.[54] Daniels, however, was well aware of the "small-navy" sentiments of many Democrats and rejected the larger request. On the surface little had changed in Congress.[55] Naval supporters like Hobson spoke of the change brought on by the dreadnought, the growth of European fleets, America's strategic commitments, its long and exposed coastline, the Monroe Doctrine, and the Philippines.[56] Crucially, Padgett, who had supported only one new battleship a year during the Taft administration, now spoke forcefully for two.[57] Those opposed, like Democrats Samuel Witherspoon of Mississippi and Walter Hensley of Missouri, poured scorn on the strategic arguments underpinning the naval bill. They denied that there was a serious threat to American security and derided what they considered the wasteful and corrupt practices of the battle-ship-building process. Witherspoon dwelt upon the "slimy fingers of commercialism clutching the white throat of the American Navy" and eventually ended up leading the House in an emotional recitation of "My Country 'tis of Thee."[58] However, in an interesting twist, the election of Wilson had dampened the anti-navy ardor of many Democrats. Many Democrats like Padgett, not wanting to embarrass the first Democratic president elected since 1892, joined with a majority of Republicans in June 1914 to authorize the construction of at least two new battleships.

It was "at least two" because the navy received an unexpected fillip. It has been mentioned earlier how in 1903 the United States built two Idaho-class battleships. These ships were too small, too slow, undergunned, and obsolete even before their completion. In 1914, however, the Greek government offered to purchase them. They were considered the perfect vessels to patrol the Aegean Sea. The U.S. Navy jumped at the chance to offload these dinosaurs and persuaded Congress to spend the proceeds from the sale on an additional battleship. Once the sale went through, three dreadnoughts of the excellent New Mexico class were constructed. It was the largest American annual building program since Theodore Roosevelt's first term. All in all it was a fitting example of the haphazard, uncertain, and capricious way in which American naval policy was made. Two obsolete and useless warships, the product of earlier congressional whims, had, without any plan or forethought, miraculously metamorphosed into one of the best dreadnoughts in the world.

## THE U.S. NAVY IN THE SUMMER OF 1914

A few weeks after the passage of the 1914 program Archduke Franz Ferdinand was gunned down in Sarajevo. At the time of the outbreak of the First World War the American navy was in an ambiguous position. Only one area had inarguably improved since President McKinley's assassination: American ship design and construction. By 1914 the United States was building some of the largest, steadiest, most heavily protected, and most heavily armed battleships in the world. America was the first country to adopt what *Jane's Fighting Ships* called the "everything or nothing" idea in warship construction.[59] While the British favored heavier broadsides over protection, and the Germans favored greater protection over offensive punch, the U.S. Navy opted for both. American dreadnoughts were usually thousands of tons heavier than their British and German counterparts and therefore could be both heavily armored and equipped with the largest batteries afloat. Compare battleships laid down in 1910, the American

*Arkansas*, the British *Orion*, and the German *Kaiser*.[60] The *Arkansas* had a displacement of 26,000 tons and carried twelve 12-inch guns. The *Kaiser* weighed 24,700 tons and sported ten 12-inch guns but could fire only eight on each broadside. The *Orion* was the smallest of the lot, weighing only 22,500 tons but, following British design principles, mounted a strong battery of ten 13.5-inch guns.

The U.S. Navy came to believe that its battleships were the best in the world. In 1914 the Naval Intelligence Department compared the relative value of the world's capital ships.[61] Using an idiosyncratic mathematical formula, it calculated that America's dreadnought-class battleships were clearly superior. It considered that the USS *New York* (27,000 tons, ten 14-inch guns), was 15 percent stronger than HMS *King George V* (23,000 tons, ten 13.5-inch guns) and almost 20 percent stronger than Germany's *Markgraf* (25,500 tons, ten 12-inch guns), all of which were laid down in the same year. This advantage increased in the navy's estimations. The New Mexico class (32,000 tons, twelve 14-inch guns) approved in 1914, was considered 25 percent stronger than Germany's Bayern class (28,000 tons and eight 15-inch guns) and a whopping 38 percent stronger that Britain's Royal Sovereigns (25,750 tons, eight 15-inch guns).

These figures were probably inflated. The British and Germans would have been shocked to see their ships ranked so low. *Jane's*, however, does provide some support for the American position, calling the Pennsylvania class, approved in 1912 and 1913, "one of the most successful if not the most successful, of all Dreadnought designs up to the present time."[62] However, if it is impossible to say definitely that American ships were the best, it is safe to say that the era of construction debacles, typified by the Idaho class, was over.

Apart from this one bright spot, however, not much had improved for the American navy. Even after all its huffing and puffing, the navy had no clear vision of its purpose. There was still no accepted policy about the relative size of the U.S. Navy. As the General Board lamented, "The creation of the existing fleet has followed no general law of policy to create a fleet for a definite purpose to meet definite needs; but has been the growth of shifting and undeveloped ideas which followed laws of expediency rather than reason."[63]

The clearest sign of this confusion was America's slide down the naval rankings. In July 1914 the American navy had slipped to become the third largest in the world, trailing the British and the Germans. By the Navy Department's own reckoning the Germans had more than twice as many completed dreadnoughts, almost three times as many cruisers, and two and a half times as many destroyers.[64] In total completed warship tonnage the German navy was clearly superior, the Germans having built 951,713 tons to the United States' 765,133. If one added warships being built to those completed, the German total would swell to 1,306,577 tons to America's 894,899.

The U.S. Navy was actually closer to the French fleet in size than to the German fleet. In 1909, when the American navy was the world's second largest, it had 366,146 tons of battleships either built or being built. The corresponding

French figure was 323,450.[65] By 1914, however, the French were threatening to push the Americans into fourth place. The United States maintained a lead in completed dreadnoughts, with eight vessels compared to France's four. However, the United States was building only four more, while the French were building eight. In terms of total warship tonnage the Americans maintained an advantage of 765,133 to 688,840. But, if tonnage built and being built were counted, the French would have surpassed the United States by 899,915 tons to 894,889.[66]

By the U.S. Navy's own estimations the British, Germans, and French all maintained many more auxiliary vessels. Even the Japanese were threatening to overtake the Americans, with one report claiming that they had only five fewer auxiliary ships.[67] The shortage of American auxiliary ships was so acute that when the United States attempted to blockade the Mexican coast in 1914, it was discovered that it had to send some of its largest battleships to do routine coastal patrolling.[68] The relative decline in America's personnel strength was similar.[69]

Interestingly, this overall decline did not go hand in hand with a decrease in funding. American naval appropriations had increased every year since 1910 and by 1914 easily surpassed those of Germany and France. The U.S. Navy had been allocated $140,736,526 for the last fiscal year before World War I, while the German navy was given only $112,037,576 and the French navy $122,493,753.[70] Some of the difference can be explained by the expense of maintaining an all-volunteer force, like the Americans, compared to the much cheaper conscript crews of the Germans. However, most of the extra American money was still the result of wasteful base expenditures. Only $35,325,695, or 25 percent of the American naval budget, was devoted to new construction. Yet, the Germans spent $53,240,546, or 47 percent, on new construction, and the French $63,655,515, or 44 percent. Even the British, with their enormous budget of $235,213,408, were able to spend $77,662,162, or 33 percent, on new warship construction.[71] At the same time, the United States maintained ten large navy yards in 1914.

In the area of strategic planning, the navy lacked cohesion as well. Instead of studying the rapidly growing European fleets, the Navy Department in 1913 and 1914 was preoccupied with Japan and Mexico. While these countries were strategically important, in neither case was the American navy planning for a conflict vital to national security. The dispute with the Japanese was the same one that had flared up periodically since Theodore Roosevelt's administration. In April 1913 the lower house of the California legislature, in one of its periodic fits of bigotry, decided to make "Orientals" ineligible for citizenship.[72] Not surprisingly, this sparked a great deal of agitation in the Japanese public, and a war scare developed.[73] Franklin Roosevelt behaved as if war was imminent, telegraphing naval commanders in the Pacific with war plans.[74]

As Japanese-American war scares went, however, the 1913 confrontation was nothing special. The Navy Department actually believed that American security had improved markedly since Theodore Roosevelt's administration. With the imminent opening of the Panama Canal, the American fleet could reach Pearl Harbor in only thirty-three days. Japanese freedom of action would thus be significantly curtailed.[75] The 1914 American war plans now assumed that the United States could fight to hold the Philippines and put up a vigorous defense of Guam.[76]

The navy's concern with Mexico was of an entirely different order. Here the fleet was to act as the proverbial "big stick" to threaten the Mexicans into compliance with President Wilson's wishes. In October 1913, Wilson, hoping to topple General Victoriano Huerta, ordered elements of the fleet to patrol off the shore of Mexico's oil fields from Vera Cruz to Tampico. It was a rather misguided and high-handed project. On 9 April 1914 a group of American sailors were arrested in Tampico, and there followed a series of recriminations and counterrecriminations.[77] The Navy Department drew up new war plans,[78] and the Treasury demanded to know the cost of a Mexican-American war at the "earliest possible moment."[79] Eventually, Argentina, Brazil, and Chile offered to mediate, and Huerta resigned from office on 15 July. It was a rather fortuitous end to what could have been a difficult conflict for the American navy.

However, while the American navy was either planning to fight a war over distant colonies or preparing to blockade a country with no naval power to speak of, European fleets were being withdrawn from colonial outposts and preparing to fight for their nation's survival. When the Great War did break out the United States was thus caught unprepared.

## THE OUTBREAK OF WAR AND NAVAL PREPAREDNESS

When the First World War began, American policy was to stand firmly aside. The great majority of Americans wanted nothing to do with this European conflict. There began a three-year period best characterized as "the struggle for neutrality."[80] For the U.S. Navy the war posed a number of very difficult questions. Who will win, and what would that mean for the United States? What can be learned from the conflict? What should the United States do to prepare itself to fight? This last question was the most pressing and divided the navy and administration into different camps. First and foremost were those, like Wilson, Bryan, and Daniels, who wanted the United States to do its utmost not to be drawn into the fighting. They wanted to avoid anything that might be construed as provocative. Wilson even urged the American people to be "impartial in thought as well as in action."[81]

Daniels also did his best to project a public air of calm. He planned to send a large part of the American fleet to the official opening of the Panama Canal, against the advice of many naval officers.[82] While Daniels was eventually thwarted by mud slides in Panama, his point had been well-made. He also denied a General Board request to increase the tempo of American battleship construction, sticking to the two-battleships-a-year program.[83]

Eventually a very loose coalition formed to oppose Daniels. Grouped under the banner of "preparedness" this coalition included important naval officers, the U.S. Navy League, a small, but vocal, bloc of congressmen, and the assistant secretary, Franklin Roosevelt. They believed that years of neglect had left the American navy undermanned, undertrained, and underequipped and wanted action now. Worries about American preparedness had been around for years. In September 1912 William Sims blasted the navy's war preparation plans, calling them "almost wholly inadequate."[84] Daniels had certainly done nothing to improve the situation. In December 1913 the General Board sent Daniels an official letter outlining areas in need of immediate attention, but it had little impact.[85] The Mexican fiasco only made things worse, as much of the fleet was deprived of training for a year and a half.[86]

The first public shot in the preparedness campaign came from Republican Augustus P Gardner, a Massachusetts representative and son-in-law to Henry Cabot Lodge. On 16 October 1914 Gardner openly criticized the state of American preparedness.[87] The administration's response was swift and harsh. Wilson personally "ridiculed and then denounced" Gardner's claims.[88] Yet, at the same time, a fierce internal debate on "preparedness" engulfed the navy. On 9 November 1914 Admiral Bradley Fiske, Daniels' aide for operations, vividly described the navy's lack of preparedness.[89] In a letter to Daniels, Fiske dwelt in particular upon two points: personnel shortages and organizational deficiencies in the Navy Department. Fiske claimed the navy needed 19,600 additional men to man the warships already on hand, to say nothing of those being built. The U.S. Navy had the worst ratio of officers to enlisted men of any major fleet. The Americans had one officer for every nineteen enlisted men, while the British ratio was one to sixteen, the French one to twelve, the Germans one to ten, and the Japanese one to nine.[90] The USS *Delaware*, a battleship of the Atlantic Fleet, carried only thirty-three officers, while Royal Navy's *Bellorophon*, a similar ship, carried fifty-three and the high seas fleet's *Helgoland* carried fifty-four.[91] The Atlantic fleet as a whole would need a whopping 40 percent increase in officers to reach wartime staffing levels.[92]

The personnel shortage failed to move Daniels. When the General Board submitted a report claiming that the navy was seriously undermanned, Daniels refused to allow it to be published.[93] His own Annual Reports, on the other hand, showed little concern, and he made no effort to persuade Congress to pay for extra officers and men. In 1914 the U.S. Navy was made up of 55,938 officers and enlisted men. By 1915 that number had grown by only 61. There was a more substantial increase of 2,105 by 1916, but that still left the fleet far below its preferred staffing levels.[94]

While these personnel debates were contentious, Fiske's organizational criticisms were political dynamite. He proposed the creation of a centralized naval staff. Such calls had previously been stymied by Congress' antipathy to anything that could diminish civilian control. Now, however, Fiske was hoping that the shadow of war might force the issue. It was a risky move, one made even more perilous by Fiske and Daniels' deteriorating relationship. These two men were vastly different. The admiral was neat and precise, a scientist and inventor with a stubborn and prickly personality. The secretary, on the other hand, was jovial but sloppy, with pacifist leanings and an innate populism that distrusted aristocratic elements in the navy. Their dealings had not been easy when the world was at peace, but now things began to fray badly. Fiske began working clandestinely with Richmond Hobson and others to attach a clause to the 1914-1915 appropriation bill reorganizing the Navy Department.[95] What they wanted was the appointment of a chief of naval operations (CNO) with a staff of fifteen officers and the ability to coordinate strategic planning. If passed, the CNO bill, as envisaged by Fiske, would have caused the most radical overhaul of the navy's structure since the American Revolution.

Surprisingly, the bill made some headway in Congress. It was moving toward passage when Daniels stepped in and drastically curtailed the powers of the CNO. By threatening to resign, Daniels forced the removal of the provision for a staff and carefully circumscribed the CNO's powers. Once this was done, the bill passed in March 1915, and Congress approved the first major overhaul of the Navy Department since the creation of the General Board. While the CNO as finally approved was a far cry from a general staff, it still represented a major change. By creating a central coordinating position, Congress set up a focal point for naval planning and reform. It took a number of years for the CNO to fully establish his preeminence. The holder had to wait until the 1940s to be given the full powers intended by Fiske, but even in its early truncated position the CNO "contributed much to the navy's efficiency."[96]

Daniels was, however, to gain a measure of revenge. For the first CNO Daniels chose Admiral William S. Benson. Benson, a devout Catholic with a solid, if unspectacular, record, was plucked out of the relative obscurity of the Philadelphia Navy Yard. Fiske, who might have expected to be named CNO, found his relationship with Daniels broken beyond repair. He was soon exiled to the Naval War College in Rhode Island and then retired in 1916. For the remainder of his life Fiske maintained a steady barrage of criticism against Daniels, criticism that eventually resulted in very partisan congressional hearings. It was a petty and rather sad end for one of the most important American naval officers of his day. Ultimately, however, Fiske's achievements far outweighed his failures, and in helping to create the chief of naval operations he was responsible for one of the most important organizational reforms in American naval history.

There were other efforts to improve elements of the navy, particularly gunnery. Gunnery training had first come into prominence under Theodore Roosevelt, when great efforts were made to improve it. By 1914 this was no longer the case. In 1913 only one American battleship was rated "excellent" in gunnery, while another was rated "good," two were rated "poor," and a shocking seventeen were considered "unsatisfactory."[97] The situation had hardly improved by 1915. During Atlantic fleet exercises only three battleships shot satisfactorily, with the rest "far from what might reasonably have been expected."[98] These poor results galvanized the navy. Training was intensified and results improved.

Soon, five battleships were considered "excellent," four were considered "good," only two were judged "fair," four "poor," and three "unsatisfactory."[99]

Taken together, there is a great deal of conflicting evidence about the state of naval preparedness before America's entry into the First World War. It is probably safe to say that while the fleet had made some important improvements, it was still far from ready in 1917. Franklin Roosevelt admitted in early 1916 that "when we come down to it and look back squarely in the face, the navy is not ready for war."[100] Edward House, Woodrow Wilson's closest confidant, was even more damning:

I am convinced that the president's place in history is dependent to a large degree on luck. If we should get into a serious war and should it turn out disastrously, he would be one of the most discredited presidents we have had. He has had nearly three years in which to get the United States into a reasonable state of preparedness and we have done nothing.[101]

## THE 1916 PROGRAM

The First World War was one of the most important events in the history of the U.S. Navy. When the war began, the American navy was fast slipping down the world's naval rankings, but by fighting's end it was second strongest in the world, with plans to challenge British supremacy. The greatest reason for this transformation was the 1916 naval program. This program was one of the most peculiar accomplishments of the Wilson administration. It was not the result of long-considered plans or policies but was the creation of a startling and totally unexpected presidential conversion. Exactly why Wilson chose to push for a dramatic increase in America's naval strength still remains a mystery.

Until the summer of 1915 the president had done everything possible to marginalize those favoring a naval buildup. Within his own government there was some support for the "preparedness" movement. Colonel House championed a stronger American fleet,[102] while the General Board pressed for a return to the forty-eight-battleship program of 1903.[103] Wilson stubbornly resisted these calls and "simply brushed aside the councils of alarm."[104] On 14 December 1914 he publicly condemned the agitation coming from the preparedness camp.[105] Wilson stuck to the two-battleship-a-year-program and in his annual message spoke vaguely of the need for a navy for national defense.[106] The president had some strong support for his stand. Traditional opponents of a large American fleet remained unbowed. Congressional opposition was strong to any move that could be considered provocative. Tillman echoed the thinking of many when he claimed that the best way for "our little navy" to improve its relative position would be for the British and German navies to sink each other![107]

At first, there seemed to be little that the navy supporters could do. In early 1915 Congress reaffirmed the two-battleship policy. Yet, just a few months later Wilson set in motion plans for the largest shipbuilding program in American history to that time. On 21 July 1915 he sent Daniels a letter calling for a "wise and adequate" naval program.[108] Exactly what Wilson wanted or why he wanted it is somewhat mysterious. The Sprouts described Wilson's conversion as "not altogether easy to explain," while Professor Link has maintained that Wilson's move "occurred with a suddenness that confused his friends as well as his political foes."[109]

When Wilson sent the letter he was becoming increasingly concerned about the course of the war. Both Germany and Britain had directly challenged the United States during the first half of 1915. After Germany's February declaration of unrestricted submarine warfare around the British Isles, the British responded by issuing an Order in Council that embargoed all trade with Germany. The United States' traditional support of neutral rights and "freedom of the seas" was thus under threat from both sides. Wilson worked hard to find diplomatic solutions to the problem and achieved a temporary success when the Germans pledged to protect American shipping. Yet, the bitterness of the dispute had done much to sour Wilson's views about all Europeans in general and Germans in particular. The torpedoing of the *Lusitania* hit the president especially hard. It cannot be a coincidence that Wilson sent his letter to Daniels on the very same day that he dispatched his most pointed note to Germany about the Lusitania.[110] For a while it seemed that the deterioration in American-German relations might eventually lead to war. With war a possibility the president had to take some action.

Wilson was not, however, just thinking about the Germans. He had no more than a passing interest in the specifics of the 1916 program. Wilson rarely intervened in technical or strategic debates, and when Edith Galt, Wilson's fiancée, first heard about the new program, she hoped it would be presented "in such digested form that you will not have to make out the plans, but only decide the method of putting it into action."[111] Indeed, Wilson refused to explain publicly why he was supporting such a massive departure from traditional American practices, saying only that the new program would provide for a "navy fitted to our needs and worthy of our traditions."[112]

Another reason for Wilson's conversion was the domestic political pressure coming from the preparedness movement. With an election looming in 1916, Wilson could not afford to look weak on defense issues. Even though many Democrats, including William Jennings Bryan and Claude Kitchin, majority leader in the House, continued to urge caution, they had lost the initiative. The "preparedness" movement came to dominate much of the national debate, especially after the sinking of the *Gulflight*, an American tanker, and the *Lusitania*. As Professor Link put it, almost overnight "a faltering movement became a crusade."[113]

While the president only obliquely discussed the political advantages of embracing "preparedness," other members of the administration were less reticent. When Franklin Roosevelt first heard about Wilson's letter to Daniels, he spoke of the political benefits of new naval policy: "I have felt for quite a long time that a good many people—more than have appeared on the surface—in the Republican and Progressive parties are going to take advantage of the national preparedness issue this Fall and also next year, basing this on what is becoming an increasingly strong public opinion on this subject. And I have felt that the administration must recognize this . . . by coming forward with a definite program."[114] Wilson's secretary, Joseph Tumulty, also warned that doing nothing could "cost the Democrats dearly" in the 1916 election.[115] Certainly the administration wasted little time in capitalizing on the 1916 program. The administration compared its construction programs with others' and proudly claimed that the fleet was being built up to "unprecedented" levels of strength.[116] Wilson also began to boast about his naval policy during campaign trips. In one particularly effusive speech, Wilson's excitement got the better of him, and he called for "incomparably the greatest navy in the world."[117] Alas, he had overstepped himself. Tillman quickly begged the president to disown this statement, and Wilson admitted that it had been an "indiscretion uttered in a moment of enthusiasm." The official transcript was rather inelegantly edited so that "incomparably the greatest" became "incomparably the most adequate."[118] Putting this one incident aside, however, Wilson was able to defuse many of his critics with the 1916 naval program.[119] While the election of 1916 was bitter, the Republicans were never able to make any headway against Wilson on the "preparedness" issue, and the president was reelected.

Ultimately, Wilson was trying to kill many birds with the 1916 program stone. He was very concerned with countering the German threat and did not want to be drawn into a war unprepared. Wilson also wanted to protect his political backside with the 1916 election approaching. Finally, the president felt he needed a multipurpose weapon to intimidate many countries, including the British. While he was generally more favorably disposed toward Britain than Germany, Wilson was not adverse to using the threat of his new navy to bring the British to heel. When, in September 1916, House had a long talk with Wilson about strains in the Anglo-American relations, the president responded, "Let us build a navy bigger than hers and do what we please."[120]

To the navy Wilson's conversion was manna from heaven. Within three weeks the General Board had drawn up a plan for the U.S. Navy to "be equal to the most powerful maintained by any other nation" by 1925.[121] They called for the construction of eight capital ships, five small cruisers, and sixty-five destroyers and submarines. Their plan would have cost $285 million, yet it was only the beginning. Two months later the General Board doubled its plan, demanding sixteen capital ships and 140 other vessels in five years, with a combined price of $481 million.[122] This second plan was the one Wilson endorsed in his annual message.

However, passage of the 1916 program did not go entirely smoothly. The remaining "small navy" faction in the House set out to whittle down the plan's grander elements. By June they had reduced the number of capital ships from sixteen to just five battlecruisers. However, this time fate intervened on the navy's side. The Battle of Jutland was fought on the same day that the House approved the reduced program. The performance of British and German battle-cruisers at Jutland was distinctly unimpressive, with the British losing three, and the Germans one.

The supporters of a large plan now felt vindicated. House, in particular, pressed Wilson not to back down.[123] In the end the Senate saved the day. Luckily for the fleet Senator Tillman was forced by illness to hand over the chairmanship of the Naval Affairs Committee to Claude Swanson from Virginia.[124] Swanson was a great supporter of the fleet (having Norfolk Navy Yard in his state did not hurt) who later became secretary of the navy in Franklin Roosevelt's administration. In 1916 he worked very closely with Henry Cabot Lodge to pass as sweeping a bill as possible. They came up with the largest program so far. They took the larger plan submitted by the General Board and proposed that it be completed in three years. Taking full advantage of the Battle of Jutland, they won a smashing 71 to 8 majority in the Senate. The administration then endorsed the Senate plan and the "small navy" faction was rocked back on its heels. It still fought bitterly in the House, but its luck had run out. The Republicans lined up almost unanimously behind the Senate program, while the Democrats split down the middle, and on 15 August the Senate program passed the House with 283 in favor, 51 opposed, and 99 abstaining.

The 1916 program thus became the law of the land. Even today its size seems staggering.[125] Ten battleships, six battlecruisers, ten scout cruisers, fifty destroyers, sixty-seven submarines, and thirteen auxiliary ships were authorized. Construction was to begin immediately on four battleships, four battlecruisers, four scout cruisers, and fifty-four of the other vessels, with the rest to be started within three years. To put this one bill into context, it called for the construction of more capital ships, destroyers, and submarines than all the authorization bills between 1905 and 1913 put together.

Views in Congress about whom the program was aimed at were complex. Representative William Stephens, Republican from California, summed up the different views best when he stated that America must be "prepared to defend herself from an attack from any other nation and be fairly prepared to repel Great Britain."[126] Worries about future conflicts with the British did play a role Congress' assumptions. When Richmond Hobson was fighting for the CNO bill, he held out the specter of a victorious Britain trying to supplant the United States in Mexico.[127] He further argued that America should have a fleet as large as the combined navies of Britain and Japan. While Hobson's views were extreme, his worries were shared by others. Many of the supporters of the 1916 program in the House stated that the United States had to be strong enough to confront whoever won the war in Europe. George Foss, the ranking Republican on the House Naval Affairs Committee, spoke of America's need for a naval force capable of dealing with a wide a range of threats, including British incursions against the Monroe Doctrine.[128] Simeon Fess, Republican from Ohio, went even further. After first proclaiming friendship for Great Britain, he added: "That does not mean that I must blind myself to the possibility of a struggle of my country with that country on the sea in due time. That is the thing I am afraid of. England's present attitude towards our rights are ominous . . . anybody who thinks that we are exempt from a contest . . . refuses to look into what has taken place in the last 100 years."[129]

These concerns were part and parcel of the Senate debate as well. When Swanson first introduced the 1916 program, he spoke more about Britain's "unjust restrictions" on American trade than the German threat.[130] In another swipe at the British, Swanson called for American naval dominance, arguing that "supremacy ultimately means national preeminence and triumph." When Lodge spoke, he supported Swanson, and in some respects he went further. Lodge called for the creation of large fleets in both the Atlantic and the Pacific, fleets strong enough to deter any enemy "either in the west or in the east."[131]

There is little evidence to support the claim that Congress or the president was concerned with one specific power. Both were content with wide-ranging generalizations about how the new fleet could or should be used. The navy, on the other hand, had to be more specific. It had to plan both how it would use the ships it had at present and what to do when the 1916 program was completed. In neither case were the Germans considered more of a threat than the Japanese or the British. In truth, between 1913 and April 1917, the U.S. Navy spent most of its time planning for a war against Britain or Japan.

Because of the disruption caused by Wilson's Mexico adventure, the fleet was unable to attempt large-scale maneuvers in 1913. This did not mean there was no planning. In October the navy submitted some tentative suggestions for joint maneuvers with the army in 1914.[132] The navy revived the old chestnut of an East Coast landing by an unnamed "European" nation. It was assumed that said "European" nation had a large enough navy to destroy an American fleet of twenty battleships and then deposit a landing force anywhere between Cape Hatteras and Maine. At that point only the British could have been capable of anything so audacious, though even they would probably have found it impossible.

The outbreak of the war changed nothing. Some in the navy even believed that the British might soon be forced to attack the United States. Daniels was sent information, supposedly gleaned from a source in the Royal Navy's Operations Division, that the British were preparing for a war.[133] According to this fantastic report, the British were willing to lose Canada if it meant stopping all neutral trade with Germany and, furthermore, they expected Japanese support against the United States. These two themes, that the British might attack America because of trade disputes and that the Japanese might draw Britain into a war with the United States, were most eagerly seized upon by the Navy Department's Anglophiles.

In one scenario Great Britain, having won the war, would use the Royal Navy to reduce American power. Captain H. P. Huse, Chief of Staff of the Atlantic fleet, outlined such a prospect:[134]

Whichever side wins in the present conflict in Europe, the prospect for the United States is one full of difficulties and problems . . . should the Allies be successful, it is difficult to see what would restrain England in her ambition to retain and extend the commercial supremacy on the seas that she has held for two centuries. . . . England fought Spain and France and Holland for this reason and was quite ready when a legitimate excuse offered to meet Germany in the present war. There is no reason to believe that the United States as a commercial rival would receive any different treatment.

Just a few months later Rear Admiral Austin Knight, president of the Naval War College, presented a paper with exactly the same theme to the General Board:[135]

The present almost world-wide war appears to be in the last analysis a struggle, primarily between Great Britain and Germany, for industrial and commercial supremacy. . . . Whichever one of these two powers is successful will find itself confronted by the certainty that sooner or later its supremacy will be challenged by the United States. . . . A nation flushed with victory with a vast army and navy of veteran soldiers and sailors, with its territory greatly enlarged by conquest and its treasury to some extent at least replenished by indemnities exacted from its defeated enemies will be in no mood to recoil from a new struggle with a new enemy rich enough, if defeated, to pay an indemnity of any conceivable size and so imperfectly prepared for defense as to make its defeat not only inevitable but comparatively extremely simple.

These ideas were swirling around the General Board at precisely the time that the 1916 program was first mooted. Admiral Knight's paper was presented one week after Wilson's letter to Daniels and ten days before the General Board called for a navy "second to none." The connection between the events is undeniable. The General Board even took Knight's analysis and included it almost verbatim in its own report.[136]

The British threat was made much more menacing by the Anglo-Japanese Alliance. Even as the war in Europe raged, the American navy kept a close watch on the Pacific. The navy's fear was that the Japanese might use the war to increase their position in the Pacific. The Naval Intelligence Department was even worried that the Japanese might take advantage of Mexico's latent anti-Americanism to whip up hostilities on the Rio Grande.[137] While the navy never explicitly practiced fighting the Japanese and British at the same time, they were worried about two scenarios. In the first, America's naval forces would be tied down by a European threat, leaving the Japanese unhindered in the Pacific. One war game even had the Japanese land 150,000 men in Puget Sound. The second scenario was that a victorious Britain might reward its Japanese ally with a gift of dreadnoughts, a gift that would shift the balance of power in the Pacific. Just three months before American entry into the war, the General Board had Japan using five "European" dreadnoughts to try to seize the Philippines, Alaska, and Guam.[138]

Distrust about British intentions remained strong until American entry into the war. The generally Anglophile Colonel House famously declared in August

1916 that in British eyes America was "rapidly taking the position Germany occupied before the war."[139] Within the navy anti-British feeling actually increased between 1915 and 1917. This was partly because William Benson became the first chief of naval operations. Benson, a gruff Georgian, was a devout Catholic of Irish ancestry and one of the most Anglophobic officers in the U.S. Navy. He had no time for the pro-British sympathies of Sims and Fiske and always did his utmost to ensure that the United States not cooperate too closely with the British. Benson also worked exceedingly well with Daniels, who grew to trust and value the businesslike and unpretentious admiral.

Between Benson's appointment in early 1915 and April 1917, American naval opinion became distinctly anti-British. In the Atlantic Fleet's 1915 spring maneuvers, Blue (US) attempted to thwart a landing by Red (Great Britain) on the East Coast of the United States.[140] A Red fleet of ten battleships and four battlecruisers overwhelmed a Blue fleet of seven battleships and then proceeded to land 120,000 men in Chesapeake Bay. In an attempt to inject a note of realism into the proceedings, the invading Red fleet was commanded by an "Admiral Beatty." In the summer of 1915, the American fleet again practiced keeping Red from landing on the Chesapeake.[141] In this maneuver Blue intercepted Red near Bermuda. These were the great strategic problems engrossing the American navy during the drafting of the 1916 program.

The 1916 program must therefore be seen for what it was, the product of a large, unstable, and in many ways contradictory set of strategic beliefs. One of the program's great selling points was that it was not aimed at a specific enemy. It could thus be nurtured and supported by a coalition made up of Anglophile-Germanophobes like Theodore Roosevelt, West Coast politicians worried about Japan, and most members of Congress, who were not sure what America might be confronted with in the future. Only with such a vast convergence of interests and viewpoints could such an enormous program have been approved. Finally, it must be recognized that hostility toward Britain played an important role in guiding the thinking of many of the program's supporters. Those who would like to downplay the importance of anti-British thinking in the American navy should look at one of the fleet's final peacetime maneuvers.[142] In an October 1916 exercise a Red force of five battleships and four battlecruisers attempted to land a force of 140,000 men and capture a port in the Northeast of the United States. They were opposed by a woefully inadequate Blue fleet of three battleships. After a week of fighting Blue was decisively defeated. Red (the British, it should be remembered), now triumphant, landed a large force at Far Rockaway on Long Island, from where, presumably, they could take the A train into Manhattan.

## 1900-1917 IN RETROSPECT

Ultimately, the period between 1900 and 1917 provides a very mixed picture for historians of the American navy. It came in with a bang and went out with a louder bang—but it had an awfully long whimper in between. Some things undoubtedly changed. This was no longer the U.S. Navy of the 1880s or early 1890s. In those years the fleet all but disappeared from public view, received little in the way of congressional beneficence, and languished at the bottom of the world naval tables. The Spanish-American War, the advent of Theodore Roosevelt, and the growth of America's export trade changed all that. By the early 1900s the United States had sizable overseas possessions and a chief executive passionately committed to American naval expansion. It seemed to follow that the U.S. Navy would inexorably move to a position of worldwide prominence, and by 1907 it was the second largest in the world. However, everything was not what it seemed.

For all that had changed in the navy's position, much had remained the same. Most important, public opinion obstinately refused to believe that there was a realistic foreign threat to American national security. Until 1905 the raw energy of President Roosevelt had served to curb congressional resistance to large naval programs. Yet, once senators and representatives learned that they could vote against the navy with impunity, the whole process went into reverse. Between 1905 and 1913 the tempo of American naval construction slowed considerably as the U.S. Navy slipped back down the world naval rankings. The Republicans, the party of Theodore Roosevelt and the party more closely aligned with large naval programs, lost ground in every election between 1906 and 1912.

It was not that the American public was hostile to the idea of a large navy; it was more that it was indifferent. Unlike in Britain, where naval issues were passionately debated by the press and where naval issues figured prominently in the public debate, in the United States hardly anyone cast his ballot because of a candidate's position on the fleet. This was the greatest hurdle that the American navy had to overcome, and in these years it failed to do so. Despite all its efforts the navy and its political supporters were unable to convince the public that the United States needed one of the largest fleets in the world. While the navy used a myriad number of rationales to support its position—defense of the Philippines, the Monroe Doctrine, the Open Door in China, growing American overseas trade, racial disputes with Japan, a growing world-wide naval race, and possible tensions with major European powers—the public remained skeptical. This was probably because no matter what the navy said, the public's instinct was right. The United States did not need one of the world's largest fleets to defend itself.

However, just when it seemed that the U.S. Navy was destined to slip back further, World War I intervened. After a year of hesitation President Wilson embraced naval preparedness. The eventual result was the massive 1916 program, which threatened to make the U.S. Navy the most powerful fleet in the world. The 1916 program was supported by an impressive coalition including the president, many other Democrats, almost the whole Republican Party, and powerful business and civic leaders. This act, much more than Theodore Roosevelt's buildup, really catapulted the U.S. Navy into its modern era of dominance.

From this point onward most American politicians would at least have to pay lip service to the idea of a "Navy second to none," the first commonly accepted naval policy the United States ever had. However, no one should be seduced into thinking that this program had changed everything. It must always be kept in mind that this impressive coalition was only made possible by one of the most brutal wars in human history and that many of its supporters had been keen "small navy" men before 1914. In one way the 1916 program represented not a repudiation but a confirmation of the unstable and pernicious way in which the United States made naval policy. It was just one more of the unexpected twists and turns that had beset the U.S. Navy since its inception.

In the end the period between 1900 and 1917 should be seen as an era of rocky transition. Certain things were definitely improving. The navy was becoming a more professional and competent service. Much, however, still needed to be done. The public still had to be convinced in peacetime that a fleet was vital to the nation's security, and Congress had to be convinced to end its long-standing habit of slashing the U.S. Navy's construction budget. A number of painful lessons still remained to be learned.

## NOTES

1. Taft Mss, Series 5, Meyer to Taft 22 October 1910.
2. GBSF, #446, General Board to Secretary of the Navy, 28 March 1913.
3. H. Sprout and M. Sprout, *The Rise of American Naval Power*, p. 297.
4. R. W. Love, *History of the United States Navy*, vol. I, p. 449.
5. W. Braisted, *The United States Navy in the Pacific, 1909-1922*, p. 24.
6. *Presidential Addresses and State Papers of William H. Taft*, vol. I, p. 34.
7. Ibid., p. 442.
8. ARSN 4 December 1909, 30 November 1910.
9. Taft Mss, Series 6, Meyer to Taft, 2 October 1911.
10. Ibid.
11. Ibid. These were twenty-six destroyers, twenty submarines and eleven others
12. ARSN, 30 November 1910.
13. Sprout and Sprout, *The Rise of American Naval Power*, p. 292.
14. Taft Mss, Series 5, Meyer to Taft, 28 October 1910, 22 October 1910.
15. Taft Mss, Series 5, Meyer to Taft, 28 October 1910.
16. Taft Mss, Series 9, Bradley to Taft, 8 July 1909.
17. Meyer Mss, Diary Entry, 21 May 1909.
18. ARSN, 30 November 1910, p. 38.
19. ARSN, 29 November 1912, p. 47.
20. P. E. Coletta ed., *American Secretaries of the Navy*, vol. 1, p. 517.
21. Meyer Mss, Box 16, Hale to Meyer, 15 May 1909
22. Meyer Mss, Box 17, Meyer to TR, 9 July 1909.
23. Meyer Mss, Box 28, Winthrop to Meyer, 6 August 1912.
24. CR, vol. 45, 61st Congress, 2d Session, pp. 6724-6727.

25. Ibid., pp. 3810-3812.

26. Ibid., p. 6603.

27. Ibid., p. 4068.

28. R. G. Albion, *Makers of Naval Policy 1798-1947*, p. 152.

29. CR, vol. 48, 62d Congress, 2d Session, p. 11178.

30. Taft Mss, Series 5, C. D. Norton Letter, March 1909.

31. CR, vol. 48, 62d Congress, 2d Session, p. 8650.

32. Meyer Mss, Lodge to Meyer, 19 July 1912.

33. Ibid., 24 July 1912.

34. Sprout and Sprout, *The Rise of American Naval Power*, p. 288.

35. GB Letters, vol. 7, p. 135, 16 November 1910.

36. GB War Plans, Box 1, #1 Atlantic Station, 19 October 1910.

37. Ibid.

38. GB Letters, vol. 7, p. 135, 16 November 1910.

39. GB War Plans, Box 1, #1 Atlantic Station, 19 October 1910.

40. GB War Plans, Box 8, Plan Orange, 14 March 1910.

41. Braisted, *The United States Navy in the Pacific, 1909-1922*, pp. 10-12.

42. GB Letters, vol. 7, 28 September 1910.

43. GBSF 420-2, Memorandum, 25 September 1912.

44. Ibid., 30 June 1912.

45. Ibid.

46. GBSF 420-2, Memorandum, 30 June 1912.

47. GBSF, #446, GB Letter, 28 March 1913.

48. R. G. Albion, *Makers of Naval Policy 1798-1947*, p. 66.

49. C. Seymour, *The Intimate Papers of Colonel House*, p. 113.

50. WW Papers, vol. 36, p. 426.

51. Love, *History of the United States Navy*, vol. 1, p. 458.

52. ARSN, 1 December 1914.

53. ARSN, 1 December 1913.

54. GBSF 420-2, Dewey to Daniels, 25 June 1913.

55. Sprout and Sprout, *The Rise of American Naval Power*, pp. 307-311.

56. CR, vol. 51, 63d Congress, 2d Session, pp. 7147-7150.

57. Ibid., pp. 8116-8117.

58. Ibid., pp. 8115-8116.

59. *Jane's Fighting Ships of World War I*, p. 134.

60. Ibid., pp. 39, 105, 135.

61. GBSF 420, "Comparison of Ship Values," 4 December 1914.

62. *Jane's Fighting Ships of World War I*, p. 133.

63. GBSF #446, Memorandum, 3 March 1914.

64. GBDC Series VIII, Book V, "Memorandum." See also Daniels Mss, #53, Reel 39, "Naval Intelligence," pp. 279-288.

65. Daniels Mss, #53, Reel 39, "Naval Intelligence," p. 286.

66. GBDC Series VIII, Box 19, Book V, "Memorandum."

67. Ibid.

68. FDR Mss, Tillman to FDR, 19 May 1914.

69. GBDC Series VIII, Box 19, Book V, "Memorandum."

70. Daniels Mss, #53, Reel 39, "Naval Intelligence."

71. Ibid.

72. See Braisted, *The United States Navy in the Pacific, 1909-1922*, pp. 125-140.

73. Daniels Mss, Series 1, Reel 1, p. 36, Diary, 14 May 1913. See also 12, 13 May.

74. Braisted, *The United States Navy in the Pacific, 1909-1922*, pp. 129-130.

75. Ibid., p. 148.

76. GB War Portfolios, Boxes 5, 6, "Orange War Plan," 14 March 1914, p. 61. See also Plans, 25 February 1914, 14 March 1914, and July 1914.

77. Love, *History of the United States Navy*, vol. 1, pp. 460-463; A. S. Link, *Woodrow Wilson and the Progressive Era 1910-1917*, pp. 122-128.

78. GBSF #423, Box 3, #125, Memorandum, 18 April 1914.

79. NDGC, #28495, Treasury Letter, 21 April 1914.

80. A. S. Link, *Woodrow Wilson: The Struggle for Neutrality 1914-1915*.

81. Ibid., p. 66.

82. Braisted, *The United States Navy in the Pacific, 1909-1922*, pp. 173-174.

83. Sprout and Sprout, *The Rise of American Naval Power*, pp. 314-315.

84. FDR Mss, ASN, Sims Memorandum, September 1912.

85. GBSF #240, "Proposed Letter," 16 December 1913.

86. Daniels Mss, Series 3, GB to Daniels, 9 September 1914.

87. See Daniels Mss, Series 3, Reel 67, "Preparedness Controversy",

88. Sprout and Sprout, *The Rise of American Naval Power*, p. 313.

89. FDR Mss ASN, Fiske to Daniels, 9 November 1914.

90. Daniels Mss, Series 3, "House Committee," 27 January 1915.

91. Ibid.

92. Daniels Mss, Series 3, Fletcher Memorandum.

93. Sprout and Sprout, *The Rise of American Naval Power*, p. 314.

94. Braisted, *The United States Navy in the Pacific, 1909-1922*, p. 190.

95. B. F. Cooling, "Bradley Allen Fiske: Inventor and Reformer in Uniform," pp. 131-134, in, J. C. Bradford, ed., *Admirals of the New Steel Navy*.

96. Albion, *Makers of Naval Policy*, p. 219.

97. Daniels Mss Series 3, Reel 37, "Gunnery," p. 105.

98. Daniels Mss Series 3, "Memorandum," 12 February 1915, p. 92.

99. Daniels Mss Series 3, Reel 37, "Gunnery," p.105.

100. FDR Mss, ASN, FDR Letter, 23 March 1916.

101. WW Papers, vol. 40, House Diary, 14 December 1916.

102. WW Papers, vol. 31, House to Wilson, 11 December 1914.

103. GBSF, 420-2, General Board to Daniels, 17 November 1914.

104. Braisted, *The United States Navy in the Pacific, 1909-1922*, p. 178.

105. Link, *Woodrow Wilson: The Struggle for Neutrality 1914-1915*, pp. 138-139.

106. AMPUSA, 8 December 1914,.

107. Daniels Mss, Series 3, Tillman to Daniels, 8 November 1914.

108. Daniels Mss, Series 2, Wilson to Daniels, 21 July 1915.

109. Sprout and Sprout, *The Rise of American Naval Power*, p. 327; Link, *Woodrow Wilson: The Struggle for Neutrality 1914-1915*, pp. 590-591

110. Sprout and Sprout, *The Rise of American Naval Power*, p. 329.

111. WW Papers, vol. 34, Gault to Wilson, 17 August 1915.

112. WW Papers, vol. 35, Annual Message, 7 December 1915.

113. Link, *Woodrow Wilson: The Struggle for Neutrality 1914-1915*, p. 590.

114. FDR Mss ASN, FDR to Daniels, 3 August 1915.

115. Braisted, *The United States Navy in the Pacific, 1909-1922*, p. 187.

116. Daniels Mss, Series 3, "The Wilson Administration and the Navy."

117. WW Papers, vol. 36, Wilson Address, 3 February 1916.

118. WW Papers, vol. 36, Tillman to Wilson, 14 February 1916, Wilson to Tillman, 14 February 1916.

119. Daniels Mss, Series 3, "Preparedness Controversy," August 1916.

120. WW Papers, vol. 38, House Diary, 24 September 1916.

121. WW Papers, vol. 34, Daniels to Wilson, 20 August 1915.

122. GBSF 420-2, "Cost Schedule of 1916 Program," 12 October 1915.

123. WW Papers, vol. 37, House to Wilson, 1 June 1916; House to Wilson, 18 June 1916.

124. CR, vol. 53, 64th Congress, 1st Session, p. 10922.

125. Daniels Mss, Series 2, Navy Department Memorandum, 21 September 1916.

126. CR, vol. 52, 63d Congress, 3d Session, p. 2667.

127. Ibid., p. 3110.

128. CR, vol. 53, 64th Congress, 1st Session, pp. 8794-8796.

129. Ibid., p. 8798.

130. Ibid., 10922-10926.

131. Ibid., p.10926.

132. FDR Mss ASN, "Maneuvers," October 1913.

133. Daniels Mss, Series 3, Preparedness Controversy, 11 September 1914.

134. Daniels Mss, Series 3, Huse to Commander in Chief, 10 February 1915.

135. GBSF 420-2, Memorandum, 28 July 1915.

136. Ibid., 6 August 1915.

137. NID, C-9-B, Box 441, 1915-1918.

138. GBSF 425-3, War Plan, 15 January 1917.

139. WW Papers, vol. 38, House Diary, 24 September 1916.

140. GBSF 434, Spring Exercises for the Atlantic Fleet, 13 March 1915.

141. GBSF 434, Strategic Maneuver for Department and Fleet, 19 August 1915.

142. GBSF 434, Strategic Maneuver #3, 9 October 1916.

# Part II

# The Interwar Years

# 6

# Anglo-American Naval Rivalry and the Paris Peace Conference

The United States' Government is adopting the view that . . . they should go on adding merchant ships to the American Flag until they have completed enough tonnage at any rate to carry the whole of the American troops' reinforcements and supplies. I realise that questions of the very greatest magnitude are involved . . . but surely the principle underlying the whole matter is one which can hardly be put second to any other question.[1]

Eric Geddes, Summer 1918

If it came to a point of England refusing to reduce naval armaments, "the United States should show her how to build a navy. We would be in a position to meet any program England or any other power might set forth," he [Woodrow Wilson] pointed out. "We have now greater navy yards, thousands more shipbuilders than we ever had before and an abundance of raw materials such as would make it possible for us to have the greatest navy in the world."[2]

Woodrow Wilson, 4 December 1918

## THE INTERWAR YEARS

An air of resignation has settled over the interwar period. It seems as if those who labored so hard in these years were somehow destined to fail. Events that were hailed in their day as great advances are now either quietly ignored or savagely dismissed. In particular the naval arms control process has come in for criticism. In the interwar years four major conferences met to discuss naval issues: the Washington Conference of 1921-1922, the Geneva Conference of 1927, the First London Naval Conference of 1930 and the Second London Naval Conference of 1935-1936. Together, they represent a concerted attempt by the great naval powers, particularly Great Britain and the United States, to regulate their strength by negotiation and not competitive building.

Since the collapse of the naval arms control system, however, the process has come in for some pointed criticism. The attacks after the Second World War were particularly sharp. Since then the general view has moderated a little, but the general tone is still skeptical. The two most recent books that cover the whole naval arms control process, the excellent works by Hall and Kaufman, both deliver very mixed reviews.[3]

The British come in for the most bitter criticism. British naval arms control policy is seen as a telling example of national decline. Many of the historians who discuss British naval power, including Marder, Roskill, Kennedy, and Hinsley, have little good to say about British policy. Another writer accuses the British of being "soundly defeated" at the Washington Conference, and another accuses them of being "reduced to the lowest point" by the First London Conference.[4] Still another has called the Washington Conference an "illusory success" and the London Conference a "passing triumph."[5] Even Hall, who is more supportive than most, damns the process with faint praise by claiming that it helped smooth the transfer of superiority from Britain to America.[6]

The Americans come in for more mixed treatment. While American diplomacy is not always seen as deft or perceptive, there is a feeling that this period was characterized by the inexorable rise of American power. The attainment of naval parity is thus seen as an important milestone in America's growth.[7] A biographer of Henry Stimson, a man instrumental in shaping the First London Naval Conference, has laid out this position:

Nothing more clearly marked the American challenge to a century of British hegemony than the American demand not only for naval disarmament, but also for naval parity with Britain. And nothing more clearly revealed the decline of both British power and British morale than Britain's willingness to concede it.[8]

If the symbolic importance of the naval arms control process for America is recognized, there are more mixed opinions about the agreements' substance. There is a feeling that the conferences were either lost opportunities for the United States or even dangerous gambles. Butler, Dingman, O'Connor, and Kaufman offer a mixture of criticism and qualified support.[9]

There is a good deal of reason for these negative views. The naval arms control process did not live up to its creator's hopes. Some nations, noticeably the Japanese, circumvented the limitations and built "illegal" ships. Anglo-American relations were also rocky, undergoing their worst crisis of the twentieth century between 1927 and 1929. Finally, the naval arms control process failed because ultimately it collapsed in 1936.

Yet, for all these flaws the question remains whether or not the process was of value to the British and American navies. In many ways the answer to this question is in the affirmative. For the U.S. Navy the arms control process focused public attention on the issue of naval parity and established building targets that could be easily presented to Congress. The immediate rush of excitement that gripped the Americans after the passage of the 1916 program was bound to subside. Without a naval arms control process it is eminently possible that the American Navy would have reverted to its earlier position of political impotence.

For the British the question of the impact of the naval arms control process is equally open-ended. Recently, two historians have argued that far from being seen as an era of decline, the 1920s and 1930s should be seen as a time when the British maintained their status as the world's most important power. McKercher and Ferris have argued that the Royal Navy maintained its supremacy throughout the 1920s and into the 1930s.[10] While it might be stretching the point to say that Britain retained its naval supremacy, they are right to call for a reevaluation of the course of British naval and other power in these years. The naval arms control agreements were not craven surrenders by different British governments unable or unwilling to spend the money needed to protect the British Empire. They were instead, with the exception of the Geneva Conference, hardheaded and logical agreements in which the British got almost everything they wanted and gave up precious little of substance.

One should be careful not to fix myopically on the Anglo-American naval balance and judge the success of the interwar period naval arms control process from that perspective. First, it was very difficult in these years to say what the Anglo-American naval balance was. The two countries had different needs and strategic goals, and to simply compare their forces ship by ship does not tell the whole story. As time went on, the British and American navies grew to be very different beasts, geared to fighting different wars. Second, we should be wary of focusing too much on the Anglo-American balance, because it was not really that important. The crucial decisions were really those affecting the naval strengths of the two greatest powers in relation to the rest of the world. Far from weakening the British and Americans, the arms control process gave them both important advantages.

## COMPETITION DURING THE FIRST WORLD WAR

The United States' 1916 program threatened to disrupt the world balance in naval power. Yet, when it had been approved, British reaction was muted. The two countries were already dueling over the question of neutral rights, and the British could not afford to antagonize America further. Not until the United States joined the war were the British to gain some influence over American construction. Indeed, while the two nations fought side by side, they were both preparing their fleets for the postwar world.

The British were determined to maintain naval supremacy. At first few in the Cabinet or Admiralty believed that the United States was planning to challenge the Royal Navy directly. It was thought that the 1916 program had been aimed at Germany and Japan. This did not keep the Lloyd George government from trying to mold American construction to serve British purposes. In 1917 Britain's first priority was to win its bitter struggle against German submarines, and the United States was encouraged to build escort vessels and merchant ships. In doing this the British thought they were serving both their short-term and long-term interests. Not only would there be more shipping to use against Germany, but America would have to curtail its construction of capital ships. Within weeks of the American declaration of war the British were urging members of Congress to suspend all work on capital ships.[11]

To begin with, the Americans played ball. In July 1917 Secretary Daniels informed President Wilson that the United States would begin no more capital ships.[12] Soon, however, the Navy Department had second thoughts. Admiral Benson and his allies had never been reconciled to the halt in capital ship construction. Benson was determined to build the United States a navy "second to none." He was also one of the most indefatigable lobbyists in the history of the U.S. Navy. As the war went on, his relentless pressure on Wilson and Daniels began to pay dividends. In a November 1917 letter to Wilson, Daniels reopened the capital ship question.[13] In June 1918 the General Board approved designs for a new class of capital ship, one displacing a mammoth 43,250 tons.[14] In July Congress gave its assent to restarting the 1916 program as soon as it was practicable. These moves reached a climax in September, when the navy submitted a new construction plan, one that dwarfed the 1916 program. It called for an additional twelve battleships, sixteen battlecruisers, 1,055 other vessels, and 2,428 aircraft.[15]

Benson and his supporters were looking far beyond the present war. They argued that if the Germans eventually triumphed, the United States had to be strong enough to fight Germany, Austria-Hungary, Turkey, and Japan single-handedly.[16] They also argued that if the Allies triumphed, the United States would need a fleet equal to the combined strength of Britain and Japan. Benson was determined that the United States should never again be inferior. It was a widely held belief in the American navy, even among those sympathetic to the British. William Pratt, Benson's deputy and an Anglophile, once argued that the United States should build twenty more capital ships to equal the Royal Navy.[17]

When stories began to circulate in Britain that the United States was poised to restart capital ship construction, the Admiralty reacted swiftly. Eric Geddes, first lord of the Admiralty from July 1917 to January 1919, began lobbying the Americans in the summer of 1918:

I would first like to refer to the question of capital ships. The strength of the Allies in capital ships . . . is preponderating, and in fact a good proportion of this strength is probably excessive. . . . We are building no battleships whatsoever, and while I appreciate that I am treading upon somewhat delicate ground . . . I venture to suggest to the United States Navy Department that . . . it is a matter for their most serious consideration whether they are justified in continuing to build capital ships.[18]

Geddes and the Admiralty were just as concerned with the future naval balance as Benson and the Navy Department. Geddes did not attach as high a value to Anglo-American friendship as most first lords, and regularly argued that more should be done to protect the Royal Navy's supremacy. His first sea lord, Admiral Sir Rosslyn Wemyss, was in many ways the mirror image of Benson, his American counterpart. Wemyss was a bluff, uncomplicated sailor with a great distrust of American intentions. However, Geddes and Wemyss were faced with a particularly thorny dilemma.

When the United States entered the war, the German submarine offensive was in full swing. Some in the Admiralty believed that without drastic action Britain might very well be knocked out of the conflict. They saw America's ability to produce merchant and auxiliary ships as a weapon that could turn the tide against the Germans. The Admiralty told Franklin D. Roosevelt, assistant secretary of the U.S. Navy, that Britain would be "unable to hold out till harvest" if there was no increase in American construction.[19] It was a refrain heard again and again. In September the Admiralty asked the United States to provide for "the rapid building of merchant ships."[20] In October Lloyd George sent a personal message to President Wilson calling for a new program of merchant ship building.[21] As late as February 1918 the British were still telling the Americans that the merchant shipping shortage was damaging the war effort.[22]

The dilemma for the British came when the submarine threat receded. It quickly became apparent that in urging America to construct merchant ships the British had created a formidable challenger to their own commercial position. In 1913 Great Britain was the world's leading builder of merchant ships, with Germany a poor second and the United States a distant third. In 1913 the United Kingdom produced 1,932,153 tons of shipping, while Germany and the United States produced 465,226 and 276,448 tons, respectively.[23] By 1918, the situation had been transformed. The United States had increased its merchant ship building dramatically. In the first six months of 1918 America produced more than 800,000 tons, and it was conservatively estimated that production for the year would be 2,237,000 tons. British production, alas, was stagnant; 760,000 tons had been built during the first six months of 1918, with little prospect for an increase.[24]

When it became apparent that the British had unwittingly undermined their own position, the Admiralty sprang into action. When Geddes met Franklin Roosevelt in July 1918, the first lord made what seemed to be a straightforward suggestion to the American: "They want to discuss the possibility of dovetailing the British program for new construction in with our program, in order that between us we may not build too many of one type of vessel."[25] It was the first in a series of attempts by Geddes to alter American merchant ship construction.

Geddes, a man of great energy, was an organizational expert who would lead the rebuilding of Britain's transportation system after the war. He had been selected as first lord to increase naval construction during the struggle against the U-boats. He was not, however, an expert in Anglo-American relations and this helped and hindered his efforts. He was not easily intimidated by the U.S. Navy or its productive capacity. To Geddes the issue was straightforward: Britain must protect its position:

The United States' Government might reasonably be asked so to adjust their shipbuilding programme that the ratio of merchant ship construction to warship construction should be the same in both countries. . . . At present Great Britain is devoting a much larger proportion of her shipyard labour to warships than is the USA: to the manifest disadvantage of Great Britain.[26]

On 2 August 1918, Geddes produced a remarkable document outlining the problem. British merchant tonnage, which stood at 18.5 million tons before the war, was now down to a little over 15 million. The United States, which possessed 3.25 million tons in 1913, now owned 6.75 million tons. [27] Geddes believed that the United States was not pulling its proper weight in the naval war and that this was preventing Britain from switching resources back into merchant ship construction. As he baldly stated, "Are we to go on losing ships in our Allies' immediate interest, and repairing ships for them while they overtake us in their mercantile marine?"[28] The "immediate interest" Geddes was referring to was the transportation of American troops to Europe, not something far removed from British interest. To rectify the situation Geddes first proposed that the United States should compensate Great Britain for ships lost to German submarines. Arthur Balfour, speaking for the Cabinet, quickly squelched that suggestion.[29] However, the August merchant ship production figures only increased Geddes' worries. The United States surpassed its June total of 180,000 tons by almost 50,000.[30] Geddes then tried to persuade the Cabinet to press the United States to produce more small warships, thereby reducing the number of vessels Great Britain would have to build and diverting American resources away from merchant ship construction:

If the Americans put into the war in European waters a reasonable number of the craft they have forecast . . . it is possible for the British Navy to decrease materially their naval construction effort, making the men available either for the Army or for what I contemplate will be the destiny approved by the Cabinet—for merchant shipbuilding.[31]

It was a far-fetched plan. The United States was already building auxiliary ships at a pace far in excess of anything Britain could manage and at the same time building many merchant ships. The true size of America's auxiliary ship program did not become apparent until later. In 1932, the United States possessed 251 destroyers to Great Britain's 150. Yet, only 12 of the American ships had been built after 1918, while the vast majority were from wartime construction programs. The situation was the same for submarines. In 1932 Britain maintained fifty-two submarines and America eighty-one. All but six of the American vessels were started during the war.[32] The United States was able to construct destroyers and other auxiliary ships at an unprecedented rate and still surpass Great Britain in merchant ship building.

Geddes, however, pressed on. His zeal and inexperience led him to make a series of potentially disastrous moves. He decided that to make the United States come to heel he would belittle America's role in the naval war. By contrasting the large burden that the Royal Navy was shouldering with what he thought was the relatively small effort of the American navy, Geddes believed he might shame the Americans into agreeing to British suggestions. When a delegation of congressmen went to London in August 1918, Geddes tried this theme out for the first time.[33] Later, he said the same thing to Colonel House.[34]

Things could have deteriorated rapidly when it was decided to send Geddes to America to argue Britain's case. The Cabinet wanted him politely to persuade the Americans to agree on a common ratio for warship and merchant ship construction.[35] Geddes, however, decided to press the issue of America's small contribution to the war effort, describing his first priority as "a general discussion on the naval situation with a view to bringing home to the United States Navy Department and its Government generally, the magnitude of our effort compared to the effort which the Americans have so far been able to put into the naval war."[36] When Geddes arrived, he did his best to convince the Americans to build auxiliary and antisubmarine vessels. He told Daniels that in exchange for the refitting work British shipyards were doing on American warships, the United States should build trawlers, minesweepers, and destroyers for Britain.[37] Later, he again tried to convince Franklin Roosevelt that the two countries should coordinate their shipbuilding programs to "avoid duplication."[38]

Geddes' trip was subject to mixed reviews. Those Americans sympathetic to the British, such as House and Pratt, thought it a success.[39] Geddes, however, was willing to describe his trip as only "partially" successful. Yet, this was probably too optimistic. Geddes' earlier attacks on America's contribution to the naval war had made him suspect in certain minds, including Woodrow Wilson's. As the president told Daniels, he did not like Geddes' argument "even a little bit."[40]

By mid-1918, Wilson had become quite suspicious of the British. He had received a number of reports written by Benson and Edward Hurley, president of the U.S. Shipping Board, predicting that the British would fight to maintain their maritime preeminence. Hurley's Shipping Board warned the White House against underestimating Britain's determination.[41] As the man in control of the construction and allocation of American merchant shipping, Hurley saw the war as a unique opportunity for the United States to grasp the lead in world commerce. The navy was also worried that friction over trade could lead to an Anglo-American conflict. The American Planning Section in London, staffed by naval officers handpicked by Benson, described these fears:

The war has caused a revival of the American Merchant Marine. The peaceful pressure it will exert towards getting its share of trade will arouse the anxiety of the British Government. Successful trade rivalry strikes at the very root of British interest and British prosperity, and may threaten even the existence of the British Empire. If British trade is seriously threatened, her people may feel that war is justified—as a measure of self preservation.[42]

Geddes' less than straightforward attempts to modify American construction so closely matched the predictions of Benson and Hurley that the first lord had made things worse. President Wilson treated Geddes very warily. Reading between the lines of Geddes' description of his meeting with the president, it is easy to see Wilson's suspicion:

He (Wilson) admitted that the British Navy had in the past acted as a sort of naval police for the world—in fact for civilisation. For his part he would be willing to leave this power to the discretion of the British people, who had never abused it, but he wondered whether [the] rest of the world would be willing to do so indefinitely. Many nations, great and small, chafed under the feeling that their seaborne trade and maritime development proceeded only with the permission and under the shadow of the British Navy.[43]

## PREPARING FOR THE PARIS PEACE CONFERENCE
Before Geddes' efforts could do irreparable damage to Anglo-American relations, the Germans sued for peace. It was not, however, an auspicious omen for the upcoming peace negotiations. Differences between the Americans and the British over "freedom of the seas" flared up immediately.[44] Admiral Wemyss, speaking for the Admiralty, thought American plans dangerous and prejudicial to British interests.[45] The U.S. Navy's Planning Department, alternatively, claimed that the British concept of freedom of the seas was not freedom "at all."[46] To Americans like Benson and Wilson the British seemed mired in the prewar world of national selfishness and petty deviousness. They were incapable of grasping the magnanimity of American plans.[47]

The president wanted to build a League of Nations and to force the Europeans to slash their armed forces. He believed the British would oppose both of these goals and seems to have decided that only brute force would break their resistance. In private he was extremely bellicose. There was one outburst taken down by Wilson's doctor when the president threatened to outbuild the British.[48] A day later the president's secretary recorded an even more extreme claim:

He (Wilson) said that if they (the British) would not [limit naval armaments] we would build the biggest navy in the world, matching theirs and exceeding it for we have the money, the men and resources to do it, and then if they would not limit it, there would come another and more terrible and bloody war and *England would be wiped off the map*.[49] (emphasis added)

The U.S. Navy benefited from Wilson's anger by becoming his weapon of choice. For the navy it was an exhilarating and deceptive development, exhilarating because the fleet seemed, for once, to have become the vital cog in the machinery of American foreign policy. Plans to make the American fleet the strongest in the world were quickly assembled. In August 1918 the General Board proposed the construction of twenty-eight new capital ships.[50] This was too large a figure even for the president, but in December Wilson proposed duplicating the 1916 program.[51] It was an awesome undertaking. Wilson proposed that the United States complete thirty-two new, powerful capital ships in seven years. Each of these vessels would have been more powerful than any ship in the Royal Navy. Marder has claimed that completing just the sixteen ships of the 1916 program would have made the American navy "qualitatively superior" to the Royal Navy.[52] An armada of thirty-two such vessels would have bested the rest of the world combined.

The Wilson administration knew there was no strategic need for such a fleet. When members of Congress began to balk at the expense, Daniels asked the president to make a public statement in favor of the extra ships. Wilson, then in Paris, responded with a diplomatic, not a strategic rationale.[53] The new program, he claimed "with very great conviction," was "necessary for the accomplishment of our objects here." For the time being it was enough. Party loyalty whipped the Democrats into line, and on 31 January 1919 the House approved the 1918 program.

This was also the time that Anglophobia in the American fleet reached its highest point. The first postwar Planning Section Memorandum talked almost exclusively about a war with the British.[54] Later, the Planning Section explained how an Anglo-American war might begin:

Four great Powers have arisen in the world to compete with Great Britain for commercial supremacy on the seas—Spain, Holland, France, Germany. Each one of these Powers in succession has been defeated by Great Britain and her fugitive Allies. A fifth commercial Power, the greatest one yet, is now arising to compete for at least commercial equality with Great Britain. Already the signs of jealousy are visible. Historical precedent warns us to watch closely the moves we make or permit to be made.[55]

Interestingly, while the Planning Section was banging this anti-British drum, it struck a placatory note about the Japanese. While opposing a Japanese takeover of the Caroline and Marshall Islands, the Planning Section suggested that Japan be given a free hand to expand in eastern Siberia.[56] A number of senior American admirals were also more worried about the British than the Japanese, among them the highly respected admiral H. T. Mayo.[57] In a lengthy memorandum Mayo, the commander in chief of the Atlantic fleet, spent 5 paragraphs discussing war with Japan and over 100 discussing war with Great Britain. He believed such a war was the "greatest danger" America faced. Admiral Hugh Roman, who had commanded an American battleship stationed at Scapa Flow, urged the administration to build a major base on either Chesapeake or Narragansett Bay.[58] Such an installation would have been needed only in a war with Great Britain.

The great paladin of the anti-British crusade remained Admiral Benson. Benson saw British plots lurking everywhere. He believed that Britain was planning to keep the defeated German navy, so as to dominate the League of Nations and preempt any American challenge.[59] Benson argued that unless the American navy equaled the Royal Navy, any league would become a tool of British influence:

It must be quite evident to you that in practically all questions that have come up Great Britain has been able to maintain her position and carry through her claims largely through the dominant influence asserted in consequence of her tremendous naval superiority. It is quite evident to my mind that if this condition of inequality of naval strength is to continue the League of Nations, instead of being what we are striving for and most earnestly hope for, will be a stronger British Empire.[60] .

Benson also muffled those voices calling for an agreement with Great Britain. Admiral Sims, who attempted to explain the British point of view to Daniels,[61] felt uneasy enough about the tenor of discussion that he wrote a letter to Benson denying that he was an Anglophile.[62] Sims' protestations fell on deaf ears. The Administration had come to believe that Sims was under a British spell. Daniels claimed all that he heard from the admiral was a rehashed version of Admiralty arguments.[63] Wilson thought Sims "utterly dominated by English influence."[64]

It must have seemed to many in the U.S. Navy that they had turned a very important historical corner. The divisions and uncertainties that had plagued the navy since the Civil War had disappeared. The navy had become the most important weapon in the arsenal of a president determined to impose his vision upon the world. However, if it was an exhilarating time, it was also terribly deceptive. The navy had been seduced into believing its status had permanently changed and ignored signs that it could easily revert to a state of political impotence.

The most important of these signals was Republican gains in the 1918 congressional elections. The Democrats were routed as the GOP gained control of both the House and Senate. While Republicans were usually stronger supporters of the navy than were Democrats, most Republicans had little sympathy for Wilson's grandiose plans, and many detested the president. Traditional naval supporters such as Henry Cabot Lodge and Theodore Roosevelt were soon attacking Wilson's programs. They saw no reason why the United States should start a new naval race.[65] As Roosevelt told Arthur Balfour, "The American people are perfectly content to say that they do not wish to rival England, but they do intend to surpass the navy of any other country."[66]

The coming of the Republican Congress forced Wilson to get House approval for the 1918 program in January 1919. Yet this authorization was not a guarantee that the ships would be built. Senate approval was still pending, and no money had been allocated. The odds were overwhelming that none ever would be. Many Democrats made it clear that they supported the 1918 program only out of party loyalty. As Walter Hensley, Democrat from Missouri, said to Daniels, "I am going to vote for the present Naval Bill, yet I do not see how it will serve any good purpose, but I am determined not to do anything that in the faintest way might be construed to mean an embarrassment to our President now at this very time when what is done will determine whether or not our boys have died in vain."[67]

With such halfhearted support the 1918 program quickly bogged down.[68] The Democrats were unable to bring the program to a vote in the Senate before the Republicans took control, at which point it was doomed. It was an important reminder of how politically weak the navy still was. The navy was still not vital to national existence but remained a weapon to be used or discarded by politicians when their mood suited. Even Wilson, for all his tough talk, saw the 1918 program as only a means to an end. He really wanted a League of Nations and disarmament, not a naval race. The threat of naval building was intended to force action on these points.[69] Wilson probably did not want, and never expected to seek, final appropriation for the program.

Members of both the British Admiralty and Cabinet were aware that Wilson was planning to use the threat of American naval power to try to get his way. Geddes assumed that Wilson wanted to "reduce comparatively the preponderance in sea power of the British Empire." [70] At the same time Geddes expected a sharp fight but did not think that the Americans would try to wrest supremacy from the Royal Navy immediately. He assumed that since the British Empire had such a large lead in completed capital ships and was so dependent on sea power for its independence, it would carry the day.[71]

At the time of the armistice Royal Navy supremacy was impressive. Britain controlled forty-two dreadnought-type capital ships. The Germans had surrendered all of their modern vessels, and the Americans had completed only sixteen and laid down four. The British could modestly claim that the Royal Navy possessed a force superior to the rest of the world's navies combined. As a sign of British confidence, the Admiralty made its first attempt in years to reinstate the two-power standard. The Admiralty's Intelligence Department asked Geddes on 21 November 1918 to reintroduce the famous standard, even if it entailed building against a combination of the United States and France.[72] Geddes wisely refused to make an official commitment and instead called for more negotiations:

I cannot believe that we shall continue in a race with America for naval supremacy on any formula at all. . . . From this it will be clear that I do not think that today we can arrive at any formula, and personally, with the uncertainty of the situation, I would not be prepared to adopt one.[73]

However, Geddes' reign at the Admiralty was drawing to a close. Lloyd George decided his energy and drive would be put to better use reorganizing Britain's transportation system. In January 1919 he was replaced by Walter Long. Long, who served as first lord until February 1921, was a peculiar choice to run the Royal Navy. His greatest value to Lloyd George was his popularity among Conservative backbenchers and his almost total lack of initiative. He was conspiratorial and easily confused, lacked nuance and was ill for long periods at a time. Once Admiral Beatty became first sea lord in November 1919, Long was completely overshadowed. There was only one subject that really seemed to interest him, "Bolshevik" infiltration of Britain. While at the Admiralty, Long was obsessed about Bolshevism and would actually have preferred to head the secret service.[74]

Under Long's supervision, the Admiralty's preparation for the Paris Peace Conference lacked coherence. The first sea lord, Admiral Wemyss, usually argued for a very forceful defense of British supremacy.[75] Wemyss disliked Americans as a matter of principle and was deeply skeptical of President Wilson's intentions.[76] He believed correctly that the president was determined to reduce British influence.[77] To counter this, Wemyss proposed continuing the construction of some battlecruisers laid down after the Battle of Jutland.[78]

However, not everyone was as pessimistic as Wemyss. When news of the 1918 program first reached the Admiralty, many assumed that the Americans were really concerned with Japan.[79] One common Admiralty belief was that the United States had never deliberately intended to challenge British supremacy but that the war had inadvertently complicated matters:[80]

The War has made the United States realise her strength. . . . There is every indication that she is endeavouring to displace the British Empire from the predominant position in regard to mercantile tonnage which the latter held before the War; but this arises rather from the fact that she now has the opportunity to do so than from any carefully planned policy on the German pattern. . . . There are undoubtedly many people working for an estrangement between the British Empire and the United States, and while it is necessary for us to be wide awake to all American policy and measures, it is undesirable to turn her natural instincts towards trade expansion into an intended threat to our own position.[81]

The dilemma for the British was how to prevent a naval race and protect their supremacy at the same time. Some perceptively saw that divisions in the

American polity could be used to Britain's advantage. Admiral Sir William Grant, who had commanded British naval forces on the North America Station, urged the Admiralty to lay low and let Wilson's domestic opposition do the Royal Navy's work.[82] Long shared this opinion, but he was also naturally concerned about the possible intervention of subversive forces: "The best citizens of the United States, especially the Republicans, are friendly to us, but our secret intelligence makes it perfectly clear that a vigorous campaign is again on foot to promote hostility to England."[83] Eventually, it was suggested that the best way forward would be to state that the Royal Navy would be kept at a high level of strength and hope that the Americans would lose the will to build to an equal level:

I would suggest we fix and publish the minimum strength we adopt as a policy . . . at the same time making it clear that this is done regardless of US. . . . Our standard will undoubtedly be adopted by US as their standard, to which they will relatively build. Then there will be great controversy in US, and on their Government will be pinned the odium of any increase in their relative power.[84]

This "wait and see" policy was by far the most sensible option for the British. The problem with the policy, however, was its passivity. Everyone in the government, Lloyd George included, was deeply attached to naval supremacy. The gut feeling was that everything should be done to cajole the United States into accepting this supremacy. Pestering the United States, however, was exactly the wrong thing to do. It was more likely to antagonize the Americans and increase their support for naval building. It was a lesson the British, much to their chagrin, were to relearn throughout the period.

There was one large difference between British attempts to maintain supremacy in 1919 and earlier efforts. The option of competitive building was generally ruled out. Hardly anyone tried to discuss how supremacy could be maintained if the United States was serious about its building programs. Earlier British governments were willing to expend large sums to deter the Germans and others. Now, the Lloyd George government was in the uncomfortable position of hoping that American inertia would maintain Britain's naval ascendancy. Britain was now dependent on the whims and fancies of another nation. Long, who was very concerned at the growth of American power,[85] admitted that a sustained American naval challenge would have been irresistible:

I do not want to get into competition with the United States for many reasons:—first, because I believe that if they chose to put all their resources into the provision of a larger navy the competition between us would be impossible, and we should in the end be beaten from the point of view merely of finance; second, because I naturally do not wish to assume that they will be hostile to us.[86]

The initiative had clearly slipped from Britain's hands. Even Wemyss never articulated a concrete policy to maintain supremacy. There was one practical plan assembled, and it came from Admiral Sir John Jellicoe.[87] Sent on a trip to evaluate the naval needs of the empire, Jellicoe drew up a detailed plan for the future of the Royal Navy. He had no time for sentimentality. It would be impossible to maintain naval supremacy over a determined United States. He even seemed willing to accept a slight inferiority.[88]

At Paris, however, the British delegation made a concerted effort to maintain their supremacy. In doing this they ran headlong into Wilson's plans for a League of Nations and naval disarmament. The ensuing negotiations were bitter and emotional and saved only by a temporary compromise. It quickly became apparent, however, that the future balance of naval power was a long way from being decided.

## BLUFF AND COUNTER-BLUFF AT THE
## PARIS PEACE CONFERENCE

When the Paris Peace Conference opened in January 1919, discussion of the Anglo-American naval balance was put off. There was some talk about "freedom of the seas," but negotiations about naval strength began only in late March. Once they began, however, Anglo-American differences threatened to disrupt the whole conference. The confrontation was bitter enough to be known as the "Sea Battle of Paris."[89] At first the chances of a settlement looked slim, probably because the negotiations were dominated by Benson, Daniels, Wemyss, and Long. There existed not one diplomatic personality among the four, and their meetings were characterized by recriminations and insults. Dealings between Benson and Wemyss were particularly volatile. Neither of these two flinty sea dogs was in any mood to compromise.

Wemyss thought it reasonable that the United States should publicly recognize Britain's "right" to naval superiority. He was supported by Long, who requested that the United States drop both the 1918 and the 1916 programs. Upon hearing these demands Benson became apoplectic. To him it was another British plot to retain world domination.[90] Exchanges became so heated that Daniels thought the American chief of naval operations and the British first sea lord might come to blows.[91] Benson charmed his British counterparts with observations like, "I don't like your King,"[92] and in response Long described Benson as a "man of mulish character" who was not "very quick at grasping any ideas other than his own."[93]

What both sets of negotiators were doing was playing a nasty game of diplomatic "chicken." The Americans claimed that they could not reduce their building programs until there was agreement on a League of Nations.[94] The British responded by threatening to veto any league unless America reduced its building plans.[95] Lloyd George told Daniels he would "not give a snap of his finger for the League of Nations if we kept on building."[96] The whole matter was threatening to boil over when Lloyd George and Wilson told Lord Robert Cecil and Colonel Edward House to search for a settlement. The navy men had been unable to settle the issue primarily because they were navy men. No American sailor could promise that America would never challenge the Royal Navy, just as no member of the Admiralty could, at this time, offer to surrender Britain's cherished supremacy.

Both Cecil and House, however, were sympathetic to the other's position. House was one of the few Anglophiles with influence over the president and often pushed for accommodation. He had played almost no role in formulating Wilson's aggressive naval policy and preferred backstairs negotiation to confrontation. House had no time for Benson's theatrics and thought the Admiral "obsessed" with the Royal Navy.[97] House also distrusted Daniels and wanted to keep him away from Paris if possible. Cecil, meanwhile, was a strong supporter of the League of Nations. He tried to convince Lloyd George not to use British support for a league to blackmail the United States.[98] To Cecil, attempts to intimidate America were bound to fail:

The more I discuss the financial and economic position of Europe . . . the more I feel the truth of the proposition that without America there is little prospect of rescuing Europe. It is therefore fatuous for us to suppose that we can impose terms on America by any devise. The most we can hope to do is persuade them to accept them.[99]

House and Cecil limited their discussions to the two most important topics, the League of Nations and American naval strength, and carefully carved a path between them. Cecil correctly surmised that the league was foremost in Wilson's mind and politely inquired what the impact would be to American building if the league were approved.[100] House's reply was encouraging. They eventually reached a working agreement that House spelled out in a confidential letter sent on 9 April. "If the kind of Peace is made for which we are working and which will include a League of Nations, it will surely be necessary for us to live up to its intentions, and in order to do this I am sure you will find the United States ready to abandon or modify our new naval program."[101]

House and Cecil were able to reach this agreement, imprecise as it was, because they avoided the emotive issue of naval supremacy. They never attempted to define a general principle governing British and American naval strength. Therefore, neither was forced to make an embarrassing climb-down. They were content with the suggestion that a naval ratio might be discussed, but only after the treaty had been signed.[102] They were admitting that, at the time, it was impossible to settle the issue of naval supremacy. Any firm agreement would have entailed a public humiliation for someone.

A number of different opinions have been expressed about who "won" the naval Battle of Paris. Many, including Marder and Braisted, believe that Wilson was the more successful for two reasons.[103] First, they believe that Wilson was really concerned only with the league and that the nebulous concession House made to "abandon or modify" the American programs was a small price to pay to get the league. That Wilson was obsessed with the league is clear, and he did support the 1918 program primarily to give himself leverage at the conference. He often used it to intimidate the British:

He (Daniels) had seen his President that morning and . . . the latter would not consent to any agreement, arrangement or proposal of any kind affecting their naval programmes, in brief, that the President would not consent to the reduction of a single ship, until the peace was signed and all the arrangements completed here.[104]

The second assumption was that British inability to secure an American recognition of their naval supremacy was the beginning of the end for their dominance. The British made major concessions and gained nothing in return.[105]

This view is not universally shared. Roskill states that House and Cecil's agreement established a truce in naval building and that the U.S. Navy made the "greater sacrifice."[106] There is something to the belief that the British were more successful than many assume. Those who claim that the Americans made no substantive concessions should admit that the British made none as well. It is hard to see what Lloyd George sacrificed to gain House's promise. Pledging British support for a League of Nations hardly represented a climb-down on Britain's part. The British had been toying with plans for a league before the war ended, and within the British delegation at Paris there was strong support for a league, particularly from Cecil. It is thus hard to see how the league as promulgated was the result of a British "concession."

Truth be told, disagreements over who "won" the naval battle of Paris are rather pointless. Eventually, no one won. The American Senate refused to ratify Wilson's league, and this refusal negated House's pledge to the British. In terms of the development of American and British naval power, the conference was irrelevant. The problem was that the talks were held too soon after the war for either government to have come to terms with America's potential naval power. Politicians and sailors in both countries knew what they wanted in an ideal world, but they were unsure about how to get it. In an ideal world every member of the British government would have liked to maintain naval supremacy. Before the conference the British spoke as if the Americans would agree to this. Yet, the Lloyd George government had no plan of action in case the Americans did not agree.

In the United States the issue was even more complicated. There were at least two distinct ideal worlds and one chaotic one. The navy, dominated by Benson, was planning for at least equality with the Royal Navy. The president, however, was more interested in establishing a new international order and viewed American naval power from that context. In Congress there was no consensus whatsoever. The hodgepodge of various factions that had so disrupted American naval policy before 1915 was still in place. These basic contradictions within the American polity had to be resolved before any consistent policy could be adopted. Since no one was sure whether this consensus could be achieved, no one, including Wilson and Lloyd George, was sure what their naval policy would be.

## NOTES

1. ADM 116/1809-A/439/2, Destroyer Refitting, Summer 1918.
2. WW Papers, vol. 53, p. 313, Grayson Diary, 4 December 1918.
3. C. Hall, *Britain, America and Arms Control 1921-1937*, pp. 193-218; R. G. Kaufman, *Arms Control During the Pre-Nuclear Era*, pp. 193-200.
4. J. L. Stokesbury, *Navy and Empire*, pp. 344-345; F. H. Hinsley, *Command of the Sea: The Naval Side of British History 1918-45*, p. 22.
5. C. L. Mowat, *Britain Between the Wars, 1918-40*, pp. 115, 375.
6. Hall, *Britain, America and Arms Control 1921-1937*, p. 218.
7. F. Costigliola, *Awkward Dominion: American Political, Economic and Cultural Relations with Europe 1919-1933*, pp. 80-81.
8. G. Hodgson, *The Colonel: The Life and Wars of Henry Stimson 1867-1950*, p. 181.
9. T. Buckley, *The United States and the Washington Conference 1921-22*, p. 190; R. G. Kaufman, *Arms Control During the Pre-Nuclear Era*, pp. 193-200; R. Dingman, *Power in the Pacific*, pp. 215-216; R. G. O'Connor, *Perilous Equilibrium: The United States and the London Naval Conference of 1930*, pp. 122-128
10. B. McKercher, "Wealth Power and the New International Order: Britain and the American Challenge in the 1920's." *Diplomatic History*, and "Our Most Dangerous Enemy: Great Britain Preeminent in the 1930's," *International History Review*; J. Ferris, *Men, Money and Diplomacy: The Evolution of British Strategic Policy 1919-1926*, and "The Greatest Power on Earth: Great Britain in the 1920's," *International History Review*.
11. AANR #377, de Chair to Jellicoe, 9 May 1917.
12. WW Papers, vol. 43, p. 178, Daniels to Wilson, 14 July 1917.
13. WW Papers, vol. 45, p. 170, Daniels to Wilson, 30 November 1917.
14. GB Hearings, "Building Program 1919," 17 June 1918.
15. GBSF 240-2, "Building Program 1920," 10 September 1918.
16. GBSF 420, Memorandum, 1 July 1918.
17. Ibid.
18. Geddes Mss A/426/1, Geddes to Franklin Roosevelt, 31 August 1918.
19. FDR Mss ASN, A. R. Miles letter, 14 April 1917.
20. Balfour Mss #49709, Admiralty Memorandum, 27 September 1917.
21. WW Papers, vol. 44, Lloyd George to Wilson, 11 October 1917.
22. Balfour Mss #49741, Spring-Rice to Balfour, 4 February 1918.
23. Geddes Mss, ADM 116/1804 26/b, undated.
24. Geddes Mss, ADM 116/1807, A/391/2, "Output of Merchant Tonnage," June 1918.
25. FDR Mss ASN, FDR to Daniels, 27 July 1918.
26. Geddes Mss, Admiralty Papers 116/1808 A/416, 16 August 1918.
27. ADM 116/1889, "Naval Effort—Great Britain and United States of America," 2 August 1918.

28. Ibid. See also ADM 116 A/439/4, Geddes to Lloyd George, 26 August 1918.

29. Lloyd George Mss 3/3/31, Balfour to Geddes, 27 August 1918.

30. Geddes Mss ADM 116/1809, A/439/16.

31. Ibid., A/439/4, Geddes to Lloyd George, 21 August 1918.

32. S. Roskill, *Naval Policy Between the Wars*, Appendix B, C. See also Hughes Mss, Reel 125, p. 600.

33. A. J. Marder, *From the Dreadnought to Scapa Flow*, vol. 5, p. 127.

34. WW Papers, vol. 51, p. 279, House Diary, 9 October 1918.

35. Lloyd George Mss 3/3/31, Balfour to Geddes, 27 August 1918.

36. Geddes Mss ADM 116/1809 A/439/17, Geddes Memorandum, 19 September 1918.

37. Daniels Mss, Series 3, Reel 56, Geddes to Daniels, 10 October 1918.

38. Daniels Mss, Series 2, Reel 59, FDR to Daniels, 21 October 1918.

39. AANR, House to Balfour, 13 October 1918; Pratt to Sims, 15 October 1918, pp. 534-535.

40. WW Papers, vol. 51, p. 179, Wilson to Daniels, 2 October 1918.

41. J. J. Safford, *Wilsonian Maritime Diplomacy 1913-21*, pp. 141-168.

42. Benson Mss #42, Planning Section Memorandum, 21 November 1918.

43. AANR Geddes Memorandum, 16 October 1918, p. 547.

44. Marder, *From the Dreadnought to Scapa Flow*, vol. 5, pp. 238-241.

45. AANR, Memorandum, #414, 17 October 1918.

46. AANR, Memorandum, #416, 7 November 1918.

47. See Daniels Mss, Series 2, Reel 42, p. 267, Benson to Daniels, 10 November 1918.

48. WW Papers, vol. 53, p. 313, Grayson Diary, 4 December 1918.

49. WW Papers, vol. 51, p. 321, Benham Diary, 5 December 1918; vol. 53, Benham Diary, 10 January 1919.

50. GBSF 240-2, "Building Program 1920," 10 September 1918.

51. WW Papers, vol. 51, p. 344, Daniels Diary, 15 October 1918.

52. Marder, *From the Dreadnought to Scapa Flow*, vol. 5, p. 225.

53. Daniels Mss, Series 2, Daniels to Wilson, 25 January 1919; Wilson response, 29 January 1919.

54. Benson Mss #42, Memorandum, 21 November 1918.

55. Marder, *From the Dreadnought to Scapa Flow*, vol. 5, pp. 226-227.

56. Benson Mss #36, Planning Section Memorandum, undated.

57. SCCCNO 138-8, Reel 38, Mayo Memorandum, 20 January 1919.

58. GB Hearings, Rodman Views, 18 January 1919.

59. Benson Mss 36, Benson to Daniels, 20 November 1918; Daniels Mss, Series 2, Benson to Daniels, 27 November 1918; WW Papers, vol. 55, Benson to Wilson, 14 March 1919.

60. Daniels Mss, Series 2, Benson to Wilson, 5 May 1919.

61. Sims Mss, Sims to Daniels, 5 February 1919.

62. Benson Mss 39, Sims to Benson, 20 December 1918.

63. J. Daniels, *The Wilson Era: Years of War and After: 1917-1923*, p. 370.

64. WW Papers, vol. 58, Benham Diary, 7 May 1919.

65. H. Sprout and M. Sprout, *Towards a New Order of Sea Power*, Chapter 7; W. Braisted, *The United States Navy in the Pacific 1909-22*, pp. 422-425.

66. Balfour Mss 49749, TR to Balfour, 15 December 1918.

67. Daniels Mss, Series 3, Hensley to Daniels, 7 February 1919.

68. Braisted, *The United States Navy in the Pacific 1909-22*, pp. 425-426.

69. Sims Mss, Daniels Correspondence, 7 January 1919.

70. Lloyd George Mss F/163/4/7, "US Naval Policy," Geddes Memorandum, 7 November 1918.

71. ADM 116/1772, Memorandum, 23 December 1918.

72. ADM 116/1605, Geddes Letter, 21 November 1918.

73. Ibid.

74. ADM 116/1677, "Secret Service," 16 January 1919.

75. AANR, Wemyss to Geddes, #400, 3 October 1918.

76. Lady Wester Wemyss, *The Life and Letters of Lord Wester Wemyss*, p. 404.

77. AANR, Memorandum, #414, 17 October 1918.

78. ADM 116/1772, "Battle Cruisers Programme," 14 January 1919.

79. AANR, Memorandum, #422, 7 November 1918.

80. ADM 116/3242, "US Policy," 14 February 1919.

81. ADM 116/3242, Memorandum, 24 February 1919.

82. ADM 116/1773, Memorandum, 25 February 1919.

83. Lloyd George Mss F/33/2/13, Long to Lloyd George, 16 February 1919.

84. ADM 116/1773, Memorandum, 25 February 1919.

85. Lloyd George Mss 33/1/48, Long to Lloyd George, 20 December 1918.

86. Lloyd George Mss F/33/2/13, Long to Lloyd George, 16 February 1919.

87. Jellicoe Mss 49045, Jellicoe to Long and Wemyss, 3 March 1919.

88. Ibid.

89. See: Sprout and Sprout, *Toward A New Order Of Sea Power*, pp. 62-72; Marder, *From the Dreadnought to Scapa Flow*, vol. 5, pp. 224-237: Daniels, *The Wilson Era*, Chapter 35.

90. Daniels Mss, Series 3, U.S. N. Advisory Staff Memorandum, 7 April 1919, pp. 114-120.

91. Marder, *From the Dreadnought to Scapa Flow*, vol. 5, p. 231.

92. Daniels, *The Wilson Era*, p. 368.

93. Lloyd George Mss 192/1/4, Long Memorandum, 29 March 1919.

94. WW Papers, vol. 56, Daniels Diary, 31 March 1919.

95. Ibid., 1 April 1919.

96. Daniels Mss, Series 2, Memorandum, 7 April 1919, p. 34.

97. WW Papers, vol. 56, House Diary, 3 April 1919.

98. Cecil Mss 51131, Journal Entry, 26 March 1919.

99. Cecil Mss 51091, Cecil to Balfour, 3 April 1919.

100. Cecil Mss 51094, Cecil to House, 8 April 1909.

101. Cecil Mss 51094, House to Cecil, 9 April 1919.

102. Lloyd George Mss 6/6/33, Cecil Memorandum, 10 April 1919.

103.Marder, *From the Dreadnought to Scapa Flow*, vol. 5, pp. 234-235; Braisted, *The United States Navy in the Pacific*, pp. 439-40.

104.Lloyd George Mss 33/2/31, Long Memorandum, 8 April 1919.

105.Marder, *From the Dreadnought to Scapa Flow*, vol. 5, p. 234.

106.Roskill, *Naval Policy Between the Wars*, vol. 1, p. 91.

# 7

# The Washington Conference and the Question of Naval Parity

On taking the chair, Hughes started his address. At the outset there was a rustling noise in the audience. It was expected that his speech would be in the nature of a polite greeting and a suggestion for permanent organization. Beginning quietly, Hughes piled point on point, and suddenly the audience realized there was a proposal coming and history was in the making. . . . Lord Lee, the First Lord of the British Admiralty, turned the several colors of the rainbow, and behaved as if he were sitting on hot coals. He glanced the plan over. He threw notes to Beatty who was sitting on the far left. He half rose and whispered to Balfour. Beatty, after the first step, sat with eyes fixed on the ceiling. Admiral Chatfield, on his left, turned red and then white, and sat immovable. Balfour did not in any way show his trend of thought, whether he was surprised or excited. . . . I have never known at any time a more dramatic moment.[1]

Theodore Roosevelt Jr., 12 November 1921

## INTERLUDE

Between the conclusion of negotiations in Paris and the opening of the Washington Conference, the American and British navies were stuck in a strategic purgatory. The situation was exacerbated by a number of important events.

President Wilson's stroke, the Senate fight over the Versailles Treaty, and the 1920 American elections all contributed to making the period very confusing. Decisions on vital naval questions had to be delayed until the American government reached a new equilibrium. The question that preoccupied both the Admiralty and the Navy Department was the fate of America's 1916 program. Once it became apparent that Wilson's 1918 program was dead, eyes turned to the sixteen capital ships approved two years earlier.[2]

The British assumed that the United States could complete the 1916 program sometime in 1924 or 1925.[3] Then the U.S. Navy would have twenty-nine first-class battleships and six battlecruisers. British strength, without new construction, would be thirty-three battleships and ten battlecruisers.[4] Britain's numerical advantage, however, was misleading. The technical advances brought on by the First World War meant that the Royal Navy would be significantly outclassed. The new American ships were much better protected and faster and fired a considerably more powerful broadside. The question facing the Lloyd George government was therefore simple: should Britain appease the United States, or should the government begin a new construction program to match American building?

Their first decision was to wait and see. Both the Cabinet and Admiralty steadfastly refused to make a decision in 1919. In June the Admiralty sidestepped the question of American naval building.[5] The Admiralty seemed to be of two minds. There were sporadic attempts to reassert Britain's "right" to supremacy. The Admiralty once devised a ratio system that supposedly accurately measured the relative needs of the world's naval powers. By assigning a numerical value to each country's coastline, reliance on naval transportation, manpower, overseas trade, merchant marine, national wealth, and "naval prestige," the Admiralty decided Britain deserved a 10, America a 6.1, France a 2.7, Japan a 2.04, and Italy a 1.4.[6]

However, such moments only masked the fact that strong momentum quickly built up in favor of accepting naval parity with the Americans. Few in the Cabinet or Admiralty had the stomach for a naval race. In the first place hardly anyone believed that a war with the United States was really possible. One of the rare Admiralty papers on the subject plaintively claimed: "War probably very unpopular—We should desire to terminate it as soon as we had shown Empire was able to contend against USA—Time all on side of USA."[7] The other reason few in the government wanted to risk a naval race with America was that most believed Britain would lose.

By 1919 the United States was, economically speaking, in a league of its own. American production of iron and coal, the twin pillars of the Industrial Revolution, was enormous. In 1913 Britain's monthly production of steel had been 855,000 tons, while the United States' was 2,581,000. By 1918 British monthly production had slipped to 753,000 tons, but America's had jumped to 3,646,000 tons. In February 1919 the figures for both were 626,000 tons and 2,941,000 tons respectively.[8] British production had fallen from 33 percent of

America's in 1913 to 21 percent in February 1919. The figures for
tion were similar. The monthly averages for coal production in Br
United States had changed from 23,953,000 and 42,408,000 tons in 1915 to
18,999,000 and 50,993,000 tons in 1918. Obviously, each country possessed
enough coal and steel to build battleships far in excess of either its wishes or
needs. However, only the United States had the excess capacity needed to increase construction dramatically. In 1920 it was estimated that no more than six
capital ships could be laid down in Britain during any calendar year, with the
optimum number being four.[9]

The shift in America's favor was even more pronounced in the areas of merchant shipping and trade. In 1913 Britain had on average 1,957,000 tons of
shipping under construction every quarter. This figure grew slightly to
1,980,000 tons in 1918 and was 2,253,000 tons for the first quarter of 1919.
American production, meanwhile, leaped phenomenally. In 1913 the United
States' quarterly average of ships under construction was a very modest 236,000
tons. In 1918, however, this figure had leaped to 3,646,000 tons, and by 1919
the British estimated it at 4,186,000 tons. In percentage terms there was a huge
shift from 1913, when American production was 12 percent of Great Britain's,
to 1919, when Britain's was 53 percent of America's. The United States had
also considerably enlarged its share of world trade. Before the First World War
Great Britain was still the world's largest trading nation. In 1913 Britain imported £54,390,000 worth of goods per month and exported £43,770,000. By
February 1919 its imports had almost doubled to £101,954,000 while its exports
had increased only marginally to £46,759,000. The United States, which had
imported £30,501,000 per month in 1913 and exported £42,505,000, had transformed its balance of payments. In February 1919 American imports were worth
£46,759,000, while American exports amounted to a whopping £120,560,000.

This shift in trading power had a material impact upon naval negotiations
between the United States and Great Britain. American statesmen and naval
officers now could justify their new fleet on the grounds of national interest.
Previously, the British had argued that the United States was a self-contained
economy impervious to blockade, while the United Kingdom was dependent on
control of the sea for its very existence. While the latter of these arguments was
still true, the former made less sense when British exports were about 40 percent
of America's.

The First World War had also increased America's financial clout. During
the war the British understandably bought enormous quantities of weapons and
supplies from America. Their total debt was difficult to measure precisely. In
1920 Lloyd George estimated that Britain owed the United States around £1
billion.[10] While the Americans were seemingly in no hurry to collect this vast
sum, they refused to accept a British suggestion that war debts should be for-
given. As Cecil said during the Paris Peace Conference: "As the Conference
goes on, the dominating position of America becomes more and more evident.

The great want of the future is money, and the only one of the Associated Governments that has money at its command is the United States."[11]

The United States had also demonstrated during the war that it could easily outspend Britain. In 1913 Great Britain spent £48,732,621 on the Royal Navy.[12] During 1915 and 1916 the British increased their spending considerably to £205,733,597 and then £209,877,218. This more than four-fold increase was impressive, but it paled in comparison to America's increase. During 1916, the United States' last full year of peace, America spent around $318,390,017, or £76,813,032, on its navy. By 1917, however, American spending had jumped to £427,281,870, and by 1918 it reached the formidable sum of £531,115,182. Even more impressive was the amount of money the Americans devoted to naval construction. In 1917 the Admiralty estimated that America spent £240 million on new construction, an amount greater than the total British naval budget. This financial advantage would be vital in an Anglo-American naval race because of the ever-growing cost of new capital ships. The first American dreadnought, USS *Michigan*, authorized in 1905, cost $6,655,773, while USS *Mississippi*, authorized in 1914, cost $13,556,324. By the end of the war even these ships seemed cheap. In 1920, the Admiralty estimated that the construction of four new capital ships alone would cost £37,500,000, or as much as the entire British naval budget for 1909, which had included eight new dreadnoughts.[13]

The economic disparity between Britain and the United States was so large that few in the Cabinet or Admiralty wanted a building race. Once the Paris Peace Conference ended, the Lloyd George government moved silently, but inexorably, to accept naval parity with America. One of its most important steps was the adoption of the Ten-Year Rule in 1919. By assuming that the British Empire would not fight a war for at least ten years, the government allowed the Royal Navy to slip into a state of parity with the American fleet.[14] Soon the number of British capital ships kept in full commission fell to twenty, while the Americans maintained seventeen. The British had an advantage in light cruisers of thirty-eight to twenty-six, but a marked inferiority in destroyers, with 90 to America's 144, and submarines, with 43 to America's 133.[15] By early 1920 the Royal Navy and the U.S. Navy were roughly comparable in fighting strength, and the Admiralty adjusted its language accordingly: "There has never been any dispute as to the fact that no one Power could be permitted to surpass us in naval strength."[16]

By the end of 1919 the Admiralty had proposed two courses of action to the Cabinet, neither of which was based on the maintenance of British supremacy. Either the Americans must be persuaded to "abandon or modify" their naval program, or the British decision to halt capital ship construction must be "reconsidered."[17] By January 1920, the Admiralty advocated "a further building programme which will ensure that we are at least equal in material strength to the United States Navy."[18] The Admiralty adopted this position, even though it was believed that the repercussions of naval equality could be unpleasant:

The fact cannot be ignored that conflict of interests may arise with the United States in the same way as with other powers in our history. It is not suggested that this involves war between the United States and the British Empire. Having deprived us by peaceful means of the supremacy of the sea, their subsequent victories are probably destined to be commercial and diplomatic, but the effect of these upon trade and Empire may be no less serious on this account.[19]

    The end of 1919 was also an important time for the British navy because of the appointment of Admiral Beatty as first sea lord. Beatty, who replaced Wemyss in unfortunate circumstances,[20] was able to arrest the drift that had taken hold of the Royal Navy since the armistice. He fused the disparate ideas emanating from the Admiralty and pressed the navy's case extremely forcefully. Surprisingly for someone who had commanded the Royal Navy at the height of its strength, Beatty was not dogmatic on the question of naval supremacy. He was worried that the U.S. Navy might surpass the Royal Navy and wanted desperately to maintain equality. The strategic situation, as Beatty saw it, was perilous.[21] While Britain and America were equal in the number of warships kept in full commission, the United States had a huge lead in ships under construction. For 1920-1921, the U.S. Navy had been given a budget of $425 million (£112 million). This covered not just the 1916 program but also ten light cruisers, 109 destroyers, and sixty submarines. The Royal Navy, meanwhile, had a budget of only £84 million, which allowed for no new capital ships and only eight light cruisers, 8 destroyers, and seven submarines. The new designs of the American capital ships also meant that the British had to react.[22] The Admiralty believed that the government had to "proceed immediately with a new building programme before it is too late to prevent us from sinking to the position of the second naval power, from which we might never be able to extricate ourselves."[23]

    Beatty supported a construction program similar to the ones approved during the naval race with Germany. He called for the construction of eight new superdreadnoughts and a few smaller vessels. Four of the dreadnoughts would be laid down in 1921, and the remainder in 1922. This program was extremely expensive, with construction alone estimated at £83.8 million.[24] Because of Britain's smaller construction capacity, Beatty believed that any delay in implementing the program could be fatal. The British could not lay down more than four capital ships in a calendar year, and if they did not do so in 1921, the United States would be able to use its excess capacity to preempt any further challenges: "If we fall further behind, the U.S. will be able to retain their supremacy, as it will be practically impossible for us to catch them up against their will once their building slips are clear of the 1916 programme."[25]

    The Lloyd George government spent much of 1920 discussing this program. The debate reached a climax during a crucial 14 December meeting of the Committee for Imperial Defence. Attending were Lloyd George, Andrew Bonar-Law, Lord Curzon, Austen Chamberlain, Winston Churchill, Eric Geddes, Air Marshal Trenchard, and Maurice Hankey. Luckily for the Admiralty

Walter Long was ill, so Beatty argued the navy's case. The admiral left Long in no doubt that he considered the meeting crucial: "I can well understand your mental tribulation at being laid by heels at this juncture which is of vital importance to the future of the Navy and the Empire. A mistake now and we shall and can never recover from it."[26]

Lloyd George, as ever, split between his affection for naval power and his predilection for slicing the Admiralty's budget,[27] opened the meeting by describing the gravity of the situation:

The Committee had to consider what was the most important question that had ever been submitted to them—the most important and the most difficult. . . . If the Committee were to decide now that Great Britain must enter into competition with the United States in naval shipbuilding, it would be the biggest decision they had taken since 1914, and conceivably, greater than that taken in 1914.[28]

The prime minister then listed a litany of the perils lurking behind a building competition with the United States. He seemed to rule out the possibility that Britain would deny America's claim to naval parity. He said the government had "no intention of embarking on a rivalry in respect of general supremacy at sea, but we propose that each nation should be superior in her own seas."

Churchill spoke next and argued passionately for the maintenance of British naval supremacy. He considered supremacy vital to the independent survival of the empire. Even Churchill, however, did not support a capital ship construction race with America. Instead, he argued that the Royal Navy should rely on its advantage in auxiliary ships, such as cruisers, destroyers, and submarines, to maintain supremacy. Then the remaining participants chipped in. Curzon, the foreign secretary, was generally uncomfortable when discussing Anglo-American relations and steered the debate toward the Anglo-Japanese Alliance. Chamberlain, one of the more "pro-American" members of the Cabinet, spoke in favor of an agreement with the United States. Only Beatty really seemed willing to face the difficult questions, and he was dismissive of Churchill's pining for naval superiority:

They (the Admiralty) had submitted a Paper showing the building programme considered necessary to give effect to what was understood to be the naval policy of the Government, namely, equality with the next strongest Power. No provision had been made in the suggested programme for superiority on all or any seas, or even for equality in capital ships.

The first sea lord considered arguments about naval supremacy to be academic. The question that concerned him was the fate of the eight dreadnoughts.

Eventually, the CID agreed to a two-track approach. The British would attempt to persuade the United States to stop its naval buildup. At the same time the Admiralty could plan for the construction of the new dreadnoughts, as long as sufficient savings were found in other parts of the naval budget. Luckily for the Admiralty, however, the Cabinet eventually backed off from the more drastic cuts. The Royal Navy was given a budget of £82,479,000. However, even then there had to be some painful reductions to pay for the capital ship program. Funding was reduced in almost every category except new construction, with victualling and clothing cut by almost £3 million and medical services by close to £1 million.

## FACT, FANTASY AND THE U.S. NAVY

While the British government was trying to come together to face the challenge of the 1916 program, the U.S. government was doing what it did best—splitting apart. The unity that the First World War had temporarily imposed upon American naval policy unraveled between 1919 and 1921. The saddest player in the whole drama was undoubtedly the U.S. Navy. While the Royal Navy was reacting to the American challenge with caution, the General Board seemed to lose all sense of proportion. While Congress and the American people moved away from confrontation, the navy just kept banging its drum louder and louder in support of larger building programs. Just weeks after House and Cecil had reached their agreement in Paris, Benson again argued for extra building. He claimed that the U.S. Navy needed to be as strong as the combined fleets of Britain, France, and Italy, or the combined fleets of Britain and Japan.[29]

This was just the opening shot. In September the General Board studied a plan for a war against the British.[30] It bore no resemblance to any plans the Royal Navy had devised. The Americans assumed that the British would wage a very aggressive campaign, with raids on the East Coast of the United States, the Panama Canal, Cuba, Haiti, Puerto Rico, and St. Thomas. The British were also supposed to send an expeditionary force to Canada and from there to fight a dogged land campaign. In September the General Board told the secretary of the navy that the policy of a "navy second to none" was now inadequate and should be replaced by a grand, new set of objectives: "The United States borders upon two oceans and the protection of our coasts together with the great increase in our merchant marine renders necessary the possession of a Navy by the United States large enough to protect our national interests in both oceans against any probable combination against us."[31] A few weeks later the General Board claimed that the British might launch a preemptive strike to head off America's coming maritime supremacy:

In the past Great Britain has resorted to war to eliminate from competition with her any nation which has seriously threatened her maritime commercial supremacy. The General Board believes that Great Britain will not hesitate to engage in war alone or to enlist the help of Japan, or any other nation against the United States to protect the interests of British maritime commerce when our merchant marine in its growth reaches such magnitude as to threaten or endanger the maritime supremacy of that of Great Britain.[32]

To protect the United States from such a strike the General Board called for a mind-boggling new program, including twelve battleships, sixteen battlecruisers, forty-four scout cruisers, forty-eight destroyer flotilla leaders, 124 destroyers, seven aircraft carriers, and a host of auxiliary vessels.

This last gambit must be seen partly as Admiral Benson's valedictory to the fleet. This unusual and stubborn man stepped down as chief of naval operations on 25 September. His replacement, Admiral Robert Coontz, while not as obsessed with the British, was still a hard-liner.[33] On 10 October the General Board again redefined American naval policy in such a way that it would have entailed overall supremacy.[34]

Under Coontz's direction the U.S. Navy continued to call for increased building programs, though more emphasis was placed on the Japanese. Within one week of his arrival the General Board had sifted through a report that described Japan as an aggressive and warlike power.[35] It was a refrain repeated throughout 1920. Japan was considered dangerously overpopulated and in need of protected markets. It was thought that the Japanese would try to dominate China to provide both an outlet for their excess population and a safe supply of natural resources.[36] The Navy Department tried to combine this fear of Japan with resentment about British behavior.[37] In April 1920, the General Board proposed the construction of an additional two battleships, one battlecruiser, ten scout cruisers, five flotilla leaders, six submarines and two aircraft carriers.[38]

The problem for the U.S. Navy was that while it pressed ahead with these plans, many Americans seemed to lose interest in the fleet. The more the First World War slipped into the background, the less people were interested in naval issues. This public apathy led to a rebirth of Congress' small-navy faction. Routed in 1916, the faction began to flex its muscles again in 1920.[39] A new generation of congressmen arose, men like Senator William E. Borah, Republican of Idaho, and Senator William H. King, Democrat from Utah, who joined forces with old small-navy warhorses like Claude Kitchin and Theodore Burton to attack plans for increasing the navy's strength.[40] They accused the navy of waste and inefficiency and saw no reason for the United States to continue building warships now that Germany had been defeated.

The 1920 presidential election and President Wilson's stroke also contributed to dislocation in American naval policy. In early 1920 Republicans in Congress launched a vicious attack against Daniels' handling of the navy. Using charges by Admiral William Sims as a pretext, the Republicans held hearings from March to May 1920 during which Daniels and others were raked over the coals.[41] Indeed, as long as the election was looming, Congress was unable to agree on any long-term naval policy. Both major party candidates, Republican Warren Harding and Democrat James Cox, resorted to vague platitudes about the fleet during the rare instances when they talked about naval policy.

Once Harding and the Republicans triumphed in the 1920 landslide, however, they were forced to confront the question of America's naval strength. Harding was, on the surface, a backer of a strong navy.[42] His Ohio newspaper had consistently supported larger construction programs. However, Harding seemed unwilling to expend much political capital on the navy. He was much more concerned with domestic matters, and during his administration Congress was able to reassert some authority over naval issues.

The man who dominated much of Congress' efforts was Senator Borah. Borah, who had supported the 1916 program, latched onto the issue of naval disarmament after the First World War. On 14 December 1920 Borah submitted a resolution in the Senate asking the president to work toward an agreement limiting naval armaments with Britain and Japan. The Borah resolution proved to be extremely popular with the American public and press. Support poured in from across the country, and soon others in Congress began echoing his call.

Alas, the American navy still underestimated the power of those massing to oppose its plans. Just six weeks before the election of 1920, the General Board submitted another construction program.[43] This time it called for the building of three battleships, one battlecruiser, thirty regular cruisers, eighteen destroyers, four aircraft carriers, and thirty-two other vessels. Even Borah's call for naval arms control and the groundswell of support that ensued did not seem to ruffle the fleet's feathers. When asked its views on naval disarmament by a member of the Senate, the General Board was unrepentant: "International limitation of armaments is practicable only as personal standards of conduct improve, and . . . the general level of the latter is not yet high enough. No power enjoying a present position of superiority is yet willing to prejudice it by placing unlimited confidence in others."[44]

## PREPARATIONS

The Navy Department would soon be forced to change its tune. The period before the Washington Conference of 1921-1922 was one of the most frustrating in American naval history. The fleet became more and more isolated by more powerful elements in the American government and found its counsel ignored or disregarded. It was the combined, if not coordinated, efforts of congressional opponents of a large navy and Secretary of State Charles Evans Hughes that were responsible for the navy's marginalization.

Many members of Congress, led by Senator Borah, continued to rail against the navy. Heartened by the response to his call for an arms control conference, Borah, who left to posterity one of the most extensive collection of congressional speeches ever, led a steady attack on the fleet's construction programs. Joined by Senators King and Norris, Borah tried to kill off the 1916 program:

We are as a matter of fact in a race for the bankruptcy of civilization. That is the thing that will come if men do not come to their reason before. Bankruptcy stares every nation in the face that engages in that race. . . . When the race is ended and we are bowed down to earth with debt and burdened with taxation, those nations that quit in the race early will be the only nations in the world standing upon their feet and doing business. We cannot engage in this race without ruin.[45]

Similar arguments were brandished in the House of Representatives. Theodore Burton, Theodore Roosevelt's great nemesis, returned to the House in 1921 and continued his lifelong crusade against naval armaments. He found a new legion of supporters, such as William Barkley, Democrat from Kentucky, the Irish-born William Cockran, Democrat from New York, and Thomas Connally, Democrat from Texas. They likewise attacked the 1916 program and proposed freezing spending on all new American naval construction.[46]

The navy was not entirely without support, however. Henry Cabot Lodge, now seventy-one, remained to parry the thrusts of the more emotional opponents of the fleet. Many Republicans also saw little reason to tie the hands of the new Harding administration. With the Republicans maintaining massive majorities in both chambers of Congress, this was a persuasive argument. Representative Patrick Kelley, Republican from Michigan, spoke for many when he warned the House against decreasing the Harding administration's leverage in any upcoming conference.[47] In the end those wanting to halt all American construction were unable to sway the bulk of the Republican Party, and the 1916 program ships continued to be built. However, the groundswell of support that had risen in favor of Borah's proposals made it clear that the administration would have to do something to pacify public opinion.

As Congress became more and more fractious, the navy began to look to the new administration for support. The incoming secretary of the navy, Edwin Denby, gave some cause for hope. Denby had been a representative from Michigan and then a Marine Corps officer during the war. He quickly endorsed the concept of a navy "second to none" and was well liked by many of the professional sailors.[48] The appointment of Theodore Roosevelt, Jr., son of the former president, as assistant secretary also seemed to bode well for the future.

However, the Harding administration did not have a unified naval policy. Realizing his own limitations, Harding appointed a number of very strong-willed men to his Cabinet. Herbert Hoover became secretary of commerce, and Andrew Mellon, the great financier, became secretary of the treasury. These men wanted to rein in government spending, which they considered a drain on the general economy. While some of Harding's other appointments were noticeably less accomplished, these men exercised great influence. The most important appointment for the navy, however, was Charles Evans Hughes' selection as secretary of state.

Hughes came to dominate the administration's naval policy. Having served as governor of New York and then run as the Republicans' presidential nominee in 1916, Hughes was an imposing figure. Later, he would become chief justice of the Supreme Court and duel with Franklin Roosevelt over the fate of the New Deal. Hughes was neither strongly in favor of, nor strongly opposed to, continuing American naval building. Instead, he saw the fleet as the means to an end. The end that most preoccupied him was the Anglo-Japanese Alliance. Hughes considered the Japanese hostile to American interests and believed that the Anglo-Japanese Alliance could make the Japanese more aggressive.

Under Hughes' direction the State Department took on a decidedly anti-Japanese tone. Within a month of Harding's inauguration the director of Far Eastern affairs circulated a memorandum claiming that the "situation of Japan is analogous to that of Germany before the war."[49] By moving the bulk of the American fleet from the Atlantic to the Pacific, the United States might deter the Japanese and, at the same time, lessen Britain's interest in maintaining the Anglo-Japanese Alliance.

Hughes quickly started to put pressure on the British to abrogate the alliance. In the spring and summer of 1921 he had a series of meetings with the British ambassador to the United States, Sir Auckland Geddes, during which he badgered the startled diplomat. Less than a month after becoming secretary of state, Hughes upbraided Geddes about Britain's agreeing to Japanese control of Germany's former Pacific colonies north of the equator. In particular Hughes thought Japan's takeover of the island of Yap a shabby deal.[50]

In June Hughes claimed that Britain might be forced to support Japan's "militaristic party" in China.[51] He was also keen to impress on the British that American public opinion was hostile toward the alliance, at one point hinting that it could provide succor to congressional supporters of Irish independence. Hughes was unrelenting.[52] By September he seemed confident enough to tell Geddes that it was high time the British chose between supporting Japan and supporting America.[53]

All this pressure undoubtedly had a great effect on the British ambassador. Geddes was an unusual man, rather pompous and with a very high opinion of his own cognitive abilities. After just a few weeks in the United States he seemed convinced that he fully understood the American political system and swamped the Foreign Office in London with wordy memoranda.[54] His views generally tended to be alarmist, but the enormous pressure being applied by Hughes seemed to unsettle Geddes. Indeed, Geddes formed an unorthodox opinion of the American. While most people have described Hughes as sober and even plodding, Geddes told the foreign secretary that the American was unbalanced.

In all sobriety and with the fullest realisation of the responsibility attaching to anyone with medical qualifications who make such a statement, I regret to have to inform you that the Secretary of State of the United States is, in my opinion, abnormal mentally and subject to attacks of very mild mania. I do not think that he can be regarded as individually responsible for what he says during these attacks.[55]

The Navy Department would have been very pleased to know that the secretary of state was being so tough. Many in the department seemed just as worried about the Japanese. Denby wrote to Hughes in April asking for his opinion about shifting almost the whole Atlantic fleet to the Pacific.[56] The General Board also spent much of 1921 updating and improving its plans for a war with Japan.[57] Reports circulated within the Navy Department that the Japanese were taking a number of steps to prepare for a conflict, including rushing ahead with the construction of battleships and battlecruisers.[58]

Where the navy split from Hughes was over the question of Anglo-American relations. Suspicion of British intentions was still strong in the Navy Department. In July 1921 the War Plans Division returned to the question of a war between the United States and the Anglo-Japanese Alliance.[59] Once again the prospect of the Royal Navy's launching attacks in the Atlantic was explored. The plan called for American assaults on Nova Scotia, Bermuda, Jamaica, and Trinidad. Hughes had little time for this type of plans. He seemed more than willing to cooperate with the British, provided the Anglo-Japanese Alliance was terminated. The differences between Hughes and the navy can best be seen in the debate over naval parity. Hughes was just as determined as any admiral to reach parity with the Royal Navy. However, he wanted parity with as little pain as possible. He saw no reason to proceed with all the ships of the 1916 program if the British could be persuaded to accept parity at a lower level. The Navy Department, meanwhile, wanted to finish the whole program and then force the British to grant parity.

These differences became accentuated once Harding on 11 July 1921 formally invited the great naval powers to a conference in Washington. The conference was set to discuss both the naval arms control and security issues in the Pacific. Hughes had pushed Harding to act both to help calm domestic unrest about American naval policy and to keep the British from acting first.[60] Once Harding issued his invitations, the Navy Department went into high gear. The General Board undertook an exhaustive study of all the issues to be discussed. Between July and October it issued a steady stream of memoranda outlining the positions it wished to see the administration take. The General Board's world was certainly a dangerous place. As the it said four days after Harding's announcement, no war was "unthinkable."[61] It also believed that the British were determined to follow their historic policy of global domination:[62]

The present British policy, a policy of long-standing and unfailingly persistent application, is to control the markets, the fuel and the communications of the world so that the needs of the empire may always take precedence over the needs of all other political organizations of the world. . . . The British attitude has been one of astonishment tinged with contempt for any who presume to question the justice of that policy. The British shield greed in the shadow of the policy of self-preservation.[63]

The Japanese were seen as equally dangerous but more unstable. Japanese overpopulation made expansion a necessity, with China their outlet of choice.[64] The Japanese ruling classes were naturally militaristic and would seek every opportunity, especially an Anglo-American conflict, to expand their influence in the western Pacific. Some in the Navy Department believed that America needed outright naval superiority to combat the threats posed by Britain and Japan.[65]

However, the General Board seemed content to call for parity with Great Britain. It was, however, an ambitious concept of parity. It wanted not just the entire 1916 program but also one new capital ship annually in 1923, 1924, and 1925 and an additional three aircraft carriers, eighteen cruisers, eighteen destroyers, and twelve submarines.[66] In one of its final plans the General Board proposed allowing the United States to complete the entire 1916 program and at the same time allowing all powers to replace all capital ships more than twenty years old.[67] This would have meant that capital ship construction in every country would have continued unabated.

Hughes was aware of the navy's views. In his private papers are copies of almost all of the Navy Department's proposals.[68] However, Hughes seems to have come to the conclusion that the navy had to be bypassed. Whether he considered the navy hopelessly unrealistic or simply tiresome is unknown, but Hughes decided to determine personally the United States' negotiating position. All of the navy's papers were politely noted and quickly disregarded. There remained a rather pathetic series of exchanges between the State and Navy Departments. State would ask the navy's opinions of many of the points Hughes would make in his dramatic opening address to the conference, and the navy would usually say it disagreed. On 20 October the General Board stated that the issue of naval bases should not be discussed.[69] On 22 October the General Board rejected the idea of a naval building holiday.[70] As late as 3 November the General Board was rejecting the idea that the conference should agree to limit gun calibers on warships.[71] All three of these proposals made their way into the eventual treaty text in one form or the other, generally with strong American support.

The Navy Department was left ignorant of Hughes' proposals until just before the conference opened. Theodore Roosevelt, Jr., assistant secretary of the navy, kept a diary throughout the preparatory period. Not until late October did he realize that Hughes was planning some very radical proposals. Even then Roosevelt was kept in the dark. As late as 25 October he was spending his time drafting the Navy Department's own plan, a plan which Hughes had no intention of following.[72]

Hughes' independence stood in stark contrast to the collective British efforts to prepare for Washington. In early 1921 the British government had given the go-ahead for the construction of eight superdreadnoughts. The government was concerned that the Royal Navy not be swamped by the 1916 program. At the same time the government wanted to go into any conference in as strong a position as possible. The new first lord, Lord Lee of Fareham, who replaced Long in February 1921, admitted as much:

I am really bound in honour to stand by the bargain which I made . . . that if the drastic reductions made last March were accepted by the Admiralty the "replacement" ships could be proceeded with. Apart from that, I could not accept any personal responsibility for a decision that would put us at the mercy of America and Japan at the approaching Conference.[73]

Lee's appointment was a sign that the British were prepared to compromise. He was married to an American and had spent a great deal of time in the United States, where he had many close friends, including the former president, Theodore Roosevelt. Lee had been present when Roosevelt charged up San Juan Hill and the Englishman been awarded the Spanish-American War Medal. He quickly made it clear that he wanted to reach an agreement with the United States.[74] To Lee it was a matter of great urgency; if the United States and Great Britain could not reach an understanding, the peace of the world was threatened:

Apart from the financial and economic impossibility of our engaging, with any hope of success, in an armament race with America, I feel that it would matter little which country emerged victorious (in a military sense) from such an insane encounter—for both nations would be irretrievably ruined and, meanwhile, civilization would have perished.[75]

Under Lee's direction the Admiralty talked almost exclusively of the "One-Power Standard" or "equality with any other power."[76] The Americans were aware of Lee's feelings. In a May 1921 meeting with the American naval attaché in London, Lee made it perfectly clear that he would accept parity with the United States and that the government would not allow the Anglo-Japanese Alliance to damage Anglo-American relations.[77]

Originally a vehicle to contain Russia and France in the Pacific, the Anglo-Japanese Alliance had served the British Empire very well.[78] It allowed the Royal Navy to concentrate in European waters while at the same time provide security for India, Australia, the Malay States, and Hong Kong. It also gave the British some influence over Japanese policy. If the Japanese were left to their own devices, it was feared that they might try to carve up China with Russia. Finally, the Japanese were very proud of their alliance with the world's greatest naval power and would view its abrogation as a severe blow to their prestige.[79] In exchange for these benefits, Britain gave up relatively little. The Japanese had become the largest naval power in the western Pacific and so were more than able to protect themselves against anybody except the Americans.

This was the one major problem with the alliance. Most Americans detested it, seeing it as a possible combination against the United States. Before the First World War the British had gone to great lengths to mollify American concerns. They privately assured the United States that the treaty would never be used against America and forced the Japanese to accept an amendment prohibiting the alliance from being invoked against countries with which Britain had signed an arbitration treaty.[80] The British then tried to negotiate such an arbitration treaty with the Americans. After the First World War the only reason for the British to let the alliance lapse was Americans' unhappiness. This was not an inconsequential point. The Admiralty saw no benefit in antagonizing the United States:[81]

It is almost inconceivable for the British Empire to consider in the future an Alliance with Japan on a basis which can only have for its object protection against the United States. . . . An Alliance or an Entente with the United States based on equality of naval material is, in fact, required to reach the ideals we each aim at.[82]

By 1919, the Admiralty seems to have convinced itself that the alliance was doomed and adjusted its war plans accordingly. Between the end of the First World War and the Washington Conference plans for an Anglo-Japanese war were revised and updated.[83] These new plans were quite elaborate, covering such questions as convoys and Japanese food supply.

The Foreign Office was at first more hopeful. However, Foreign Office opinion, like that in the Admiralty, was decidedly suspicious of the Japanese. Curzon's personal view was that the alliance was needed to keep the Japanese, who were "insidious and unscrupulous," in line.[84] The Foreign Office at first tried to redesign the alliance to make it less offensive to the United States. In doing this it had to rely on the reports filed by Auckland Geddes. The British ambassador in Washington made it perfectly clear that American popular and political opinion was opposed to the alliance in almost any form.[85] By June 1921 Geddes became convinced that unless the alliance were emasculated, the effect upon American opinion would be disastrous.[86] Eventually and somewhat reluctantly, the rest of the Foreign Office reached the same conclusion. However, the Foreign Office realized that getting rid of the alliance was a dangerous move. Curzon, while always interested in improving Anglo-American relations, realized that closer friendship with America could be obtained only at a steep price.

We shall lose the advantages of the Anglo-Japanese Agreement, which have been and are considerable. I do not allude to the obligations of military support which are obsolete, but to the steadying influence which the Agreement has exercised in international politics, the gain to our Eastern policy of having a close alliance with the most powerful Eastern nation, the help given us in war by the Japanese, and the undeviating support which we receive from them in Allied Conferences. I regard the loss of these advantages (if we do lose them) with no small apprehension and am not at all sure that they will be compensated by a temporary conquest of the beaux yeux of America.[87]

The Foreign Office decided that British interests would now best be served by further embroiling the United States in the Pacific. They were very interested when it was reported that American naval strength would be shifted to the Pacific.[88] The Philippines was another case in point. The British had encouraged the United States to take control over this archipelago since the Spanish-American War. The American presence kept other more threatening countries, such as Germany, from controlling a vital strategic area. Now, with reports circulating that the United States might grant the Philippines independence, British policy was to encourage further American control of the archipelago.[89]

By January 1921 the British government was moving more and more into the American camp. The Anglo-Japanese Alliance Committee proposed the following solution:

A careful consideration of all the arguments, both for and against renewal of the Alliance, has resulted in the unanimous conclusion that it should be dropped, and that in its stead should, if possible, be substituted a Tripartite Entente between the United States, Japan and Great Britain. . . . In submitting these recommendations to your Lordship we desire to add that we have approached the question not solely as a matter affecting the Far East, but from the broader standpoint of world politics, which are dominated by our relations with the United States as constituting the prime factor in the maintenance of order and peace throughout the world.[90]

Once Harding had issued his invitation, the British were forced to fuse their naval and Pacific policies into a coherent block. However, there was a great deal of pessimism in the government about whether anything of real substance would be achieved in the upcoming talks. Both the Admiralty and the Foreign Office assumed that the Americans would complete the entire 1916 program.[91] All sixteen of the capital ships authorized in 1916 were under construction by 1921, and the British could not believe that anything would convince the Americans to give them up.[92]

The most depressing thing for the Lloyd George government was the prospect of coming up with the millions needed to match these American ships. The eight new capital ships approved in early 1921, which were supposed to ensure only British parity with the United States, would cost at least an additional £80 million over the next few years. Yet, at the same time the CID was listing "the largest possible reduction in expenditure on armaments" as the goal of the government's arms control policy. Any tax increases, on the other hand, were viewed as "politically undesirable and economically most prejudicial to the nation's interests.[93] With all this economic pressure the idea of fighting for British naval superiority evaporated. While the Cabinet and Admiralty were not thrilled by the prospect of surrendering naval supremacy, they could see no other option: "Neither is it likely that the U.S. would be prepared to agree to anything less than equality with the British Empire, and we are not in a position to make any more favourable demand."[94]

With the British willing to accept parity with the Americans, the next question was the ratio of superiority they would need over Japan. With the Admiralty taking an increasingly anti-Japanese line, the Royal Navy wanted a large measure of supremacy to protect the British Empire in the Pacific. The Admiralty wanted "a total naval strength equal to that of Japan, plus the percentage necessary to give reasonable certainty of success in battle, plus the percentage necessary to compensate us for the disadvantage of operating at a great distance from our main bases . . . plus the percentage necessary to enable us to retain in Home

Waters a force capable of dealing with any European Powers."[95] Eventually the Admiralty opted for a 50 percent advantage over the Japanese, or a 3 to 2 ratio. It was hoped that the Americans would be happy with this ratio and that the naval balance between the three countries could be settled at 3-3-2.

To get such an agreement, the Admiralty was more than willing to sacrifice the Anglo-Japanese Alliance.[96] The policy they pressed for, instead, was "containment." First, the Admiralty wanted increased American involvement to keep the Japanese in line, and, second, it wanted an agreement limiting the establishment of new naval bases in the western Pacific. It was hoped that Japan could be prevented from establishing bases "any further to the southward than Formosa" while at the same time allowing the British to develop Singapore.

The other department to prepare extensively for the conference was the Foreign Office. Like the Admiralty, the Foreign Office was willing to sacrifice the Anglo-Japanese Alliance to get a naval agreement with the United States. If the British had to toe the American line in the Pacific to get a naval arms control agreement, then so be it:

A successful Disarmament Conference may mark an epoch in the history of mankind. But a successful Disarmament Conference is impossible without a successful Pacific Conference preceding it. If the latter is a failure the former will fail also; and failure in either case will not leave matters where they were. It will leave them incomparably and it may be fatally worse. All our efforts therefore should be devoted to creating the antecedent conditions which will make Disarmament possible by making Pacific solutions certain.[97]

Yet, for all their preparatory work the British went into the Washington Conference with little optimism. They mistook Hughes' reticence to have preliminary discussions as a sign of confusion in the American government. Lloyd George thought the preparations for the talks "amateurish in the extreme."[98] It also seemed to the British government that whatever the conference achieved, the full American 1916 program would be built, a large and expensive program of British construction would be started, and the Anglo-Japanese Alliance would have to be ended without any concrete agreements aiding British security in the Pacific. In late September 1921 the American naval attaché in London described the depth of British pessimism.[99] While claiming that the British preferred cooperation with the United States over the Anglo-Japanese Alliance, the attaché made it clear that the British expected few tangible accomplishments from the upcoming talks. The U.S. Embassy in London described British expectations in a similar vein.[100] At this point the British government had no idea of Charles Evans Hughes' dramatic plans. If it did, it would have realized that of all people, the American secretary of state was about to give it almost everything that it wanted with relatively little cost.

## THE WASHINGTON CONFERENCE

Charles Evans Hughes' speech opening the Washington Conference on 12 November 1921 is one of the more famous in diplomatic history. In place of high-minded platitudes he offered the assembled dignitaries a detailed plan to halt the embryonic naval building race between the United States, Great Britain, and Japan. It was a bold and savvy gamble that not only determined the course of the conference but also set the tone for negotiations between the major naval powers for the next decade.[101] The scope of Hughes' plan took almost the whole hall by surprise. First, he offered to scrap every American capital ship laid down as part of the 1916 program. Then he told the British and the Japanese that they would have to halt all capital ship construction and scrap a large number of older vessels and that the three countries should stabilize their capital ship strengths using the famous 5-5-3 ratio. Hughes proposed maintaining this balance by instituting a ten-year capital ship building holiday and regulating building afterward. While Hughes did not explicitly say so, in exchange for this plan he wanted a Pacific settlement that would take into account American displeasure with the Anglo-Japanese Alliance.

After Hughes' speech almost three months were needed to hammer out the details of a final settlement. The naval discussions were complicated by Japanese and French objections. The Japanese were unhappy with the 5-5-3 ratio and wanted a capital ship fleet 70 percent as strong as Britain's or America's. For the first month of the talks they held firm. The British delegation, however, led by Arthur Balfour, who was assisted by Lord Lee and Admiral Beatty, made a united front with the Americans against the Japanese. Eventually, the Japanese were unwilling to risk being blamed for the conference's collapse and grudgingly accepted the 5-5-3 ratio. As a means of saving public face they asked for, and were granted, permission to retain the *Mutsu*, Japan's newest battleship. Under Hughes' plan the *Mutsu* was to be scrapped, so in compensation the United States was allowed to keep USS *West Virginia* and USS *Colorado*, two of the 1916 program battleships, while the British were given the right to build two new capital ships.

The Americans, British, and Japanese then hammered out an agreement regulating the construction of new fortifications in the Pacific. The Japanese wanted to protect their security in the western Pacific, while at the same time the Americans and British wanted to make sure that the Japanese did not establish any naval bases in Germany's old colonies. In the end new fortifications were banned from a large area. The British were allowed to build at Singapore but were forbidden from developing any other of their holdings to the northeast, Hong Kong included. The United States renounced the right to put any more fortifications on either the Philippines or Guam, while the Japanese promised to build new bases only on their home territory, excluding Formosa and the Ryukyu Islands.

French objections had as much to do with hurt pride as strategic considerations. The French delegation to the conference was the most senior in Washington, including both the present prime minister, Aristide Briand, a former prime minister, Rene Viviani and France's long-serving ambassador to the United States, Jules Jusserand. The French still considered themselves a major naval power, even though French naval building had been drastically curtailed since 1914. The French felt slighted when Hughes ignored them in his opening address and were even more unhappy when it became clear that the Americans and British wanted France to be allowed a navy much smaller than Japan's. After making a great fuss, the French, following Hughes' personal intercession with Briand, eventually gave in and accepted a capital ship ratio of 1.75, the same as Italy's.

Once the French gave in, the naval part of the conference was as good as over. After scrapping, the Royal Navy would retain twenty-two capital ships, weighing 580,400 tons, the United States would retain eighteen, weighing 525,800 tons and the Japanese ten, weighing 301,320 tons.[102] The larger British allowance was to compensate the Royal Navy for its older and less sophisticated ships. Eventually, the Americans and British were to be restricted to fifteen capital ships weighing no more than 525,000 tons, the Japanese to nine ships weighing 315,000 tons, and the French and Italians to five ships weighing 175,000 tons. Also, all new capital ships were to be limited to 35,000 tons and could carry nothing larger than sixteen-inch guns.

Auxiliary ship strength, including cruisers, destroyers, aircraft carriers, and submarines, was also discussed in Washington. Hughes had put forward no specific auxiliary ship plan in his opening address, but he hoped that an agreement could be reached in negotiation. His expectations foundered on the submarine question. The British, after their experiences in the First World War, were particularly interested in limiting the use of submarines and would have liked to see them banned. The French, however, still angry after accepting what they considered to be an insulting capital ship allowance, refused to agree to any meaningful submarine limitation. In the end the issue was dropped.

More progress was made on the issue of aircraft carriers. At the time of the Washington Conference these vessels, which would eventually come to dominate naval warfare, were still in their infancy. No country was quite sure how many it would need and for what they would be used. After some discussion the delegates agreed to relatively generous aircraft carrier tonnage limitations. The United States and Great Britain were allowed 135,000 tons, Japan 81,000 tons, and France and Italy 60,000 tons. At first it was hoped to limit all aircraft carriers to a maximum of 27,000 tons, but the United States asked to be allowed to rebuild some of the 1916 program capital ships as carriers, and so the maximum was raised to 33,000 tons.

The final two classes of auxiliary ship that were discussed were cruisers and destroyers. Hughes' original idea was that such vessels should be subject to the 5-5-3 ratio. The British, however, believed that the Royal Navy needed considerably more of these ships than anybody else. Unlike the United States, Great Britain was dependent on overseas trade for vital supplies of raw materials and foodstuffs. Unlike Japan, the British Empire's trade routes were worldwide, stretching from the North and South Atlantic, through the Mediterranean and Indian Oceans, and into the Pacific. Without a significant advantage in auxiliary craft the government believed that British trade could be savaged.

When Hughes tried to extend the capital ship ratio to auxiliary ships, the British were therefore quick to object. The Royal Navy had on hand a substantial advantage in cruisers, and the British proposed that all building should be halted, and the present balance frozen. Eventually, the British wanted the Royal Navy to have fifty cruisers, the United States thirty, and Japan eighteen. There was little chance of this happening. Having secured the right to equality with Great Britain in capital ships, the Americans were not going to renounce this right for auxiliaries. All the conference could finally agree upon was technical cruiser limitations. From now on, a cruiser could not exceed 10,000 tons or mount anything larger than eight-inch guns. There were no restrictions placed on destroyers. At the time the auxiliary ship agreements, or lack thereof, were ignored in the rush to celebrate the Washington Treaty. However, the inability of the United States and Great Britain to agree on a ratio for auxiliary ships would soon return to jeopardize Anglo-American relations.

The naval settlements made up only half of the Washington Treaty. Just as controversial were the Pacific settlements. These were enshrined in two agreements; the Four-Power and Nine-Power Treaties. The Four-Power Treaty was an attempt by the British and Americans to find a face-saving way for Britain to withdraw from the Anglo-Japanese Alliance. During the talks the Japanese, on a number of occasions, approached the British delegation with requests to renew the alliance. After Hughes' offer to scrap the entire 1916 program, this was not going to happen. Instead, the British and Americans came up with a nonaggression treaty whereby each signatory pledged itself to respect the others' possessions. It was eventually made into a Four-Power Treaty by the inclusion of the French, an attempt to comfort French feelings after their earlier reverses. The Japanese, with no other options, grudgingly accepted this new arrangement.

The second Pacific agreement was the Nine-Power Treaty. It was an attempt to preempt any coming trouble over China but was really more an exercise in public relations than anything else. The delegates agreed to a group of nebulous principles that were intended to protect the sovereignty of the Chinese state from foreign encroachment. However, the Nine-Power Treaty had no method of enforcement, and the Japanese believed that it did not apply to Manchuria, the part of China they were intent on controlling. In the end it was the least important understanding reached in Washington.

The signing of most treaties is usually accompanied by a degree of hyperbole, yet few have matched the euphoria that surrounded the end of the Washington Conference on 6 February 1922. To many, the naval limitation agreements and the Four-Power and Nine-Power Treaties heralded a new era in international relations. Now, it was hoped, national cooperation and disarmament would take the place of alliances and arms races. President Harding, in his closing address, stated that the treaties marked "the beginning of a new and better epoch in human affairs."[103] Arthur Balfour in a similar vein described the treaties as an "absolute unmixed benefit to mankind, which carried no seeds of future misfortune."[104]

History, however, has not been as kind to the Washington Conference as Harding and Balfour might have hoped. Since the Second World War, most opinions about the agreements reached at Washington have oscillated between ambivalence and hostility. The American delegation has generally received relatively moderate criticism, and on a number of occasions Hughes' efforts have been portrayed sympathetically.[105] The secretary of state is seen as a man struggling gamely to satisfy domestic political critics, end the Anglo-Japanese Alliance, and gain naval parity for the Americans. From these perspectives his performance was a success of some kind. The treaties were all ratified relatively quickly by the Senate and received overwhelming popular support. The United States and Great Britain were now established as equals in capital ship strength, and at the same time the Anglo-Japanese Alliance was replaced by a rather innocuous nonaggression pact.

Praise for Hughes' tactical maneuverings, however, has not generally been extended to his strategic thinking. While Hughes got what he wanted at Washington, this has not always been seen as the best thing for the United States or the world. The Washington agreements have been called inherently unstable and even dangerous. In fact, American critics of the Washington Conference appeared as soon as the meeting broke up. Originally, the U.S. Navy was most bitter. Admiral Benson, now retired but in no way mellowed, thought the agreements left the British "decidedly superior" to the American navy.[106] The secretary of the navy poetically described the impact of the agreements on the fleet as "the worst smash it ever got."[107] Even ten years after the fact many in the American navy saw the Washington Conference as a great defeat. Admiral William Moffett, one of the most respected officers of his day, claimed in 1933 that "Uncle Sam lost everything but his shirt tail when he signed the Washington Treaty."[108]

In the immediate aftermath of the Second World War these views received even more support. Dean Acheson described the Washington Conference as a "disaster."[109] This type of criticism was aimed at the idealism of the Washington Conference, which supposedly left the U.S. Navy with an inadequate level of superiority over the Japanese. Upon reflection, however, these views seem harsh. The Washington Conference gave the U.S. Navy two crucial things that it had always lacked. First, it made equality with Great Britain the fleet's accepted standard of strength. Since the American Revolution the U.S. Navy had never been given a realistic "policy." Now it had something to aim at that both the public and Congress could understand, if not wholeheartedly support. Second, the agreements removed Congress temporarily from the equation. One should not hastily assume that Congress would have engaged in a capital ship building race with either Great Britain or Japan. The average legislator's instinct was to resist building expensive ships, and the longer the war slipped into the background, the more this instinct reappeared. During the 1920s, as the United States fell further and further behind Britain and Japan in cruiser strength, Congress waited for years before approving even a paper cruiser program. Secretary of State Hughes understood Congress' basic instinct not to build up the fleet and at Washington did his best to neutralize it. What critics like Benson and Acheson have overlooked is that without Washington all bets were off, and the U.S. Navy might have slipped back down the world's naval rankings just as it did after the administration of Theodore Roosevelt.

In the last few decades the critics of the American position at the Washington Conference have been more measured. Some have praised the naval agreements while dwelling upon the inadequacies of the Pacific settlements. Supposedly, the Washington agreements left the Japanese too secure in the western Pacific while providing for a dangerous gap between America's naval strength and its commitments to China.[110] In particular the agreement prohibiting the United States from building more fortifications on the Philippines and Guam, coupled with the Nine-Power Treaty, seems contradictory.[111] Again, these criticisms might not be entirely realistic. If Congress was reluctant to appropriate funds to build warships, it was even more averse to spending money on projects outside America that had no possibility of employing the hometown voter. Before the First World War Congress starved America's foreign bases of cash while lavishing money on home ports. Even during the numerous war scares with Japan the Philippines and Guam were not properly funded. Also after Washington the United States was still allowed to develop its naval facilities in Hawaii. A strong American base there coupled with an equally strong British establishment at Singapore would have allowed the two countries to choke off the supply of many vital raw materials to Japan.

Inasmuch as the Japanese could now protect their main fleet by keeping it close to home, Japan was in a safer position. However, the First World War demonstrated that a country needed more than an intact main battle fleet. The Royal Navy was dominant throughout the war, but Britain was almost defeated through an assault on its trade. What was true for Britain was doubly true for Japan—especially in the case of oil. At the time of the Washington Conference, Japan imported almost all its oil from the United States. The only other source within close proximity to Japan was the Dutch East Indies. However, if the Americans decided to cut off supplies, a strong base at Hawaii coupled with a powerful British facility at Singapore would have been more than adequate to cut off the flow of oil to Japan.

What the United States really gave up in Washington was the right to build new, expensive naval facilities in the Pacific that would have allowed the U.S. Navy to fight the Japanese fleet in the western Pacific. Perhaps, if Washington had never occurred, sometime between 1922 and 1936 Congress would have appropriated the vast sums needed to fight such an aggressive campaign. If it had done so, it would have run counter to the whole history of American naval appropriation. It was a risk that Hughes was wisely unwilling to run.

If the critics of American policy at Washington have generally been measured, those displeased with British policy have often been scathing. Perhaps the most controversial British decision was agreeing to the capital ship limitation ratios. Naval supremacy had been a British policy for centuries and had been thought vital to Germany's defeat in the First World War. Recognizing another power as an equal, even if it was the United States, was bound to cause some resentment. Admiral Wemyss, the former first sea lord, felt aggrieved. He remained convinced that Britain should maintain naval supremacy, even if it involved a building race with the United States.[112] Wemyss' position has some support. Corelli Barnett has described the Washington ratios as a "disastrous mistake" and the conference as "one of the major catastrophes of English history . . . which was to exercise a cumulative and decisive effect on the future of English power."[113] Paul Kennedy speaks of Hughes' proposals as arousing "the most angry protests from the Admiralty . . . for the first time for centuries the Royal Navy had declared itself content with mere parity rather than naval mastery," while Dopson has claimed that the acceptance of parity was "not agreeable to most navy chiefs."[114] Even Arthur Marder has characterized the Washington agreements as "not a good bargain" for the British.[115]

These objections are in many ways as shaky as the ones directed at the American delegation. Far from arousing anger in the Admiralty, Hughes' offer was greeted with a sense of relief. The British delegation at Washington included the first lord of the Admiralty, the first sea lord and other senior British naval officers. Had they accepted the 5-5-3 ratio more quickly it would have been unseemly.[116] This was because Hughes, in his opening address, offered the British more than they had ever imagined.

Before the conference began, both the Cabinet and the Admiralty had come to believe that capital ship parity with the Americans was inevitable. However, both also believed that the United States was bound to complete the full 1916 program. This meant that the Lloyd George government, whatever the outcome of the conference, was expecting to find a massive amount of money to build an equivalent force. When Hughes opened the conference by offering to scrap the whole 1916 program, it was as if British prayers had been answered.[117] Hughes was offering to destroy 845,740 tons of American capital ships, while the Royal Navy needed to scrap only 583,375 tons, mostly made up of nineteen old, obsolete vessels and a paper program of new construction. Hughes had offered the British everything they wanted, and it cost almost nothing. There was no possibility that the British delegation, including high Admiralty officers, would reject the 5-5-3 ratio:

The British Delegation are fully in accord with the proposals of the United States Government in regard to capital ships to be retained, arrested in construction and scrapped respectively by the British Empire, the United States and Japan in the immediate future, and wish to record their sincere appreciation of the high motives with actuated the United States Government in making these proposals which involve them in heavy relative financial losses.[118]

Even the most pessimistic paper to come out of the Admiralty at this time never challenged the new ratios.[119] What Admiralty objections there were centered on the ten-year holiday. Beatty and others believed that such a holiday would seriously damage Britain's shipbuilding capacity.[120] Beatty was opposed not by the Americans, however, but by the British Cabinet. The Cabinet was so pleased by Hughes' proposals that it wanted to do nothing that could slow down the conference's momentum.[121] Building new battleships seemed to the Cabinet to be an expense that Great Britain could do without. All was not lost for Beatty, however; the Japanese eventually came to his rescue. By demanding to keep the *Mutsu*, their newest battleship, the Japanese caused some alterations in Hughes' proposals. In exchange the Americans kept two battleships of the 1916 program, while the British were allowed to build two completely new vessels during the ten-year holiday.[122]

One of the problems with criticizing British acceptance of the 5-5-3 ratio is that at the time no one opposed it. Even Winston Churchill, who had been the Cabinet's strongest supporter of continuing naval supremacy, accepted Hughes' proposal. Churchill was even willing to sacrifice the Anglo-Japanese Alliance to keep the Americans happy.[123] He maintained that Great Britain could agree to Washington but still retain supremacy through superiority in auxiliary ships:

[Churchill] stated that it would be nothing less than a calamity to surrender our sea supremacy which we had held for so many centuries to any other power, and that he could not agree to any such decision; that he was not of the opinion that it was necessary to have a superiority of the Post-Jutland design; that the superiority might be made up of a proper proportion of other units—cruisers, destroyers and particularly submarines.[124]

At the time Churchill was alone in believing this was possible. The Admiralty scoffed at his plan, believing that the balance of capital ship strength was what really mattered.[125] Churchill, however, would cling to his beliefs throughout the 1920s, ultimately with disastrous repercussions.

If one accepts that the 5-5-3 ratio, or some kind of agreement establishing capital ship parity, was inevitable, then the naval clauses of the Washington Conference were decidedly advantageous to the Royal Navy. After deciding that the Royal Navy needed a 50 percent margin of capital ship superiority over the Japanese, the Washington Conference gave the British 60 percent. The Washington agreements also gave the British better than a two-power standard and total dominance in European waters. A combined Franco-Italian capital ship force would be less than 70 percent as strong as the Royal Navy's. Even a Franco-Japanese combination would have been smaller than the Royal Navy. It is hard to imagine the British obtaining better ratios of strength in a world with unrestrained building.

The British were also generally successful in shaping the treaties' auxiliary ship clauses. Both the Admiralty and the Cabinet believed that Great Britain had a special need for auxiliary ships, especially destroyers and cruisers. Hughes, however, wanted the capital ship ratio to be extended to auxiliary ships. During negotiations the British refused to compromise, and in the end there was no explicit agreement calling for auxiliary parity. There were also no numerical restrictions placed on the building of destroyers and cruisers, another British victory. There was an agreement to limit aircraft carrier construction, with Britain and the United States restricted to 135,000 tons. However, all earlier aircraft carrier construction, in which the British had a big lead, was excluded from the allowances so the Royal Navy could start from scratch. The one area where the British delegation was noticeably unsuccessful was in limiting submarines. Ideally, it would have liked to see these vessels outlawed. The French, however, refused to accept any limitations, and in the end the conference could agree on nothing. It was a rare setback for the British but at the time was forgotten in the approving clamor.

If the British were successful in shaping the naval clauses, they had a more difficult time with the Pacific questions. The scrapping of the Anglo-Japanese Alliance and the naval bases agreement have both been seen as dangerous British concessions.[126] The ending of the alliance has received the most criticism. The Four-Power Treaty was a "mere understanding"[127] and "a poor substitute for a concrete alliance."[128] British possessions in the Pacific were now no longer protected by Japanese power but subject to the whims of the fickle American republic.

There is certainly some substance to these remarks. It is true that in sacrificing the Anglo-Japanese Alliance to appease the Americans, the British both insulted and angered the Japanese. Yet, it is hard to see another option for the British. There was almost no support in the British government for maintaining the alliance. Even Winston Churchill, with his fondness for naval supremacy, was more than willing to sacrifice the Japanese to keep the Americans happy.[129] Within the empire there was also little support for maintaining the alliance in any meaningful form. At the 1921 Imperial Conference the issue received a full airing. This meeting is often seen as a turning point in the debate over the Anglo-Japanese Alliance.[130] On one side were those hostile to the agreement, including South Africa and Canada. These dominions were extremely sensitive to American concerns and argued strongly against continuing to ally with Japan.[131] Roskill goes as far as to call the Canadians part of an "American lobby," and Barnett says they were the party "which finally sank the Japanese Alliance."[132]

Supposedly opposed to this group were those in favor of the alliance, including the Australians and New Zealanders. Yet, these distinctions are somewhat artificial. It is true that the Australians, led by Prime Minister William Hughes, called for the renewal of the Anglo-Japanese Alliance. However, at the same time Hughes made an impassioned plea to make the agreement less offensive to the United States:

Any future Treaty with Japan, to be satisfactory to Australia, must specifically exclude
the possibility of a war with the United States of America. . . . In any future Treaty we
must guard against even the suspicion of hostility and unfriendliness to the United States
. . . the only path of safety for the British Empire is a path on which she can walk together with America.[133]

Reshaping the alliance in the manner proposed by the Australians was impossible. The Americans were determined to see it ended and would not have
accepted any naval agreement with the British otherwise. No one, not the Admiralty, Foreign Office, Colonial Office, or the major dominions, wanted the alliance to be extended in its present form if that was the case.

If one accepts the fact that the Anglo-Japanese Alliance was doomed, then
the remaining Pacific agreements were advantageous to the British. Unlike
America and Japan, Great Britain would not be prohibited from establishing
naval bases in important strategic areas. While the United States could not develop the Philippines or Guam, and the Japanese could not develop the Ryukyus
or Formosa, the British were able to exempt Singapore from the agreement. The
only British base of any note to fall in the exclusion zone was Hong Kong, but
there were no plans to build there. Once again the agreements at Washington
had met or exceeded the Admiralty's earlier expectations

Those who criticize British choices have yet to propose a realistic alterna-
tive. The choice confronting the Lloyd George government was clear. It could
keep the Anglo-Japanese Alliance, dash any hopes of reaching a naval settlement with the United States, seriously damage relations inside the empire, embark on an enormously expensive round of naval construction, and hope that the
United States stopped building once the 1916 program was completed. Such a
course of action was fraught with peril. Rejecting America's claim to parity was
probably the one thing that would have guaranteed that the American Congress
continue naval building. If the United States pressed ahead, the British, even
combined with the Japanese, could not have kept up. The Admiralty estimated
that if no agreement was reached, American construction would have been able
to overwhelm the British by the late 1920s.[134]

One of the problems with the Washington Naval Conference is that it never
lived-up to its high-toned rhetoric. It did not prevent the next great naval war
and provided only a temporary reprieve against naval building. It did not usher
in a "new order" of sea power. Yet, to consider it a failure for these reasons is
harsh. The Washington Conference, and the whole naval arms control process,
were considerably more beneficial than harmful to both the United States and
Great Britain. The security of both nation's was protected and a useless naval
building race was preempted. Within the confines of realistic expectations, the
Washington Conference was an important success.

## NOTES

1. Theodore Roosevelt Jr. Mss, Diary, 12 November 1921.

2. H. Sprout and M. Sprout, *Toward a New Order of Sea Power*, p.52.

3. Lloyd George Mss 60/3/22, "Notes on the Peace Strength of the U.S. Navy," November 1919.

4. ADM 167/59, Memorandum, 17 July 1919.

5. ADM 116/1773, Memorandum, 19 June 1919.

6. ADM 1/8592/131 A, "Admiralty Policy and the League of Nations," 11 August 1920.

7. Beatty Mss 8/1, Plans Division Memorandum, 4 January 1921.

8. Lloyd George Mss 195/2/1 "State of Trade since the Armistice." See also ADM 116/3448, "Statistics Prepared for the British Delegation."

9. Beatty Papers, Tennyson d'Eyncourt to Beatty, 3 December 1920.

10. Lloyd George Mss 192/1/5, Draft Minutes, 14 December 1920.

11. Cecil Mss #51131, Journal Entry, 26 March 1919.

12. ADM 116/3448 , "Statistics Prepared for the British Delegation."

13. ADM 116/1775, "Naval Policy and Construction," 22 November 1920.

14. ADM 1/8549/18, Memorandum re Postwar Fleet, September 1919.

15. ADM 167/61, DNI Memoranda, 1, 6 May 1920.

16. ADM 116/1774, "Post-War Naval Policy," 12 August 1919.

17. ADM 116/1774, "Naval Policy and Expenditure," 24 October 1919.

18. ADM 116/1772, "Naval Policy" 7 January 1920.

19. Beatty Mss 13/28, Draft Memorandum 1920-1921 Naval Estimates.

20. S Roskill, *Naval Policy between the Wars*, vol. 1, pp. 42-44.

21. Beatty Papers, Beatty to Long, 8 July 1920.

22. ADM 167/61, Memorandum, 6 May 1920.

23. Ibid.

24. ADM 116/1776, Memorandum, 22 November 1920.

25. ADM 167/61, Staff Memorandum, 6 May 1920.

26. Beatty Papers, Beatty to Long, 13 December 1920.

27. Beatty Papers, Lloyd George to Long, 14 December 1920.

28. Lloyd George Mss F 192/1/5, Minutes of CID Meeting, 14 December 1920.

29. Daniels Mss, Series 2, Benson to Wilson, 5 May 1919, Benson to Daniels, 5 May 1919. See also Benson Mss #39, "Naval Armaments," May 1919.

30. GBSF 425, "The Strategy of the Atlantic," September 1919.

31. SCCCNO 138-9, General Board Letter, 11 September 1919.

32. GBSF 240-2, Memorandum, 22 September 1919.

33. R. Love ed., *The Chiefs of Naval Operations*, pp. 23-35.

34. GBSF 240-2, Memorandum, 10 October 1919.

35. GB Hearings, "Conditions in Japan," 1 October 1919.

36. FDR Mss ASN. General Correspondence—Japan, 13 January 1920; SCCCNO File 178, Gleaves Memorandum, 8 September 1920.

37. SCCCNO 138-12, Plans Division Memorandum, 8 June 1920.

38. GBSF 420-2, Memorandum, 2 April 1920.

39. W. Braisted, *The United States Navy in the Pacific 1909-1922*, pp. 491-504

40. CR, vol. 59, pp. 4699-4700, 22 March 1920 and pp. 6161-62, 27 April 1920.

41. FDR Mss ASN, Sims Hearings Transcripts and Notes, March-May 1920. See also P. Coletta, "Naval Lessons of the Great War: The William Sims-Josephus Daniels Controversy," *American Neptune*.

42. R. G. Kaufman, *Arms Control During the Pre-Nuclear Era*, pp. 28-29.

43. GBSF 420-2, General Board Memorandum, 24 September 1920.

44. GBSF 446, General Board, 19 January 1921.

45. CR, vol. 61, Senate, Norris speech, 13 May 1921, p. 1415.

46. CR, vol. 61, House, 25, 26 April 1921.

47. CR, vol. 61, 26 April 1921, p. 685.

48. P. E. Coletta, *American Secretaries of the Navy*, vol. 2, pp. 583-604.

49. State Department, Box 7496, 8.11/30/131, Director of Far Eastern Affairs, 21 April 1921.

50. Hughes Mss, Reel 122, p. 179, Memorandum, 12 April 1921.

51. Ibid., p. 212. Memorandum, 23 June 1921.

52. Ibid., Memorandum, 6 July 1921.

53. Ibid., p. 234, Memorandum, 20 September 1921.

54. FO 371/4612, Geddes Letter, 18 October 1920.

55. Lloyd George Mss 13/2/19, Geddes to Curzon, 15 April 1921.

56. State Department, Box 7496, 811.30/53-304/85, Denby to Hughes, 15 April 1921.

57. GB Hearings, Recommendations, 3 September 1921. See also WPL 1, War Portfolio, Orange War Plans, July 1921.

58. Rodgers Mss, Box 34, "Extracts," 1 July 1921.

59. WPL-1, War Portfolio, Red-Orange Plan, 1 July 1921.

60. Castle Mss, Diary, 21 December 1922.

61. GBSF 420-2, Memorandum, 15 July 1921.

62. GBDC, Series 1, "Limitation of Naval Armaments," 23 August 1921; Series 1, "Limitation of Naval Armaments," 12 September 1921; Series 1, Report of the General Board, September 1921.

63. GBDC Series 1, "Limitation of Naval Armaments," 23 August 1921.

64. Ibid., 12 September 1921

65. GBDC Series 1, "Memorandum," 13 August 1921.

66. GBSF 420-2, "Naval Policy" Memorandum, 15 July 1921.

67. Hughes Mss, Reel 125, Memorandum, 11 October 1921.

68. Hughes Mss, Reel 125, p. 370, Memorandum, 11, 14 October 1921.

69. Hughes Mss, Reel 125, General Board Memorandum, 20 October 1921.

70. TR Jr., Mss, "WNC," General Board Memorandum, 22 October 1921.

71. Hughes Mss, Reel 125, General Board Memorandum, 3 November 1921.

72. TR Jr., Mss, "Diary," 20, 21, 24 October 1921.

73. Lloyd George Mss 31/2/61, Lee to Lloyd George, 16 July 1921.

74. Lloyd George Mss 31/2/52, Lee to Lloyd George, 19 March 1921.

75. Lloyd George Mss 31/2/50, Lee to Lloyd George, 10 February 1921.

76. ADM 116/1776, Admiralty Memorandum for Cabinet, 28 February 1921.

77. SNGC 7266-275, Naval Attaché to ONI, 19 May 1921.

78. FO 371/5359, Sir C. Eliot to Curzon, 17 June 1920; Wellesley Memorandum, 1 September 1920.

79. FO 371/5359, Eliot to Curzon, 17 June 1920.

80. FO 371/5359, 13 July 1911.

81. ADM 116/3124, "Changes in War Plans," 12 January 1920.

82. ADM 116/1774, "Naval Policy," 13 February 1920.

83. ADM 1/8571/295, "Naval Situation in the Far East," 1919. See also Beatty Mss 8/1/4, "War Plans," 4 January 1921; ADM 116/3124, "Changes in War Plans," 12 January 1920.

84. Lloyd George Mss 192/1/5, Minutes of CID Meeting, 14 December 1920.

85. BFP Documents, vol. 14, # 24. See also 162, 175.

86. BFP Documents, vol. 14, #294.

87. Ibid., #405.

88. Lloyd George Mss 210/2/11, "American Policy in the Far East," 16 June 1921.

89. BFP Documents, vol. 14, #404.

90. Ibid., # 212.

91. FO 371/4614, "US Naval Appropriations," 11 November 1920.

92. ADM 116/3447, Memorandum by DNI, 25 June 1921. See also Memorandum, 4 July 1921.

93. ADM 116/3445, CID Memorandum, October 1921.

94. ADM 116/3447, Memorandum by DNI, 25 June 1921.

95. ADM 116/3445, Lee Memorandum, 5 October 1921.

96. Ibid.

97. BFP Documents, vol. 14, #337.

98. WSC vol. 4, Companion, p. 1557, Lloyd George to Churchill, 18 July 1921.

99. TR Jr., Mss, "WNC," Naval Attaché Report, 29 September 1921.

100. Castle Mss, "England 1920-1925," Boylston to Castle, 7 October 1921.

101. T. Buckley, *The United States and the Washington Conference 1921-22*; R. Dingman, *Power in the Pacific,* pp. 196-214; Roskill, *Naval Policy between the Wars,* vol. 1, pp. 300-330; Kaufman, *Arms Control During the Pre-Nuclear Era,* pp. 43-68; J. MacDonald, "The Washington Conference and the Naval Balance of Power," in J. Hattendorf, R. Jordan eds. *Maritime Strategy and the Balance of Power, Britain and America in the 20th Century.*

102. Roskill, *Naval Policy between the Wars*, vol. 1, p. 331.

103. Buckley, *The United States and the Washington Conference 1921-22*, p. 172.

104. Roskill, *Naval Policy between the Wars*, vol. 1, p. 330.

105. M. J. Pusey, *Charles Evans Hughes*, pp. 507-22

106. Daniels Mss, Series 2, Benson to Daniels, 16 March 1922.

107. Roskill, *Naval Policy between the Wars*, vol. 1, p. 333.

108. FDR Mss, Official File, Bureau of Aeronautics, Moffett Speech, 18 February 1933.

109. Dingman, *Power in the Pacific*, p. 216.

110. Buckley, *The United States and the Washington Conference 1921-22*, pp. 188-190; B. Glad, *Charles Evans Hughes and the Illusions of Innocence*, pp. 325-326; Kaufman, *Arms Control During the Pre-Nuclear Era*, p. 68.

111. C. Hall, *Britain, America and Arms Control 1921-1937*, p. 30.

112. Wemyss, W., "Washington and After," *Nineteenth Century*.

113. C. Barnett, *The Collapse of British Power*, pp. 271-272.

114. P. Kennedy, *The Rise and Fall of British Naval Mastery*, p.325; A. P. Dobson, *Anglo-American Relations in the 20th Century*, p. 51.

115. A. J. Marder, *Old Friends, New Enemies*, vol. 1, p. 6.

116. Domville Mss, Diary.

117. BFP Documents vol. 14, #448, Balfour to Curzon, 24 November 1921.

118. ADM 116/2149, 13 November 1921.

119. ADM 116/1776, Oliver Memorandum, 21 November 1921.

120. BFP Documents, vol. 14 #417, Balfour to Curzon. See also ADM 116/1776, Oliver Memorandum, 30 November 1921.

121. ADM 116/3445, Lloyd George to Balfour, 15 November 1921.

122. BFP Documents, vol. 14, #417. See also #s 463, 494, 501-4.

123. WSC, vol. 4, Companion 3, Churchill Memorandum, 4 July 1921; Cabinet Minutes, 30 May 1921.

124. Beatty Mss 13/28/14, Notes of CID Meeting, 14 December 1920.

125. ADM 116/3442, "Battleship vs. Submarine," 16 December 1920. See also Beatty Mss 13/28/14.

126. C. J. Lowe and M. L. Dockrill, *The Mirage of Power*, p. 303.

127. M. Beloff, *Imperial Sunset, Britain's Liberal Empire*, p. 336.

128. Hall, *Britain, America and Arms Control*, p. 30.

129. Lloyd George Mss 192/1/5, Minutes of CID Meeting, 14 December 1920.

130. Roskill, *Naval Policy between the Wars*, vol. 1, pp. 292-99.

131. BFP Documents, vol. 14, # 261.

132. Barnett, *The Collapse of British Power*, p. 266.

133. Command Papers, # 14, 1921.

134. ADM 116/3448, "Statistics prepared for the British Delegation."

# 8

# The Geneva Conference. A Crisis in Anglo-American Relations

No doubt it is quite right in the interests of peace to go on talking about war with the United States being "unthinkable." Everyone knows that this is not true . . . We do not wish to put ourselves in the power of the United States. We cannot tell what they might do if at some future date they were in a position to give us orders about our policy, say, in India, or Egypt, or Canada . . . tonnage parity means that Britain can be starved into obedience to any American decree. I would neither trust America to command, nor England to submit. Evidently on the basis of American naval superiority speciously disguised as parity immense dangers overhang the future of the world.[1]

Winston Churchill, 20 July 1927

We have not only a long coastline, distant outlying possessions, a foreign commerce unsurpassed in importance, and foreign investments unsurpassed in amount . . . but we are also bound by international treaty to defend the Panama Canal. Having few fueling stations, we require ships of large tonnage, and having scarcely any merchant vessels capable of mounting 5 or 6 inch guns, it is obvious that, based on needs, we are entitled to a larger number of warships than a nation having these advantages.[2]

Calvin Coolidge, 11 November 1928

## THE CALM BEFORE THE STORM: 1922-1926

Most Americans viewed the results of the Washington Conference with a great deal of satisfaction. Popular opinion strongly backed the agreements, and even after some moaning, a large majority of the Senate voted to ratify the treaties.[3] Only the U.S. Navy seemed unimpressed. While the Washington Conference gave the fleet something it had always craved, the right to equality with Great Britain in capital ships, it did not cure the navy's chronic political weakness. Soon after the conference ended, Congress and the American people again lost interest in naval affairs. In many ways the situation between 1922 and 1926 was a mirror image of that between 1909 and 1914. While the Navy Department assembled plans for more construction, hardly anyone paid attention. It was as if the fleet was operating in a vacuum.

Committed antinavalists such as Senator King even attacked the navy while the conference was ongoing. King claimed that the "foolish reactionary naval policy" of the United States had been the greatest "menace to the peace of the world."[4] Others, not as extreme, saw the Washington Conference as the perfect excuse to slash the naval budget. By April 1922 a heated congressional debate was raging about reducing America's naval personnel. Some wanted to limit the fleet to 67,000 men, a figure more than 30 percent smaller than the size of the Royal Navy.[5] Theodore Roosevelt, Jr., the assistant secretary of the navy, accused Congress of having a "witches Sabbath" over the naval budget,[6] and some in the fleet wanted the president to intervene.[7] While this move was eventually rebuffed, the debate marked the beginning of a steady decline in the navy's budget. Between fiscal years 1922 and 1926 spending on the fleet plummeted from $476,775,000 to $312,743,000. Spending on the Royal Navy, on the other hand, was relatively flat, moving from £64,884,000 in fiscal year 1922-1923 to £58,100,000 in fiscal year 1926-1927.[8]

For a while, however, the U.S. Navy gamely tried to pretend that things had not changed. The Navy Department still drew up large building programs. The ships it most wanted were cruisers. Cruisers were fast, relatively lightly armed vessels of between 5,000 and 10,000 tons. They were used mostly for two purposes: scouting and trade warfare. In the first role cruisers used their high speed to operate as the eyes of the main battle fleet. In their second role cruisers were sent out singly or in small units to protect or destroy commerce.

By the mid-1920s the United States had far fewer cruisers than the British. Only the ten cruisers of the Omaha class, part of the 1916 program, were of any value to the Americans. Every year between 1922 and 1926 the General Board complained about this deficiency. In July 1922 it called for eight new cruisers and a number of other vessels.[9] In 1925 and 1926 it repeated this call, demanding eight new cruisers for fiscal years 1927 and 1928.[10]

Its efforts had only mixed results. In 1922 and 1923 no new cruisers were approved. In 1924, however, Congress, under the prompting of Representative Thomas Butler, Republican of Pennsylvania and chairman of the House Naval Affairs Committee, finally authorized the construction of eight large Washington-class cruisers. However, this authorization was not a guarantee that the cruisers would be built. Congressional authorizations did not obligate Congress to appropriate money. They were merely congressional notices of intent, notices that could take years to be fund and notices that Congress could revoke at will. Congress actually had scant desire to build the eight cruisers authorized in 1924. It was stipulated that they could be halted if an international agreement on cruisers was reached, and building proceeded painfully slowly. By the end of 1926 only one of the eight cruisers had been laid down. This one cruiser, along with one submarine and six river gunboats, constituted the totality of American naval construction between 1922 and 1926.

It was all a very disheartening turn of events for the U.S. Navy. It still had some friends in Congress like Representatives Butler, Fred Britten (Republican, Illinois), and William Ayres (Republican, Kansas) and senators like Jesse Metcalf (Republican, Rhode Island) and Frederick Hale (Republican, Maine). Butler and Hale, chairman of the Senate Naval Affairs Committee and, ironically, the son of Senator Eugene Hale, were particularly active. However, instead of pushing for greater construction, much of their time was tied up resisting attempts to cut the naval budget.[11]

Nor could the navy turn to the executive branch for succor. By the middle of 1922 Secretary of the Navy Denby indicated that he wanted increased economy in naval spending.[12] A few months later Denby publicly stated that it was not his intention, "considering the financial shape of the country, to ask for any increase" in the navy.[13] President Harding's death on 2 August 1923, which brought Calvin Coolidge to the presidency, made little difference. Coolidge was by nature even more parsimonious than Harding and made repaying the national debt one of his great objectives. When the new president came to power, he immediately stated that he favored more naval arms control.[14] Under Coolidge's direction the naval budget dropped to its lowest level of the interwar period, bottoming out at $318,909,000 in 1926. Coolidge also was responsible for choosing a new secretary of the navy in the wake of the Teapot Dome scandal, which brought about the resignation of Denby.[15] His choice, Curtis Dwight Wilbur, the chief justice of the California Supreme Court, was a graduate of Annapolis.[16] While Curtis believed that the U.S. Navy should be built to its full Washington Treaty strength, he was unable to bring the president around to his way of thinking.

The inability to get approval for new construction led many in the U.S. Navy once again to question the fleet's role. Most saw the fleet as a vital instrument of national power, one that should be strong enough to dominate the Japanese and match the British. Great Britain and the British Empire were still seen as America's most formidable potential foe. It was thought the British would do anything possible, both scrupulously and otherwise, to further their aims.[17] Plans were still drawn up for an Anglo-American war. In January 1924 the navy and army held a joint exercise during which American forces tried to repel an assault on the Western Hemisphere by a European power.[18] The European power, called

"Black" in the exercise, could only have been Great Britain. Later, in April 1924, the Navy Department simulated an Anglo-American capital ship duel.[19] In four different simulations the British fleet, because of the greater range of its guns, damaged at least 80 percent of the American ships.[20]

However, the Anglophobia that had gripped the American navy since the First World War had abated a little by the mid-1920s. While the Navy Department was still drawing up plans for an Anglo-American war, it did so with less urgency. In 1925 Captain L. McNamee, American naval attaché in London, told the General Board it could "dismiss the possibility" of Great Britain's going to war with the United States.[21] In some quarters there was even talk of cooperating with the British. In 1924 Captain C. L. Hussey of the Naval War College specifically advocated increasing Anglo-American naval cooperation.[22]

War with Japan, meanwhile, was now thought considerably more likely.[23] Right after the Washington Conference the War Plans Division claimed that the 5-5-3 ratio was insufficient to protect American interests in the Pacific and asked that it be viewed as an "experiment."[24] The General Board also wanted the American fleet to be strong enough to engage and defeat the Japanese in the western Pacific.[25] The Orange war plans were updated and revised to reflect this. In 1924 a joint army-navy plan was approved that called for bold, aggressive action, including possible amphibious assaults on Japan's imperial possessions.[26]

However, while the navy came up with these plans, whenever the General Board asked Congress for the ships needed to implement them, it was usually rebuffed. The general futility of its struggle led many in the U.S. Navy to question American policy. In much the same way that its predecessors before the First World War sought to define the fleet's role, in the 1920s a great deal of effort was expended trying to define explicitly American naval policy. Within two months of the end of the Washington Conference a paper on the subject had been drawn up.[27] It divided American naval policy between a nebulous "fundamental" objective and ten other "general" goals. This document was only the beginning. In May 1922 another paper, entitled "Naval Policy," was put forward, claiming that the navy's ultimate purpose was to ensure world peace.[28]

The question of what was America's naval policy was never really answered. When the General Board took the lead, it usually plumped for an aggressive policy that committed the United States to all sorts of overseas objectives, including the Open Door in China and the Monroe Doctrine.[29] When the Coolidge administration intervened, usually in the person of Secretary of the Navy Wilbur, the importance of economy in expenditure was stressed.[30] It was a rather odd, if slightly touching, process that reached a kind of conclusion in October 1928. Then, Wilbur put his signature to an enormous chart that purported to spell out American naval policy.[31] While it adopted the fundamental and ten general principles first laid out in 1922, this extensive document listed a "building and maintenance" policy for every type of vessel in the navy, a four-clause "organization" policy, an eleven-clause "operating" policy, a twelve-clause "personnel" policy, a six-clause "base and shore stations" policy, a seven-clause "communications" policy, a four-clause "inspection" policy, a thirteen-clause "information" policy, and, finally, a one-clause "publicity" policy. For all the navy's efforts, however, little was achieved. At this time the U.S. Navy had but one real "policy," parity with Great Britain, the policy Hughes had given the navy at Washington. It was the only "policy" that Congress, the administration, the Navy Department, and the American populace could understand in common. No matter how hard the Navy Department tried, it could not get beyond it. That being the case, as long as Congress and the administration believed the United States' right to naval parity with Great Britain was not being questioned, they were willing to ignore the Navy Department's pleas for cruisers. Not until the Baldwin government tried to deny this right, in an astonishing act of hubris, did the U.S. Navy once again return to prominence.

The story of how the Baldwin government came to the rescue of the U.S. Navy is not flattering. For a while after the Washington Conference the Royal Navy seemed to be thriving, particularly with its cruiser strength. However, when it seemed that the United States was not going to make an issue of British cruiser supremacy, the Baldwin government opted for such an antagonistic policy at the Geneva Conference of 1927 that Coolidge had little option but to fight back.

Instinctively, it is easy to see how the cruiser question could have divided the two governments. To the British, cruisers were of vital importance. With a widely dispersed empire and a home country dependent on imports, the British could claim with justification that they needed many more cruisers than the self-sufficient Americans.[32] Within the U.S. Navy there was even some sympathy for Britain's position.[33] By early 1925 the British had considerable cruiser supremacy. The Royal Navy had forty-nine cruisers either built or being built, to the Americans' ten.[34] While the U.S. Navy had vainly struggled to interest Congress in constructing cruisers, different British governments had continually increased the Royal Navy's strength. In 1924 Britain's first Labour government approved a very generous construction program of five new cruisers. It seemed that as long as the British kept quiet about their lead, the Americans would leave them to it.

Unfortunately, the unchallenged growth of British cruiser strength eventually went to some people's head. The Admiralty began to press for an even more massive advantage. The Royal Navy started to claim that it needed at least seventy cruisers to protect the empire, irrespective of the strength of other powers: "The number of British cruisers must be based not upon the number of cruisers maintained by other powers, but upon the length and variety of sea communications over which food and other vital supplies for the United Kingdom must be transported."[35] To reach such a grand figure, the Admiralty pressed for another program in 1925 of five new cruisers.[36]

On the surface things should have been easier for the Royal Navy in 1925 than in 1924. The Conservatives, led by Baldwin, were back in power. The new chancellor of the exchequer, Winston Churchill, had been first lord of the Admiralty before the First World War and was a staunch supporter of British naval supremacy. The new first lord, William Bridgeman, was not particularly influential but was well liked. Also, Admiral Beatty remained first sea lord, ready to add his considerable muscle to the Admiralty's arguments.

However, things did not turn out exactly as the Admiralty had planned, and there ensued a rather bitter Cabinet debate. Unable to hold the Americans up as a cruiser threat, the Royal Navy had to rely on the Japanese menace. The Japanese had continued to build up their fleet. Between 1919 and 1924 the Japanese had laid down eighteen new cruisers, more than the British and Americans combined. Now, the Admiralty claimed Britain needed to respond:

Japan . . . owing to her geographical position can deal us a serious blow, by attacking our trade and outlying portions of the Empire, without having to engage in a naval battle . . . a war with Japan would certainly, for the first twelve months or more, be a cruiser war of oceanic proportions . . . The Far East covers a vast expanse and in it are situated much British possessions. . . . They are at the present moment dominated by Japan. It is the Admiralty's responsibility to neutralise this domination as far as possible.[37]

However, the Admiralty found itself opposed by, of all people, Winston Churchill. Churchill's behavior at this period seems odd, to say the least. While he had taken the lead in fighting for the retention of naval supremacy, Churchill never seemed willing to spend much money to protect that supremacy. He was not an insignificant threat to the Admiralty at this time. Not only was he chancellor of the exchequer, but the Baldwin government was composed of men often unwilling to parry his thrusts into strategic policy.[38] Baldwin cared little about naval issues, while the foreign secretary, Austen Chamberlain, was mostly absorbed in European matters. Gone were such strong members of the Lloyd George government as Lord Curzon and Andrew Bonar-Law, and in their place were more allies of Churchill, such as Lord Birkenhead and William Joynson-Hicks, and less assertive personalities such as the fourth marquess of Salisbury and Baron Cushendun. Only two people, Lord Robert Cecil and Admiral Beatty, were really equipped to withstand Churchill's forays into naval policy. Eventually, Cecil and Churchill would fall out spectacularly over naval policy, but in 1925 they were on the same side of the argument. Cecil was a firm champion of disarmament and the League of Nations, and Churchill made appeals to his idealism.[39]

Churchill believed that the Royal Navy already had a large supremacy in cruiser strength and that any additional naval spending would be a drag on the national economy.[40] He estimated that the construction program planned by the Admiralty would eventually bring the naval budget up to £90 million and he had no desire to part with such vast sums.[41] This was partly because he did not share the Admiralty's fears about Japan. Churchill claimed that the Royal Navy had at least twice as many effective cruisers as the Japanese.[42] Furthermore, he ridiculed the notion that Britain and Japan might eventually go to war. "Why should there be a war with Japan? I do not believe there is the slightest chance of it in our lifetime. The Japanese are our allies."[43] Churchill also believed that the Royal Navy had effectively seen off the American challenge. He claimed that there was "absolutely no doubt" that the Royal Navy was stronger in capital ships than the U.S. Navy, while the latter was "astonishingly weak" in cruisers and even lagged behind in aircraft carriers.[44]

The deadlock between the Admiralty and Churchill dragged on through the first few months of 1925. Bridgeman continued to fight gamely,[45] and in the end both sides compromised. The Admiralty was allowed to build four of the five cruisers it requested, but its hoped-for £10 million increase was sliced in half. Churchill was also successful in getting an official Cabinet statement discounting the notion that Britain and Japan could go to war anytime soon.[46]

The debate over the 1925-1926 estimates was one of the few moments between the Washington and Geneva Conferences when British naval policy received a wide airing. There were a number of things the Royal Navy could be satisfied with. Even though no other power was close to Britain in cruiser strength, within two years nine large cruisers had been approved by two different governments. The Admiralty's budget was beginning to recover from the cuts imposed after Washington, while the American navy was continually having its funding reduced. Indeed, the greatest danger for the British was that things were looking too easy.

One of the most interesting aspects of the 1925 debate was that for the first time in centuries, the Royal Navy had difficulty spelling out who its greatest enemy was. For the first time ever the two powers the Admiralty compared itself to were not European. The naval balance in Europe tilted so much in Britain's favor that it was impossible to portray any country on the continent as a naval threat. The Admiralty felt so secure in home waters that a large number of vessels were shifted from the Atlantic and North Seas to the Mediterranean.[47]

This left the Americans and the Japanese, and the Admiralty certainly used them to its advantage. Most attention was given to the Japanese. Since the Washington Conference, extremely elaborate war plans had been developed for an Anglo-Japanese conflict.[48] Whenever the Admiralty justified its construction plans, the Japanese usually received the most comment.[49] In 1923 the Admiralty Plans Division was pushing for the construction of seventeen new cruisers to offset the growth of the Japanese fleet.[50] After the debate over the 1925 estimates, a Cabinet committee, chaired by Lord Birkenhead, was charged with laying out a British naval construction program for the next few years.[51] Almost all of its calculations were based on Anglo-Japanese comparisons.

Yet, for all their efforts the Admiralty could not really bring itself to fear the Japanese too much. Like Churchill some in the Admiralty believed that there was little reason for Britain and Japan to quarrel. Admiral Beatty is recorded as saying as much only a few months after the 1925 estimates quarrel, during which the Admiralty held Japan up as a potentially fierce competitor:

In conversation today Sam Hoare outlined a policy towards Japan very similar to your ideas. "Let them alone," he said in effect, "provided they don't interfere in our commerce." I suspect you converted Trenchard at the C.O.S. meeting and that he converted Hoare.[52]

The Royal Navy was experiencing the same kind of problem that had plagued the U.S. Navy for over a century. Because the present naval balance seemed so propitious, the Admiralty had to bring forward policies that were not based on realistic threats. The intellectual poverty of the Admiralty's position can be seen in the seventy-cruiser fleet. First articulated in the early 1920s, the seventy-cruiser force was an Admiralty policy until into the 1930s. Yet, as the Admiralty admitted, the number seventy bore no relation to the cruiser strengths of the other naval powers. The contrast with earlier policies like the two-power standard could not have been more striking. The two-power standard was an attempt to determine the Royal Navy's strength in relation to the rest of the world. The standard was easily understood and very popular. The seventy-cruiser policy, on the other hand, was more of a bargaining ploy designed to put pressure on politicians. In the mid-1920s the British had no need for such a massive force, but if the United States, Japan, and the European naval powers embarked upon a cruiser-building race, seventy quite easily could have been inadequate.

Eventually, the lack of a realistic naval threat, when coupled with the combined authorization of nine new cruisers in 1924 and 1925, created an unstable level of confidence in the Baldwin government. Churchill, and others who thought that the British needed no additional cruisers in 1925, began to believe that with a little push formal supremacy could be regained for the Royal Navy. At the Geneva Conference they tried to give the United States that little push. This was the disastrous move that eventually winched the U.S. Navy out of the doldrums it had been in since the Washington Conference.

## THE GENEVA CONFERENCE

The Baldwin government should have let sleeping cruisers lie. With the balance so much in its favor, it had little to gain by having a public debate on the subject. By late 1926, Thomas Butler, chairman of the House Naval Affairs Committee, told President Coolidge that the British had, since 1922, laid down three times as many cruisers as America. Furthermore, Butler claimed that his committee was willing to proceed with the cruisers authorized in 1924 to give the administration some leverage with the British.[53] On 10 February 1927, Coolidge finally grasped the bull by the horns and invited the British, Japanese, French, and Italians to a conference in Geneva. He wanted to apply the 5-5-3 ratio to cruisers and other auxiliary ships.[54]

The British reacted cautiously to Coolidge's invitation. The Admiralty had known for years that the Americans might call a conference, but it was determined to maintain Britain's cruiser supremacy. In 1926 the Admiralty made a survey of defensive requirements of the empire and reaffirmed that the Royal Navy needed seventy cruisers as well as seven aircraft carriers, 162 destroyers, and seventy-eight submarines.[55] All of the arguments in support of British cruiser supremacy hinged upon Britain's greater reliance on trade. In some ways the British case had strengthened since 1918. Then, Eric Geddes was worried that the United States might soon become the world's largest shipping power. By 1927 it was clear that his fears had been exaggerated. By 1927 the British had recovered their position as the global leader in merchant ship production. British merchant shipping tonnage was now almost twice as large as America's and more than one-third of the whole world's total.[56] The British also had considerably more tonnage under construction, with 633,622 tons being built to the United States' 106,835 tons.[57]

In terms of trade, the picture was still mixed. Great Britain remained the world's largest importer, buying more foreign goods than the United States every year between 1919 and 1927. The United States was still a net exporter of food, while Great Britain was still vulnerable to blockade. The United States was also self-sufficient in oil, accounting for almost 72 percent of world crude production, while the British Empire produced less than 2 percent.[58] To the Admiralty these were the most compelling arguments in favor of its call for more cruisers than the Americans had.[59]

What the Admiralty wanted at Geneva was to make a distinction between two cruiser classes. The first were Washington-class cruisers, those built up to the treaty's limits of 10,000 tons and armed with eight-inch guns. These ships were considered ideal for fleet work, and the Admiralty was willing to extend the 5-5-3 ratio to cover them. The other class of cruiser, however, sporting guns of six-inches or less and weighing around 7,000 tons, was thought ideal for commerce protection. The Admiralty wanted as little restriction on their building as possible.

The sailors, however, could not dictate policy to the Cabinet. The first lord of the Admiralty, William Bridgeman, was not the fleet's strongest advocate and, when compared to earlier first lords like Churchill or McKenna, had relatively little Cabinet clout. Indeed, after the Geneva Conference Bridgeman seemed to lose control over British naval policy. In 1927 Bridgeman was one of the two leading British delegates to Geneva, and his lack of decisiveness was not helpful. In Geneva Bridgeman mimicked much of the conciliatory rhetoric of Lord Robert Cecil, the other leader of the British delegation.[60] However, once back in London and confronted by the formidable Churchill, Bridgeman reverted to being a "big-navy" man.

For Cecil, the chancellor of the duchy of Lancaster, Coolidge's invitation was seen as a real opportunity.[61] Cecil firmly believed in the League of Nations and was committed to the arms control process.[62] In 1925 he had joined Winston Churchill to fight against the Admiralty's five-cruiser program and remained suspicious of the navy's demands.[63] Cecil also believed in bettering Anglo-American relations. At the Paris Peace Conference he pressed Lloyd George to cooperate with Wilson and then helped to negotiate a compromise with the Americans.

Cecil described Coolidge's arms control proposals as "attractive" and seemed willing to concede the principle of cruiser parity to the Americans.[64] He could not imagine that the cruiser question could lead to a rupture in Anglo-American relations and fully expected to negotiate a compromise. In his quest Cecil believed his strongest support would come from Arthur Balfour, lord president of the council, and the foreign secretary, Austen Chamberlain. He was right in the first instance. Balfour, the head of the British delegation at the Washington Conference, wanted to continue with the naval arms control process and provided Cecil with relatively constant support. Chamberlain, on the other hand, was not so steady. The foreign secretary was generally more interested in European questions and ignored the signs of American resentment over British attempts to maintain cruiser superiority.[65] Chamberlain admitted that he "was not well informed" on the upcoming disarmament questions.[66] When the cruiser issue came up before the Cabinet in July 1927, Chamberlain's inability to resist the more strident demands of Churchill led the government to take the disastrous step that it did.

Just how Winston Churchill came to play this crucial role is somewhat unusual. Since the end of the First World War he had been both the staunchest defender of British naval supremacy as well as the most determined opponent of increased spending on the fleet. By 1927 Churchill had become extremely influential in the Baldwin government and decided to use his influence to reassert the Royal Navy's supremacy. He and his allies, such as Lord Birkenhead and the home secretary, William Joyson-Hicks, believed that extending the 5-5-3 ratio to cruiser strength would mean the British fleet would be dangerously inferior to that of the Americans:

In this case ostensible parity is actual disparity. If America builds in light cruisers upon a scale which challenges the arteries of this Empire we must respond without examining our financial situation. . . . In such a situation we become vassals of the U.S.A. . . . The only safe and sane course is to remain faithful to the maritime traditions of our people.[67]

Before the conference began, neither Churchill nor Cecil was able to gain the upper hand. This was partly due to the prime minister's general indecisiveness about naval issues. Baldwin tackled maritime questions with Asquithian directness, very rarely expressing his own opinion and, probably, just as rarely having one. He normally tried to find a Cabinet consensus and proceed from there. But since consensus was not possible between Cecil and Churchill, Baldwin entered the Geneva Conference unsure of what he wanted.

It was just as well that the Coolidge administration did not know that some in the British Cabinet wanted to reassert the Royal Navy's "right" to supremacy. The American administration's preparations for Geneva were based on the assumption that, whatever the outcome, the United States' right to equality would be recognized. The Americans knew that their position before the Geneva Conference was not as strong as that before Washington. In 1921 the 1916 program was under construction, providing the Harding administration with a great deal of leverage. In 1927 the United States had but a paper program of eight large cruisers, only two of which had been laid down. The British, meanwhile, had nine large cruisers under construction in 1926, with a further five to be started in 1927.

The Coolidge administration believed that it could get around this imbalance by using America's enormous latent power to compel the British to recognize America's right to equality. William Castle, the chief of the State Department's Western European Affairs Division, reported in his diary that the British were willing to concede the principle of cruiser parity, as long as the Americans did not actually build up to the Royal Navy's strength.[68] Castle's opinion mattered because he played a central role in the State Department's preparations for Geneva. The secretary of state, Frank Kellogg, was not a details man and gave Castle a great deal of independence. Therefore, Castle communicated with Alanson Houghton, the American ambassador in London, about British plans.[69] Houghton had told him in January and February that the British were willing to recognize America's right to cruiser parity.[70] In March the American ambassador warned that the British were approaching the Geneva talks with "tremendous seriousness."[71] After meeting Bridgeman, Houghton was further impressed with British seriousness.

Castle took these warnings to heart. He came to believe that the Coolidge administration was not approaching its own conference with enough commitment. He bemoaned the fact that the American delegation was to be led by Hugh Gibson, a man Castle believed to be insufficiently important. Instead, he proposed that Kellogg be sent.[72] Castle also believed that the U.S. Navy might prove to be one of the biggest obstacles to any settlement. The rest of the administration, unlike the navy, saw the conference as an opportunity to have America's right to parity recognized. It had no desire for a massive cruiser construction program and wanted to establish Anglo-American parity at as low a level as possible. One of the reasons Castle wanted Kellogg to go to Geneva was his fear of the navy's "obstructive tactics."[73]

This was not a substanceless fear. The General Board did seem to see the Geneva Conference as an opportunity to reignite American interest in naval construction. Having suffered through almost five years of marginalization, the Navy Department assumed that the United States would have to begin a large new construction program to reach naval equality with the British. Like the State Department, the General Board was being told that the British were approaching the talks with great seriousness.[74] Unlike the State Department, however, the General Board maintained that the British would fight to maintain their cruiser supremacy.

Talk of "Perfidious Albion" once again echoed around the American navy. The General Board was particularly unimpressed with the British argument that the Royal Navy legitimately needed more cruisers:[75] "Any plea for ships to guard commerce disguises the equally important missions which they have of denying the sea to enemy commerce and of controlling neutral commerce."[76] The General Board's preparatory memoranda were based on the assumption that the British were out to regain naval supremacy.[77] The old shibboleths of British "domination of world markets" and " control of global communications" were once again trotted out.

In April the General Board stated that the Royal Navy's total force of cruisers built, being built, and appropriated for amounted to 387,410 tons, while the United States' figure was a paltry 166,250 tons.[78] Even the Japanese had more cruisers than the Americans, with over 175,000 tons. The General Board planned to improve its position by applying the 5-5-3 ratio to all auxiliary ships. It preferred a cruiser limit of 300,000 tons but would accept 400,000 if it kept the British happy. It also rejected outright the British proposal to divide cruisers into two classes and limit only the larger class.[79] As the navy knew, getting the conference to agree to a limit of 300,000 tons would have required the United States to authorize and construct at least thirteen new Washington-class cruisers, a daunting figure considering Congress' and Coolidge's proclivities. However, just having a commonly accepted figure was seen as in the fleet's interest. At least then it would have a target with which to approach Congress.

It should have been apparent to the Americans that the cruiser limitations being proposed by the General Board were totally unacceptable to the British Admiralty. The Admiralty believed that a 70-cruiser force, its ideal, could be accommodated only within a limitation of 600,000 tons. If things had gone to form, the American government would have ignored the General Board's objections and tried to make a deal with the British. However, fate was to smile on the General Board.

The Geneva Conference officially opened on 20 June 1927. Robert Cecil and William Bridgeman led the British delegation, while Hugh Gibson, the American ambassador to Belgium, and Admiral Hilary P. Jones represented the United States. There were early signs of hope. In picking Cecil the Baldwin government had sent the most pro-American man in the Cabinet, as well as someone committed to disarmament. Cecil was determined not to do anything to make the conference fail.[80] Gibson, alternatively, was a man used to negotiation in the League of Nations and not averse to making a deal.

The conference was supposed to discuss a great number of issues, including the tonnage allowances for all classes of auxiliary ships and further restrictions on capital ships.[81] The Americans eventually proposed relatively low auxiliary ship allowances for themselves and the British: 250,000 to 300,000 tons of cruisers, 200,000 to 250,000 tons of destroyers, and 60,000 to 90,000 tons of submarines. The Japanese were to be allowed 60 percent of the final agreed-upon figure. The British proposals were very different and could hardly be called arms control. They would accept the 5-5-3 ratio for Washington-class cruisers, those weighing 10,000 tons and carrying eight-inch guns, but wanted as few restrictions as possible on cruisers not exceeding 7,500 tons or mounting anything larger than six-inch guns. Destroyers, likewise, would be subject to only qualitative limitations. The British would have preferred to outlaw submarines but, as this did not seem realistic, pushed for a maximum size of 1,600 tons.

As a way of soothing anger at the lack of any substantive disarmament in their proposals, Cecil and Bridgeman went to great lengths to assure the Americans that the United States' right to naval parity was not being questioned. On 29 June the British delegates told Gibson that the British recognized the United States' right to parity in all classes of vessel. Their promise was quickly relayed to the State Department and then to President Coolidge.[82] For the next two days it seemed that Cecil and Bridgeman did nothing but assure Americans about the right to naval parity. Bridgeman kept a diary in which he recorded his efforts:

June 29th . . . I undertook to repeat to an American pressman that we were not out for superiority.
9:30 (p.m.) Important interview with . . . Associated Press of America, to explain that the idea that we are contesting parity is a myth.
June 30th . . . 9:30 (a.m.) . . . I gave similar remarks on parity . . .
11:00 (a.m.) His (Gibson) impression was that English opinion would favour such a statement as I had made last night on parity.
12:00 (a.m.) Cecil came—and warmly approved my message to the American press.[83]

Bridgeman's later comments were also passed to Coolidge[84] and Kellogg, and the secretary of state was so pleased he exclaimed that his "misapprehension had been swept away."[85] Even the naturally skeptical General Board recorded that the principle of parity had been "recognized" by the British.[86] After all these assurances the Americans began to rest a little easier, and the two sides settled down to try to reach an acceptable compromise.

The ensuing negotiations were far from easy. The British attempt to put limits on only the largest class of cruiser seemed self-serving to the Americans. With the majority of British cruisers weighing less than 7,000 tons, the Royal Navy feared a worldwide spurt in the construction of 10,000-ton, eight-inch-gun vessels. The U.S. Navy, on the other hand, thought the larger Washington-class cruiser ideally suited to its purposes.[87] With no vital lines of trade to protect, the Americans wanted the most powerful individual units possible. Also, the comparative lack of American overseas bases meant that the Washington class' extended cruising radius was coveted. As the Americans were quick to point out, the British Empire had an unparalleled string of bases, which allowed the Royal Navy to resupply and reprovision anywhere in the world.

The Admiralty, naturally, took a different position in the negotiations. With their vast lines of communications the British claimed they needed a large number of smaller cruisers. The American proposal for a 250,000-ton to 300,000-ton cruiser limit would have allowed the Royal Navy only half of the vessels it thought necessary for national defense. The British therefore began the talks by claiming that they needed about 600,000 tons of cruisers, a figure one American admiral at Geneva termed "catastrophical."[88]

Through the first half of July the two delegations tried to reach a compromise. Their negotiations were not always easy. At one point the British vice admiral, Frederick Field, the Admiralty's deputy chief of naval staff, called the American proposals "unintelligible to the naval mind," while the mild-mannered Cecil called another American idea "nonsense."[89] Eventually, however, there were signs of movement. The British grudgingly admitted that they could accept a 462,000-ton cruiser allotment, at least until 1936.[90] The Americans likewise compromised by claiming they could accept a ceiling of 400,000 tons for cruisers instead of 300,000.[91] No one could say with any assurance what the eventual figure would be; however, these were hopeful signs. Yet, it was the prospect of just such a compromise that caused the Baldwin government, led by Winston Churchill, to panic.

Early in the negotiations the British Cabinet had supported Cecil and Bridgeman. When Cecil assured the Americans that their right to naval parity was not being questioned, Austen Chamberlain told him that the government was "quite clear that they must support Bridgeman and yourself, and that to use any other language in Washington than that which you had used in Geneva was unthinkable."[92] One member of the Cabinet, in his copy of the 4 July Cabinet minutes, wrote that "the principle of cruiser parity had been conceded."[93]

However, to some people in the Cabinet the principle of American parity was far from conceded. In late June Winston Churchill had written a memorandum outlining his fears about such a move:

There can really be no parity between a power whose navy is its life and a power whose navy is only for prestige. . . . It always seems to be assumed that it is our duty to humour the United States and minister to their vanity. They do nothing for us in return, but exact their last pound of flesh. [94]

Churchill had some powerful support. Beatty had tried to convince Baldwin not to issue a public communique to the Americans about parity.[95] Lord Birkenhead also lobbied the prime minister.[96] In the end, however, it was up to Churchill to kill off any chance of an agreement, a job he did with consummate skill. During a CID meeting on 7 July, Churchill, aided stoutly by Beatty, dominated the discussion and made it known that he was not in the least concerned about the prospect of a breakdown at Geneva.[97] Only Austen Chamberlain tried to counter the rambunctious chancellor, but he was never his best when discussing naval issues. On 20 July Churchill circulated an even more aggressive memorandum, calling parity with the United States "fatal to British naval security" and mentioning the possibility of an Anglo-American war.[98]

Churchill saw the Geneva Conference as Britain's last chance to reassert its strategic independence from the United States. He even thought about reinvigorating the Anglo-Japanese Alliance to rein in the Americans.[99] The rather alarming nature of his arguments began to win over converts in the Cabinet. By the middle of July the telegrams being sent from London to Cecil and Bridgeman had a much harsher tone.[100] Even Baldwin, who generally avoided naval questions, began to adopt much of Churchill's rhetoric. The prime minister stated that cruiser parity with America would make Britain "vassals of the United States. . . . In my opinion the moment has quite definitely come when we must stand up to them."[101] However, when Baldwin recorded these ideas, he was not in London but on a steamship bound for Canada. His departure, on 21 July, was crucial.

On 19 July the Cabinet decided to recall Cecil and Bridgeman from Geneva. Cecil had been growing increasingly worried by the change in tone coming from London and feared that the Cabinet was thinking of disavowing his earlier promises to the Americans.[102] With Baldwin absent, Churchill was in a very powerful position to confront the returning delegates. He eventually used his power to make sure the Geneva Conference collapsed. At first Churchill wanted Bridgeman to claim that he had exceeded his instructions and state that he had had no right to say what he had about naval parity to the Americans. Bridgeman wisely declined to do so.[103] Next, Churchill decided to wreck the conference by refusing to compromise on the question of eight-inch guns. The Americans had the right, according to the Washington Treaty, to arm all their new cruisers with eight-inch guns. Churchill, however, wanted to limit all new American cruisers of less than 10,000 tons to six-inch guns. Cecil was appalled at the chancellor's maneuverings and attacked.[104] However, Cecil's protests were in vain. When Churchill brought his proposal before the Cabinet in Baldwin's absence, he was supported by a vote of 10 to 6.[105] His policy thus became the official negotiating position of the British government. It was widely known that Churchill's proposals were unacceptable to, and would be thought deeply offensive by, the Americans. This did not make the slightest difference. As Maurice Hankey related the story to Baldwin, "I think most people in their hearts think the Conference will now break-down. . . . I would mention some people who rather hope it will."[106]

In Geneva and Washington the Americans had little knowledge of the machinations under way in the Baldwin Cabinet. The American ambassador to London claimed he had no idea why Cecil and Bridgeman had been recalled but claimed that a deal was still possible.[107] However, when the two Britons returned to Geneva on 28 July, the Americans were quickly disillusioned. Secretary of State Kellogg told President Coolidge that the British had reverted to demanding 650,000 tons of cruisers and at the same time wanted to limit the United States to only twelve 10,000-ton vessels.[108] Kellogg, strongly supported by Coolidge, immediately rejected this one-sided British plan.[109]

Unfortunately, the tragicomedy in Geneva went on for a few days more. Cecil and Bridgeman tried to find a way around their own government's policy. They eventually telegraphed London, claiming that while the Americans were holding firm on the eight-inch-gun question, they were "not regarding any of our other proposals as insuperably objectionable."[110] The Cabinet, however, would have none of it and rejected any talk of a compromise.[111]

The Geneva Conference duly broke up on 4 August. The blame for the conference's collapse rests almost entirely with the British government. Laboring under the influence of Winston Churchill, the Cabinet chose to recall Cecil and Bridgeman from Geneva and then forced the two to adopt a position that the Americans were bound to reject. But that, indeed, was Churchill's hope. He and his allies did not want any agreement because whatever the compromise, the British would have had to formally guarantee the Americans the right to naval parity in all classes of warship. This they were unwilling to do. As Churchill remarked a few weeks later: "It is not true that a concession on the eight-inch gun w[oul]d have turned the scale at Geneva. The basis of agreement never existed."[112]

## A CRISIS IN ANGLO-AMERICAN RELATIONS

The fallout from the collapse of the Geneva Conference was dramatic. For a while all trust between the British and American governments disappeared. Secretary of State Kellogg accused the British of going back on their word and told President Coolidge that he saw no reason to negotiate with them.[113] William Bridgeman now referred to his American counterparts as a "terrible lot of people."[114] Even the usually mild-mannered Austen Chamberlain called Hugh Gibson, the head of the American delegation at Geneva, a "dirty dog."[115] Within the British government, however, there was also a split. When Cecil returned from Switzerland, he was exhausted, emotional, and determined to resign from the Cabinet. The final draft of his resignation letter was published. However, it paled when compared to his private sentiments. Chamberlain tried to mollify Cecil but failed miserably.[116] Cecil blamed the intransigence of his own government for the failure at Geneva.[117] He was equally direct in his correspondence with the prime minister.

There was no hope of an agreement unless it included a limitation of the smaller cruisers, and an unqualified acceptance of the principle of parity. So clear was this, not only to us, but to the Cabinet, that we received an urgent telegram from them directing us to agree to parity. . . . Parity in our minds and in those of the other negotiators meant what is now called "mathematical equality.". . . At last it seemed that we were well on the road to an agreement. . . . But it was just the prospect of success which was agitating those of our colleagues who had come to believe that what is now called mathematical equality between us and the Americans in the smaller cruisers was a danger to the Empire, and accordingly, notwithstanding our protests, the Cabinet sent us a peremptory summons to come home.[118]

Cecil singled out Winston Churchill for particular criticism.[119] During his recall from Geneva, Cecil had accused Churchill of believing "that future war is practically certain."[120] Now he was even more blunt, saying that war was the only thing that interested Churchill in politics.[121] However, in resigning from the government, Cecil succeeded in making Churchill only more powerful. Indeed, for the next year or so British naval policy would be very much under Churchill's influence. What he did with this influence was disastrous.

This was mostly because Churchill did not understand how the collapse of the Geneva Conference had changed American opinion. British antics had lit a fire under Calvin Coolidge. The president, who had expected an agreement that would both limit spending and keep taxes down, changed his tune as soon as he heard the proposals put forward by Cecil and Bridgeman after their recall.[122] At that point he favored breaking off, rather than adjourning the talks.[123] The State Department's reaction to the British proposals was equally fierce. Secretary of State Kellogg claimed that the British never intended "to agree to anything" and were probably out to regain naval supremacy.[124] William Castle, now promoted to assistant secretary of state, believed that the American position at Geneva had been "impregnable." He was as angry with the British as his boss. "They [British] did not want limitation—at least not reasonable limitation—and within the limits they wanted to dictate to us what kind of ships we could build."[125]

The U.S. Navy, on the other hand, was delighted by the breakdown in relations. By the end of September 1927 the General Board had come up with a new five-year plan of naval construction, including twenty-five Washington-class cruisers, forty destroyers, thirty-five submarines, five aircraft carriers, and even five capital ships.[126] It was the kind of program that would have been brushed aside by the president and Congress between 1922 and 1926, but Coolidge was now so enraged that he decided to make it the center point of a new American naval policy. In his Annual Message to Congress, delivered on 6 December 1927, the president made a plea for increased cruiser construction.[127] His specific plan, revealed a few days later, was to build a total of seventy-one new vessels, including the twenty-five Washington-class cruisers proposed by the General Board in September.[128]

If the United States went ahead with this program, then British naval policy, as promulgated by Churchill, would have been in tatters. This policy was based on two premises. The first was that the Washington system and the concept of naval parity between the United States and Great Britain were not in British interests. Cecil claimed that Churchill mentioned pulling out of the Washington system as early as August 1927.[129] In early 1928 Churchill gave a fuller exposition of his ideas to his private secretary, P. J. Grigg. Grigg made a note of them, which he passed on to Hankey:

The most we can hope to do in the twenty or thirty years lying before us is to have the best and strongest Navy. . . . Even now we have only just escaped binding ourselves to a mathematical parity with the United States, which would in fact make it impossible for us to protect our vital overseas supplies in any war with them. . . . A sound good British fleet operating through a well-conceived and well-maintained system of fueling bases ought to be able to keep us going at heavy expense until our unique resources in ship-building and ship-manning power gave us decisive preponderance. . . . These hideous and remote and improbable wars must be considered for they affect the foundations of the state. . . . We should reject all proposals for a treaty of mathematical parity with the United States . . . we should preserve entire liberty in numbers and design; and lastly, we should do our utmost to keep a Navy which as a whole is stronger and better than that of the United States.[130]

Churchill, in his early years, was never as fond of the United States as his later career might indicate. His antipathy toward America was probably at its peak after the Geneva Conference. There are a number of reasons for this. First, he saw no strategic justification for the American demand for cruiser parity. He grew more and more irritated at America's inability to recognize Britain's special cruiser needs. Second, his experiences while chancellor of the exchequer had not served to endear him to Americans, nor they to him. Squabbling over the payment of Britain's wartime debt and other financial issues had led to friction. Churchill thought the Americans were excessively domineering and wanted Britain to have the power to resist American dictation.[131] In his view American policy was "selfish," "extortionate," and the result of "avarice."[132] The American people, likewise, were "sunk in selfishness."[133]

The second premise on which Churchill's policy was based, was that naval supremacy could be achieved without undue expense. This was the policy's fatal weakness. Churchill fought against making concessions to the Americans and at the same time continued his crusade against new British cruiser construction. When he was leading the Cabinet to scupper the Geneva Conference, Churchill also began a fresh campaign against the Royal Navy's cruiser plans.[134] It would have been difficult to devise a more passive policy than the one Churchill proposed. He fought hard against Admiralty plans to lay down three cruisers in both 1927 and 1928, not wanting to build any cruisers in these years.[135] Eventually, the Cabinet appointed a special committee, including Churchill, to study the question of naval building. The committee, following the forceful lead of the chancellor, ended up endorsing his "wait and see" approach.[136] With this support Churchill was able to reduce substantially the Admiralty's requests. The Royal Navy would get only one new cruiser in 1927 and none in 1928.[137]

With the benefit of hindsight Churchill's actions seem more than slightly contradictory. He was, however, involved in a high-stakes gamble that he believed would maintain Britain's naval superiority. Churchill was growing increasingly skeptical about the United States' will to maintain its naval power. He believed that the Americans were "hopelessly" behind the Royal Navy, estimating that Britain was four times as strong in cruisers.[138] Moreover, American apathy, or so he reasoned, meant that they would find it extremely difficult to catch the Royal Navy:

As to the naval race, I hope it will not come off. At any rate I hope we shall let them (USA) pump themselves up for the next two years, while we rest on our enormous lead. . . . It is often not profitable to look too far ahead. But in principle I think it should be agreed that if the United States wish for the supremacy of the seas, they will find it very expensive to obtain.[139]

He thought American cruiser building would be limited to two or three ships annually, so that the British could delay their new building for a number of years.[140] In a sense he believed the Royal Navy could have its cake and eat it too: "Winston talked very freely about the USA. He thinks they are arrogant, fundamentally hostile to us, and that they wish to dominate world politics. He thinks their "Big Navy" talk is bluff which we ought to call."[141]

Churchill's estimation of the Coolidge administration might have been correct if the British had not so offended the Americans. If he did not understand this, more acute analysts of the American political scene did. Secretary of State Kellogg claimed that there was now in Congress "a pretty strong feeling that we should extend our building program."[142] William Castle, in an even more prophetic passage written just days after the Geneva Conference collapsed, described the predicament the British had made for themselves:

The tragic part of the whole business, from the British point of view, was that if there had been a perfectly frank agreement as to parity instead of a specious statement in favor of parity backed up by specific demands which made parity out of the question, Great Britain would have undoubtedly remained the mistress of the seas. I am afraid the conference has done a good deal toward creating a big navy party in this country, and although I do not think that there will be a feverish attempt to build up to what the British have and intend to have, I am afraid the big navy people may try to carry on their campaign through quite gratuitous insults of the British.[143]

The big-navy people in Congress acted precisely according to Castle's plan.[144] Thomas Butler took his cue from the General Board and President Coolidge. In December 1927 he introduced a bill calling for the construction of seventy-one new warships, including twenty-five Washington-class cruisers. If passed, this bill would have revolutionized the world cruiser balance. With these ships added to the eight cruisers authorized in 1924 and the ten Omahas of the 1916 program, America's cruiser force would be the most modern and powerful in the world. During the Geneva Conference, the British had wanted to limit the Americans to fifteen or even twelve Washington-class cruisers. The prospect of the United States' possessing thirty-three 10,000-ton eight-inch-gun cruisers meant that the British, who had only fourteen such vessels built, being built, or authorized, would have had to stretch their resources just to stay equal.

It was unlikely, however, that the American navy was going to get all twenty-five new cruisers. A strong, if outmaneuvered, small-navy faction remained in the House and Senate. Senator King continued to rail against the big-navy faction, which had supposedly "flagellated" the American people into supporting cruiser building.[145] He was supported by the maverick Senator Gerald Nye from North Dakota, who would be one of the country's leading "isolationists" in the late 1930s. However, the big-navy group had been reinvigorated by the collapse at Geneva. Men like Butler, Frederick Hale, and Jesse Metcalf, who had unsuccessfully fought for increased authorizations between

1922 and 1926, felt that the tide had turned in their favor. With people like Senator Borah admitting that the United States needed some new cruisers, some kind of large appropriation was bound to be passed.[146]

The first great debate over the naval bill was in the House of Representatives, and it was clear that the navy's support had increased. In a heated debate on the floor of the House on 13 and 15 March, the small-navy faction was pressed back.[147] Opponents of the bill complained that supporters were acting as if "the British were advancing on this capital as they did in 1812."[148] A young Fiorello LaGuardia made swinging attacks on the cruiser plan, but it was all to no avail.[149] On 17 March 1928 the House went ahead and approved a program of fifteen Washington-class cruisers, the largest American authorization since the end of the First World War. However, there still remained work to do, work which was made considerably easier for the U.S. Navy by one more British blunder.

This blunder was, ironically, part of a British attempt to improve Anglo-American relations. By early 1928 some in the British government came to believe that, far from meekly accepting cruiser superiority as Churchill prophesied, the United States was going to press ahead. Previously, the Cabinet and Admiralty had been seduced by Britain's numerical lead in cruisers into overestimating the depth of their supremacy. They had relatively few of the large, 10,000-ton, eight-inch-gun cruisers.[150] In 1927, when Churchill wanted to halt all British cruiser construction, the Royal Navy had only twelve either built or being built.[151]

Neither the Cabinet nor the Admiralty wanted to build many more of these larger cruisers. First, they threatened to make earlier classes obsolete. If the Americans went ahead and built an additional fifteen Washington-class cruisers on top of the eight authorized in 1923, the British fleet would look decidedly long in the tooth. Also, the large cost of the Washington-class cruisers made them undesirable. A single 10,000-ton, eight-inch-gun cruiser cost about £2,200,000, while a 7,500-ton cruiser with six-inch guns required only £1,400,000.[152] If the British were to match an American fleet of twenty-three Washington-class cruisers, it could cost an additional £20 million annually for four or five years. This is why the Baldwin government went to the Geneva Conference hoping to limit American building of Washington-class cruisers. It was even willing to scrap some British vessels if the Americans would agree to parity at twelve ships each.

When the American House of Representatives passed the fifteen-cruiser bill, this Achilles' heel in Britain's position was revealed. In May the Admiralty asked the Cabinet to reconsider the cruiser question.[153] Soon more moderate Cabinet voices, such as Lord Cushendun, Cecil's successor, and Lord Salisbury, leader of the House of Lords, also showed concern. Previously, these two had been mostly passive, but the obvious failure of Churchill and his allies to predict the Coolidge administration's reaction to Geneva brought them to the forefront.

Salisbury wrote directly to Baldwin, while Cushendun circulated a memorandum attacking both Churchill and Bridgeman.[154]

Out of this anxiety emerged the Anglo-French compromise. It was an attempt by the British to reach an understanding with the French over land armaments and at the same time get French backing for the limitation of eight-inch-gun cruisers.[155] Under the terms of the compromise gun caliber, not tonnage, would be the primary determinant in cruiser arms control. A country could have as many 10,000-ton cruisers as it wanted but would be restricted in the number of ships that could carry guns larger than six-inches. This, it was hoped, would soothe American nerves.[156]

It did not have the desired affect. In 1928 the Americans were deeply suspicious of British behavior. Castle wrote in his diary that any new naval initiatives would have to come from London.[157] Admiral Hilary Jones, one of the leaders of the American delegation to Geneva, blasted the British for dishonesty and accused them of going back on their word.[158] When the Anglo-French proposals were first revealed to the Americans in August 1928, they plopped down into this sea of animosity. From the White House to the State Department and through to the Navy Department, there was a unanimous view that the compromise was sneaky and self-serving.

When Kellogg first learned of the Anglo-French proposal, he said that he could not see how the United States would agree.[159] Others in the State Department knew right away that the ultimate impact of the compromise would be to strengthen the big-navy forces in America.[160] To the U.S. Navy the compromise offered few advantages. If America was to build 10,000 cruisers, then the navy wanted to be able to arm them with the most powerful gun possible.[161] Otherwise, all the Americans would be doing is neutering a large number of their new vessels to help prolong the useful life of Britain's smaller, older cruisers. The General Board suggested that the British be told that these new proposals were "even more unacceptable" than the ones put forward at Geneva.[162]

The person who became most enraged by the Anglo-French compromise was Calvin Coolidge. The president had been on a slow burn since the collapse of the Geneva Conference, and the Anglo-French compromise caused him to explode. Castle claimed that Coolidge now hated the British so much that he was refusing to see Sir Esme Howard, the United Kingdom's ambassador in Washington.[163] In public, Coolidge was able to hold his tongue as long as the 1928 presidential campaign was ongoing. In his speeches the president often referred to the need to build more American cruisers, but his language was usually moderate.[164] Once Herbert Hoover was elected, however, Coolidge lost his inhibitions. On 11 November, during his official Armistice Day address, the president publicly called for American naval superiority. He also vented his anger at British behavior, starting with the fiasco at Geneva and ending with the Anglo-French compromise:

I requested another conference which the British and Japanese attended, but to which Italy and France did not come. The United States there proposed a limitation of cruiser tonnage of 250,000 to 300,000 tons. As near as we could figure out their proposal, the British asked for from 425,000 to 600,000 tons. As it appeared to us that to agree to so large a tonnage constituted not a limitation, but an extension of war fleets, no agreement was made.

     Since that time no progress seems to have been made. In fact, ⌣ ⌣ movements have been discouraging. During last summer France and England made a tentative offer which would limit the kind of cruisers and submarines adapted to the use of the United States, but left without limit the kind adapted to their use. The United States of course refused to accept this offer.[165]

The passion of the president was crucial. After the House passed the fifteen-cruiser bill, known as the Second Butler Cruiser Act, progress in the Senate was slowed by the 1928 elections. After November the debate resumed. A vocal small-navy faction dominated by Borah, King, and Nye still opposed the cruiser plan.[166] However, with the president willing to press hard, much of the Senate gave in. On 5 January 1929 the act finally passed. For the Baldwin government it was a terribly depressing turn of events. When the Americans had reacted skeptically to the Anglo-French proposals, Cushendun, who was sitting in for Foreign Secretary Austen Chamberlain during the latter's illness, tried to calm their nerves.[167] However, as things spun more and more out of control, a sense of panic set in.[168] The British government began to cast around frantically to find ways of placating the Americans.

Some believed that the Americans might be won over by a concession on neutral rights or "freedom of the seas." Austen Chamberlain thought disagreements on this issue, which had plagued Anglo-American relations from the War of 1812 through to the First World War, had been the cause of some friction at the Geneva Conference.[169] However, as Chamberlain was still ill during the fallout over the Anglo-French compromise, others in the Cabinet took up the issue at first.[170] The Admiralty opposed the idea of a compromise, but they were overruled.[171] When Chamberlain returned to work, he put a great deal of pressure on Baldwin to support a compromise with the Americans. Soon there was a rush of diplomatic activity in both Washington and London.[172]

It was a well-meaning, if ultimately subsidiary, exercise. The Americans were pleased that the British were being accommodating on neutral rights, but they considered it secondary to the overall question of naval parity. Without a concession on this issue Anglo-American relations could not be materially improved, something that became more and more obvious as time went on. In October 1928 Esme Howard, who was probably the Briton with the most first-hand knowledge of American resentment, called for a new policy. In a private memorandum sent to Baldwin, he suggested that the Anglo-French compromise be withdrawn and attacked the Royal Navy for measuring itself against the U.S. Navy.[173] In January Howard again said that the United States would accept nothing but parity and that all discussions with the Americans had to proceed along that basis.[174] The next Foreign Office mandarin to strike was Robert Craigie, a counselor who had previously been first secretary at the British Embassy in Washington. Craigie wrote a powerful memorandum, which was passed to the Cabinet.[175] Craigie was convinced that the Americans were not bluffing and believed that a long period of strained Anglo-American relations could be very damaging to British interests. Like Howard, he dismissed the notion that the Americans would be content with anything less than complete parity:

Another illusion which it would be dangerous to preserve is that any United States Government would be prepared or able to accept anything less than some form of "mathematical parity," If this illusion is still to prevail, it will be far better not to attempt any further negotiations with the United States on this subject. The attempt to substitute some other form of parity for "mathematical parity" . . . would appear to the Americans as yet a further British "dodge" to retain supremacy in practice.[176]

Winston Churchill had obviously been stung badly by this turn of events. Coolidge's Armistice Day speech and Craigie's memorandum had begun to expose the weaknesses inherent in his naval policy. His first reaction was to lash out. The chancellor of the exchequer called the American president a "New England backwoodsman" who would "soon sink back into the obscurity from which only accident extracted him," while Craigie was accused of trying to "inculcate meekness and caution."[177] Beyond launching personal attacks, however, Churchill had precious few options. He returned to his refrain of "wait and see" which day by day was becoming more and more untenable. Any move by Churchill to argue for the resumption of British cruiser construction or to press for a negotiated settlement with the United States would have been an admission of his misjudgment. All he could do was to continue to fight against the Admiralty's requests for new ships and hope that the United States once again lost interest in building new ships.[178]

If Churchill was left with no room to maneuver, the rest of Cabinet was not so restricted. The Admiralty pressed for the construction of five new Washington-class cruisers.[179] Most in the government, however, were more interested in improving Anglo-American relations. With a general election due in 1929, the continuing, damaging rift with the United States was bound to be exploited by the opposition. Lord Cushendun explicitly mentioned the "unfortunate influence" the present state of Anglo-American relations could have on the voters.[180]

Eventually, Stanley Baldwin, with his trusty political instincts, realized that something dramatic had to be done. The prime minister decided that he should pay a personal visit to the United States. When William Castle visited Europe in late 1928, the prime minister took him aside and practically pleaded for an invitation to go to America:[181] "I want to go to America and if you would give me any excuse I should go. It would mean a lot."[182] Baldwin seemed to hold out great hopes for reaching an accommodation with the president-elect, Herbert Hoover, and began to swamp him with hints. The prime minister took time out to talk to newspaperman Edward Price Bell, a known conduit of information to

Hoover, and again said he wanted to visit America.[183] Next, the American Embassy in Paris passed along similar gossip to the president-elect.[184]

Once Hoover assumed power in March 1929, the Baldwin government went public with its desire to make a deal. Responding to a conciliatory speech by Hugh Gibson, Austen Chamberlain stated that the British government would now take American naval arms control proposals, even involving cruisers, very seriously.[185] The foreign secretary followed this statement up with his own meeting with Edward Price Bell, where he repeated many of the earlier assurances given by Baldwin.[186] Perhaps the best example of the seriousness of the prime minister lay not in his hints to the Americans but in his plans for his own Cabinet. In March Baldwin was contemplating demoting Winston Churchill, the creator of the government's disastrous naval policy, from the Treasury to the India office if the Conservatives won the upcoming election.[187] Unfortunately for him, Stanley Baldwin was never able to make his trip to the United States. In the May 1929 general election his ruling Conservative Party was rejected by the voters, and a new Labour government, headed by Ramsay MacDonald, assumed power. Ultimately, it is impossible to tell whether the strains in Anglo-American relations brought on by the Baldwin government's naval policy played a large role in this defeat, but they certainly did not help.[188]

## NOTES

1. WSC, vol. 5, Companion, Cabinet Memorandum, 20 July 1927, pp. 1030-35.

2. GBDC, Series 8, Book 2, Coolidge Speech, 11 November 1928.

3. T. Buckley, *The United States and the Washington Conference 1921-22*, pp. 172-184.

4. CR, 67th Congress, 9 March 1922, p. 3598.

5. Ibid., 10, 11 April 1922, pp. 5234-55, 5333.

6. Roosevelt. Jr., Mss #39, Roosevelt to Harvey, 23 March 1922.

7. SCCCNO, File 109, Reel 17, Rowcliff to CNO, 12 May 1922.

8. S. Roskill, *Naval Policy between the Wars*, vol. 1, Appendix D, E.

9. GBSF, 420-2, FY 1924 Construction Program, 12 July 1922.

10. GBSF, 420-2, FY 1927 Construction Program, 3 April 1925, FY 1928 Construction Program, 30 March 1926.

11. CR, 69th Congress, p. 2371, 19 January 1926, pp. 2606-10, 22 January 1926.

12. SCCCNO, 109:13, Reel 17, Secretary to All Bureaus, 12 July 1922.

13. ARSN, 15 November 1922, p. 38.

14. D. Richardson, *The Evolution of British Disarmament Policy in the 1920s*, p. 104

15. P. E. Coletta, ed., *American Secretaries of the Navy*, vol. 2, pp. 598-600.

16. Ibid., pp. 605-630.

17. GBDC, Series 4, "British Fundamental Policy," 17 April 1925.

18. WPL 11, Report of Chief Umpire Joint Army-Navy Exercise, January 1924.

19. GBSF 420, Comparison of Blue-Red Capital Ship Strength, April 1924.

20. GBSF 420, Memorandum, 29 November 1922, Memorandum, 19 December 1922.

21. GB Hearings, The Situation in Great Britain, 10 October 1925.

22. GBSF 429, Hussey Lecture, 5 December 1924.

23. SCCCNO 109: 14, War Plans Memorandum, 27 March 1923. See also GBSF 425, Director of War Plans Memorandum, 17 March 1924.

24. SCCCNO File 203, War Plans Division to CNO, 13 April 1922.

25. SCCCNO 109: 14, War Plans Memorandum, 27 March 1923. See also GBSF 425, Director of War Plans Memorandum, 17 March 1924.

26. SCCCNO File 178, War Plan Orange, 15 August 1924.

27. SCCCNO File 203, U.S. Naval Policy, 29 March 1922.

28. See GBSF 420-2, General Board Memorandum, 31 May 1922.

29. GBDC, Series 4, General Board Draft Policy, 24 July 1925.

30. SCCCNO, 109: 14, Wilbur to Bureaus, 15 April 1926.

31. Hoover Mss, "US Naval Policy," Approved by Wilbur, 6 October 1928.

32. ADM 116/2311, "Empire Naval Policy and Cooperation," April 1926.

33. GB Hearings, "The Situation in Great Britain," 20 October 1925.

34. CAB 24/171, "Navy Estimates," 5 February 1925.

35. CAB 24/171, "Navy Estimates 1925-26," 27 January 1925.

36. Ibid.

37. CAB 24/171, "Navy Estimates," 5 February 1925.

38. B. J. C. McKercher, *The Second Baldwin Government and the United States 1924-1929*, pp. 5-19.

39. Cecil Mss #51073, Churchill to Cecil, 20 January 1925.

40. Baldwin Mss #232, Churchill Memorandum, 25 March 1925.

41. WSC, vol. 5, Companion, vol. 1, Churchill Memorandum, 29 January 1925, pp. 359-368.

42. CAB 24/171, Churchill Memorandum, 7 February 1925.

43. Baldwin Mss #2, Churchill to Baldwin, 15 December 1924.

44. WSC, vol. 5 Companion, vol. 1, Cabinet Memorandum, 29 January 1925, p. 364.

45. CAB 24/171, Bridgeman Memorandum, 5 March 1925.

46. CAB 24/172, "Naval Policy," 3 April 1925.

47. CAB 24/165, "Naval Estimates 1924-25."

48. ADM 116/3123, 116/3167, Anglo-Japanese War Plans.

49. Baldwin Mss #2, Bridgeman Memorandum, March 1925.

50. Roskill Mss, Admiralty Plans Division Memorandum, 31 January 1923.

51. CAB 24/174, Naval Programme Committee Report, 13 July 1925.

52. Beatty Mss 8/8, Hankey to Beatty, 13 July 1925.

53. Coolidge Mss 18, Butler to Coolidge, 15 December 1926.

54. AMPUSA, 10 February 1927, p. 7.

55. ADM 116/2311. "Empire Naval Policy and Cooperation 1926," April 1926.

56. ADM 116/2609, "Papers Prepared for the British Empire Delegation to the 1927 Geneva Conference."

57. Ibid.

58. Ibid.

59. ADM 116/3371, "Plan for Naval Limitation and Disarmament Conference at Geneva," 17 March 1927.

60. Baldwin Mss #130, Hankey to Baldwin, 29 June 1927.

61. Baldwin Mss #130, Cecil to Baldwin, 9 March 1927.

62. D. Carlton, "Disarmament with Guarantees: Lord Cecil 1922-27," *Disarmament and Arms Control*, vol. 3, #2.

63. Cecil Mss #51073, Cecil to Churchill, 24 July 1925.

64. Baldwin Mss #130, Cecil to Baldwin, 9 March 1927.

65. Vansittart Mss 2/5. "The Foreign Policy of His Majesty's Government," Memorandum, April 1927.

66. D. Dutton, *Austen Chamberlain: Gentleman in Politics*, p. 276.

67. Baldwin Mss #130, Birkenhead to Baldwin, probably July 1927.

68. Castle Mss, Diary, 4 January 1927.

69. Castle Mss, "England," Castle to Hougton, 15 April 1927.

70. Castle Mss, "England," Houghton to Castle, 28 February 1928.

71. Ibid., 10 March 1927.

72. Castle Mss, "England," Castle to Houghton, 2 May 1927.

73. Ibid.

74. GBDC, Series 5, Admiral H. P. Jones to Wilbur, 9 March 1927.

75. Hoover Mss, Naval Disarmament, General Board 1927, GB Memo, 2 June 1927.

76. Roskill Mss, General Board Meeting Conclusions, 21 April 1927.

77. Hoover Mss, Naval Disarmament, General Board 1927, GB Memo, 21 April 1927.

78. Ibid., 25 April 1927.

79. Ibid., p. 14. See also GB Memo, 1 June 1927.

80. Cecil Mss #51118, Cecil to Tyrell, 24 June 1927.

81. Roskill, *Naval Policy between the Wars*, vol. 1, pp. 498-516; McKercher, *The Second Baldwin Government and the United States 1924-1929*, pp. 119-139; L. E. Ellis, *Frank B. Kellogg and American Foreign Policy 1925-1929*, pp. 167-184, or D. Carlton, "Great Britain and the Coolidge Naval Disarmament Conference of 1927," *Political Science Quarterly*.

82. Coolidge Mss, Series 20, Gibson to Secretary of State Kellogg, 29 June 1927.

83. Bridgeman Mss #1, Bridgeman Diary, 29, 30 June 1927.

84. Coolidge Mss Series 20, Gibson to Secretary of State Kellogg, 29 & 30 June 1927.

85. Royal Institute of International Affairs, *Survey of International Affairs, 1927*, p. 51.

86. GBDC, Series 6, Committee Minutes, 28 June 1927.

87. Hoover Mss, Naval Disarmament, General Board 1927, GB Memo, 25 April 1927.

88. GBDC, Series 6, Admiral Schofield Diary, 28 June 1927.

89. Ibid., 9 July 1927.

90. Castle Mss, Castle Diary, 9 July 1927. See also GBDC, Series 6, Schofield Diary, 1 July 1927.

91. GBDC, Series 6, Admiral Schofield Diary, 5 July 1927.

92. Cecil Mss #51078, Chamberlain to Cecil, 5 July 1927. See also Cecil Mss #51104, Foreign Office cable, 4 July 1927.

93. Templewood Mss C 4, Cabinet Minutes, 4 July 1927.

94. CAB 24/187, Churchill Memorandum, 29 June 1927.

95. Baldwin Mss #130, Beatty to Baldwin, 30 June 1927.

96. Baldwin Mss # 130, Birkenhead to Baldwin, probably July 1927.

97. CAB 24/187 CID Proceedings Organized by Hankey, 12 July 1927.

98. WSC, vol. 5, Companion, Cabinet Memorandum, 20 July 1927, pp. 1030-35.

99. CAB 24/187 CID Proceedings Organized by Hankey, 12 July 1927.

100. BFP Documents, Series 1A, vol. 3, #446, p. 683.

101. CAB 24/188, Baldwin Memorandum, 21 July 1927.

102. BFP Documents, Series 1A, vol. 3, #457, p. 693.

103. WSC, vol. 5, Companion, Davidson to Baldwin, 27 July 1927, pp. 1037-38.

104. Cecil Mss #51073, Cecil to Churchill, 26 July 1927.

105. Baldwin Mss #230, Hankey to Baldwin, 28 July 1927.

106. Ibid.

107. Castle Mss, "England," Houghton to Castle, 21 July 1927.

108. Coolidge Mss, Series 20, Kellogg to Coolidge, 29 July 1927.

109. Coolidge Mss, Series 20, Kellogg, Coolidge Conversation, 29 July 1927.

110. BFP Documents, Series 1A, vol. 3, #474, p. 705.

111. Ibid., #477, p. 707.

112. WSC, vol. 5, Companion, Churchill to Cecil, 14 September 1927, p. 1049.

113. Coolidge Mss, Series 20, Kellogg to Coolidge, 10 August 1927.

114. Baldwin Mss #131, Bridgeman to Baldwin, 7 August 1927.

115. Bridgeman Mss #3, Chamberlain to Bridgeman, 5 August 1927.

116. Cecil Mss #51078/79, Chamberlain to Cecil, 14 August 1927.

117. Cecil Mss #51078/79, Cecil to Chamberlain, 10 August 1927.

118. Baldwin Mss #131, Cecil to Baldwin, 9 August 1927.

119. Bridgeman Mss #1, Cecil to Bridgeman, 18 November 1927.

120. Cecil Mss #51073, Cecil to Churchill, 26 July 1927.

121. Cecil Mss #51078/79, Cecil to Chamberlain, 18 August 1927.

122. NID Papers, C9B, Box 442, "Exchange of President and Secretary of State," 29 July 1927

123. Ibid., 30 July 1927.

124. Coolidge Mss, Series 20, Kellogg to Coolidge, 10 August 1927.

125. Castle Mss, Diary, 2 August 1927.

126. GBSF 420-2, Proposed Building Plan, 27 September 1927.

127. AMPUSA, 1927, pp. 2-4.

128. G. Davis, *A Navy Second to None*, p. 326.

129. Cecil Mss #51078/79, Cecil to Chamberlain, 18 August 1927.

130. Hankey Mss #5/1, Churchill Comments Recorded by P. J. Grigg, 10 February 1928.

131. WSC, vol. 5, Companion, Churchill to Leith-Ross, 23 September 1928, Churchill to Baldwin, 30 September 1928.

132. WSC, vol. 5, Companion, Churchill to Niemeyer, 2 January 1925, Cabinet Memorandum, 12 January 1925, Churchill to Amery, 21 March 1926.

133. WSC, vol. 5, Companion, Churchill to A. Chamberlain, 1 September 1925.

134. WSC, vol. 5, Companion, Cabinet Memorandum, 25 July 1927.

135. WSC, vol. 5, Companion, Churchill to Bridgeman, 28 October 1928, Churchill to Bridgeman, 4 November 1927, Cabinet Memorandum, 6 November 1927, Cabinet Memorandum, 17 November 1927, Churchill to Bridgeman, 28 November 1927.

136. ADM 116/3439, "Extract from the Conclusions of a Meeting of the Cabinet . . ." 27 December 1927.

137. Roskill, *Naval Policy between the Wars*, vol. 1, pp. 555-59.

138. WSC, vol. 5, Companion, Churchill to Bridgeman, 4 November 1927, Cabinet Memorandum, 12 November 1927.

139. Bridgeman Mss #3, Churchill to Bridgeman, 16 September 1927.

140. WSC, vol. 5, Companion, Cabinet Memorandum, 6 November 1927, Churchill to Douglas-Hogg, 14 November 1927.

141. WSC, vol. 5, Companion, J. Scrymegour-Weddeburn (11th Earl of Dundee) diary, 21 September 1928.

142. Coolidge Mss, Series 20, Kellogg to Coolidge, 10 August 1927.

143. Castle Mss, England, Castle to Houghton, 12 August 1927.

144. Davis, *A Navy Second to None*, pp. 322-333.

145. CR, vol. 69, pp. 3101-07, 16 February 1928.

146. Borah Mss, Box 256, Magruder Memorandum, 1928.

147. CR, vol. 69, pp. 4650-54, 4836-41.

148. Ibid., p. 4653.

149. CR, vol. 69, pp. 4839-41. See also vol. 70, p. 3010.

150. CAB 24/173, Bridgeman Memorandum, 30 April 1925.

151. Alexander Mss #5/2, Alexander to MacDonald, 18 September 1929.

152. ADM 116/2578, Cabinet Memorandum, 11 May 1928.

153. Ibid.

154. Baldwin Mss #2, Salisbury to Baldwin, 22 May 1928.

155. ADM 116/2578, Cabinet Memorandum, 26 June 1928; CAB 24/197, Memorandum, 28 August 1928.

156. CAB 24/197, Admiralty Memorandum, 5 October 1928.

157. Castle Mss, Diary, 4 January 1928.

158. NID Papers, C-9-B Box 442, Jones Lecture, 19 January 1928.

159. Coolidge Mss, Series 20, Kellogg to Coolidge, 3 August 1928.

160. Castle Mss, "England," Castle to Cox, 8 October 1928.

161. GBSF 420-8, Schofield Memorandum, 26 November 1928; Long Memorandum, 27 November 1928.

162. GBSF 438-1, General Board Memorandum, 21 September 1928.

163. Castle Mss, Diary, 22, 23 October 1928.

164. GBDC, Series 8, Book 2, Coolidge Speech, 30 May 1928.

165. Ibid., 11 November 1928.

166. CR, vol. 70, pp. 2589-94 & pp. 4836-41.

167. GBDC, Series 8, American Embassy to Secretary of State, 10 August 1928.

168. See Baldwin Mss #230, Bridgeman to Baldwin, 5 October 1928.

169. CAB 24/189, Chamberlain Memorandum, 17 November 1927.

170. CAB 24/201, Memorandum, 16 January 1929, Memorandum 11 February 1929.

171. CAB 24/201, Admiralty Memorandum, 21 February 1929.

172. McKercher, *The Second Baldwin Government and the United States 1924-1929*, pp. 176-94.

173. Baldwin Mss #109, Howard Memorandum, 17 October 1928.

174. Baldwin Mss #109, Howard to Vansittart, 24 January 1929.

175. CAB 24/198, Craigie Memorandum with Cushendun Note, 14 November 1928.

176. Ibid.

177. CAB 24/199, Churchill Memorandum, 19 November 1928.

178. Ibid., 15 December 1928.

179. CAB 24/199, Admiralty Memorandum, December, 1928.

180. CAB 24/198, Craigie Memorandum with Cushendun Note, 14 November 1928.

181. Hoover Mss, Kellogg Correspondence, Castle to Kellogg, 21 November 1928.

182. Castle Mss, Diary, 16 November 1928. See also Houghton to Castle, 17 December 1928.

183. Hoover Mss, Bell to Hoover, 2 May 1929.

184. Hoover Mss, Maclean to Hoover, 19 February 1929.

185. Hoover Mss, Disarmament, Atherton to State Department, 24 April 1929.

186. Hoover Mss, Presidential, Bell to Hoover, 15 May 1929.

187. WSC, vol. 5, Companion, Irwin to Baldwin, 28 March 1929.

188. Richardson, *The Evolution of British Disarmament Policy in the 1920s*, pp. 197-211

# 9

# The Highpoint and Collapse of the Naval Arms Control Process

You asked me about the reduced figure of 50 cruisers when 70 cruisers was given in 1927. It is somewhat difficult to explain but the facts of the situation are that the figure 50 now represents the only figure practicable under a reasonable building programme of 3 cruisers a year. The situation has got into a bad state owing to the dropping of 3 cruisers as a gesture by the Conservative Government after the 1927 Conference. We are now in the position that even with a building programme of 3 cruisers a year we shall not have 50 up-to-date cruisers in ten years time.[1]

    Roger Bellairs, Admiralty Director of Naval Intelligence, 13 December 1929

The building program is a veritable Godsend. Few people realize how far below treaty strength and relative strength we have sunk, and also how badly, in some instances, we need replacements. Your action will also go a long way towards saving a starving national asset in the case of our shipbuilding yards, not to mention the great help to our own people in our own navy yards.[2]

    Admiral Harold Stark to Franklin Roosevelt, 22 June 1933

## THE FIRST LONDON NAVAL CONFERENCE

With Herbert Hoover and Ramsay MacDonald now in charge of American and British naval policy, the chances for a new arms control agreement were considerably enhanced. Coolidge had left office still bitter.[3] Hoover, on the other hand, immediately began looking for a solution. A Quaker, he was probably the most "pacifist" president in American history. Like Coolidge before the Geneva Conference Hoover wanted to spend as little on the armed forces as possible. To help improve the chances of an agreement, Hoover appointed the Republican Party stalwart Henry Stimson, someone determined to improve Anglo-American relations, as his secretary of state.[4] Together they set out to try to find some common ground with the British.[5]

The idea that the new president hit upon was the "yardstick" proposal. Instead of using gross tonnage to establish cruiser parity, Hoover was willing to let the newer, more powerful American ships count for more than an equal tonnage of older or smaller ships. Thus, the Royal Navy would be allowed a greater overall cruiser tonnage of older vessels. In late April 1929 Hugh Gibson gave the first public hint that the United States was willing to accept some sort of "yardstick."[6] The reaction to his remarks by both the British press and government was very favorable.[7] To try to take advantage of this development the new American ambassador in Great Britain, Charles Dawes, was told to immediately begin talks with the British.[8]

By June 1929, once MacDonald and the Labour Party took power, Hoover seemed even more eager. He asked the secretary of the navy, the somewhat ineffectual Charles F. Adams, to find out how many new American cruisers it would take to provide for a force equal in strength, if not number, to the Royal Navy's.[9] In MacDonald, Hoover knew he was facing a man with similar aspirations. The new British premier quickly started dropping hints that he was just as willing as Baldwin to go to America. In late June MacDonald used Edward Price Bell to tell Hoover that he agreed with the American president completely on the question of arms control and that he was "ready and eager" to visit Washington.[10] The make up of MacDonald's Cabinet also boded well for a naval agreement. The arch supremacist Churchill was succeeded at the Treasury by Philip Snowden, a long-time member of the labor movement who had opposed the First World War. The new first lord of the Admiralty, A. V. Alexander, a leader in Britain's Cooperative movement, also promised change. A strong supporter of the arms control process, Alexander had praised Cecil for resigning after the Geneva Conference.[11] He was also considerably more energetic and daring than his predecessor. While Bridgeman refused to tamper with the vested interests in the Admiralty, Alexander attempted to reform some of the fleet's more traditional elements.[12]

This new government quickly made it clear that it was willing to use the "yardstick" to give the United States cruiser parity.[13] To facilitate agreement, it was even willing to reduce temporarily the Royal Navy's cruiser target from seventy vessels to fifty. This was made possible by the upcoming block obsolescence of many British cruisers. Thirty-five of Britain's fifty-nine front-line cruisers would become obsolete in the next ten years.[14] The MacDonald government therefore felt it could promise to limit the Royal Navy to fifty cruisers until 1936.[15] Even the new Director of the Admiralty's Intelligence Division, Admiral Roger Bellairs, grudgingly admitted that the idea made some sense.

As the preliminary contacts between the Americans and British seemed so promising, it was decided that MacDonald should visit America. With a naval arms control conference scheduled to be held in London in 1930, MacDonald's trip was seen as an ideal way to prepare the upcoming negotiations. Hoover seemed as pleased as the British prime minister at the prospect of a face-to-face meeting. He hoped their meetings might relieve the United States from proceeding with the full fifteen-cruiser construction program. As Hoover told Stimson:

It seems to me that there is the most profound outlook for peace today that we have had at any time in the last half century, more especially if we succeed in our conference of January next, yet in effect we are plunging along building more ships at fabulous expense only with the hope and aspiration that at the end of a period so short as six years we shall be able to sink a considerable part of them.[16]

From 4 to 10 of October Hoover and MacDonald held talks at the president's retreat in rural Virginia.[17] The main issue under discussion was the number of Washington-class cruisers the United States would build and how much extra tonnage of smaller cruisers the British were to be allowed.[18] MacDonald would have preferred to see the Americans limited to fifteen 10,000-ton, eight-inch-gun cruisers, though he would accept an American allowance of eighteen.[19] While Hoover said the United States needed twenty-one large cruisers, he was so excited at the prospect of an agreement that he was willing, indeed eager, to come down to eighteen.[20] One of the most striking things about the talks was not just how close the sides were to an agreement but how the whole tone of Anglo-American relations had changed since the departure of Coolidge and Churchill.

The new British Labour government had no time for Churchill's apocalyptic pronunciations and ruled out the prospect of the United States and Great Britain's ever going to war. As MacDonald told Dawes:

If I had the shadow of dread that the United States and ourselves would ever be at war, it would be impossible for me to agree to parity being expressed by any number of 8-inch cruisers beyond our own—e.g. 15. . . . Everybody here is anxious to accommodate themselves to an agreement with you on the assumption that there will be no war and no interference in which our fleets are involved. But I am not justified in making the same assumption as regards the rest of the world.[21]

Hoover and Stimson likewise had no trace of Coolidge's Anglophobia. They termed any idea of an Anglo-American war "unthinkable."[22] The one body that was still mostly immune to this lovefest was the U.S. Navy. When Hoover had come to power, the navy had worked hard to convince the new president that the

British were a legitimate threat. It knew that Hoover had little desire to build the fifteen new cruisers authorized by Congress. As soon as Hoover took office, a retired admiral sent him a memorandum that claimed that even if the whole cruiser program were completed, the United States would still lag behind the British.[23] The General Board also worked over the new secretary of the navy. It tried to convince Adams to support the construction of five additional Washington-class cruisers.[24] When the issue of the "yardstick" was first mooted, the American navy thus reacted with skepticism.[25] Having striven hard for full tonnage parity, the General Board did not want to see the Royal Navy's ending up with a larger, if older, force.[26]

However with Hoover and MacDonald working toward an agreement, the American navy was starved of crucial anti-British oxygen. There were worrying signs that the fleet was reverting back to its pre-Geneva position of relative unimportance. While Hoover was agreeing to an American limit of eighteen Washington-class cruisers, the General Board was claiming that the number twenty-one was its "absolute minimum."[27] As the London Naval Conference came closer, the navy's position did not improve. In early January 1930, the General Board still maintained that anything less than twenty-one Washington-class cruisers was "unacceptable."[28] However, when a tentative plan for the American delegation was drawn up in late January, the administration opted for a limit of eighteen.[29] The navy still argued its case, with Admiral Hilary Jones taking the lead.[30] Yet, the navy had seemed to have little influence.

The First London Naval Conference began on 21 January 1930. It was a very different affair from the Washington and Geneva meetings that had preceded it. There had been very little preparatory negotiations for either of the earlier conferences. At Washington this had been surmounted by Hughes' dramatic proposals, but the lack of preparation was one of the reasons for the debacle at Geneva. The London meeting, meanwhile, was easily the best prepared and best organized of all the naval arms control conferences. The Americans and British had been in close contact for almost nine months before the opening session and had already hammered out the framework of an agreement.

The end result was that the Anglo-American naval rivalry that had dominated both naval policies since 1918 was settled. A yardstick agreement was instituted for cruisers, with the United States allowed 323,500 tons and the British 339,000 tons. The British were allowed the larger figure but they were limited to fifteen Washington-class cruisers, while the United States could build eighteen. Parity was also agreed to for destroyers and submarines, with America and Britain agreeing to limits of 150,000 tons and 52,700 tons, respectively.

These were liberating agreements for the Americans and British. While the debate about the advisability of the tonnage allowances continued, the amount of time wasted in each country worrying about the other's naval strength was now drastically reduced. For the last twelve years, especially over the preceding two and a half, the British and American governments and navies were preoccupied with a question that was not vital to their national security. The Anglo-

American naval balance was important for reasons of prestige and politics, but it was not an issue of national life and death. By settling most of the outstanding Anglo-American naval issues at London, both were allowed to concentrate on legitimate issues of national or imperial security.

The first of these was the Japanese navy. The Japanese had benefited from the split in Anglo-American relations. At Geneva they were able to play the middle-man between the two larger naval powers. Afterward, while Coolidge and Churchill exacerbated the Anglo-American split, the Japanese attended to their own needs. With plans to expand their influence in Manchuria and China, the Japanese decided they needed more than the 5-5-3 ratio.[31] However, when Hoover and MacDonald began patching up Anglo-American differences, the Japanese feared that they might be the odd men out.[32]

When the conference began, the Japanese tried to increase their relative auxiliary ship strength by replacing the 5-5-3 ratio with one of 10-10-7. This would have presented enormous problems for the Anglo-American compromise over eight-inch-gun cruisers. The Japanese had twelve eight-inch-gun cruisers, weighing 108,400 tons, either built or being built.[33] If America was to be allocated 180,000 tons of Washington-class cruisers, the Japanese wanted 126,000 tons, or the right to build a total of fourteen, only one less than the Royal Navy had.[34]

Both the Americans and British were determined to limit the Japanese from building any more Washington-class cruisers. Though the two Western powers tried to make it seem that they were not acting jointly, they eventually came up with a plan that the Japanese had to accept. In exchange for building no more large cruisers the Japanese were given the 10-10-7 ratio for smaller cruisers and destroyers and the right to parity with the British and Americans in submarines. As at Washington, a united Anglo-American front forced the Japanese to agree to something that they knew would be domestically unpopular. In the case of the London Treaty it was a very serious development. The concession on cruiser strength caused a great resentment among Japanese nationalists. This faction, which had been considerably strengthened by the Great Depression, led a bitter campaign against the London Treaty. While they were unsuccessful in the short term, the London Treaty marked the last time that the Japanese would consent to having a smaller naval allowance than that of the Americans and British.

While both the Americans and British were concerned with the Japanese, there still remained the question of the European naval balance. To the British this was always a question of central importance. At the Washington Conference the French and Italians had agreed to limit their capital ship strength to 35 percent of the Royal Navy's. The French only grudgingly accepted this settlement. They found it insulting to accept the same capital ship allowance as the Italians. As a way of recouping some pride the French had refused to accept any numerical limitations on auxiliary ships. Like the Japanese they had benefited from the split in Anglo-American relations in the late 1920s. However, when the British and Americans began to cooperate, the French feared that they might once again be backed into a corner.

At London the French argued that, like the British, they had a special need for cruisers. They wanted a nation's entire coastline, including that of their imperial possessions, to be used as a measure of auxiliary ship need.[35] This, naturally, ruled out any chance of the French's accepting auxiliary ship parity with the Italians. Since parity with France was the sole object of Italian policy, it became impossible to incorporate these powers into the London settlement. It was a worrying omission for the British, who were determined to maintain their European supremacy. To protect their position, the British included an article in the London Treaty that allowed the signatories to exceed the tonnage ratios if other powers, not party to the agreements, engaged in a naval race. Though this exception could hardly be described as a triumph of British policy, it was a sign of how things had changed for the better. By not having to worry about American support, the British were able to cope with Japanese and French recalcitrance in a level-headed and sensible manner.

The last meeting of the London Conference was held on 22 April 1930. Hoover and Stimson seemed particularly pleased with the results.[36] Though some of the big-navy supporters in the United States saw the agreements as a lost opportunity, the Senate overwhelmingly approved. In Britain there was less rejoicing, but MacDonald felt he had gotten the best deal possible for the Royal Navy.[37] It was an important moment in interwar-period history. With the First London Conference the naval arms control process reached its apex.[38] The struggle for naval supremacy between America and Britain that had begun with Woodrow Wilson's 1916 program was finally settled. Parity between the two was agreed to for every type of warship while Japan had accepted a smaller ratio for every category except submarines. The tragedy of the London Conference is that while it marked a considerable success in the arms control process, it was not a lasting achievement. Within six years naval arms control would be at an end. While those responsible for the London agreements thought them positive, they have since come in for a rough ride.

For the United States and the American navy the London treaties were less evocative and less controversial. The one full-length work on the American role in London has delivered a mixed verdict.[39] Most other studies share this sense of underachievement.[40] The American navy supposedly gained the acknowledgment of its right to parity and a tonnage target at which to aim. On the other hand, the Japanese were able to increase their share above the 5-5-3 ratio in certain categories. On balance the tangible gains that the United States secured probably outweigh the sacrifices. While a year earlier Congress had passed a large cruiser bill, since then there were worrying signs that the American navy was losing influence. The new secretary of the navy was not a political heavyweight. The new president and the secretary of state were instinctively opposed to large building programs. Stimson even privately believed that the United States did not need as many cruisers as Great Britain.[41] Once the Great Depression began in late 1929, public interest in naval matters eroded even further. Without public interest Congress could easily buckle. In the past Congress had shown a propensity not to fund ships that had previously been authorized, so there were no guarantees that the ships approved in 1929 would be completed. The London Treaty headed off any potential trouble in Congress by giving the American navy's supporters a firm program to support. For that reason, if no other, it was in the fleet's interest.

For the British the London Conference was an altogether more serious affair. The general verdict rendered by historians was that the MacDonald government made some serious mistakes. Corelli Barnett has claimed the London agreements were responsible for maiming British sea power, Paul Kennedy has accused the Labour government of abandoning the Royal Navy, and Roskill agreed that the building restrictions were "misplaced."[42] The most criticized decision was the reduction of the Royal Navy's cruiser target from seventy vessels to fifty. Jellicoe, among others, thought a British limit of fifty cruisers inadequate.[43] Criticism has also been leveled at the decision to surrender Britain's claim to superiority in auxiliary ships.

A close examination of the decisions made by the MacDonald government makes it difficult to support these objections. While the London Naval Treaty was undoubtedly swathed in the idealistic rhetoric that MacDonald and Hoover loved, it was really a hard-nosed bargain. First and foremost it was not a disarmament agreement like the Washington Treaty. No ships were scrapped, and naval construction, particularly British construction, increased markedly after the conference. From 1931 until the outbreak of the Second World War the British government never authorized fewer than three cruisers a year. While two British cruisers had been authorized between 1927 and 1929, nine were approved between 1930 and 1932. The Japanese, in comparison, approved only four cruisers between 1930 and 1932.

It must also be kept in mind that the London Naval Treaty was a temporary agreement. The limitations on auxiliary ships were applicable only until 31 December 1936. With many of Britain's cruisers becoming obsolete in this period, it would have been impossible for the Royal Navy to maintain seventy effective cruisers. This was the reason the MacDonald government was able to accept the much-maligned limit of fifty, a fact well known in the Admiralty, if not in the outside world. The director of naval intelligence, Admiral Roger Bellairs, regularly wrote confidential letters to the now retired Admiral Beatty. In them he laid out exactly why the fifty-cruiser limit was accepted. He was particularly scathing about the self-defeating naval policy hoisted upon the Admiralty by Churchill when compared to the sensible actions of MacDonald:[44]

Actually, we can say that, under the present state of affairs, 50 represents for us what is practically possible during the forthcoming years. . . . The last Government may have talked about 70 but they made little effort to provide for this. What did they do? After the failure of the Geneva Conference in 1927, when it was apparent that we could not obtain agreement for reduction, they took the extraordinary step of dropping two cruisers from the 1927 programme and one from the 1928 programme.[45]

Admiral Chatfield, one of the most perceptive first sea lords in British history, also claimed in a letter to Beatty that it would have been practically impossible to exceed the fifty-cruiser limit before the end of 1936.[46] The British were careful to tell the Americans that the London agreements extended only until 1935, after which the Royal Navy "would have to have more cruisers."[47] If one accepts the word of Bellairs, Chatfield, and the American General Board, then it is hard to see how the London Conference was detrimental to Britain's cruiser position.

Also, contrary to what might be expected, the Admiralty thought there was merit in Hoover's yardstick proposal.[48] When negotiations began with the Americans the Admiralty's main objectives were to limit the United States to eighteen Washington-class cruisers and to make sure that the Royal Navy's cruiser allowance exceeded 325,000 tons.[49] The first sea lord, Admiral Madden, was particularly adamant on this last point.[50] In the end the Admiralty was completely successful on both fronts, limiting the Americans to eighteen large cruisers while getting a 339,000-ton cruiser allocation for themselves.

Nor does it make much sense to argue that the MacDonald government was somehow naive. When the French and Italians chose not to sign the London agreements, the British inserted an opt-out clause for themselves. With the Japanese some concessions were made, but some important victories were won. Because of this not all historians have harshly criticized British behavior. One of MacDonald's biographers has termed the conference a "limited" success.[51] However, a few go much further than this concession and challenge the whole notion of British decline. McKercher and Ferris see the naval arms control process, capped by the Washington and London meetings, as part of a British policy to keep naval supremacy.[52] Thus, Washington left Britain "the greatest power at sea," while the London Conference was an example of "British resolve to remain first in the naval tables."[53]

While the challenges posed by these arguments to traditional notions of British decline are extremely important, they should not be overstated. It is extremely difficult in this period to define exactly what naval supremacy was, let alone to say that the British maintained it. Those who argue for the continuation of British supremacy tend to focus on the Royal Navy's undoubtedly impressive cruiser advantage. In 1925, the British had forty-nine effective cruisers to the Americans' ten.[54] By 1929, the British had fifty-four cruisers on active service and were building a further five, while the United States still had the ten and were building only eight. In 1930 the American navy believed that the Royal Navy's cruiser advantage could be decisive in any Anglo-American war.[55] The huge cruiser program supported by Coolidge threatened to upset the balance, but it was still only a paper plan. By almost any numerical measure Britain's cruiser position was comfortable, though there were some hidden weaknesses. Much of the British cruiser advantage came from ships built during the First World War. Between 1934 and 1938 twenty-five of these cruisers would become obsolete.[56] Also, as more and more eight-inch-gun cruisers were completed by other powers, the relative value of Britain's large number of smaller ships was being eroded. However, even with these problems, British cruiser supremacy was undeniable.

Yet, the Royal Navy's cruiser advantage did not mean that Britain had maintained naval supremacy. A brief examination of other classes of warship goes some way to highlight this problem. Capital ships (battleships and battlecruisers) had been regulated by the Washington Conference, and American and British strength was approximately equal. Aircraft carriers presented a more confusing picture. The United States and Britain were assigned equal amounts of carrier tonnage by the Washington Treaty but constructed quite different forces.[57] During the 1920s many Americans and Britons thought that the Royal Navy's more numerous force of smaller aircraft carriers was worth considerably more than America's few large flattops. However, in retrospect the U.S. Navy in the 1920s, with the *Lexington* and *Saratoga*, had by far the better carrier strike force. In one of the unusual twists so common to American naval history these two large carriers were built only because the United States had some unwanted battlecruiser hulls after the Washington Conference. Through this unforeseen stroke of luck the U.S. Navy ended up with the world's two best carriers of the 1920s, ships capable of carrying almost 100 planes each. The smaller British carriers could embark only 135 planes in total. The Americans were also considerably more advanced than the British in the nuts and bolts of naval aviation.[58] By 1931 the United States had almost 1,000 naval aircraft to Britain's 261. Also, while the Royal Navy was locked in a fierce battle to retain control of its own air assets, the American navy department was allowed to develop its own forces unhindered.

British superiority in cruisers could also be counterbalanced by American strength in destroyers and submarines. Enormous First World War construction programs left America with huge numbers of these vessels. In 1925 the United States had 289 destroyers, 109 in full commission, while the Royal Navy had 205 destroyers, 63 in full commission.[59] This American advantage was retained well into 1930s. In 1932 the United States possessed 251 destroyers and eighty-one submarines, while the Royal Navy had 150 and fifty-two, respectively.[60] Many of these vessels were soon to be threatened by block obsolescence, but at the time the American lead in destroyers and submarines was just as valid as the Royal Navy's in cruisers.

Above and beyond the raw data, however, it is extremely difficult to define exactly what it would have meant for Britain to retain naval "supremacy" over America. Comparing the numerical strength of each fleet gives only part of the story. Their different responsibilities also have to be considered. Strategically, the Royal Navy was considerably more stretched than the U.S. Navy. The British not only had to defend vital trade routes but also had imperial possessions in every ocean. Beyond a few islands in the Pacific and Caribbean, which were in no way vital to the national economy, the United States had to protect only its home territory. In any conflict the U.S. Navy would have had more discretion in the disposition of its naval power. By the Admiralty's own estimations the Royal Navy needed twenty-nine more cruisers and thirty-two more destroyers to be equal in striking power to the U.S. Navy.[61] An American fleet equal in size to the Royal Navy would in fighting terms have been navally "superior."

In the end it is safe to say that the First London Conference was not an extremely good indicator of the decline of British power or the rise of America. It was also probably not a sign that the British had retained naval supremacy. Instead, the London Treaty was a thoughtful solution to an unnecessary and damaging rift in Anglo-American relations. Its naval clauses were short-term, and left both the United States and Great Britain with a tremendous naval advantage over all the other nations. It also freed both governments from having to waste time on Anglo-American naval relations and allowed them to focus on more legitimate issues of national security.

## THE U.S. NAVY FROM 1930 TO 1935

By the end of the First London Conference something had changed for the U.S. Navy. For the first time in peacetime the navy had what could unironically be called a "policy." The Washington and London Treaties had spelled out exactly how much tonnage the United States was allowed for each class of warship. Now all the navy had to do was get the ships built. This was not going to be easy. Even though Congress had passed a large cruiser program, not all the ships had been funded. A large number of American destroyers and submarines were also about to become obsolete. Meanwhile, America could still build about 55,000 tons of aircraft carriers before reaching its treaty limit.

During the First London Conference plans was assembled to make up all these deficiencies.[62] President Hoover, however, had other ideas. His natural pacifism had been fortified by the Great Depression and the London settlement. Hoover viewed spending on the armed services as an unnecessary drain on the economy, and once Anglo-American differences had been settled, he moved quickly to reduce the naval budget.[63] He praised the London Conference for making "important economies" possible.[64] Naval personnel was reduced by 4,800, and two aircraft carriers, three cruisers, one destroyer, and six submarines were deleted from the navy's building program.[65]

These cuts hit hard. Once again it seemed that a naval arms control agreement had sapped public interest in the fleet.[66] Frustration in the fleet threatened to boil over. A number of retired naval officers publicly attacked naval arms control,[67] and the U.S. Navy League viciously criticized President Hoover. If not for the efforts of Admiral William Veazie Pratt, chief of naval operations from September 1930 to June 1933, things might have unraveled. Pratt was the right man at the right time. Hoover's secretary of the navy, Charles Francis Adams, was ineffectual, and it was left to Pratt to maintain good relations with the White House. It was a task he did with great skill.

Pratt was one of the least orthodox members of his profession. A flexible thinker, he strongly supported the arms control process.[68] Having been on the American delegation to the First London Conference, Pratt supported the agreements.[69] Later, he toyed with the idea of a four-year naval "holiday."[70] and publicly defended Hoover from attacks by the Navy League and others.[71] In 1932 Pratt even charged Hoover's critics with damaging the fleet's interests.[72]

Pratt maintained good relations with the president, even while Hoover continued to demand savings.[73] During one 1931 conference at the president's retreat in West Virginia, Hoover pressured Pratt for spending reductions.[74] The president saw no reason for the United States to build a full treaty navy.[75] During his tenure naval spending dropped from $374 million in fiscal year 1930 to $349 million in fiscal year 1933. Only in the area of cruiser construction was the navy to gain a few victories. By the end of 1931 the United States had laid down fifteen of the eighteen large cruisers allowed it by the London Treaty.

Interestingly, in one way it was to the navy's advantage not to begin new ships at this time. The navy was 55,000 tons short of its Washington Treaty allotment for aircraft carriers, but Hoover allowed only one new carrier, the 14,000 ton *Ranger*, to be built. This was undoubtedly a boon for the fleet. The navy department had miscalculated in these years, favoring smaller aircraft carriers.[76] The *Lexington* and *Saratoga*, giants weighing almost 35,000 tons, were thought to be inefficient behemoths.[77] World War II, however, would demonstrate the value of the larger ship. While the *Lexington* and *Saratoga* were vital to holding the line after the Japanese attack on Pearl Harbor, the *Ranger* was used only for escort duty. By being restrained from laying down its next two carriers, the *Yorktown* and *Enterprise*, until 1934, the U.S. Navy was spared from constructing small, ineffective vessels.

At the time it was not seen as a victory. Hoover remained committed to the naval arms control process until the end of his term in office. He seemed so determined that even Secretary of State Stimson started to oppose the president's proposals.[78] The most effective opposition to Hoover would come not from the Cabinet or navy, however, but, astonishingly, from Congress.

The Great Depression was one of the best things that ever happened to the U.S. Navy. The American electorate turned strongly against the Republicans as more jobs disappeared, and businesses collapsed. In the 1930 congressional elections a huge Republican majority in the House of 267 to 167 was replaced by a Democratic majority of 220 to 214. In the Senate the Republican majority was cut from 56 to 39 to only 48 to 47, with one independent. Normally, the rise of the Democratic Party would not have heralded a positive change in the American navy's fortunes. Democrats had supplied much of the opposition to the Coolidge cruiser bill and historically were less inclined to support large building programs. However, the navy was extremely lucky with the Democrats who came to power during the Great Depression. After capturing the House, the

Democrats installed Carl Vinson of Georgia as chairman of the House Naval Affairs Committee. A longtime supporter of a strong fleet, Vinson was one of the most effective naval advocates in American congressional history. He was determined to see the fleet built up to its full treaty strength. Vinson worked closely with Pratt and Frederick Hale, the Republican chairman of the Senate Naval Affairs Committee. After a series of "extended" conferences they drew up a bill calling for a full treaty fleet.[79] Then, using his formidable powers of persuasion, Vinson got the House Naval Affairs Committee to support the measure by 18 to 0.[80] Hale introduced a similar bill in the Senate.[81]

Without Hoover's support these efforts at first stumbled. Soon, however, a sympathetic figure would be in the White House. With Hoover's popularity in tatters, whomever the Democrats chose to be their candidate was bound to become the next president. The leading prospect going into 1932 was Franklin Delano Roosevelt, the progressive governor of New York who had been assistant secretary of the navy under Woodrow Wilson. Roosevelt was not a shoe-in, however. The Democratic nominee from 1928, Al Smith, beat Roosevelt in a number of New England primaries, and soon other candidates, such as John Nance Garner, the speaker of the House, talked about running.[82] In the end Roosevelt was able to wear down his opponents. After a few tense ballots at the Democratic convention, he was finally selected to be the nominee.

Roosevelt was chosen for a number of reasons, none of which had anything to do with his affection for a strong navy. A winning politician with a proven ability to capture votes in a swing state like New York, Roosevelt offered optimism and hope to a restless electorate. During the 1932 campaign he avoided specifics and never said anything of substance about naval policy. The economic downturn made his election a foregone conclusion, however, and in November he and the congressional Democrats won a crushing victory. Soon afterward Roosevelt met with Vinson. While the chairman of the House Naval Affairs Committee was encouraged by the talks, the president remained noncommittal.[83] Roosevelt was still unwilling to talk publicly about his plans for the fleet. In his inaugural address, the new president refused to say anything about the navy.

Yet, for all his public ambivalence, Roosevelt remained very interested in naval power. His previous experience meant that he knew more about the United States navy than any other president when taking office. Within the navy his election was greeted with real satisfaction. Admiral Harold Stark, who would be chief of naval operations from 1939 to 1942, wanted Roosevelt to know that he "was just bustin' to see that smile in the White House."[84]

Roosevelt revealed his intentions a little by appointing Senator Claude Swanson of Virginia to be secretary of the navy. An elderly, patrician Virginian, Swanson had been the ranking Democrat on the Senate's Naval Affairs Committee and had consistently supported a navy "second to none."[85] While he was ill for much of his tenure, Swanson always pushed the president to spend more on the fleet. On 13 April 1933 Swanson told the president that the navy needed an additional $10 million immediately and would eventually need an extra $230 million.[86] A few weeks later he told Roosevelt that there would be little congressional opposition to an immediate $46 million increase in naval construction.[87]

Pratt also lobbied the new president. A few days after Roosevelt's inauguration the chief of naval operations helped draw up a paper outlining the navy's needs.[88] He called for the expenditure of $944 million to bring the American navy up to full treaty strength, to provide for new airplanes, and to improve shore establishments. A few weeks later the General Board called for an additional two aircraft carriers, seven cruisers, twenty-four destroyers, and nine submarines.[89] It is impossible to say what would have become of these plans under normal economic circumstances. It is unlikely that Roosevelt would have had either the desire or the nerve to push for such expensive undertakings. However, the Great Depression had played into the navy's hands. Roosevelt decided that the federal government needed to play an active role in reducing unemployment and reflating the American economy. A large program of naval construction, repairs, and base improvements was seen as a way to kill two birds with one stone. Such a program could ease unemployment and, correspondingly, build up the fleet.

Roosevelt decided to come out of his shell. He diverted a great deal of the money appropriated under the National Industrial Recovery Act (NIRA) to the navy. The NIRA passed Congress on 15 June 1933, and a few days later funds started flowing. A whopping $238 million was earmarked for naval building, and work started immediately on thirty-two new vessels, including two aircraft carriers and four cruisers.[90] Naval spending for the whole of fiscal year 1934 exceeded $530 million, more than $180 million more than the previous year. Not all this money was spent on naval building, however. A great deal of cash found its way to traditional "pork barrel" projects. A few days after the NIRA's passage more than $37 million had been allocated to improve dockyards and bases.[91] In October the assistant secretary of the navy, Henry L. Roosevelt, a distant relation of the president, asked for $93 million more, mostly for work on shore installations.[92] A few months later the assistant secretary asked for the release of $6.9 million from the Public Works Administration to support the politically sensitive Brooklyn Navy Yard.[93]

To the American navy it was an astonishing turn of events. Stark called the building program a "veritable Godsend."[94] However, Roosevelt still trod carefully.[95] While the Great Depression had created much support for unemployment relief, it had not done much to increase public backing for a powerful American navy. Opposition to a large American fleet remained. Roosevelt was even rebuked by Reverend Malcolm Peabody, the headmaster of Groton, his old prep school, for building up the fleet.[96] Roosevelt was therefore careful to describe his naval spending as part of a plan to combat unemployment. The idea of the United States' playing a larger role in the world was correspondingly downplayed. This was particularly the case during the debate over the Vinson Trammell Naval Act of 1934.

This act can be seen either as a turning point in American naval history or as a cautious, incremental move. Named after its sponsors, Carl Vinson and Park Trammell, the latter chairman of the Senate Naval Affairs Committee, the bill called for the American navy to be built up to full treaty strength. It called for 102 new vessels, including sixty-five destroyers, thirty submarines, one aircraft carrier, and six cruisers.[97] It was the second largest American peacetime naval plan to that time, eclipsed only by the 1916 program. Yet, compared to earlier efforts the Vinson Trammell act flew through Congress. Introduced in late January 1934, the bill was signed by Roosevelt on 27 March 1934.

Psychologically, it was a great boost for the navy. Yet, in reality it was an important, but not a dramatic, step. Ninety-three percent of the ships covered by the act were needed to replace the huge numbers of American destroyers and submarines that were soon to become obsolete. They would lead to little real increase in the navy's strength. Also, not until 1938/39 would all the destroyers be laid down. Excepting the destroyers and submarines, the rest of the Vinson Trammell bill was really quite moderate. The building program initiated after the NIRA passed had already made up much of the United States' naval deficiencies. In January 1934 the navy department admitted that it needed only one large cruiser, one aircraft carrier, and 35,000 tons of smaller cruisers to reach the treaty limits.[98]

The Vinson Trammell act was probably not a watershed in American naval history. It was a moderate step made possible only by an unusual convergence of events. Popular support for job creation programs was coupled with a massive Democrat majority in Congress devoted to its new president. Furthermore, for the first time in American history both internationalists and isolationists supported the same naval bill. Seventy-eight percent of all senators voted in favor of the Vinson Trammel act.[99] Those looking forward to more naval arms control conferences supported the bill to give America greater leverage. Vinson stressed this point: ."A conference composed of delegates from the British Empire, Japan and the United States must convene to revise, continue or abandon the London Treaty of 1930. If our delegation goes to that conference without a definite declaration of this Nation's policy with regard to its Navy, its prestige is almost nil."[100] On the other hand, a number of isolationists supported the Vinson Trammell act because they saw it as a way of separating the United States from the world. Senator Marne Logan, Democrat of Kentucky, outlined the isolationist view in a rather convoluted manner: "If we have decided—and it seems to me we have—that America must be self-contained, that she must be self-sufficient, that she will depend upon economic self-sufficiency, then it follows as a matter of course, it seems to me, that we must be prepared to protect America to the fullest extent against the other nations of the world."[101]

The unpredictability that was endemic to American policy had for once worked very much to the navy's advantage. Within a few months the pacifism and obstruction of Hoover had been replaced by the support of Roosevelt, Vinson, and an eclectic coalition in Congress. The Great Depression, party politics, and economic considerations had all played a role in this transformation. It was certainly not a preordained change, but the navy accepted it gladly nonetheless. However, this was not all. International changes also played into the U.S. Navy's hands.

In 1930 the navy still lacked a credible enemy in the eyes of many. Britain and Japan received the most attention, but the idea of an Anglo-American or Japanese-American war caused little panic. In 1930 separate studies were made of a cruiser war with both nations.[102] The Red-Blue, or Anglo-American, plan was supposed to demonstrate that the United States would be unable to hamper British trade without new cruiser construction. The Orange-Blue plan also supposedly showed that without new cruisers the United States could do little in the western Pacific. Both plans were more political than strategic, drawn up to give the American navy more evidence with which to fight its case. In fact of all the war plans maintained by the fleet in 1930—Orange, Red, Orange-Red, Green (Mexico), Tan (Cuba), Violet (China), and White (Domestic)—only the latter was amended significantly.[103]

The impact of the Great Depression had led to an updating of plans for controlling domestic disturbances. First established in 1924, these "White" plans had grown to twenty-seven pages and eight appendixes by November 1930.[104] It was clearly stated that all action had to be constitutionally sanctioned, and, happily, the plans were never employed. However, it was a good sign of where the fleet's priorities lay for much of the Hoover administration.

For a while this was tolerable. With Anglo-American disagreements settled at London the idea of war with Britain received less attention.[105] This was not the case with Japan. Soon after the London Conference relations with Japan were to be tested by disagreements over China. Japan's interference in Chinese affairs had been noted by the Americans throughout the 1920s.[106] While most Americans sympathized with the Chinese, the situation was never considered serious enough to lead to war. In September 1931, however, Japan's Kwantung Army, which was stationed in Korea, manufactured an excuse to move into the northern Chinese province of Manchuria. The Japanese government, meanwhile, took on a decidedly more nationalistic hue. In 1932, in response to anti-Japanese rioting, the Japanese bombed Shanghai and later took over the city.

Japanese aggression caused a number of different reactions. Hoover appealed for calm and resisted calls for sanctions against Japan. Secretary of State Stimson also called for caution.[107] The American navy, meanwhile, saw this as a chance to refocus attention on a plausible war involving the United States. Only weeks after the bombing of Shanghai the navy ran a war exercise that had an American force retaking Hawaii from an invading foreign power.[108] A few months later the General Board informed the secretary of the navy that the Orange war plans needed to be changed to reflect Japan's hostile actions.[109]

Once Franklin Roosevelt took over, the navy was allowed to fan further the flames of anti-Japanese feeling. This task was abetted by Japan's withdrawal from the League of Nations and Roosevelt's almost paranoid fear of Japanese intentions. Roosevelt seemed convinced that the Japanese were up to no good. In November 1933 he asked the navy department to investigate stories that Japanese fishing boats were surveying the American coast.[110] In early 1934 he wanted to call a conference to discuss Japanese infiltration of Panama.[111] A few months later Roosevelt's suspicions reached the level of farce when reports reached the White House that a hermit living on the Galapagos Islands reported that Japanese fishing boats were surveying there.[112] Talk like this, as strange as it was, was most welcome to the American navy. It represented the first significant change in American perceptions since the Washington Conference. Even though there had been international incidents since 1921, a war involving America never seemed very likely. With the Great Depression, the election of Franklin Roosevelt and Japan's aggressive actions in China things had changed.

## BRITISH NAVAL POLICY 1930-1935

The MacDonald government initially reacted to the Great Depression much like the Hoover administration, by rooting around for budgetary savings. Admiralty funding was hit hard, dropping from £56 million in 1929-30 to £50 million in 1932-33. Naturally, these cuts have not been seen as a sign of British commitment to a naval build up. Roskill has called the period one of "reluctant" rearmament, a view shared by others.[113] This notion is correct. Hardly anyone in either the Labour government of 1929-1931 or the National government afterward, wanted to spend much money on the Royal Navy. Yet, for all their reluctance, Britain's naval position probably improved between the First and Second London Conferences.

In these years the Royal Navy, unlike every other fleet, received a regular building allotment. While the Admiralty's budget was reduced, every year but one between 1930 and 1935 saw the laying down of three cruisers, nine destroyers, and three submarines. The exception was 1934, when one aircraft carrier and four cruisers were started instead.[114] Even when the Treasury tried to reduce construction, as it did in 1931, the full program was approved.[115] This meant that, excepting the Americans, who were making up their cruiser deficiencies, the British comprehensively outbuilt every other power, including the Japanese.

Nor was it the case that the British were somehow naive in the period. British naval policy was hardheaded and sensible, with close attention being paid to the Japanese and Germans. Anglo-Japanese relations caused disquiet soon after the First London Conference.[116] Japanese aggression in Manchuria and Shanghai led to a rethinking of Admiralty and Cabinet policy. The most significant change occurred when the services attacked the Ten-Year Rule.[117] This rule, which stated that the armed services should plan not to be in a war for at least ten years, had been in place since 1919. At that time, It was seen as a bulwark against unnecessary rearmament. None of the crises of the 1920s were serious enough to threaten the rule's integrity, but Japanese behavior changed all this.

In February 1932 the CID's Chiefs of Staff Sub-Committee called for the rule's cancellation.[118]

Cabinet reaction to this proposal was surprisingly swift.[119] Within a month of the chiefs of staff's paper, the Ten-Year Rule had been repealed. Sir Bolton Eyres-Monsell, the National government's first lord of the Admiralty, claimed that the change was due to "the ominous character of recent events in the Far East."[120] What was then decided was that Britain needed to maintain a fleet strong enough to engage the bulk of the Japanese navy and at the same time control European waters. It was an important change. The British were moving from a numerical naval policy, like the old two-power or one-power standards, to one that was objective-oriented. It was an example of how British policy had been liberated by the rapprochement with America and the First London Conference. Now, the British could define a set of specific, realistic goals and build their fleet accordingly.

It cannot be said that these goals were indicative of a decline in Britain's position. This first set helps demonstrate how serious the Cabinet and Admiralty were. It would have been impossible in 1914, say, to assign the Royal Navy the task of engaging the bulk of the Japanese fleet and maintaining control of European waters. At the beginning of the First World War the Royal Navy had to concentrate every front-line battleship in local waters. The dispatching of the fleet's three oldest battlecruisers to the South Atlantic, in the pursuit of a German force of small cruisers, was considered risky. In 1914 the Japanese had five dreadnoughts and were building another five. To confront such a force would have left the Germans in control of European seas.

However, in 1932 the Admiralty believed that the Royal Navy should be strong enough to do just this. By 1933 worries about a possible conflict with Japan had increased. Under the strong leadership of the talented new first sea lord, Admiral Ernle Chatfield, the Admiralty began to press the government for immediate changes. It applied for emergency funding to increase fuel stocks and to purchase defensive equipment for naval bases.[121] Plans were also assembled to complete the remaining improvements to the Singapore Naval Base.[122] Two plans were put forward to correct Singapore's weaknesses, one taking five years and another just three and a half. A meeting of the CID on 6 April 1933 approved the quicker of the two proposals and approved the emergency funding measures as well.

If the Admiralty was mostly successful in getting what it wanted in the short term, it was even more successful in the long term. In late 1932 the Admiralty first began planning for what it wanted once the arms control agreements expired in 1936.[123] It began planning for a larger fleet than the present tonnage allowance provided for.[124] The Admiralty eventually settled upon a force of fifteen capital ships, seventy cruisers, and five large aircraft carriers. In addition it wanted to begin a new nine-ship destroyer flotilla and three submarines a year. A ten-year plan of construction was drawn up incorporating these goals.[125] It was a reasonable, farsighted, and politically astute program. Every ship that the

Royal Navy thought it needed in 1932 was laid down before the outbreak of the
Second World War, as well as a significant number of additional and more powerful vessels.

In 1933 the Admiralty originally planned on proceeding with four new
cruisers, one of the Leander class weighing 7,500 and three Arethusas weighing
5,200 tons. Later, however, the Admiralty decided that to compete with the
Japanese, it needed a larger cruiser and designed the Minotaur class, which
weighed about 9,000 tons. It was an expensive change. One Arethusa cost
£1,400,000, and one Leander £1,600,000, but one Minotaur cost £2,100,000.[126]
Yet, the Admiralty thought the Minotaurs so much stronger that it was willing
to sacrifice three of the smaller vessels to get two of the larger.[127] Though both
short-term and long-term costs would rise if the Minotaurs were approved, the
government did not flinch. In doing so it only whetted the first sea lord's appe-
tite.[128] In 1934 the Admiralty was originally to get three smaller cruisers and
one aircraft carrier. Instead, Chatfield pressed for four cruisers, all Minotaurs.[129]
The government accepted this change without much discussion.

The year 1934 was also important because of the increased attention being
paid to German naval strength. Even though Hitler came to power in 1933, the
German navy posed no immediate threat to the British.[130] An examination of
German infringements of the naval clauses of the Versailles Treaty showed only
small infractions.[131] In March 1934 the British Embassy in Berlin reported that
there was "no reason to suppose that the naval clauses" were being infringed to
any notable extent.[132] A Foreign Office report claimed that the Germans would
not build anything larger than 10,000 tons before 1935 at the earliest.[133]

These optimistic naval reports did not mean that the Admiralty or Foreign
Office discounted the German threat. The foreign secretary, Sir John Simon,
was originally deeply distrustful of the national socialists. He even considered
the idea of a preventive war against the Nazis, "before Germany is strong
enough to attack anyone else."[134] His skepticism was shared by Robert Vansittart, the Foreign Office's permanent undersecretary. Two months after Hitler
came to power, Vansittart called the German leadership an "alarming and insane gang," while prophesying that Britain would have both to rearm and to ally
with France.[135] He produced a number of such sobering papers and also coun-
seled the most extreme measures.[136]

The Admiralty was in a bind. On one hand, it was eager to take advantage
of any issue that could lead to increased appropriations, but, on the other, the
German navy was still woefully inadequate. All the Admiralty could do was
dwell on Germany's potential strength:

Germany . . . is not yet fully armed. She has considerable elements of force, but her permanent system, with its full complement of armaments and trained reserves, has not yet
taken shape, though it is rapidly doing so. Surrounded by armed and suspicious neigh-
bours she is not at present a serious menace to this country, but within a few years will
certainly become so. . . . In her case we have time, though not too much time, to make
defensive preparations.[137]

What the potential German threat did do was give greater definition to the task-oriented naval policy begun in 1932. The Royal Navy began to study how much strength it would need both to engage the Japanese and to keep the Germans at bay. The British estimated that the Japanese navy would contain nine capital ships, four aircraft carriers, and twenty-nine cruisers by 1940. To meet this force the Admiralty planned to dispatch twelve capital ships, five aircraft carriers, and forty-six cruisers to the Pacific.[138] Under the Washington and London limits the Royal Navy would be left with only three capital ships, one aircraft carrier, and four cruisers in local waters. However, as the Admiralty was expecting to be rid of the London limit of fifty cruisers by 1936, it was planning on having twenty-four free cruisers by 1940.

Such a force might not seem large, but in 1934 it was more than enough to handle the tiny German navy. In late 1933 the Germans possessed only three prewar capital ships and three "pocket" battleships and had six cruisers built or being built.[139] By November 1934 only one additional "pocket" battleship was being built.[140] There were no German vessels capable of standing up to British capital ships, and there was no way the Germans could do much damage to British commerce.

Yet, the Admiralty was able to combine the potential threat posed by Germany with the Japanese menace to raise interest in rearmament. Soon the service chiefs drew up a wide-ranging deficiency program.[141] First assembled in 1934, the program was a blueprint for modernizing and strengthening all the armed services within five years. It was intended to make the Royal Navy strong enough to fulfill its Pacific "commitment," to defend India, and to deter Germany in Europe. Needless to say, it was ambitious, calling for capital ship modernization, a larger fleet air arm, more personnel, improvements in antisubmarine equipment and land defenses, greater fuel reserves, a general stockpiling of stores, and significant upgrading of Singapore Naval Base. It was also very expensive, with an estimated price tag of £21,067,600.[142]

The 1934 deficiency program marked a transition in the period of British naval rearmament initiated after the First London Conference. Since 1930 British naval construction, both numerically and technologically, had been upgraded, and Admiralty policy had evolved from a rigid numerical standard to a more sensible, task-oriented plan. Close attention was paid to the growing naval power of Japan and the naval potential of Germany. In 1935 planning had to be replaced by decision making. The first question was Anglo-German naval relations. On the surface things seemed calm. The government approved another installment of its regular building program.[143] Yet, a note of caution appeared:

Public opinion in this country has tended to assume that nothing is required for the maintenance of peace except the existing international machinery. . . . The force of world events, however, has shown that this assumption is premature. Nations differ in their temperaments, needs and state of civilisation. Discontent may arise out of various causes . . . and it has been found that once action has been taken the existing international machinery for the maintenance of peace cannot be relied upon as a protection against an aggressor. . . . If peace should be broken, the navy is, as always, the first line of defence for the maintenance of our essential sea communications.[144]

The Admiralty had known for a while that German naval strength would be a crucial determinant in setting British naval strength. Control of German rearmament was considered "essential for the security and peace of Europe," and changes in German naval strength were closely monitored.[145] Since 1933 the Germans had tried to convince the British that they posed little danger to the Royal Navy.[146] Admiral Raedar had personally assured the Admiralty on this point.[147]

On 25 and 26 March 1935, the Germans went further and offered to limit their navy to 35 percent of the Royal Navy.[148] A high-ranking British delegation in Berlin, led by Simon and Anthony Eden, the lord privy seal, was swamped with pledges of Germany's peaceful intentions. This move posed a dilemma for the British government. The Versailles Treaty had imposed severe restrictions on German construction, depriving Germany of submarines and limiting surface ships to only 10,000 tons. Now, the British had to decide whether to stick to these limits and treat excessive German building as a breech of international law or anger countries such as France and Italy by unilaterally repudiating a part of the Versailles system. They chose the latter.

Simon, who only a few years earlier had contemplated a preemptive strike against Hitler, now raved about the German plan: "This German offer is of such outstanding importance that it would be a mistake to withhold acceptance merely on the ground that other powers might feel some temporary annoyance at our actions."[149] This memorandum was written on the same day that Simon was replaced as foreign secretary by Sir Samuel Hoare, and MacDonald stepped down as prime minister in favor of Stanley Baldwin. British policy, however, was not affected. A German delegation arrived in London a few days later, and the two sides agreed that German surface ships would be limited in strength to 35 percent of the Royal Navy, while German submarines would be limited to 45 percent.[150]

As one of the textbook examples of appeasement, the Anglo-German Naval Agreement has been harshly criticized. Roskill called it the "crowning folly" of British policy, while Corelli Barnett has described it as an "abject surrender."[151] The splitting of the "Stresa" Front, the grouping of Britain, France, and Italy set up to restrain Germany, has been seen as a great loss.[152] This criticism about the "Stresa" Front carries real force. The naval side of the agreements, meanwhile, was probably in Britain's interest.[153] The Versailles Treaty had been showing signs of collapse for a while. Just two months earlier, in March 1935, Hitler had announced the existence of a German air force, something forbidden by Versailles. It was inevitable that some kind of modern German fleet would be built. The Anglo-German agreement kept the German fleet at a level below what Germany's natural industrial muscle could have attained. Nor were the British naively lulled into a false sense of security. The Admiralty realized that the agreement might lead to a spurt in German construction and kept a close watch on German naval developments.[154] Within two months of the agreement the Admiralty revised the deficiency program in response to an "acceleration" of German naval rearmament.[155]

On the downside there is evidence that the agreement caused resentment among the French and Italians.[156] British eagerness to cut a deal with the Germans did not augur well for the "Stresa" Front. The French seemed particularly angry that the British could unilaterally offer the Germans a fleet 35 percent as large as the Royal Navy. However, if one accepts that the method behind British diplomacy was far from ideal, that does not mean that the results were necessarily injurious to French interests. Before the First World War the Germans had proven that they could easily outbuild every other nation on the European continent. In the mid-1930s Germany's industrial advantage still existed. The Anglo-German agreement meant that, at least for a little while, German naval strength would be limited to a level the French could match. In fact the French were trying to maintain a fleet half the size of the Royal Navy, which meant, said the Foreign Office, that the agreement offered France "permanent naval superiority over Germany."[157]

It should also be noted that by the time the Second World War started, the Germans had not exceeded the surface vessel restrictions of the Anglo-German agreement. In 1939 the British had twenty capital ships built or being built to Germany's six, thirteen aircraft carriers built or being built to Germany's none, seventy-nine cruisers built and being built to Germany's eleven cruisers and three "pocket" battleships, and 187 destroyers built or being built to Germany's 40.[158] Only in the area of submarines had the Germans exceeded the Anglo-German agreement's limitations, with seventy-nine submarines to Britain's sixty-nine. However, only forty-nine of the German submarines were operational. Even the French navy was considerably larger than the German fleet, containing nine capital ships, one aircraft carrier, eighteen cruisers, and seventy destroyers either built or being built.

What else was the government to do? It could have rejected the proposals and stuck to the letter of the Versailles Treaty, which no other power was doing. Since there was no possibility that Britain would go to war to stop the Germans from building a larger navy, clinging to Versailles would have accomplished little. Ultimately, the Anglo-German Naval Agreement was far from a panacea and, as it turned out, did not act as a long-term brake on German intentions. It was, however, a modest and prudent step that allowed for easier planning in the next few years.

## THE SECOND LONDON CONFERENCE AND THE END OF THE NAVAL ARMS CONTROL PROCESS

By 1934 the naval arms control process seemed doomed. Little had gone right since the First London Conference. In 1932 a general disarmament conference was held in Geneva, during which nothing of substance was agreed.[159] This failure was compounded by Japan's new assertiveness. Not only did Japanese aggression in China damage relations with the United States and Great Britain, but Japan's desire for full naval equality with the two largest naval powers threatened to kill off arms control. A new naval conference was scheduled to be held in London in 1935. The British and Americans began preparing for these talks in early 1934.[160] Both still believed the upcoming conference had something to offer, primarily in the area of qualitative restrictions.[161] The British still wanted to abolish submarines and to prolong the useful lives of their older warships. They wanted all new capital ships limited to twelve-inch guns and favored increased size restrictions on cruisers. The United States, meanwhile, wanted to retain the present size restrictions but was willing to approve new numerical limits.

These qualitative agreements, however, could be achieved only if Britain, America, and Japan could agree to extend the 5-5-3 ratio. Chances of such an agreement looked slim. The Japanese were pushing for full naval parity with Britain and America. They wanted a "common upper limit," whereby each country would be given the same overall tonnage limit within which they could build any fleet they wanted. These demands presented the Americans and British with different challenges.

The American government knew from the beginning that the Japanese wanted parity.[162] The General Board began discussing the problem in February 1934.[163] There was no chance that the American government, dominated by Franklin Roosevelt, would ever accept a common upper limit. Doing so would significantly reduce American leverage and leave the western Pacific in Japanese hands. To head off Japan's efforts, the Roosevelt administration sent envoys to work out a common front with the British. Norman Davis, the chief American delegate to the 1932 Geneva Conference, started talks in London in March 1934.[164] In June an American naval delegation, led by the chairman of the General Board, also visited Britain to discuss the upcoming conference.[165] The Americans believed that there was enough common ground between them and the British to thwart any compromise with the Japanese.

The Americans were not entirely right on this point. Within British circles there was a split between those favoring cooperation with the United States and those wanting to improve Anglo-Japanese relations. The Foreign Office and Admiralty inclined toward the former. In 1933 Simon called American friendship "more important than ever," while Vansittart warned that Britain "should have to keep in as close as we could with the U.S.A."[166] Alternatively, the Foreign Office was less than enamored of the Japanese.[167] In early 1934, the Foreign Office balked at a proposal to resuscitate the Anglo-Japanese Alliance.[168]

The Admiralty also tended to prefer the Americans to the Japanese. It considered the Japanese a "warlike race" whose confidence had grown because for "centuries they have not had a thrashing."[169]

Some, however, had other ideas. Warren Fisher, permanent secretary at the Treasury, wanted desperately to improve Anglo-Japanese relations. In a series of exchanges with Admiral Chatfield, Fisher argued that Britain should move closer to Japan, even if this ended up antagonizing the United States: "It is high time that our masters should stop the game of make believe amongst themselves and should face up to the facts. It is not Japan that should be in the dock, but the USA; yet never once have our political spokesmen told the Americans the truth."[170] While having some sympathy for this point, Chatfield argued against improving relations with Japan at the expense of American friendship.[171] This did not stop Fisher. He believed that the United States did not need a large fleet, while Britain and Japan were dependent on the sea for their survival. If Britain could resist America's unwarranted demands, a naval agreement could quickly be reached with Japan.[172] By reaching such an agreement, Britain could stop worrying about security in the Pacific and could concentrate on the German threat. Fisher's boss, Neville Chamberlain the chancellor of the exchequer, shared these beliefs. It has even been argued that the Treasury "hankered" for a return of the Anglo-Japanese Alliance.[173] Eventually, Fisher produced a memorandum summarizing his different points, and Chamberlain circulated it as a document reflecting the Treasury's views.[174]

Had the Japanese not called for a common upper limit, Anglo-Japanese relations might have improved. Simon and Chamberlain tried to reach common ground on the question.[175] However, once the Japanese started demanding parity, they lost any hope of improving relations with the British.[176] Under no condition could the Cabinet accept the Japanese as equals.[177] It considered Japanese demands unwarranted and dangerous and was compelled to a common position with the Americans.

The Americans were partly aware of the arguments circulating within the British government. The British and American governments were in constant touch.[178] Norman Davis regularly sent Roosevelt reports from London.[179] The president seemed convinced that the British had no choice but to cooperate with the United States. He was certainly not afraid of applying pressure on the Mac-Donald government. While Roosevelt greatly preferred cooperation with the British to agreement with Japan, he never fully trusted the British. Even after Davis reported that it was unlikely that the British would make a deal with the Japanese, Roosevelt told his negotiator to threaten the MacDonald government: "If Great Britain is even suspected of preferring to play with Japan to playing with us, I shall be compelled, in the interest of American security, to approach public sentiment in Canada, Australia, New Zealand and South Africa in a definite effort to make these Dominions understand clearly that their future security is linked with us in the United States. You will best know how to inject this thought into the minds of Simon, Chamberlain, Baldwin and MacDonald in the most diplomatic way."[180]

In the end such threats were unnecessary. With the Japanese determined to press their case for naval parity, the British cooperated with the Americans. By the time Norman Davis left Great Britain in late 1934, he believed that the MacDonald government was prepared to present a united front to the Japanese.[181] The Japanese further compounded their isolation by announcing on 29 December 1934 that they were ready to withdraw from the Washington Treaty. Roosevelt seemed heartened enough by these developments to propose that Britain, France, and the United States join together to blockade Japan if the Japanese did not give way on the parity question.[182]

With most Anglo-American differences settled, the final year before the opening of the Second London Conference was an anticlimax. It was well known that Japan might withdraw if it did not get a common upper limit, but there were no serious attempts made to head off a confrontation.[183] Instead, the American and British governments kept in close contact. Only Warren Fisher tried to argue that concessions should be made to the Japanese, but he was very much in the minority.[184] When the Second London Conference officially opened on 9 December 1935, there were no surprises. By 15 January 1935 the Japanese were forced to withdraw from the talks. Instead of trying to avoid the issue or reach a compromise, the Americans and British made it perfectly clear that they would give no ground on the issue of naval parity.[185] Norman Davis was effusive in his praise of Anglo-American cooperation.[186]

From then on the Japanese attended the conference as observers. Both the British and Americans still pressed ahead with their plans for qualitative limitations. The powers still participating agreed to limit capital ships to 14-inch guns and 35,000 tons, aircraft carriers to 6.1-inch guns and 23,000 tons, cruisers to 8,000 tons, and submarines to 2,000 tons. However, the treaty also contained a safeguarding clause that allowed the signatories to respond to moves by outside powers.[187]

Ultimately, the Second London Conference achieved very little, and it is not uncharitable to describe the event as a "colossal waste of time and effort."[188] Because it was a failure, the conference is often seen as a watershed, marking the end of the naval arms control process and the belated beginning of rearmament. British and American faith in arms control had finally been shattered, leaving both countries with little choice but to rearm.[189]

However, it must be remembered that British and American expectations were extremely limited long before the talks began. As early as December 1934 Franklin Roosevelt was giving the navy department a "highly confidential" order to design new warships on the assumption that naval arms control would end in 1936.[190] Both governments knew it was very likely that Japan would withdraw from the naval arms control process. There was certainly little idealism displayed in either British or American preparations. Instead of trying to find a face-saving way of including the Japanese, the Americans and British made a point of showing them the door. Yet, even though both countries had very limited expectations for the talks, there were still practical, political reasons for pressing ahead. By forcing the Japanese to withdraw from the talks, the British and Americans were able to blame them for the collapse of the naval arms control process. The Admiralty and Foreign Office pointed out that with a British election scheduled for 1936, it made sense to go through with the talks, even if they were to achieve little.[191]

It is also exaggerating to credit the Second London Conference with changing Great Britain and the United States from indolent powers into desperately rearming nations. Rearmament in both had been under way for years before the talks began. Between 1930 and 1935 British naval building exceeded Japan's by a considerable margin. Excepting the United States, the British built at a rate greater than that of any other naval power and maintained a fleet equal in fighting strength to the combined forces of Japan, Germany, and Italy. The United States had undertaken even a more massive rearmament program before the Second London Conference. The Great Depression and the election of Franklin Roosevelt had combined to create a large American coalition supporting naval building. Under the auspices of the NIRA and the Vinson-Trammell act, the U.S. Navy was allowed to build the fleet to its full treaty strength. If the Second London Naval Conference did not represent a major substantive break, it was important for symbolic reasons. With Japan's withdrawal from the ratio system the interwar period naval arms control process was at an end. Thus, the Second London Naval Conference provides one of the best possible moments for evaluating the impact of the whole process on American and British naval strength.

Naval arms control did not live up to the expectations of its most committed supporters. Less than fifteen years after the Washington Conference a new naval arms race had started, and a few years later a new world war would begin. This objective failure does not mean, however, that the process itself was a bad thing for either Great Britain or the United States. Indeed, for a number of reasons it improved the strategic position of both countries.

Starting with the Washington Conference, the naval arms control process kept both Britain and America from wasting huge sums of money building relatively unimportant capital ships. In essence it kept them from building catapults just before the age of cannons. In 1921 the United States had sixteen capital ships in various stages of construction, while the British had plans to build eight of their own. However, capital ships were becoming progressively less and less central to naval warfare. The development of aircraft carriers, naval airpower, and submarines diminished the value of capital ships in the Second World War. These large-gunned vessels were mostly relegated to escort or coastal bombardment duties. Without the naval arms control process America and Britain might have not only completed their approved capital ship programs but pressed on with new construction. Paying for even more capital ships would have not only strained both countries' financial resources but would in all probability have led to very damaging cuts in other more vital areas of naval spending. For this reason alone the naval arms control process paid some important dividends.

Also, in an era of uncertainty, the process gave the American and British navies concrete building targets. For the American fleet this was very important. Before the naval arms control process the Americans never had what could really be called a naval "policy." Instead, different administrations and various Congresses either built, or more often resisted building, a motley collection of warships. There was never a long-term purpose or strategic vision guiding the laying down of American vessels. Someone like Theodore Roosevelt might envisage a global role for a strong American fleet, while a more moderate personality like William Howard Taft might see little reason to use American naval power. The naval arms control process, by giving the United States the right to parity with Great Britain and fixed tonnage limits for all classes of warship, gave the American navy the closest thing it ever had to a naval policy before the Second World War. This was borne out by the pattern of American naval construction in these years. Only three times could both Congress and the president motivate themselves to support new naval construction. The first was during the last years of Coolidge's tenure, when the British tried to reject the United States' right to cruiser parity, and the Americans responded with the 1929 program. The third was the famous Vinson-Trammell act, whereby Congress and the president used the naval arms control limitations as their target for American naval strength. Only during the second time, when Franklin Roosevelt first came to office and naval building was being driven by the impact of the Great Depression, did the naval arms control process did not play a central role.

For the Royal Navy the tonnage limitations were also useful. Through the process that seventy-cruiser target became British naval policy. Before the First London Conference a seventy-cruiser force was an Admiralty wish that had never been officially approved by a government. After London the British began an ambitious program of cruiser construction designed to give the Royal Navy its full cruiser tonnage quota of seventy ships.

Finally, the naval arms control process was important for Great Britain and the United States because it gave each a large measure of security. The ratios gave both nations naval superiority over all potential enemies except each other. Compared to the situation before the First World War, the position of Britain and America improved markedly. In the interwar period the Royal Navy dominated European waters in a way unmatched since Trafalgar. Even combined, the only two European powers with sizable fleets, France and Italy, were no match for the British. Indeed, the rest of Europe combined could not compete with the Royal Navy. The extent of Britain's naval advantage can be seen by the great shift in Admiralty attentions back to the Pacific. From the signing of the Anglo-Japanese Alliance in 1902 until the First World War the Royal Navy had to rely on Japanese strength to protect the British Empire in the Pacific. The situation was considered so dangerous in Europe that all the British could station in the Pacific were auxiliary vessels. After the Washington Conference the Royal Navy was able once again to focus on the Pacific. The Singapore Naval Base was improved, and extensive war plans for an Anglo-Japanese conflict were assembled.

The United States likewise stopped worrying about threats in home waters and looked outward. Before and during the First World War the American navy spent much of its time planning for a war in the Western Hemisphere, either a German attack in the Caribbean or South America, a British landing in the Chesapeake, or a Japanese attack on the West Coast. In the interwar period the focus switched to Japan and the western Pacific. More and more of the U.S. Navy's strongest units were switched to the Pacific. Critics of the process sometimes use this shift to support their arguments, claiming that naval arms control gave Japan too much security in the western Pacific. There is something to this point, but it should be placed in context. By being allowed a fleet 60 percent as strong as Great Britain's or America's and larger than that of any other naval power, the Japanese had improved their relative position markedly. However, Japan's global position had not improved. Before the First World War Japan had great leverage over European powers. As the only country capable of basing its whole fleet in the western Pacific, the Japanese were courted and prized as allies. Naval arms control brought this to an end. One of the prices Britain paid for the Washington Treaty was the sacrificing of the Anglo-Japanese Alliance, something Japan was desperate to maintain. While the Japanese ratio would have made it difficult for Britain or America to launch offensive naval action in Japanese waters, this was nothing new. Before the First World War most British and American planners saw little likelihood that their fleets could strike Japan in the western Pacific. It is somewhat harsh to criticize the naval arms control process for making something difficult that would have been impossible before.

Finally, the naval arms control process was important because it helped make the Second World War winnable for Great Britain and the United States. By restraining other countries' naval building in the interwar period, as well as their own, the process made everybody start from a relatively low level in the mid-1930s. This was in Britain's, and particularly in America's, interest. No Axis naval power went into the Second World War armed in breadth and depth. The Japanese had a very powerful front-line striking force of aircraft carriers and capital ships, but little in reserve. Much has been made of the effectiveness of Japan's carrier strike force, which within a few months bombed Pearl Harbor, sank the *Prince of Wales* and *Repulse*, and spearheaded Japan's early advances. Yet, partly because aircraft carrier building had been restrained by the naval arms control process, the Japanese had only six large carriers when they entered the war. These six ships, the *Akagi, Kaga, Hiryu, Soryu, Shokaku,* and *Zuikaku,* were excellent offensive machines, if prone to exploding when bombed, but they were all the Japanese had. At the Battle of Midway when the *Akagi, Kaga, Hiryu,* and *Soryu* were sunk, the Japanese were unable to recover. From then on the Japanese were ground into dust.

The Germans were also unable to realize their full naval potential. While not part of the arms control process, they in no way represented a naval threat to the British or the Americans until years after the Second London Conference. British war plans drawn up in April 1936, during a period of tension, discounted the German naval threat almost entirely:

14. German naval forces are hopelessly outnumbered compared to those of Britain and France. Germany cannot seek a fleet action. She would try to secure her Baltic trade, probably relying on airforces to assist this task. Outside the Baltic she would realise that her trade is bound to suffer almost complete severance.
   15. Germany might cause considerable interference to our trade at the outset of hostilities by passing "Deutschlands" [pocket battleships] or raiders into the Atlantic; and she might attempt coastal raids. But there is no doubt that all such interference must eventually be overcome. In effect, Germany could not hope to win the war by action at sea.[192]

When the Second World War did break out, the German navy had to be content with inconsequential, if dramatic, raids. Only through submarine warfare could Great Britain and, later, the United States be attacked. Yet, of all the German submarines used in the Second World War hardly any were laid down before the collapse of the naval arms control process. At the beginning of the war the Germans had only forty-nine operational U-boats.

The naval arms control process was far from perfect. It was prone to fits and starts, occasionally led to acrimony, and eventually collapsed. Yet, for all its faults it was set up for, and served the interests of, its major sponsors: the United States and Great Britain. By preempting a useless naval race, providing security in home waters, and forcing the other naval powers to restrain their building until 1936, it was a valuable contributor to the Allied victory in the Second World War.

## NOTES

1. Beatty Mss 13/2/3, Bellairs to Beatty, 13 December 1929.
2. FDR Mss, Personal File, Stark to FDR, 22 June 1933.
3. Hoover Mss, Disarmament, Coolidge to Hoover, 30 March 1929.
4. G. Hodgson, *The Colonel: The Life and Wars of Henry Stimson 1867-1950*, pp. 183-186.
5. R. G. Kaufman, *Arms Control during the Pre-Nuclear Era*, pp. 113-118.
6. C. Hall, *Britain, America and Arms Control, 1921-37*, p. 60.
7. Hoover Mss, Disarmament, Atherton to State Department, 24 April 1929.
8. R. O'Connor, *Perilous Equilibrium; The United States and the London Naval Conference of 1930*, pp. 29-32.
9. Hoover Mss, Hoover to Adams, 14 June 1929.
10. Hoover Mss, Bell Memorandum, 9 July 1929.
11. Alexander Mss 7/2, Alexander Article in the Sheffield Cooperate.
12. S. Roskill, *Naval Policy between the Wars*, vol. 2, pp. 31-36.
13. BFP Documents, MacDonald to Dawes, Second Series , vol. 1, p. 19, #12.

14. Beatty Mss 13/2/3, Bellairs to Beatty, 13 December 1929.

15. CAB 24/204, Alexander Memorandum, 25 June 1929.

16. Hoover Mss, Disarmament, Hoover to Stimson, 17 September 1929.

17. Stimson Mss, Reel 126, Memorandum, 7 October 1929. See also Roskill, *Naval Policy between the Wars*, vol. 2, pp. 45-49.

18. BFP Documents, Second Series , vol. 1, p. 84, #62, Draft Foreign Office Note, September 1929.

19. Ibid., p. 33, #25, MacDonald Memorandum, 29 July 1929.

20. Hoover Mss, Disarmament, Hoover to Stimson, 17 September 1929. See also; CAB 24/207, MacDonald Memorandum, November 1929.

21. BFP Documents, Second Series, vol. 1, p. 96, #67, MacDonald to Dawes, 23 September 1929.

22. Stimson Mss, Reel 126, Memorandum, 9 October 1929.

23. Hoover Mss, Niblack to Hoover, March 1929.

24. GBSF 420-2, Memorandum, 4 April 1929.

25. GBDC, Series 8, Box 19, Book 1, Jones to Secretary of Navy, 18 June 1929.

26. Hoover Mss, Disarmament, Memorandum, 23 August 1929. See also GB 438-1, Memorandum, 13 July 1929.

27. GBDC, Series 9, Box 24, Memorandum, 21 December 1929.

28. GBDC, Series 8, Box 20, Book 12, Memorandum, 8 January 1930. See also GBDC, Series 9, Box 24, Memorandum, 4 January 1930.

29. GB 438-1, Tentative Plan, 28 January 1930.

30. GBDC, Series 9, Box 23, Jones Memoranda, 28 January, 5 February 1930.

31. O'Connor, *Perilous Equilibrium*, pp. 51-54.

32. Hoover Mss, Disarmament, Gibson to Stimson, 6 May 1929.

33. ADM 116/2686, Plans Division Memorandum, 13 April 1929.

34. BFP Documents, Second Series, vol. 1, #91, p. 139.

35. ADM 116/2717, Draft Memorandum, 27 December 1930.

36. Kaufman, *Arms Control during the Pre-Nuclear Era*, pp. 138-139.

37. Roskill, *Naval Policy between the Wars*, vol. 2, pp. 65-66.

38. Hall, *Britain, America and Arms Control*, p. 88.

39. O'Connor, *Perilous Equilibrium*, pp. 122-128.

40. Kaufman, *Arms Control during the Pre-Nuclear Era*, pp. 138-145; R. Albion, *Makers of Naval Policy 1798-1947*, pp. 242-243; S. Howarth, *To Shining Sea*, pp. 349-350.

41. Hodgson, *The Colonel*, p. 183

42. C. Barnett, *The Collapse of British Power*, p. 290; P. M. Kennedy, *The Rise and Fall of British Naval Mastery*, p. 278; Roskill, *Naval Policy between the Wars*, vol. 2, p. 67. See also: B. Collier, *Barren Victories: Versailles to Suez*, p. 110.

43. ADM 116/2717, Jellicoe Memorandum, 3 January 1930.

44. Beatty Mss 13/2/2, Bellairs to Beatty, 22 November 1929.

45. Beatty Mss 13/2/4, Bellairs to Beatty, 19 February 1930.

46. Chatfield Mss. 4/2, Chatfield to Beatty, 10 October 1933.

47. GB 438-2, Memorandum, 18 January 1933, p. 14.

48. ADM 116/3371, Plans Division Memorandum, 26 June 1929.

49. ADM 116/2717, Draft Memorandum, 27 December 1930.

50. Templewood Mss, C VII 8, Madden Memorandum, 17 January 1930.

51. D. Marquand, *Ramsay MacDonald*, p. 517.

52. J. Ferris, "The Greatest Power on Earth, Great Britain in the 1920s;" B. McKercher, "Our Most Dangerous Enemy: Great Britain Preeminent in the 1930's," *International History Review*.

53. J. Ferris, *Men, Money and Diplomacy: The Evolution of British Strategic Policy 1919-1926*, p. 100; B. McKercher, "Wealth, Power and the New International Order: Britain and the American Challenge in the 1920's," *Diplomatic History*.

54. CAB 24/171, Navy Estimates, 5 February 1925. See also: Navy Estimates 1925-1926, 27 January 1925.

55. GBSF 420-8, "Red-Blue Cruiser War," 18 February 1930.

56. ADM 116/2686, Plans Division Memorandum, 13 April 1929.

57. CAB 24/171, Navy Estimates, 5 February 1925.

58. CAB 24/220, "The Disarmament Conference," 10 April 1931.

59. CAB 24/171, Navy Estimates, 5 February 1925.

60. Roskill, *Naval Policy between the Wars*, vol. 1, Appendix B.

61. ADM 116/3371, Plans Division Memoranda, 10, 17 March 1927.

62. Yarnell Mss, Yarnell Memorandum, 17 February 1930.

63. Albion, *Makers of Naval Policy*, pp. 244-251.

64. PPPUSAHH, Annual Message 1930, #390, p. 518.

65. PPPUSAHH, News Conference, 10 October 1930, #321, p. 428; GBSF 420-2, 1933 Building Program, 20 April 1931.

66. GBDC, Box 56, Series XVI, Memorandum, 28 May 1931.

67. Hoover Mss, C/P 33, Statements by Naval Officers, 25 August 1930.

68. Pratt Mss, Box 17, Pratt Memorandum, 13 February 1930.

69. GBDC, Series 10, Box 26, War Plans Division Memorandum, 29 April 1931.

70. Pratt Mss, Box 4, Pratt to Adams, 12 October 1931.

71. Hoover Mss P/S 213, "Navy League 1931-35," Jahncke to Hoover, 30 October 1931.

72. Hoover Mss P/C 35, Pratt Article, May 1932.

73. PPPUSAHH, News Conference, 29 July 1931, #327, pp. 444-445.

74. Hoover Mss P/C 38, Naval Conference at Camp Rapidan, 6 June 1931.

75. G. E. Wheeler, *Admiral William Veazie Pratt USN*, pp. 339-340.

76. Pratt Mss, Box 17, Memorandum, 4 March 1930; Moffett Memorandum, 30 March 1930.

77. GBDC, Series 9, Box 24, Moffett Memorandum, 31 March 1930.

78. Stimson Mss, Reel 126, Stimson Memorandum, 25 May 1932.

79. GBSF 420-2, Pratt Memorandum, 2 January 1932.

80. CR, 72d Congress, 1st Session, vol. 75, p. 2663.

81. Ibid., pp. 3003-11.

82. W. E. Leuchtenburg, *Franklin D. Roosevelt and the New Deal 1932-40*, pp. 4-8.

83. FDR Mss, PP File 5901, Carl Vinson, Vinson to FDR, 28 December 1932.

84. FDR Mss, Personal File, Stark, 21 March 1933.

85. P. E. Coletta ed., *American Secretaries of the Navy*, vol. 2, pp. 655-65. See also H. C. Ferrell, *Claude A. Swanson of Virginia: A Political Biography*, pp. 200-218.

86. FDR Mss, Secretary's File, Navy Confidential, Swanson to FDR, 13 April 1933.

87. FDR Mss, Official File, Navy Department, Swanson to Early, 9 May 1933.

88. Ibid., Miscellaneous, Swanson to FDR, 5 April 1933.

89. GB 420-2, GB Memorandum, 10 May 1933.

90. FDR Mss, Official File, Swanson Memorandum, 6 November 1934.

91. Ibid., Navy Department, 19 June 1933.

92. Ibid., H. Roosevelt to FDR, 16 October 1933.

93. Ibid., 8 January 1934.

94. FDR Mss, Personal File, Stark to FDR, 22 June 1933.

95. R. Dallek, *FDR and American Foreign Policy 1933-1945*, pp. 75-76.

96. E. E. Nixon and D. B. Schewe eds., *Franklin D. Roosevelt and Foreign Affairs*, FDR to Peabody, 19 August 1933.

97. CR, 73d Congress, 2d Session, vol. 78, 30 January 1934, p. 1597.

98. FDR Mss, Official File, Miscellaneous Naval Building, H. Roosevelt to FDR, 5 January 1934.

99. W. S. Cole, *Roosevelt and the Isolationists 1932-43*, p. 266.

100. CR, 73rd Congress, 2nd Session, vol. 78, 30 January 1934, p. 1598.

101. Ibid., 6 March 1934, p. 3804.

102. GBSF 420-8, "Red-Blue Cruiser War," 18 February 1930, "Blue-Orange: Cruiser Operations in the Far East," 15 April 1930.

103. WPL 8, Navy Basic Plans, June 1930.

104. WPL 9, Basic White Plan, November 1930.

105. W. R. Braisted, "The Evolution of the United States Navy's Strategic Assessments in the Pacific: 1919-1931" p. 119, in E. Goldstein and J. Maurer eds., *The Washington Conference 1921-22: Naval Rivalry, East Asian Stability and the Road to Pearl Harbor*.

106. R. Love, *History of the United States Navy*, vol. 1, pp. 565-577.

107. Borah Mss, Box 278, "9-Power Treaty," Stimson to Borah, 23 February 1932.

108. WPL 28, "Report of Chief Umpire," February 1932.

109. GBSF 425, Box 131, General Board to Secretary of the Navy, 4 May 1932.

110. FDR Mss, Secretary's File, Navy Department, Swanson to FDR, 8 November 1933.

111. FDR Mss, Official File, Japan, FDR letter, 26 March 1934.

112. Ibid., White House Telegram, 8 November 1934.

113. R. P. Shay, *British Rearmament in the Thirties*, pp. 3, 11.

114. S. Roskill, *Naval Policy Between the Wars*, vol. 1 Appendix C.

115. CAB 24/219, Snowden Memorandum, 23 January 1931.

116. S. Hiroharu, "The Manchurian Incident 1931;" A. Iriye, "The Extension of Hostilities, 1931-32;" in W. Morley ed., *Japan Erupts: The London Naval Crisis and the Manchurian Incident, 1928-32*. See also W. R. Louis, *British Strategy in the Far East 1919-1939*, pp. 172-205.

117. CAB 24/228, "New Construction Programme 1931," 5 February 1932.

118. CAB 24/229, "Imperial Defence Policy," February 1932.

119.CAB 24/237, "Navy Estimates," Appendix 1, 8 February 1933.

120.CAB 24/232, "Singapore Naval Base," 11 July 1932.

121.CAB 24/237, "Navy Estimates for 1933," 8 February 1933.

122.CAB 24/239, Report by the Chiefs of Staff Sub-Committee, 7 April 1933.

123.ADM 116/2860, "Fleet Committee 1st Report," December 1931.

124.Chatfield Mss 3/1, Sea Lords Memorandum, 3 November 1932.

125.Ibid.

126.CAB 24/243, Monsell Memorandum, 24 October 1933.

127.CAB 24/243, "Programme of New Construction, 1933," 31 August 1933.

128.Chatfield Mss 4/2, Chatfield to Beatty, 10 October 1933.

129.CAB 24/245, "Programme for New Construction for 1934," 21 December 1933.

130.W. Wark, *The Ultimate Enemy: British Intelligence and Nazi Germany 1933-1939*, pp. 124-54.

131.ADM 116/2945, Memorandum, 5 July 1933. See also ADM 116/2945, "Instances of Alleged Infringement of Treaty of Versailles."

132.CAB 24/248, Simon Memorandum, 21 March, 1934.

133.ADM 116/2890, Foreign Office Report, 25 January 1934.

134.CAB 24/241, Simon Memorandum, 16 May 1933.

135.Vansittart Mss 1 2/2, Memorandum, 26 February 1933.

136.CAB 24/243, Vansittart Memorandum, 28 August 1933. See also Vansittart Mss 1 2/6, Vansittart Note, July 1933, and CAB 24/248, Vansittart Memorandum, 7 April 1934.

137.CAB 24/247, CID Defence Sub-Committee Report, 28 February 1934.

138.CAB 24/244, CID Chiefs of Staff Sub-Committee Report, October 1933.

139.Ibid., Appendix.

140.CAB 24/251, CID Report on German Rearmament, 23 November 1934.

141.CAB 24/247, CID Defence Sub-Committee Report, 28 February 1934.

142.Ibid., Table B.

143.CAB 24/251, Monsell Memorandum, 6 December 1934.

144.CAB 24/253 Cabinet Statement (Revised) Relating to Defence, 11 March 1935.

145.CAB 24/251, "Committee on German Rearmament," December 1934.

146.E. W. Bennet, *German Rearmament and the West 1932-1933*, p. 496.

147.ADM 116/2890 British Naval Attaché in Berlin Report, 30 November 1933.

148.CAB 24/254, "Notes of the Anglo-German Conversations," March 1935.

149.CAB 24/255, Simon Memorandum, 7 June 1935.

150.Hall, *Britain, America and Arms Control*, pp. 174-180; Roskill, *Naval Policy between the Wars*, vol. 2, pp. 302-8; Wark, *The Ultimate Enemy*, pp. 130-45.

151.Roskill, *The Strategy of Sea Power*, p. 147; Barnett, *The Collapse of British Power*, p. 407.

152.W. R. Rock, *British Appeasement in the 1930's*, p. 37.

153.Templewood Mss VIII 1, Craigie Memorandum, June 1935.

154.BFP Documents, Second Series, vol. 13, Naval Staff Memorandum, #305.

155.ADM 116/3437, Plans Division Memorandum, 6 August 1935.

156.Roskill, *Naval Policy between the Wars*, vol. 2, pp. 307-8.

157.Templewood Mss VIII 1, Craigie Memorandum, June 1935.

158.Roskill, *Naval Policy between the Wars*, vol. 1, Appendix B, Tables II and III.

159.Ibid., vol. 2, pp. 134-44.

160.Ibid., pp. 284-321; Hall, *Britain, America and Arms Control*, pp. 116-142.

161.FDR Mss, Navy Department, GB Memorandum, 25 May 1934.

162.FDR Mss, LNC, "Forecast of Japanese Attitude," 22 March 1934.

163.GBSF 438-1, GB Memorandum, 26 February 1934, GB Memorandum, 1 March 1934.

164.FDR Mss, LNC, Davis to FDR, 6 March 1934.

165.GBSF 438-1, Leigh Memorandum, 30 July 1934.

166.CAB 24/239, Simon Memorandum, 28 February 1933; Vansittart Mss 1 2/2, Vansittart Memorandum, 26 February 1933.

167.CAB 24/254, "The Far East," April 1935.

168.CAB 24/248, "Imperial Defence Policy," 16 March 1934.

169.ADM 116/3338, "The General Strategic Situation in the Western Pacific," c. August 1935.

170.Chatfield Mss 3/2, Fisher to Chatfield, undated.

171.Baldwin Mss #131, Chatfield to Fisher, 16 July 1934.

172.Chatfield Mss 3/2, Fisher Notes, 7 November 1934.

173.G. C. Peden, *British Rearmament and the Treasury 1932-1939*, p. 110. See also Chatfield Mss 3/2, Fisher Memorandum, 12 November 1934.

174.BFP Documents, Second Series, vol. 13, Appendix 1.

175.CAB 24/250, "The Future of Anglo-Japanese Relations," 16 October 1934.

176.CAB 24/251, "The Naval Conference 1935," 30 October 1934.

177.CAB 24/251, Cabinet Statement, 7 November 1934.

178.GBDC, Series 13-14, Box 50, London Naval Conversations, March 1935.

179.FDR Mss, LNC, Davis to FDR, 6 March 1934, 4 June 1934, 27 June 1934, 28 June 1934, 20 August 1934, 31 October 1934, 6 November 1934, 27 November 1934, 14 December 1934.

180.FDR Mss, LNC, FDR to Davis, 9 November 1934.

181.FDR Mss, LNC, Davis to FDR, 14 December 1934.

182.Morgenthau Mss, Diary, 18 March 1935.

183.GBSF 438-1, Memorandum, 4 October 1935; GBDC, Series XIII-XIV, Box 50, Memorandum, 8 July 1935.

184.GBDC, Series XIV, Box 52, Memorandum, 17 December 1935.

185.ADM 116/3332, "The Position of the Naval Conference," 21 February 1936.

186.FDR Mss, LNC, Davis to FDR, 30 January 1936.

187.BFP Documents, Second Series, vol. 13, #718.

188.Roskill, *Naval Policy between the Wars*, vol. 2, p. 320.

189.Ibid., p. 322; S. W. C. Pack, *Sea Power in the Mediterranean*, p. 36; S. E. Pelz, *Race to Pearl Harbour:The Failure of the Second London Naval Conference and the Onset of World War II*, p. 97; F. H. Hinsley, *Command of the Sea*, p. 31; Love, *History of the United States Navy*, vol. 1, p. 595.

190.FDR Mss, LNC, Roosevelt Memorandum, 17 December 1934.

191.ADM 116/3332, "Future Course of Naval Negotiations," July 1935.

192. Templewood Mss, C VII 9, CID Paper, 29 April 1936.

# Conclusion

Between 1936 and the outbreak of the Second World War, naval building picked up worldwide. For the British and Americans it was time to restart the construction of capital ships and aircraft carriers, vessels that had been limited by the Washington Treaty. In 1937, the single greatest year of British naval construction since the First World War, work began on five King George V-class capital ships and four Illustrious-class aircraft carriers. American building was more spread out. The NIRA program and the Vinson-Trammell act meant that the United States had a large number of warships, including the modern aircraft carriers *Yorktown* and *Enterprise*, under way before the Second London Conference ended. In 1936 an additional American carrier, the *Wasp*, was started, while in 1937 the *North Carolina*, America's first modern capital ship since the Washington Conference, was laid down.

The Americans and the British were not alone. The Japanese, freed from the restrictions of the naval arms control process, started building some very large ships. Three of the Imperial Japanese Navy's best carriers, the *Hiryu*, *Shokaku* and *Zuikaku*, were laid down between 1936 and 1938, while the two largest battleships ever built, the 62,000-ton *Yamato* and *Musashi*, were also begun. The famous German battleships *Bismarck* and *Tirpitz* were also laid down in 1936. The German battleship *Deutschland* and the aircraft carrier *Graf Zeppelin* were also started, but neither would ever be completed. Other powers such as the French and Italians joined in by laying down additional capital ships, though none were completed in time to have much impact during the Second World War.

What did all this mean for Great Britain and the United States? One of the most interesting aspects of the years between 1900 and 1939 was how naval power did not evolve smoothly. People looking for a long, slow decline in Britain's naval position and a corresponding even rise in America's are bound to be disappointed. In many ways Britain's position had improved over the years. Certainly, British policy and preparations were more measured and considerate in the interwar period than before 1914. Prior to the First World War British naval policy was erratic and unstable. In 1900 the Royal Navy, still by far the world's largest, was without allies. France and Russia remained Britain's traditional naval competitors, but at the same time new fleets were being built in Germany, America, and Japan. This relative decline in Britain's naval position forced the British to take some dramatic steps. The two-power standard was abandoned, and an alliance with Japan was soon followed by an entente with France. Then British confidence recovered dramatically. The Japanese defeat of Russia in 1905 and the construction of HMS *Dreadnought* led to a return of bravado and a reassertion of the two-power standard. In 1909, however, this new sense of security collapsed in the space of a few months when it was thought that the Germans were secretly set on grabbing naval superiority. From the 1909 naval estimates crisis onward the Royal Navy spent most of its time worrying about the German threat. However, even after "winning" the Anglo-German naval race, British security was far from assured. For all Britain's advantages—its excellent geographical position and alliances with Japan, France, Russia, and eventually the United States—the British in the First World War were almost brought to their knees by the German navy. In 1917 it seemed that the Royal Navy was powerless to stop German submarine attacks. Had it not been for the timely introduction of the convoy system and massive American aid, Britain might have been forced out of the war.

Instead of swinging between moments of despair and overconfidence, British decision making between 1919 and 1939 was mostly sober and effective. After realizing that the United States could not be bluffed into a position of inferiority, it was decided to accept the Americans as naval equals. In making this symbolic concession, the British were to gain more from the Washington Conference of 1921-1922 than they had thought possible. The Americans scrapped their entire 1916 program, while the ratios agreed to by the other powers left the British in total control of European waters. Prewar tendencies reasserted themselves temporarily in 1927 and 1928, when Winston Churchill cajoled the Baldwin government into taking a much more aggressive line with the United

States. This rash policy was the one serious British miscalculation of the inter-war period but was quickly made good at the First London Conference. After 1930 British naval rearmament took decisive, if incremental, steps. Throughout the period the British maintained their commitment to the naval arms control process only when it was in their national interest. When the Japanese tried to get naval parity, the British cooperated with the Americans to thwart the attempt.

The rise of America in these years was the only significant sign of a British naval decline. Yet, too much should not be made of this. The rise of America did not pose any new threats to the British Empire. Whether or not the United States possessed the world's strongest or fourth strongest fleet, it still presented the same formidable challenge. Canada remained a geographic hostage, while the size of the American economy meant that it could eventually ground any opponent into dust. British governments began adjusting policy accordingly as early as 1900, when the Royal Navy was far larger than the American fleet. The British really needed to worry about the naval strength of more realistic potential enemies such as Germany, Japan, and Italy. This was what was done so well in the interwar period.

When the naval arms control process ended after the Second London Conference, the British took part in the worldwide naval construction boom. They moved more quickly than both the Americans and Japanese in resuming the construction of battleships, starting five before the other powers had begun their first. The sensible policy paid its dividends after 1939. While not part of this study, I think it is safe to say that the Royal Navy's performance during the Second World War was superior to that in the First World War. At the beginning of the Second World War the Royal Navy controlled all the waterways vital to the British war effort. The German navy, aside from a few insignificant sorties by raiders like the *Graf Spee*, was bottled up. Even German submarines were mostly ineffectual at this point. Things changed rapidly for the worse in 1940. The German capture of Denmark and Norway, Italy's decision to fight as Germany's ally, and finally the fall of France were a potentially disastrous triple blow. It is highly unlikely that the British would have been able to survive the First World War if such a string of catastrophes had occurred. The 1914-1918 war presented the British with a much simpler geographic task. German access to the sea was limited to a small number of ports on the North Sea. After the early duels in the South Atlantic, all major naval combat occurred within a few hundred miles of the British Isles.

In 1940, however, the British home islands were outflanked to the north and south, while the Mediterranean was reopened to naval conflict in a way not seen since Nelson fought the Battle of the Nile. Yet, the Royal Navy was able to fight on and fight on well. For over a year and a half the British survived without a naval ally worth speaking of. They were able to hold the line against German submarines. When the Germans launched surface raids, such as the famous sortie of the *Bismarck*, the Royal Navy's strength was sufficient to sink the attackers or force them back to port. The Italian navy, which looked strong on paper, was defeated, and British communications were maintained in the Mediterranean. It was a performance worthy of admiration. The British had handled the naval side of the Second World War so well that when the Japanese declared war, some powerful surface units could be sent to the Pacific and Indian Oceans. The British decision to dispatch the *Prince of Wales* and *Repulse* to Singapore was somewhat hasty, but the fact that they both could be spared is illuminating. It is unlikely that the Royal Navy could have dispatched about 10 percent of its capital ship strength to the Pacific at any time between 1914 and 1918. During the Second World War the Royal Navy thus had to contend with four major geographic changes, any one of which might have tipped the balance against Great Britain between 1914 and 1918.

If British naval power evolved somewhat fitfully between 1900 and 1939, American naval power was even more unpredictable. This is not to say that the American navy did not grow, because it did. In 1900 the American navy was still a relatively small force, but by 1939 it was a world leader. Yet, American naval strength did not grow along some preordained path. Indeed, the American navy between 1900 and 1939 grew because of four unconnected, random events.

The first of these was the assassination of President William McKinley, which brought Theodore Roosevelt to the White House. The assassin's hand had unwittingly brought the most pro-navy politician in America to the pinnacle of power. For the next five years the American fleet would grow at an unprecedented pace, eventually becoming the second strongest in the world. Yet, Roosevelt was an anomaly, pushing Congress and the American people further than they really wanted to go. By 1907 there were worrying signs that things were reverting to course. Congress started reducing the president's proposed construction programs, while the American people stood aside uninterested.

For the next six years the American navy was left behind as the major European powers engaged in a building race. Passed by the Germans and threatened by the French, the American navy seemed powerless. Presidents Taft and Wilson had little interest in naval power and saw no reason to expend political capital pulling the navy's chestnuts out of the fire. Redemption came about only through a combination of the tragedy of the First World War and President Wilson's messianic tendencies. At first Woodrow Wilson tried to play down American naval construction, not wanting to look provocative to the European powers. However, the longer the war went on, and the more both sides encroached on American principles, the more Wilson craved American force. In 1915 he changed course abruptly and proposed the largest naval building program in American history. After languishing for years, the American navy now found itself being built up to match the largest fleet in the world.

Needless to say, this fervor could not last. After the war, while the American navy continued to press for more and more building, the consensus in favor of naval building began to erode. The American navy thrived on crisis and confrontation, not peace and domestic self-absorption. It is impossible to say what would have happened to American naval strength without the arms control process. Maybe enough political will might have remained to keep the U.S. Navy up to strength with the British, but maybe not. The naval arms control process, inaugurated at the Washington Conference, gave the Americans the public "right" to parity, which tided the fleet over until the next international confrontation created a political consensus for more ships.

The confrontation in question was the Baldwin government's decision to question America's right to cruiser parity. Between 1922 and 1926 American naval construction proceeded at a glacial pace, with only a handful of new ships being laid down. However, once the British government, very undiplomatically, refused to make a deal with the Americans at the Geneva Conference, things changed rapidly. Calvin Coolidge, who previously had been as interested in naval power as William Taft, believed he had fallen victim to a dastardly British plot. He soon called for a massive new construction program of Washington-class cruisers, the largest possible that could be built. After another disastrous move by the British, the famous Anglo-French compromise, Coolidge became so enraged that he called for American naval supremacy.

Eventually, the British were forced to accept parity in all classes of naval vessels at the First London Conference. Once again the U.S. Navy was pushed into the background. Coolidge's successor, Herbert Hoover, was a pacifist by nature and a hostile opponent of spending on the armed services. When the Great Depression hit, he moved to restrain government spending on the fleet, believing it a wasteful drain on the national economy. Yet, the Great Depression ultimately and unpredictably served the American navy's interest. By severely damaging the popularity of the Republicans, the Great Depression helped bring Democrats like Carl Vinson and, most important, Franklin Roosevelt to power. These Democrats, unlike most in their party, were committed to a strong American fleet. They used the economic dislocation caused by the depression to rally support behind huge injections of cash for American shipbuilding. Within months of Roosevelt's coming to power an extra $240 million had been redirected to the fleet. A year later the Vinson-Trammel act was passed, and the United States started building all the ships allowed it by the naval arms control process.

It had been, in the words of a popular song, "a long, strange trip" for the U.S. Navy. Between 1900 and 1936 American naval building progressed only in four short bursts. The first years of Theodore Roosevelt's presidency, the 1916 program, the Coolidge cruiser bill, and the Great Depression building plans were almost entirely responsible for building up the American fleet in these years. However, none of these events were preordained, and most were the result of chance or luck.

The role of chance or luck in American naval power should not be minimized. For the British, chance played an important role before the First World War, but in the interwar period good planning was essential. The U.S. Navy was never able to shake off its more unpredictable tendencies. Take, for instance aircraft carriers. After the Washington Conference the United States was left with the *Lexington* and *Saratoga*, at 33,000 tons each the largest carriers in the world. However, both had actually been designed as battlecruisers and had been redesigned as carriers only because of the Washington Conference. Within a few years of their completion, both were thought to be dinosaurs. In the late 1920s the American navy became increasingly fond of small carriers and would gladly have scrapped the *Lexington* and *Saratoga*. However, as Congress was in no mood to spend more money on the fleet, these large flattops were maintained. It was a very good thing for the United States. When the Second World War started, the *Lexington* and *Saratoga* would prove their worth as two of the best carriers in the world.

In general today there is a distressing tendency for historians to write that things were bad, and then they got worse. This was certainly not the case for the American and British fleets in these years. While this study has pointed out a number of blunders or mistakes on both sides, this is something that should not be forgotten. Two world wars were fought, and both were won. For all the miscalculations, panics, and frustration, both fleets triumphed doing what they were built to do. Not only that—both improved their position at different points during these years. Royal Navy planning became more sensible, and for all the American fleet's political problems, things were better before the Second World War than the First World War. With this in mind it might be best to end with the old adage that the proof of the pudding was in the eating. In both cases it was ultimately tasty.

# Appendix I

# United States Navy Annual Construction Programs and Recommendations: 1900-1914

| Year and (fy) | General Board Recommendation | Navy Dept. (Presidential) Recommendation | Congressional Authorization |
|---|---|---|---|
| 1900 (1901–02) | 2 Battleships 2 Armored Cruisers 6 Gunboats 2 Destroyers 6 Others | 12 Gunboats | No New Construction |
| 1901 (1902–03) | 4 Battleships 2 Armored Cruisers 18 Gunboats 11 Others | 3 Battleships 2 Armored Cruisers 6 Gunboats 11 Others | 2 Battleships 2 Armored Cruisers 2 Gunboats 2 Others |
| 1902 (1903–04) | No Specific Recommendation | 2 Battleships 2 Armored Cruisers | 5 Battleships 2 Others |

| 1903<br>*(1904–05)* | 2 Battleships<br>1 Armored Cruiser<br>7 Light Cruisers<br>3 Destroyers<br>2 Colliers | 1 Battleship<br>1 Armored Cruiser<br>5–7 Light Cruisers<br><br>2 Colliers<br>4 Others | 1 Battleship<br>2 Armored Cruisers<br>3 Light Cruisers<br><br>2 Colliers<br>6 Others |
| --- | --- | --- | --- |
| 1904<br>*(1905–06)* | 3 Battleships<br>6 Destroyers<br>18 Others | 3 Battleships<br>6 Destroyers | 2 Battleships |
| 1905<br>*(1906–07)* | 3 Battleships<br>4 Submarines<br>16 Others | 2 Battleships<br>2 Submarines<br>9 Others | 1 Battleship<br>8 Submarines |
| 1906<br>*(1907–08)* | 2 Battleships<br>4 Destroyers<br>14 Others | 2 Battleships<br>4 Destroyers<br>14 Others | 1 Battleship<br>2 Destroyers |
| 1907<br>*(1908–09)* | 4 Battleships<br>10 Destroyers<br>4 Submarines<br>2 Colliers<br>12 Others | 4 Battleships<br>10 Destroyers<br>4 Submarines<br>4 Colliers<br>8 Others | 2 Battleships<br>10 Destroyers<br>8 Submarines<br>5 Colliers |
| 1908<br>*(1909–10)* | 4 Battleships<br>10 Destroyers<br>4 Submarines<br>3 Colliers<br>8 Others | 4 Battleships<br>10 Destroyers<br>4 Submarines<br>3 Colliers<br>8 Others | 2 Battleships<br>5 Destroyers<br>7 Submarines<br>1 Collier |
| 1909<br>*(1910–11)* | 4 Battleships<br>10 Destroyers<br><br><br>7 Others | 2 Battleships<br>6 Destroyers<br><br><br>1 Other | 2 Battleships<br><br>4 Submarines<br>2 Colliers |
| 1910<br>*(1911–12)* | 4 Battleships<br>16 Destroyers<br><br>23 Others | 2 Battleships<br>8 Destroyers<br>2 Submarines<br>6 Others | 2 Battleships<br><br>4 Submarines<br>7 Others |
| 1911<br>*(1912–13)* | 4 Battleships<br>1 Battlecruiser<br>16 Destroyers<br>5 Submarines<br>17 Others | 2 Battleships<br><br>6 Destroyers<br>8 Submarines<br>2 Others | 1 Battleship<br><br><br><br>5 Others |

| 1912 | 4 Battleships | 3 Battleships | 1 Battleship |
|---|---|---|---|
| (1913–14) | 2 Battlecruisers | 2 Battlecruisers | |
| | 16 Destroyers | 16 Destroyers | 6 Destroyers |
| | 6 Submarines | 6 Submarines | 4 Submarines |
| | 12 Others | 12 Others | 2 Others |
| | | | |
| 1913 | 4 Battleships | 2 Battleships | 3 Battleships |
| (1914–15) | 16 Destroyers | 8 Destroyers | 6 Destroyers |
| | 8 Submarines | 3 Submarines | 8 Submarines |
| | 11 Others | | |
| | | | |
| 1914 | 4 Battleships | 2 Battleships | 2 Battleships |
| (1915–16) | 12 Destroyers | 6 Destroyers | 6 Destroyers |
| | 19 Submarines | 8 Submarines | 18 Submarines |
| | 15 Others | 2 Others | 1 Other |

# NOTE

1. Daniels Mss, Series 3, Microfilm Reel 36, Memorandum, 2 April 1920.

# Appendix II

# Surface Warships Begun by Great Britain, the United States, Japan and Germany: 1930-1939

| Great Britain | United States | Japan | Germany |
|---|---|---|---|
| | | **1930** | |
| 1 Aircraft Carrier[2] | 3 Cruisers | 5 Destroyers | |
| 1 Cruiser | | | |
| | | **1931** | |
| 3 Cruisers | 1 Aircraft Carrier[3] | 2 Cruisers | 1 Pocket Battleship |
| 9 Destroyers | 4 Cruisers | 3 Destroyers | |
| | | **1932** | |
| 1 Cruiser | 3 Destroyers | | 1 Pocket Battleship |
| | | **1933** | |
| 5 Cruisers | 1 Cruiser | 1 Cruiser | 1 Cruiser |
| 18 Destroyers | 8 Destroyers | 5 Destroyers | |
| | | **1934** | |
| 3 Cruisers | 2 Aircraft Carriers[4] | 1 Aircraft Carrier[5] | 2 Destroyers |
| 9 Destroyers | 2 Cruisers | 2 Cruisers | |
| | 21 Destroyers | 3 Destroyers | |

| Great Britain | United States | Japan | Germany |
|---|---|---|---|

### 1935

| Great Britain | United States | Japan | Germany |
|---|---|---|---|
| 1 Aircraft Carrier[6] | 7 Cruisers | 1 Cruiser | 2 Battleships[7] |
| 4 Cruisers | 14 Destroyers | 8 Destroyers | 2 Cruisers |
| 9 Destroyers | | | 13 Destroyers |

### Total for 1930–1935

| Great Britain | United States | Japan | Germany |
|---|---|---|---|
| 2 Aircraft Carriers | 3 Aircraft Carriers | 1 Aircraft Carrier | 2 Battleships |
| 17 Cruisers | 17 Cruisers | 6 Cruisers | 2 Pocket Battleship |
| 45 Destroyers | 46 Destroyers | 24 Destroyers | 3 Cruisers |
| | | | 15 Destroyers |

### 1936

| Great Britain | United States | Japan | Germany |
|---|---|---|---|
| 5 Cruisers | 1 Aircraft Carrier[8] | 1 Aircraft Carrier[9] | 2 Battleships[10] |
| 24 Destroyers | 2 Cruisers | 6 Destroyers | 1 Aircraft Carrier[11] |
| | 8 Destroyers | | 2 Cruisers |
| | | | 4 Destroyers |

### 1937

| Great Britain | United States | Japan | Germany |
|---|---|---|---|
| 5 Battleships[12] | 1 Battleship[13] | 1 Battleship[14] | 1 Cruiser |
| 4 Aircraft Carriers[15] | 19 Destroyers | 1 Aircraft Carrier[16] | 2 Destroyers |
| 6 Cruisers | | 5 Destroyers | |
| 15 Destroyers | | | |

### 1938

| Great Britain | United States | Japan | Germany |
|---|---|---|---|
| 10 Cruisers | 1 Battleship[17] | 1 Battleship[18] | 1 Battleship[19] |
| 8 Destroyers | 7 Destroyers | 1 Aircraft Carrier[20] | 2 Destroyers |
| | | 2 Cruisers | |
| | | 7 Destroyers | |

### 1939
### (not including war programs)

| Great Britain | United States | Japan | Germany |
|---|---|---|---|
| 4 Cruisers | 3 Battleships[21] | 6 Destroyers | 3 Destroyers |
| 8 Destroyers | 1 Aircraft Carrier[22] | | |
| | 9 Destroyers | | |

### Total for 1936–1939

| Great Britain | United States | Japan | Germany |
|---|---|---|---|
| 5 Battleships | 5 Battleships | 2 Battleships | 3 Battleships |
| 4 Aircraft Carriers | 2 Aircraft Carriers | 3 Aircraft Carriers | 1 Aircraft Carrier |
| 25 Cruisers | 2 Cruisers | 2 Cruisers | 3 Cruisers |
| 55 Destroyers | 43 Destroyers | 24 Destroyers | 11 Destroyers |

## NOTES

1. This appendix lists naval vessels whose construction was actually begun in a certain year, as opposed to those whose construction was simply approved. There are a number of different reference books listing the naval vessels laid down by the great powers before World War II but they do not, however, agree on everything. In areas of conflict I have tried to take the most commonly accepted dates. Among the sources

consulted are: *Jane's Fighting Ships of World War II*, R. Chesneau, *Aircraft Carriers of the World*, N. Friedman, *United States Battleships*, and *United States Cruisers*, B. Gordon and A. Watt, *The Imperial Japanese Navy*, A. Raven and J. Roberts, *British Battleships of World War II*, and *British Cruisers of World War II*, J. Reilly, *United States Destroyers of World War II*, S. Terzibaschitsch, *Cruisers of the United States Navy*, M. Whitley, *Destroyers of World War II*, and *German Cruisers of World War II*, and *German Destroyers of World War II*.

2. *Glorious*
3. *Ranger*
4. *Yorktown, Enterprise*
5. *Soryu*
6. *Ark Royal*
7. *Gneisenau, Scharnhorst*
8. *Wasp*
9. *Hiryu*
10. *Bismarck, Tirpitz*
11. *Graf Zeppelin* (never finished)
12. *King George V, Prince of Wales, Duke of York, Howe, Anson*
13. *North Carolina*
14. *Yamato*
15. *Illustrious, Formidable, Victorious, Indomitable*
16. *Shokaku*
17. *Washington*
18. *Musashi*
19. *Deutschland* (never finished)
20. *Zuikaku*
21. *South Dakota, Indiana, Massachusetts*
22. *Hornet*

# Bibliography

**PRIMARY SOURCES**

**PERSONAL PAPERS**
*British*

| | |
|---|---|
| Alexander Mss | Churchill College, Cambridge |
| Asquith Mss | Bodleian Library, Oxford |
| Baldwin Mss | Cambridge University Library |
| Balfour Mss | British Library, London |
| Beatty Mss | National Maritime Museum, Greenwich |
| Bridgeman Mss | Churchill College, Cambridge |
| Cecil Mss | British Library, London |
| Chatfield Mss | National Maritime Museum, Greenwich |
| Corbett Mss | National Maritime Museum, Greenwich |
| Domville Mss | National Maritime Museum, Greenwich |
| Esher Mss | Churchill College, Cambridge |
| Fisher Mss | Churchill College, Cambridge |
| Geddes Mss | Public Records Office, London |
| Grey Mss | Public Records Office, London |

| | |
|---|---|
| Haldane Mss | National Library, Scotland |
| Hankey Mss | Churchill College, Cambridge |
| Hardinge Mss | Cambridge University Library |
| Jellicoe Mss | British Library, London |
| Lloyd-George Mss | House of Lords Library, London |
| McKenna Mss | Churchill College, Cambridge |
| Roskill Mss | Churchill College, Cambridge |
| Selborne Mss | Bodleian Library, Oxford |
| Slade Mss | National Maritime Museum, Greenwich |
| Templewood Mss | Cambridge University Library |
| Vansittart Mss | Churchill College, Cambridge |
| Wemyss Mss | Churchill College, Cambridge |

*American*

| | |
|---|---|
| Benson Mss | Library of Congress, Washington, DC |
| Bonaparte Mss | Library of Congress, Washington, DC |
| Borah Mss | Library of Congress, Washington, DC |
| Castle Mss | Hoover Presidential Library, West Branch, IA |
| Coolidge Mss | Library of Congress, Washington, DC |
| Daniels Mss | Library of Congress, Washington, DC |
| Hoover Mss | Hoover Presidential Library, West Branch, IA |
| Hughes Mss | Library of Congress, Washington, DC |
| Lodge Mss | Massachusetts Historical Society, Boston |
| Meyer Mss | Massachusetts Historical Society, Boston |
| | Library of Congress, Washington, DC |
| Moody Mss | Library of Congress, Washington, DC |
| Morgenthau Mss | FDR Presidential Library, Hyde Park, NY |
| Pratt Mss | Naval Historical Society, Washington, DC |
| Rodgers Mss | Naval Historical Society, Washington, DC |
| Roosevelt, Franklin D. Mss | FDR Presidential Library, Hyde Park, NY |
| Roosevelt, Theodore Mss | Library of Congress, Washington, DC |
| Roosevelt, Theodore, Jr., Mss | Library of Congress, Washington, DC |
| Root Mss | Library of Congress, Washington, DC |
| Sims Mss | Library of Congress, Washington, DC |
| Stimson Mss | Library of Congress, Washington, DC |
| Taft Mss | Library of Congress, Washington, DC |
| Yarnell Mss | Naval Historical Society, Washington, DC |

## OFFICIAL PAPERS

*British*

| | |
|---|---|
| Admiralty Papers | Public Records Office, London |
| Cabinet Papers | Public Records Office, London |
| Command Papers | Public Records Office, London |
| Committee for Imperial Defence | Public Records Office, London |
| Foreign Office Papers | Public Records Office, London |
| Treasury Papers | Public Records Office, London |

*American*
*Congressional Record*, various volumes.

General Board Disarmament Conference          National Archives, Washington, DC
General Board Letter Books                    National Archives, Washington, DC
General Board Subject File                    National Archives, Washington, DC
General Board War Plans Division              National Archives, Washington, DC
Navy Department General Correspondence        National Archives, Washington, DC
Naval Intelligence Department                 National Archives, Washington, DC
Secret and Confidential Correspondence
    of the Chief of Naval Operations          National Archives, Washington, DC
State Department Papers                       National Archives, Washington, DC

## PUBLISHED DOCUMENT COLLECTIONS
*British*
Butler, R., W. N. Medlicott, et al., eds. *Documents on British Foreign Policy 1919-1939*.
    London, 1949-1955.
Gooch, G. P., H. Temperley, eds., *British Documents on the Origins of The War*. Various
    vols., London, 1926-1938.
Marder, A. J., *Fear God and Dreadnought*. vol. 2, London, 1956
Ranft, B. M., ed. *The Beatty Papers*. London, 1993.
Simpson, M., ed. *Anglo-American Naval Relations 1917-1919*. Aldershot, 1991.


*American*
*Annual Message of the President of the United States*. Various issues, Washington DC.
*Annual Report of the Secretary of the Navy*. Various issues, Washington DC.
*Foreign Relations of the United States*. Various vols, Washington DC.
Link, A., ed., *The Papers of Woodrow Wilson*. Various vols, Princeton, 1968-1983
Morison, E. E. ed., *The Letters of Theodore Roosevelt*. Vols 4-6, Cambridge, 1952.
Nixon, E. E., D. B. Schewe, eds., *Franklin Roosevelt and Foreign Affairs*. Cambridge,
    1969.
*Presidential Addresses and State Papers of William H. Taft*. Vol 1., London, 1910.
*Public Papers of the Presidents of the United States: Herbert Hoover*. Washington DC.
Seymour, C. ed.. *The Intimate Papers of Colonel House*. Boston, 1926-1928.

## REFERENCE MATERIAL
Chesneau, R., *Aircraft Carriers*, London, 1984
Friedman, N., *United States Cruisers*, London, 1986.
Friedman, N., *United States Battleships*, London, 1985.
*Historical Statistics of the United States*. White Plains, NY, 1987.
*Jane's Fighting Ships 1906*. London, 1906
*Jane's Fighting Ships 1909*. London, 1909.
*Jane's Fighing Ships of the First World War*. London, 1992.
*Jane's Fighting Ships of the Second World War*. London, 1989.
Mitchell, B. R., *British Historical Statistics*. Cambridge, 1988.
Raven, A. & Roberts, J., *British Cruisers of World War II*, London, 1980.
Raven, A. & Roberts, J., *British Battleships of World War II*, Naval Institute Press 1976.
Reilly, J.C., *United States Navy Destroyers of World War II*, Dorset, 1983.
Royal Institute of International Affairs, *Survey of International Affairs—1927*. Oxford,
    1929.
Showell, J.P.M., *The German Navy in World War II: A Reference Guide*, London, 1979.

Terzibaschitsch, S., *Cruisers of the United States Navy*, London, 1984.
Watts, A.J., & Gordon, B.G., *The Imperial Japanese Navy*, London, 1971.
Whitley, M.J., *Destroyers of World War II: An International Encyclopedia*, London,
    1988.
Whitley, M.J., *German Cruisers of World War II*, London, 1985
Whitley, M.J., *German Destroyers in World War II*, London, 1983.

## SECONDARY SOURCES

Albion, R. G. *Makers of Naval Policy 1798-1947*. Annapolis, MD, 1980.

Alch, M. W. "Germany's Naval Resurgence, British Appeasement, and the Anglo-German Naval Agreement of, 1935." Diss, University of California-Los Angeles, 1977.

Allard, D. "Anglo-American Differences during World War I." *Military Affairs* 44, #2, 1980.

Asquith, H. H. *The Genesis of the War*. London, 1923.

Ayerst, D. *Garvin of the Observer*. London, 1985.

Bailey, T. A. *Theodore Roosevelt and the Japanese-American Crises*. Stanford, CA, 1934.

Barnes, J., and K. Middlemas, K. *Baldwin*. London, 1969.

Barnett, C. *The Collapse of British Power*. London, 1972.

Beach, E. L. *The United States Navy: A 200 Year History*. Boston, 1986.

Beale, H. K. *Theodore Roosevelt and the Rise of America to World Power*. Baltimore, 1956.

Beloff, M. *Imperial Sunset, Britain's Liberal Empire*. Vol. 1. London, 1969.

Bennet, E. W. *German Rearmament and the West, 1932-1933*. Princeton, NJ, 1979.

Berkowitz, B. D. *Calculated Risks, a Century of Arms Control, Why It Failed and How It Can Be Made to Work*. New York, 1987

Borg, D. *The United States and the Far Eastern Crisis of, 1933-38*. Cambridge, MA, 1964.

Borg, D. and S. Okamoto eds. *Pearl Harbor as History: Japanese-American Relations, 1931-41*. New York, 1973.

Bourne, K. *Britain and the Balance of Power in North America*. London, 1967.

Bradford, J. C. ed. *Admirals of the New Steel Navy*. Annapolis, MD, 1990.

Braisted, W. R. *The United States Navy in the Pacific, 1897-1909*. Austin, TX, 1958.

――――*The United States Navy in the Pacific, 1909-1922*. Austin, TX, 1971

Brune, L. H. *The Origins of American National Security Policy: Sea Power, Air Power and Foreign Policy*. Manhattan, KA, 1981.

Bryce, J. *The American Commonwealth*. London, 1908.

Buckley, T. *The United States and the Washington Conference, 1921-22*. Knoxville, TN, 1970.

Burk, K. "Great Britain and the United States, 1917-18: The Turning Point," *International History Review* 1, #2, April 1979.

――――*Britain, America and the Sinews of War*. Boston, 1985.

Campbell, F. *F. E. Smith, First Earl Birkenhead*. London, 1983.

Carlton, D. "Great Britain and the Coolidge Naval Disarmament Conference of 1927." *Political Science Quarterly* 83, 1968.

――――"The Anglo-French Compromise on Arms Limitation, 1928." *Journal of British Studies* 8, #2, 1969.

――――"Disarmament with Guarantees: Lord Cecil, 1922-27." *Disarmament and Arms Control* 3, #2, 1964.

Cecil of Chelwood, Viscount. *A Great Experiment*. London, 1941.

Chace, J. *American Invulnerable: The Quest for Absolute Security from 1812 to Star Wars*. New York, 1988.

Challener, R. D. *Admirals, Generals and American Foreign Policy 1898-1914*. Princeton, NJ, 1973.

Chamberlain, J. A. *Down the Years*. London, 1935.

Charmley, J. *Chamberlain and the Lost Peace*. London, 1989.

Chatfield, A. E. *It Might Happen Again*. Vol. 2. London, 1947.

Churchill, R. S. *Winston S. Churchill*, Vol. 2. London, 1969.

Churchill, W. S. *The World Crisis, 1911-1914*. London, 1923.

Clayton, A. *The British Empire as a Superpower, 1919-39*. Basingstoke, 1986.

Cogar, W., ed. *Naval History: The Seventh Symposium of the United States Naval Academy*. Wilmington, DE, 1989.

Cohen, W. I. *Empire without Tears: American Foreign Relations, 1921-33*. Philadelphia, 1987.

Cole, W. S. *Roosevelt and the Isolationists 1932-43*. London, 1983.

Coletta, P. *A Survey of U.S. Naval Affairs 1865-1917*. London, 1987.

————"Naval Lessons of the Great War: The William Sims-Josephus Daniels Controversy." *American Neptune* 51, #4, 1991.

————ed. *American Secretaries of the Navy*. 2 vols. Annapolis, MD, 1980.

Collier, B. *Barren Victories: Versailles to Suez*. London, 1964.

————*The Lion and the Eagle, Britain and Anglo-American Strategy 1900-1950*. London, 1972.

Colvin, I. *Vansittart in Office*. London, 1965.

Costigliola, F. *Awkward Dominion, American Political, Economic and Cultural Relations with Europe 1919-1933*. Ithaca, NY, 1984.

Cowling, M. *The Impact of Hitler: British Politics and British Policy, 1933-1940*. Cambridge, 1975.

Cowman, I. "An Admiralty Myth: The Search for an Advanced Far Eastern Fleet Base before the Second World War." *Journal of Strategic Studies* 8, #3, 1985.

Cross, J. A. *Sir Samuel Hoare*. London, 1977.

Davis, G. *A Navy Second to None: The Development of Modern American Naval Policy*. New York, 1940.

Dallek, R. *Franklin D. Roosevelt and American Foreign Policy, 1933-1945*. New York, 1979.

Daniels, J. *The Wilson Era: Years of War and After, 1917-1923*, Westport, CT, 1974.

Dayer, R. A. "The British War Debts to the United States and the Anglo-Japanese Alliance, 1920-23." *Pacific Historical Review* 45, #4, November 1970.

Dingman, R. *Power in the Pacific: The Origins of Naval Arms Limitations*. Chicago, 1976.

Dobson, A. P. *Anglo-American Relations in the 20th Century*. London, 1995.

Dockrill, M. I., and Z. S. Steiner. "The Foreign Office at the Paris Peace Conference in 1919." *International History Review* 2, #1, January 1980.

Dunbabin, J. P. D. "British Rearmament in the, 1930's." *Historical Journal* 3, 18, 1975..

Dutton, D. *Austen Chamberlain: Gentleman in Politics*. Bolton, 1985.

Ellis, L. E. *Frank B. Kellogg and American Foreign Policy in the 1920's*. New Brunswick, NJ, 1966.

————*Republican Foreign Policy, 1921-33*. New Brunswick, NJ, 1968

Esthus, R. A. *Theodore Roosevelt and Japan*. Seattle, 1967

Ferrell, H. C. *Claude A. Swanson of Virginia: A Political Biography*. Lexington, KY, 1985.

Ferris, J. "A British Unofficial Aviation Mission and Japanese Naval Developments 1919-1929." *Journal of Strategic Studies* 5, #3, 1982.

————*Men, Money and Diplomacy: The Evolution of British Strategic Policy 1919-1926*. London, 1989.

———— "The Greatest Power on the Earth: Great Britain in the 1920s." *International History Review* 13, #4, November 1991.

Fraser, P. *Lord Esher: A Political Biography*. London, 1973.

Friedberg, A. L. "The Weary Titan: Britain and the Experience of Relative Decline 1895-1905." *The Journal of Strategic Studies* 10, #3, 1987.

————*The Weary Titan: Britain and the Experience of Relative Decline 1895-1905*, Princeton, NJ, 1988.

Fry, M. G. "The North Atlantic Triangle and the Abrogation of the Anglo-Japanese Alliance." *Journal of Modern History*, Vol 39, 1, 1967.

————*Illusions of Security: North Atlantic Diplomacy, 1918-22*. Toronto, 1972.

George, M. *The Warped Vision: British Foreign Policy, 1933-39*. Pittsburgh, 1965.

Gibbs, N. "The Naval Conferences of the Interwar Years: A Study of Anglo-American Relations." *Naval War College Review* 50, 1977.

Gilbert, B. B. *David Lloyd-George*. London, 1987.

Gilbert, M. *The Roots of Appeasement*. London, 1966.

————*Winston S. Churchill*, Various vols. London, 1975-1990.

Gilbert, M., and R. Gott. *The Appeasers*. London, 1963.

Glad, B. *Charles Evans Hughes and the Illusions of Innocence*. London, 1966.

Goldstein, E. and J. Maurer, eds. *The Washington Conference, 1921-22: Naval Rivalry, East Asian Stability and the Road to Pearl Harbor*. Ilford, 1994.

Graham, G. S. *The Politics of Naval Supremacy*. Cambridge, 1965.

Greenaway, J. R. "Warren Fisher and the Transformation of the British Treasury 1919-39," *Journal of British Studies* 23, #1, Fall 1983.

Grey, E. *Twenty-Five Years*. London, 1925.

Hagan, K. J. *In Peace and War: Interpretations of American Naval History 1775-1978*. Westport, CT, 1978.

————*This People's Navy: The Making of American Seapower*. New York, 1991

Haggie, P. *Britania at Bay: The Defence of the British Empire against Japan*. Oxford, 1981.

————"The Royal Navy and War Planning in the Fisher Era." *Journal of Contemporary History* 8, #3, 1973.

Hall, C. *Britain, America and Arms Control: 1921-1937*. London, 1987.

Harrod, F. S. *Manning the New Navy: The Development of a Modern Naval Enlisted Force*. Westport, CT, 1978.

Hart, R. A. *The Great White Fleet*. New York, 1965.

Hattendorf, J. and R. Jordan, eds. *Maritime Strategy and the Balance of Power, Britain and America in the 20th Century*. Oxford, 1989.

Herwig, H. *Politics of Frustration: The United States in German Naval Plans 1889-1941*. Boston, 1976.

————*'Luxury' Fleet: The Imperial German Navy 1888-1918*. London, 1980.

————*Germany's Vision of Empire in Venezuela 1871-1914*. Princeton, 1986.

Hiley, N. "The Failure of British Counter-Espionage against Germany, 1907-14." *The Historical Review* 28, 1985.

Hinsley, F. H. *Command of the Sea: The Naval Side of British History, 1918-45*. London, 1950.

————ed. *British Foreign Policy under Sir Edward Grey*. Cambridge, 1977.

Hodgson, G. *The Colonel: The Life and Wars of Henry Stimson, 1867-1950*. New York, 1990.
Hone, T. C. "The Effectiveness of the 'Washington Treaty' Navy." *Naval War College Review* 32, #6, 1979.
Hough, R. *First Sea Lord*. London, 1969.
Howard, E. (Lord Howard of Penrith). *Theatre of Life*. London, 1936.
Howarth, S. *Morning Glory: A History of the Imperial Japanese Navy*. London, 1983.
———*To Shining Sea: A History of the United States Navy*. London, 1991.
James, R. R. *Churchill, a Study in Failure 1900-39*. London, 1970.
Jenkins, R. *Asquith*. London, 1964.
———*Baldwin*. London, 1987.
Jordan, G., ed. *Naval Warfare in the 20th Century*. London, 1977.
Kaufman, R. G. *Arms Control During the Pre-Nuclear Era*. New York, 1990.
Kennedy, P. M. *The Samoan Tangle: A Study in Anglo-German-American Relations 1878-1900*, Dublin, 1974.
———*The Rise and Fall of British Naval Mastery*. London, 1976.
———"The Tradition of Appeasement in British Foreign Policy." *British Journal of International Studies* 2, #3, 1976.
———*The Rise of the Anglo-German Antagonism*. London, 1980.
———*The War Plans of the Great Powers: 1880-1914*. Boston, 1985.
———*The Rise and Fall of the Great Powers*. New York, 1987.
Kennedy, M. D. *The Estrangement of Great Britain and Japan*. Manchester, 1969.
Kittredge, T. B. *Naval Lessons of the Great War*. New York, 1920.
Klachko, M., and D. Trask. *Admiral William Shepherd Benson, First Chief of Naval Operations*. Annapolis, MD, 1987
Klein, I. "Whitehall, Washington and the Anglo-Japanese Alliance, 1919-21." *Pacific Historical Review* 41, #4, 1972.
Lamb, R. *The Drift to War, 1922-1939*. London, 1989.
Lambi, I. N. *The Navy and German Power Politics, 1862-1914*. Boston, 1984.
Layne, C. "British Grand Strategy, 1900-39; Theory and Practice in International Politics." *Journal of Strategic Studies* 2, #3, 1979.
Lees-Milne, J. *The Enigmatic Edwardian: The Life of Reginald 2nd Viscount Esher*. London, 1986.
Leuchtenburg, W. E. *Franklin D. Roosevelt and the New Deal, 1932-1940*. New York, 1963.
Leutze, J. R. *Bargaining for Supremacy: Anglo-American Naval Collaboration 1937-41*. Chapel Hill, NC, 1977.
Link. A. S. *Woodrow Wilson and the Progressive Era, 1910-1917*. New York, 1954.
———*Woodrow Wilson: The Struggle for Neutrality, 1914-1915*. Princeton, NJ, 1960.
Long, W. (Viscount Long of Wrexall). *Memories*. London, 1923.
Louis, W. R. *British Strategy in the Far East, 1919-1939*. Oxford, 1971.
Love, R. W. *History of the United States Navy*. (2 vols.) Harrisburg, PA, 1992.
———ed. *The Chiefs of Naval Operations*. Annapolis, MD, 1980.
Lowe, C. J., and M. L. Dockrill. *The Mirage of Power*. London, 1972.
MacDonald, C. A. *The United States, Britain and Appeasement*. London, 1981.
Mackay, R. F. *Fisher of Kilverstone*. Oxford, 1973.
———*Balfour, Intellectual Statesman*. Oxford, 1985.
Maddox, R. *William E. Borah and American Foreign Policy*. Baton Rouge, LA, 1969.

Marder, A. J. *British Naval Policy 1880-1905: The Anatomy of British Sea Power*.
        London, 1940.
————*From The Dreadnought to Scapa Flow*, (5 vols.) 1961-1970.
————*Old Friends, New Enemies*, Volume I, Oxford, 1981.
Marks, F. W. *Velvet on Iron, the Diplomacy of Theodore Roosevelt*. Lincoln, NE, 1979.
————*Wind Over Sand, the Diplomacy of Franklin Roosevelt*. Athens, GA, 1988.
Marquand, D. *Ramsay Macdonald*. London, 1977.
May, E. ed *Knowing One's Enemies: Intelligence Estimates Between the Two World
        Wars*. Princeton, 1984.
May, E. R. *The World War and American Isolation, 1914-17*. Cambridge, MA, 1959.
McDonald, A. "The Geddes Committee and the Formulation of Public Expenditure
        Policy." *Historical Journal* 32, 1989.
McCoy, D. *Calvin Coolidge, the Quiet President*. New York, 1967.
McKenna, S. *Reginald McKenna*, London, 1948.
McKercher, B. J. C. *The Second Baldwin Government and the United States, 1924-1929*.
        Cambridge, 1984.
————"Wealth Power and the New International Order: Britain and the American
        Challenge in the 1920's." *Diplomatic History* 12, #4, 1988.
————*Anglo-American Relations in the, 1920's*. London, 1991.
————"Our Most Dangerous Enemy: Great Britain Preeminent in the 1930's."
        *Internaional History Review* 13, #4, November 1991.
McNeill, W. H. *The Pursuit of Power*. Oxford, 1983.
Monger, G. *The End of Isolation: British Foreign Policy, 1900-07*. London, 1963.
Morgan, A. *J. Ramsay MacDonald*. Manchester, 1987.
Morison, E. E. *Admiral Sims and the Modern American Navy*. New York, 1968.
Morley, J. W., ed. *Japan Erupts: The London Naval Crisis and the Manchurian Incident,
        1928-32*. New York, 1984.
Morris, A. J. A. *The Scaremongers: The Advocacy of War and Rearmament*. London,
        1984.
Morrison, J. L. *Josephus Daniels: The Small-d Democrat*. Chapel Hill, NC, 1966.
Mosley, L. *Curzon, The End of an Epoch*. London, 1960.
Mowat, C. L. *Britain Between the Wars, 1918-40*. London, 1955.
Munro, D. C. *Intervention and Dollpar Diplomacy in the Caribbean, 1900-1921*.
        Princeton, NJ, 1961.
Murfett, M. *Fool-Proof Relations: The Search for Anglo-American Naval Cooperation,
        1937-1941*. London, 1981.
Neidpath, J. *The Singapore Naval Base*. Oxford, 1981.
Neilson, K. "The Russo-Japanese War and British Policy." *Journal of Strategic Studies*
        12, #1, March, 1989.
————"Greatly Exaggerated: The Myth of British Decline Before 1914." *International
        History Review* 13, #4, November 1991.
Nish, I. H. *The Anglo-Japanese Alliance*. London, 1985.
————ed. *Anglo-Japanese Alienation, 1919-52*. Cambridge, 1982.
Noel-Baker, P. *The First Disarmament Conference, 1932-1933*. Oxford, 1979.
Northedge, F. S. *The Troubled Giant*. London, 1966.
O'Connor, R. G. *Perilous Equilibrium: The United States and the London Naval
        Conference of 1930*. New York, 1969.

Offer, A. "Morality and Admiralty: "Jacky" Fisher, Economic Warfare and the Laws of
        War." *Journal of Contemporary History* 23, #1, April, 1988.
———*The First World War: An Agrarian Interpretation*. Oxford, 1989.
———"The Working Classes, British Naval Plans and the Coming of the Great War."
        *Past and Present* #107.
Offner, A. A. *The Origins of the Second World War: American Foreign Policy and World
        Politics, 1917-41*. New York, 1975.
O'Gara, G. C. *Theodore Roosevelt and the Rise of the Modern American Navy*.
        Princeton, NJ, 1943.
O'Halpin E. *Head of the Civil Service: A Study of Sir Warren Fisher*. London, 1989.
Pack, S. W. C. *Sea Power in the Mediterranean*. Essex, 1971.
Padfield, P. *The Great Naval Race*. London, 1974.
Parker, R. A. C. "Treasury, Trade Unions and Skilled Labour: British Rearmament
        1936-1939." *English Historical Review* 94, 1973.
———*Winston Churchill: Studies in Statesmanship*. London, 1996.
Paullin, C. *Paullin's History of Naval Administration, 1775-1917*. Annapolis, MD, 1968
Peden, G. C. "Sir Warren Fisher and British Rearmament against Germany." *English
        Historical Review* 94, 1973.
———*British Rearmament and the Treasury, 1932-1939*. Edinburgh, 1979.
Pelz, S. E. *Race to Pearl Harbor: The Failure of the Second London Naval Conference
        and the Onset of World War II*. Cambridge, MA, 1974.
Pollard, S. *Britain's Prime and Britain's Decline: The British Economy 1870-1914*.
        London, 1989.
Pusey, M. J. *Charles Evans Hughes*. New York, 1963.
Ranft, B. *Technical Change and British Naval Policy 1860-1939*. London, 1977.
Rappaport, A. *The Navy League of the United States*. Detroit, 1962.
Reckner, J. R. *Teddy Roosevelt's Great White Fleet*. Annapolis, MD, 1988.
Reuterdahl, H. "The Needs of Our Navy," *McClures*, January 1908.
Reynolds, D. *The Creation of the Anglo-American Alliance, 1937-41*. London, 1981.
———*Britannia Overruled: British Policy and World Power in the 20th Century*.
        London, 1991.
Richardson, D. *The Evolution of British Disarmament Policy in the, 1920's*. London,
        1989.
Richmond, H. *Economy and Naval Security*. London, 1931.
Robbins, K. *Sir Edward Grey*. London, 1971.
Robertson, E. M. ed. *The Origins of the Second World War*. London, 1971.
Rock, S. "Risk Theory Reconsidered: American Success and German Failure in the
        Coercion of Britain 1890-1914." *Journal of Strategic Studies* 11, #3, 1988.
Rock, W. R. *British Appeasement in the, 1930's*. London, 1977.
Rodger, N. A. M. *The Admiralty*. London, 1979.
Roskill, S. W. *The War at Sea*, Vols 1-3. London, 1956.
———*Naval Policy Between the Wars*. Vol 1, London, 1968; vol 2. London, 1976.
———*Hankey: Man of Secrets*, 3 vols, London, 1970-1974.
———*The Strategy of Seapower*. London, 1986.
———*Admiral of the Fleet, Earl Beatty the Last Naval Hero*. London, 1986.
Rowse, A. L. *Appeasement: A Study in Political Decline, 1933-1939*. New York, 1961.
Safford, J. J. *Wilsonian Maritime Diplomacy, 1913-21*. New Brunswick, NJ, 1978.

Schmidt, G. *The Politics and Economics of Appeasement: British Foreign Policy in the 1930's*. Hamburg, 1981.

Schurman, D. M. *The Education of a Navy: The Development of British Naval and Strategic Thought, 1867-1914*. London, 1965.

Seager, R. *Alfred Thayer Mahan: The Man and His Letters*. Annapolis, MD, 1977.

Semmel, B. *Liberalism and Naval Strategy*. Boston, 1986.

Shay, R. P. *British Rearmament in the Thirties*. Princeton, NJ. 1977.

Smith, M. "Rearmament and Deterrence in Britain in the, 1930's." *Journal of Strategic Studies* 1, #3, 1978.

Spector, R. "Roosevelt, the Navy and the Venezuelan Controversy, 1902-03." *American Neptune* 32, #4, 1972.

Sprout, H. and M. Sprout. *The Rise of American Naval Power 1776-1918*. Princeton, NJ, 1939.

———*Towards a New Order of Sea Power*. Princeton, NJ, 1943.

Steinberg, J. *Yesterday's Deterrent*. London, 1965.

Stokesbury, J. L. *Navy and Empire*. London, 1983.

Steiner, Z. S. *The Foreign Office and Foreign Policy 1898-1914*. Cambridge, 1969.

Still, W. *American Sea Power in the Old World*. Westport, CT, 1980.

Sumida, J. T. "British Capital Ship Design and Fire Control in the Dreadnought Era." *Journal of Modern History* 51, #2, 1979.

———*In Defence of Naval Supremacy, Finance, Technology and British Naval Policy*. Boston, 1989.

Taylor, A. J. P. *Origins of the Second World War*. London, 1961.

Taylor, A. J. P. ed. *Lloyd-George*. London, 1971.

Thorne, C. *The Limits of Foreign Policy, The West, the League and the Far Eastern Crisis of 1931-33*. London, 1972.

Till, G. *Air Power and the Royal Navy, 1914-1945*. London, 1979.

Tillman, S. P. *Anglo-American Relations at the Paris Peace Conference*. Princeton, NJ, 1961.

Towle, P. "Winston Churchill and British Disarmament Policy." *Journal of Strategic Studies* 2, #3, December 1979.

Trask, D. F. *Captains and Cabinets: Anglo-American Naval Relations, 1917-1919*, New York, 1972.

———*The War With Spain in 1898*, New York, 1981.

Turk, R. W. "The United States Navy and the Taking of Panama, 1901-03." *Military Affairs* 38, #3, 1974.

———*The Ambiguous Relationship: Theodore Roosevelt and Alfred Thayer Mahan*. New York, 1987.

Van Meter, R. H. "The Washington Conference of, 1921-22: A New Look." *Pacific Historical Review* 46, #4, 1977.

Vansittart R. *The Mist Procession*. London, 1958.

Wark, W. *The Ultimate Enemy: British Intelligence and Nazi Germany, 1933-1939*. Oxford, 1986.

Watt, D. C. "The Anglo-German Naval Agreement of 1935." *Journal of Modern History* #28, 1956.

———*Personalities and Policies*. London, 1965.

———"Appeasement: The Rise of a Revisionist School?" *The Political Quarterly* 36, #2, 1965.

Weinroth, H. "Left-Wing Opposition to Naval Armaments in Britain before 1914."
    *Journal of Contemporary History* 6, #4, 1971.
Wemyss, R. W. "Washington and After." *Nineteenth Century* 91, March 1922.
Wester-Wemyss, Lady. *The Life and Letters of Lord Wester-Wemyss*. London, 1935.
Wheeler, G. E. *Admiral William Veazie Pratt, USN*. Washington, DC, 1974.
Wilson, K. *The Policy of the Entente*. Cambridge, 1985.
Winton, J. *Jellicoe*. London, 1981.
Woodward, E. *Great Britain and the German Navy*. Oxford, 1935.
Wrench, D. J. "The Influence of Neville Chamberlain on Foreign and Defence Policy,
    1932-35." *RUSI Journal* 125, 1979.
Young, K. *Stanley Baldwin*. London, 1976.
Zebel, S. *Balfour, a Political Biography*. Cambridge, 1973.

# Index

**About the Author**

PHILLIPS PAYSON O'BRIEN is a lecturer in Modern History at the University of Glasgow in Scotland. From 1991 until 1996 he was both the Mellon Research Fellow in American History at Cambridge University and a Drapers Research Fellow at Pembroke College, Cambridge.

ISBN 0-275-95898-1

90000>

EAN

9 780275 958985

HARDCOVER BAR CODE